CROD

KEY GUIDE

Australian Wildlife

First published in 2007

Jacana Books, an imprint of
Allen & Unwin
83 Alexander Street
Crows Nest NSW 2065
Australia
Phone: (61 2) 8425 0100
Fax: (61 2) 9906 2218
Email: info@allenandunwin.com
Web: www.allenandunwin.com

National Library of Australia
Cataloguing-in-Publication entry:

Cronin, Leonard.
  Cronin's key guide to Australian wildlife.

  ISBN 9781741750751.

  1. Natural history - Australia. 2. Plants - Australia.
  3. Animals - Australia. I. Title. (Series : Cronin's key guides).

508.94

A LEONARD CRONIN PRODUCTION

Text: Leonard Cronin
Illustrations: Marion Westmacott, Nicola Oram, Barbara Duckworth,
Mike Gorman, Leonard Cronin, Jenny Taranto, Ruth Berry, Roslyn Devaux
Photography: Leonard Cronin
Distribution Maps: Laurel Cohn
Design: Robert Taylor
Editor: Laurel Cohn

Printed in China by Everbest Printing Co., Ltd

10 9 8 7 6 5 4 3 2 1

CRONIN'S
KEY GUIDE

Australian Wildlife

Leonard Cronin

JACANA
BOOKS

ALLEN&UNWIN

Contents

◊

Introduction

◊

Australia is a land of extremes, from scorching deserts to tropical reefs, and supports an enormous variety of life. It has been estimated that there are more than one million different plant and animal species in Australia, yet only a fraction of these have been studied. Among them are some 2000 land vertebrates, 54,000 insects, 3600 fishes and more than 30,000 different plants.

With such a vast natural flora and fauna, how can we begin to understand and appreciate the diversity of life in Australia? Part of the answer is to become familiar with a number of key species and then apply that knowledge to further observations and different habitats.

The seeds of this knowledge are contained within the pages of this book. Here you will find some of the key species of plants and animals from around Australia. Many are commonly encountered, such as the kangaroos; some, like the river red gum, typify a particular habitat; while others, like the honey pot ant, have outstanding features or lifestyles.

Working within the limitations of a portable field guide I have attempted to give the reader an overview of the different animal groups by including both vertebrates and invertebrates; and this has allowed me to introduce many fascinating creatures from different parts of the continent.

I have grouped the plants into four major habitat types: rainforests, forests and woodlands, coastal heaths, and dry country. Some species are found in a number of different habitats, but overall I find this the most useful way to present the plants in a field guide format.

Australia's Gondwanan ancestry and long isolation from the rest of the world have allowed the evolution of many unique plants and animals. Some species that dominate the landscape, including most of the eucalypts and marsupials, are found nowhere else in the world. Yet this high natural diversity has left Australian wildlife particularly susceptible to extinction and decline.

In the last 200 years 18 species of mammals and about 100 species of plants have become extinct, while another 40 species of mammals (16 per cent of the living species) and 209 species of plants (1.4 per cent of the living species) are threatened with extinction. These shocking figures are the worst in the world.

Land clearing for agriculture, urban and other development is a major cause of extinctions. Fragmentation of habitat often leads to loss of species, and even though areas are often set aside as wildlife corridors and reserves, many are too small to support viable populations. Events such as fire can easily wipe out a population, and plants may lose the animals that pollinate them.

Population declines can, in some cases, be reversed, and a few endangered species, such as the numbat, have been saved from extinction. Continued research may improve the prospects for survival of some other endangered species, but the outlook gets bleaker as governments pursue policies of economic growth and pay lip service to the reduction of greenhouse gases.

We need to commit ourselves now to fundamental changes to the way we manage our natural resources. If we do not grasp the nettle, then the outlook for life in Australia, and for the planet as a whole, is bleak indeed, and our grandchildren will be deprived of the rich and diverse wildlife heritage and wonders of nature that sustain and fulfil us today.

My aim in producing this book is to help as many people as possible become familiar with the nature of Australia. The benefits of identifying the plants and animals around us are enormous, and as we learn more about our natural environment a new, fascinating, and infinitely variable world opens up before us.

◊

Australian Habitats

SPINIFEX AND HUMMOCK GRASSLANDS cover much of inland Australia where annual rainfall is often less than 125 mm. The dominant grasses grow in spiny hummocks.

HEATHS are found in patches along the coast, in the southeastern highlands and southwestern sandplains. They are dense communities of hard-leaved shrubs and low trees.

- Saltbush & Bluebush Shrublands
- Spinifex & Hummock Grasslands
- Mulga and Malleee Woodlands
- Heaths
- Woodlands
- Wet & Dry Sclerophyll Forests
- Rainforests

MULGA AND MALLEE WOODLANDS cover large parts of the arid and semi-arid inland. They are dominated by low mallee eucalypts or several hardy species of acacia (mulga).

WOODLANDS dominated by eucalypts extend right around Australia, intergrading with forests and grasslands. The medium-high trees are well scattered above a grassy understorey.

RAINFORESTS grow in scattered communities in high rainfall areas of the east coast and Tasmania. A variety of trees and palms form an almost continuous canopy.

WET AND DRY SCLEROPHYLL FORESTS dominated by eucalypts grow along the coast and ranges. The canopy is fairly open with an understorey of hard-leaved shrubs, ferns and grasses.

SALTBUSH AND BLUEBUSH SHRUBLANDS cover much of the southern inland including the Nullarbor, on saline and limestone soils where rainfall is less than 500 mm.

9

Mammals

Australian mammals have penetrated even the most remote and inhospitable parts of the continent, surviving on the meagre food sources of the arid regions, developing strategies to deal with bush fires, droughts, high summer temperatures and freezing winters. But the greatest diversity of species is found in our coastal forests, and the wet tropics of northern Queensland are particularly rich in mammalian life.

Most Australian mammals are active during the night and around dawn or dusk, and these are the best times to see them. Many live in trees, and some possums have a membrane between the forelimbs and hindlimbs enabling them to glide. Bats have modified limbs with large flight membranes giving them the freedom of the skies, while other mammals have adopted a fast hopping gait, or taken to the water where they use flippers instead of feet.

In the hot, arid interior many mammals hide from the heat of the sun by burrowing into the ground. They can survive without drinking by producing highly-concentrated urine and dry faecal pellets, obtaining sufficient free water from their diet or by the chemical breakdown of carbohydrates.

All mammals have hair and produce milk to feed their young, but apart from these defining characteristics, there are striking differences among the mammals. Monotremes lay eggs with a leathery shell, while the eutherians (or placental mammals) give birth to fully-formed young. Marsupials, on the other hand, are born in an embryonic form and crawl up their mother's belly to attach to her teats. Some marsupials suckle their young in the security of a well-developed pouch, while others offer the newborn little protection, dragging them around while they cling helplessly to the mother's teats.

While there are marsupials in the Americas, and a single monotreme species in New Guinea, only in Australia can all three subclasses of mammal easily be seen.

FAMILY **TACHYGLOSSIDAE** SPECIES *Tachyglossus aculeatus* SIZE **TO 45 CM**

SHORT-BEAKED ECHIDNA

This monotreme has stout spines, a tubular snout with a long, sticky tongue, a tiny tail, spade-like claws on its forefeet for digging and long claws on its hindfeet for grooming. Males have a small spur on the rear ankle. **Behaviour** They forage by day, probing for ants with their snout and digging them out with their forefeet. They sleep under vegetation, in hollow logs, rock crevices or burrows, and hibernate in cold climates. If threatened they curl up and may bury themselves on the spot. **Reproduction** Females mate in winter and lay a single, soft-shelled egg into their pouch. The newborn emerges 10 days later and suckles from 2 milk patches. At 6-9 weeks it is left in a sealed burrow while the mother forages. She returns every 3-10 days and suckles it for another 4-5 months. **Diet** Mainly ants and termites. **Habitat** Most habitats from forests to deserts.

FAMILY **ORNITHORHYNCHIDAE** SPECIES *Ornithorhynchus anatinus* SIZE **TO 58 CM**

PLATYPUS

This monotreme has webbed feet, a flattened tail and a very sensitive rubbery, duck-shaped bill. The feet have long, sharp claws and males have a short, hollow, venomous spur on the rear ankle. Its fur is soft, dense and water-repellent. **Behaviour** Active from evening to early morning, and by day in cold weather, it swims fast, closing its eyes under water, detecting and catching aquatic animals on the river bed with its bill, and eating them on the surface. It basks on logs, sleeps in burrows along the river bank and hibernate in cold climates. **Reproduction** They mate in winter and the female lays 2 soft-shelled eggs in a burrow and curls around them until they hatch about 10 days later. The young suckle milk from pores on her belly for 3-4 months, and are often left in the nest while she forages. **Diet** Insects, aquatic animals, small vertebrates. **Habitat** Streams and lakes in forests and rainforests.

FAMILY **DASYURIDAE** SPECIES *Dasyurus maculatus* SIZE **BODY TO 76 CM TAIL TO 55 CM**

SPOTTED-TAILED QUOLL

This ferocious marsupial has a long tail for balance, sharp curved claws, ridged pads on its feet, and an opposable clawless thumb on its hindfoot for gripping branches. **Behaviour** It is active at night, moving slowly on the ground sniffing for food and climbing trees to spot prey and catch sleeping birds. It runs with a bounding gait and is an agile climber. During the day they sleep in a den in a tree hollow, log, cave, rock crevice or abandoned burrow, and this is shared with family members after mating. Males fight for dominance in the breeding season. **Reproduction** Females breed in winter, giving birth to 6 young some 21 days after mating. They suckle in the mother's shallow, rear-opening pouch for about 7 weeks, and are then left in the den while she forages, until independent at about 18 weeks old. **Diet** Birds, reptiles, insects, small mammals. **Habitat** Sclerophyll forests, rainforests, woodlands, coastal heaths.

| FAMILY **DASYURIDAE** | SPECIES *Dasyurus viverrinus* | SIZE **BODY TO 45 CM TAIL TO 28 CM** |

EASTERN QUOLL

This carnivorous marsupial has short legs and 4 toes on its hindfeet. It is black with a brown belly or fawn with a white belly; both forms have white spots on the back but not on the tail. **Behaviour** It is active at night, hunting in grasslands, among undergrowth and the lower branches of trees, often standing on its hindlegs sniffing the air. It sleeps in a grass-lined den in a burrow, hollow log, rock pile or dense vegetation, often changing dens. **Reproduction** Females breed from May to June, giving birth to 8 or more tiny young 20-24 days after mating. They have 5-8 teats in a rudimentary pouch, and only those attached to a teat survive. They are dragged around for 6-8 weeks, then left in the den until weaned at about 16 weeks, becoming independent at 20-29 weeks. **Diet** Small mammals, birds, insects, fruit, seeds, grass, carrion. **Habitat** Sclerophyll forests, heaths, scrubs.

| FAMILY **DASYURIDAE** | SPECIES *Sarcophilus harrisii* | SIZE **BODY TO 71 CM TAIL TO 31 CM** |

TASMANIAN DEVIL

This carnivorous marsupial has small eyes set in a short, broad head with a sparsely-haired muzzle and short, strongly clawed limbs. It is black with white patches on the neck and rump and stores fat in its tail. **Behaviour** They sleep by day in grass-lined dens in burrows, hollow logs, caves and rock piles, using several dens and sometimes sharing them. They are inept killers and feed mainly on carcasses, fighting noisily among themselves. They move with a slow lope and a rocking run, and can climb trees. Males fight for dominance in the breeding season. **Reproduction** They breed in March, and the female gives birth to 2-3 young 21 days after mating. They suckle in her shallow, backward-opening pouch for 13-16 weeks and are then left in the den while she forages. They are weaned at 28-30 weeks and independent at 40 weeks. **Diet** Carrion, insects, small animals. **Habitat** Most habitats, preferring sclerophyll forests, scrubs, woodlands.

| FAMILY **DASYURIDAE** | SPECIES *Phascogale tapoatafa* | SIZE **BODY TO 26 CM TAIL TO 23 CM** |

BRUSH-TAILED PHASCOGALE

This marsupial has a pointed head with bulging eyes, clawed toes and small opposing, clawless first toes on the hindfeet for gripping. **Behaviour** They sleep in nests on the ground or use bird nests, emerging at night to forage, extracting insects from the bark with their long fingers. They can run beneath branches and leap between trees. In the breeding season females build nursery nests in tree hollows and males search frantically for females, becoming so stressed that they all die a few weeks after mating. **Reproduction** They breed in May and June and the female gives birth to 8 or more young some 30 days after mating. They have 8 teats in a shallow pouch and only those able to attach to a teat survive. At about 7 weeks old they are left in the nest while the mother forages, and are weaned between 14 and 25 weeks. **Diet** Insects, small vertebrates, nectar. **Habitat** Eucalypt forests, woodlands.

FAMILY **DASYURIDAE** SPECIES *Sminthopsis crassicaudata* SIZE **BODY TO 9 CM TAIL TO 7 CM**

FAT-TAILED DUNNART

This carnivorous marsupial has a pointed head with bulging eyes and stores fat in its short tail.
Behaviour They sleep by day in cup-shaped nests of dried grass beneath logs, in rocky crevices or soil cracks.
They often huddle together in cold weather and become torpid for a few hours each day if food is short, utilising fat reserves in the tail. They are generally solitary and hunt for invertebrates on the ground, sometimes in open areas, within large home ranges that change according to the food supply. **Reproduction** They breed from July to February, and the female gives birth to 2 litters of 8-10 young 13 days after mating. They suckle in her circular pouch for about 60 days and are then left in the nest while the mother forages, until weaned at about 10 weeks. **Diet** Insects, small invertebrates, rarely small vertebrates. **Habitat** Woodlands, shrublands, tussock grasslands, gibber plains, farmland.

FAMILY **DASYURIDAE** SPECIES *Antechinus flavipes* SIZE **BODY TO 16 CM TAIL TO 15 CM**

YELLOW-FOOTED ANTECHINUS

This carnivorous marsupial has a pointed head with bulging eyes and thin, crinkled ears. The hindfeet have a small, opposing, clawed inner toe for gripping. **Behaviour** They sleep in a rough nest in a hollow log, rocky crevice, cave or building, emerging at night, moving fast and erratically in short bounds and running underneath branches. They pounce on prey, killing quickly with bites to the head and neck, leaving the skin inverted. All males die from stress soon after mating.
Reproduction They breed in winter and the female gives birth to up to 14 young 23-26 days after mating. Only those that attach to the 8-14 teats in her rudimentary pouch survive. They are dragged around for about 5 weeks and then left in the nest or carried on the mother's back until weaned at 3-4 months. **Diet** Insects, other invertebrates, small vertebrates, flowers, nectar. **Habitat** Rainforests, sclerophyll forests, dry mulga woodlands.

FAMILY **NOTORYCTIDAE** SPECIES *Notoryctes typhlops* SIZE **BODY TO 16 CM TAIL TO 26 MM**

MARSUPIAL MOLE

This burrowing marsupial is blind with tiny vestigial eyes. It lacks external ears and has a horny shield protecting its nostrils. The forefeet have 2 spade-like shovelling claws, the hindfeet are clawless and the tail is reduced to a leathery stub. It has long, silky, golden-brown fur. **Behaviour** They live mostly underground, digging into sandy soil with their forefeet, travelling horizontally about 10 cm deep and suddenly descending to 2.5 m or more. The burrow fills in behind so that the mole appears to swim through the sand. They often feed on the surface, pulling themselves along in a rapid shuffle, leaving parallel furrows. Pregnant females construct deep permanent burrows.
Reproduction Little is known about their reproduction. Females have a rear-opening pouch completely covering 2 teats. **Diet** Ants, termites, beetles, larvae, seeds. **Habitat** Sandy soils in desert regions.

| FAMILY **PERAMELIDAE** | SPECIES *Macrotis lagotis* | SIZE **BODY TO 55 CM TAIL TO 29 CM** |

BILBY

This endangered, delicate marsupial has long, silky fur, a narrow head with large ears, a pointed snout and a long tongue. The forelimbs have 4 clawed digits. The hindfeet have a large, strongly-clawed fourth toe and a double claw on the fused second and third toes. **Behaviour** They sleep in a burrow in a termite mound, beneath a grass tussock or shrub, sometimes shared by a family group. They emerge after midnight, running with the tail held up like a flag, often standing upright sniffing for insects and fungi, which are dug out with the forefeet. Males establish a rigid dominance hierarchy without fighting. **Reproduction** They breed from March to May and the female gives birth to 1-3 young 21 days after mating. They suckle in her rear-opening pouch for 70-80 days, and are weaned some 14 days later. **Diet** Termites, ants, larvae, seeds, bulbs, fruit, fungi. **Habitat** Arid and semi-arid shrublands, spinifex, tussock grasslands.

| FAMILY **MYRMECOBIIDAE** | SPECIES *Myrmecobius fasciatus* | SIZE **BODY TO 27 CM TAIL TO 21 CM** |

NUMBAT

This endangered marsupial has a long, sticky, cylindrical tongue to collect termites, large ears and sharply-clawed forefeet. **Behaviour** They sleep in nests of soft plant material in a hollow log or at the end of a shallow burrow, using different burrows for sheltering and rearing their young. Numbats are solitary with home ranges of 25-50 ha, although males roam over large areas in the breeding season searching for females. They walk on all-fours frequently standing up and sniffing for termites. They cannot breach hard termite mounds so dig into the runways. **Reproduction** They breed from January to March, and the female gives birth to up to 4 young some 14 days after mating. They suckle from her 4 exposed teats, clinging to hairs surrounding them, and are dragged around until furred in late July. They are then left in the nest while the mother forages, becoming independent in November. **Diet** Termites. **Habitat** Wandoo or Jarrah-dominated eucalypt forests.

| FAMILY **PERAMELIDAE** | SPECIES *Perameles nasuta* | SIZE **BODY TO 43 CM TAIL TO 16 CM** |

LONG-NOSED BANDICOOT

This compact marsupial has a long head with a slender muzzle and long pointed ears. Its short forelimbs have strong, curved claws. The hindlegs have a very long fourth toe and a double claw on the fused second and third toes for grooming. **Behaviour** They sleep in a well-concealed nest of dry plant matter in a shallow depression, sometimes covered with soil. They emerge at night, move on all fours and dig conical holes with their forefeet while probing with the snout for food. Males establish dominance hierarchies and follow receptive females looking for a chance to mate. **Reproduction** They breed most of the year and the female gives birth to several litters of 1-5 young 12.5 days after mating. They suckle in her rear-opening pouch until 45-50 days old and stay in the nest until weaned at about 2 months. **Diet** Worms, insects, larvae, eggs, fungi, seeds, roots. **Habitat** Rainforests, sclerophyll forests, woodlands, heaths, grasslands.

FAMILY **PARAMELIDAE**   SPECIES *Isoodon obesulus*   SIZE **BODY TO 36 CM TAIL TO 14 CM**

SOUTHERN BROWN BANDICOOT

This solidly-built marsupial has a long head with a naked, pointed nose, small rounded ears and small eyes. Its short forelimbs have strong, curved claws. The hindlegs have a very long fourth toe and a double claw on the fused second and third toes for grooming. **Behaviour** They sleep in an oval nest of plant matter and soil usually in a shallow depression, sometimes in a decaying log, rabbit warren, or on a raised soil platform in wet sites. They emerge at night, moving on all-fours around a large home range, digging conical pits with the forefeet while probing with the snout for food. **Reproduction** They breed most of the year and the female gives birth to 2-3 litters of up to 6 young 12.5 days after mating. They suckle in her rear-opening pouch and become independent at 60-70 days old. **Diet** Fungi, seeds, ants, worms and other invertebrates. **Habitat** Dry sclerophyll forests and woodlands, grasslands, heaths and shrublands.

FAMILY **VOMBATIDAE**   SPECIES *Vombatus ursinus*   SIZE **BODY TO 1.2 M TAIL TO 3 CM**

COMMON WOMBAT

This large, squat marsupial has a broad head with a flattened nose, small eyes, small ears, and a very short tail. It has stout, flattened claws on its forelimbs for digging. The hindfeet have a very small first toe and fused second and third toes with a double claw for grooming. **Behaviour** They shelter by day in burrows to 30 m long, dug into the banks of gullies, often with several entrances, nesting chambers and connecting tunnels. They graze mostly at night, have poor vision and are slow and clumsy, but can bound at 40 km/h. **Reproduction** They breed in winter in Tasmania and year-round elsewhere, and the female gives birth to a single young 3 weeks after mating. It suckles in her rear-opening pouch for 6-10 months, then stays in the burrow until weaned at 15 months, remaining at heel until 20 months old. **Diet** Grasses, rushes, sedges, roots, tubers, mosses, fungi. **Habitat** Open forests, woodlands, scrubs, wet heaths to 1800 m.

FAMILY **PHASCOLARCTIDAE**   SPECIES *Phascolarctos cinereus*   SIZE **TO 82 CM**

KOALA

This stocky marsupial has a broad, flat head with large ears, a flat nose and small eyes. Its long limbs have strongly-clawed feet for climbing. The hindfeet have opposing first toes and the first 2 digits of the forefoot oppose the other 3, giving it a vice-like grip. **Behaviour** Solitary and nocturnal, koalas spend much of their time resting or feeding high up in gum trees within a home range of about 1.5 ha. They climb slowly, grasping the trunk with the forefeet and pulling the hindlimbs up, and can jump 2 m between branches. On the ground they walk on all-fours, run with a bounding gait, and can swim if necessary. In the breeding season males bellow and grunt loudly to establish dominance hierarchies and territories. **Reproduction** They breed in late spring and the female gives birth to a single young 34-36 days after mating. It suckles in her rear-opening pouch for 6-7 months, then rides on her back until weaned at 11-12 months. **Diet** Eucalypt leaves. **Habitat** Eucalypt forests and woodlands.

FAMILY **PSEUDOCHEIRIDAE**   SPECIES *Pseudocheirus peregrinus*   SIZE **BODY TO 35 CM TAIL TO 35 CM**

COMMON RINGTAIL POSSUM

This arboreal marsupial has a long prehensile tail and strongly clawed feet. The first 2 fingers of the forefeet and the first toe of the hindfoot oppose the others. The second and third toes of the hindfeet are fused with a long, split claw used for grooming.
Behaviour Active at night, they forage in trees and leap between branches. On the ground they move on all-fours and can swim well. They live in family groups and build several spherical nests in trees, shrubs or in tree hollows within their home range. Juveniles are forced to dis-perse. **Reproduction** Females usually give birth to 2 young from late April to November. They suckle in the mother's forward-opening pouch for about 4 months, and are then left in the nest or carried on her back while she forages until 5-8 months old. **Diet** Leaves, flowers, fruit. **Habitat** Forests, woodlands, rainforests, dense shrublands, to around 1200 m high.

FAMILY **PHALANGERIDAE**   SPECIES *Trichosurus vulpecula*   SIZE **BODY TO 55 CM TAIL TO 40 CM**

COMMON BRUSHTAIL POSSUM

This arboreal marsupial has large pointed ears and a moderately prehensile tail. The clawless first toe of the hindfoot opposes the others for gripping, while the second and third toes are fused with a long, split claw for grooming. **Behaviour** Active at night, they forage in trees and shelter in tree hollows, logs, dense undergrowth, rabbit holes and roof spaces. Several dens are used within a home range of 5-7 ha and adults often travel long distances, scent-marking their den sites. They have a large vocal repertoire including coughs, sharp hisses, loud chattering and screeching. **Reproduction** They breed year round in the north, mainly autumn and spring elsewhere, and the female gives birth to a single young 16-18 days after mating. It suckles in her forward-opening pouch for 4-5 months and is then left in the den or rides on her back until 7-9 months old. **Diet** Leaves, fruit, blossom, grass, insects. **Habitat** Sclerophyll forests, woodlands.

FAMILY **PHALANGERIDAE**   SPECIES *Trichosurus caninus*   SIZE **BODY TO 57 CM TAIL TO 42 CM**

MOUNTAIN BRUSHTAIL POSSUM

This arboreal marsupial has short rounded ears, a pink nose and a prehensile tail. Clawless opposing first toes on the hindfeet are used for gripping while the second and third toes are fused with a long, split claw for grooming. The forefeet have 5 strongly-clawed, non-oppos-ing fingers. **Behaviour** Active mainly at night, they crash through the for-est canopy and often descend to the ground to feed. They walk on all-fours with a rolling gait and can swim if necessary. Adults form monogamous pairs and sleep in dens in tree hollows, hollow logs, stumps or in large epi-phytic ferns within a home range of 5-7 ha. **Reproduction** They breed from February to May and the female gives birth to a single young 15-17 days after mating. It suckles in her forward-opening pouch for 5-6 months then rides on her back until weaned at 8-9 months. **Diet** Leaves, fungi, lichen, bark, pine cones. **Habitat** Wet sclerophyll forests, rainforests.

FAMILY **TARSIPEDIDAE**   SPECIES *Tarsipes rostratus*   SIZE **BODY TO 95 MM TAIL TO 110 MM**

HONEY POSSUM

This arboreal marsupial has a long snout and a long, brush-tipped tongue. The eyes are near the top of the head, the ears are rounded and the tail is strongly prehensile. The hands and feet have opposing first digits and large rough pads for gripping. The second and third toes of the hindfeet are fused for grooming. **Behaviour** Active at night, they dart between blossoms, extracting pollen and nectar with their brush-tipped tongue, running beneath branches and climbing vertically. They shelter in the hollow stems of grass trees or abandoned bird nests, huddling together on cold days and becoming torpid for short periods when food is scarce. **Reproduction** Females breed throughout the year producing 2-3 litters of up to 4 young 21-28 days after mating. They suckle in the mother's forward-opening pouch for about 65 days, then are left in a shelter while she forages, until weaned at 90 days. **Diet** Pollen, nectar. **Habitat** Sandplain heaths, shrublands.

FAMILY **BURRAMYDAE**   SPECIES *Cercartetus nanus*   SIZE **BODY TO 11 CM TAIL TO 11 CM**

EASTERN PYGMY-POSSUM

This small arboreal marsupial has very large eyes and ears, long whiskers and stores fat in the base of its prehensile tail. The first 2 toes of the hindfeet oppose the other 3 for gripping, while the second and third toes are fused with a double claw for grooming. **Behaviour** They shelter in tree hollows, under bark, in dense vegetation or disused bird nests within a home range less than 1 ha, emerging at night to feed in the trees, sometimes suspended by their tail. Breeding females build small spherical nests of shredded bark, lined with fresh leaves. **Reproduction** Females breed from spring to autumn (late winter and spring in Tasmania), producing up to 3 litters of 2-4 young some 30 days after mating. They suckle in the mother's shallow pouch for 33-37 days and then cling to her belly fur until weaned at 60-65 days. **Diet** Pollen, nectar, insects, seeds, soft fruit. **Habitat** Wet sclerophyll forests, rainforests, heaths, shrublands to about 1600 m.

FAMILY **PETAURIDAE**   SPECIES *Petauroides volans*   SIZE **BODY TO 45 CM TAIL TO 60 CM**

GREATER GLIDER

This arboreal marsupial has a weakly-prehensile tail and a square gliding membrane between the flanks, elbows and ankles. The first 2 toes of the forefeet oppose the other 3 for gripping. The hindfeet have an opposing first toe and a long, split claw on the fused second and third toes for grooming. **Behaviour** They emerge at dusk from dens high up in tree hollows within home ranges of 1-6 ha, and follow established routes to feeding sites. They are agile climbers and can glide more than 100 m with their limbs outstretched, steering with the tail and gliding membrane. **Reproduction** They breed from March to June and the female gives birth to a single young that suckles in her forward-opening pouch for 3-4 months. It is then left in the den or rides on the her back for the next 3 months. **Diet** Eucalypt leaves and buds. **Habitat** Sclerophyll forests and tall woodlands with tree hollows, to 1200 m.

FAMILY **PETAURIDAE**   SPECIES *Petaurus breviceps*   SIZE **BODY TO 21 CM TAIL TO 21 CM**

SUGAR GLIDER

This arboreal marsupial has a prehensile tail and a square gliding membrane between the fifth finger, first toe and the flanks. The first 2 toes of the forefeet oppose the other 3 for gripping. The hindfeet have an opposing first toe and a split claw on the fused second and third toes for grooming. **Behaviour** Active at night, they are agile climbers and can glide more than 50 m, making gashes in trees and licking the sap. They nest in tree hollows, often shared by 2-3 males, 3-4 females and their young, scent-marked by the dominant male. **Reproduction** Females breed from June to November, rearing up to 2 litters of twins born 16 days after mating. They suckle in the mother's forward-opening pouch for 60-70 days, are then left in the nest for 50 days and become independent at 7-10 months. **Diet** Sap, nectar, pollen, invertebrates, small birds, mammals. **Habitat** Eucalypt forests, woodlands to 1200 m.

FAMILY **ACROBATIDAE**   SPECIES *Acrobates pygmaeus*   SIZE **BODY TO 8 CM TAIL TO 8 CM**

FEATHERTAIL GLIDER

This arboreal marsupial has a brush-tipped tongue and a feather-like prehensile tail with long stiff hairs on each side. A small gliding membrane extends from the flanks to the elbows and knees. The feet have sharp claws, grooved pads and opposing toes for gripping, and a double claw on the fused second and third toes of the hindfeet for grooming. **Behaviour** Active at night, they leap through the canopy and glide more than 20 m steering with the tail. Up to 40 individuals may share a nest in a tree hollow, huddling together in cold weather, and becoming torpid when food is scarce. **Reproduction** Females breed year round in the north and from March to February in the south, raising 2-3 litters of usually 2-3 young. They suckle in the mother's forward-opening pouch for 60-65 days, then stay in the nest until independent at 95-100 days. **Diet** Pollen, nectar, insects, manna, sap. **Habitat** Sclerophyll forests, woodlands to 1200 m.

FAMILY **PHALANGERIDAE**   SPECIES *Spilocuscus maculatus*   SIZE **BODY TO 58 CM TAIL TO 43 CM**

SPOTTED CUSCUS

This arboreal marsupial has a prehensile tail, large red-rimmed eyes and long canine teeth. The thick fur is grey above and creamy-white below and males have creamy-white spots on the back. They have strong curved claws and the first 2 toes of the forefeet oppose the other 3 for gripping. **Behaviour** Active at night and on cool overcast days, they rest on branches in dense foliage and sleep on a small platform of leaves and twigs. They climb slowly through the canopy, leap between trees, and use a bounding gait on the ground. Males defend an area defined by scent-marking. If stressed they secrete a reddish-brown substance on the bare facial skin, particularly around the eyes. **Reproduction** Females probably breed throughout the year, giving birth to 1-3 young 2 weeks after mating. They suckle in the mother's forward-opening pouch for some 6-7 months and are then carried on her back. **Diet** Leaves, fruit, insects, small vertebrates. **Habitat** Rainforests.

FAMILY **POTOROIDAE**　　SPECIES *Potorous tridactylus*　　SIZE **BODY TO 40 CM TAIL TO 26 CM**

LONG-NOSED POTOROO

This kangaroo-like marsupial has a long tapering nose with a naked tip, long canine teeth, rounded ears and a scaly tail used to gather nesting material. The forefeet have spatulate claws for digging. The fourth toes of the hindfeet are long, the second and third toes are shorter and fused with a double claw for grooming. **Behaviour** They forage on the ground at night, moving slowly with a short hop, digging for underground fungi with the forefeet, rarely venturing far from cover and sometimes gathering in small groups. They sleep in nests of grass and other vegetation placed in scrapes below dense scrub, grass tussocks or grass trees. **Reproduction** Females breed year-round, giving birth to a single young 38 days after mating. It suckles in the mother's pouch for 15 weeks and at foot for 5-6 weeks. **Diet** Fungi supplemented by insects, roots, seeds, fruit. **Habitat** Coastal heaths, rainforests, sclerophyll forests, woodlands.

FAMILY **POTOROIDAE**　　SPECIES *Aepyprymnus rufescens*　　SIZE **BODY TO 39 CM TAIL TO 39 CM**

RUFOUS BETTONG

This kangaroo-like marsupial has a hairy muzzle, long fourth toes on its hindfeet and a double claw on its fused second and third toes for grooming. It has long, curved claws on its forefeet for digging, and uses its prehensile tail to carry nesting material. **Behaviour** They forage at night, digging for food with their forefeet, and often feeding in small groups. When alarmed they stand with their arms by their sides and stamp their hindfeet before hopping away. They sleep in grass nests below grass tussocks, under logs or rocks, and may travel 4 km overnight using up to 5 nests within a home range of 45-110 ha. **Reproduction** Females breed throughout the year and give birth to a single young 22-24 days after mating. It suckles in the mother's pouch for 14-16 weeks and at foot for 7 weeks. **Diet** Tubers, roots, herbs, fungi, insects, seeds, tree exudates, flowers. **Habitat** Open forests, woodlands.

FAMILY **POTOROIDAE**　　SPECIES *Hypsiprymnodon moschatus*　　SIZE **BODY TO 30 CM TAIL TO 16 CM**

MUSKY RAT-KANGAROO

This is our smallest macropod. It has an opposing, clawless first toe on the hindfoot, enabling it to climb and grip branches. The other 4 toes have curved claws, the second and third toes are fused, and the palms and soles have striated pads. **Behaviour** Active by day, they forage on the forest floor, sometimes in small groups, and climb among fallen trees. They move with a slow hop with the tail held out behind and run with a galloping gait. They carry grass, ferns and lichen in their curled tail to build nests in clumps of lawyer vines, tree buttresses or rock piles. Individuals use several nests and females build larger maternity nests. **Reproduction** Females breed from October to April and give birth to 1-3 young. They suckle in the mother's pouch for about 21 weeks and spend several weeks in the nest before accompanying her to feed. **Diet** Insects, small animals, fungi, fruit and seeds. **Habitat** Tropical rainforests.

| FAMILY **MACROPODIDAE** | SPECIES *Petrogale penicillata* | SIZE **BODY TO 59 CM TAIL TO 70 CM** |

BRUSH-TAILED ROCK-WALLABY

This kangaroo is brown with a rufous rump and black furry feet. Southern animals have a black tail, pale stripes on the sides, white cheek stripes and a black stripe on the forehead. The hindfeet have granulated pads for gripping, no first digit, and a double claw on the fused second and third toes for grooming. **Behaviour** They shelter by day in caves, rocky crevices and dense vegetation, forming small colonies with dominance hierarchies. Females often share den sites with female relatives. They hop on rocks with their tail arched over the back, and can climb almost vertical rock faces. **Reproduction** Females breed all year, giving birth to a single young 31 days after mating. It suckles in the mother's pouch for about 29 weeks, then is left in the den while she forages for another 3 months. **Diet** Grass, some leaves, sedges, ferns, roots, bark, fruit, flowers. **Habitat** Rocky sites near grassy areas.

| FAMILY **MACROPODIDAE** | SPECIES *Thylogale stigmatica* | SIZE **BODY TO 54 CM TAIL TO 47 CM** |

RED-LEGGED PADEMELON

This kangaroo has rounded ears, a naked nose and a short, thick tail. The hindfeet have no first digit, the second and third are fused with a double claw for grooming, and the fourth is much longer than the others. **Behaviour** Active most of the day and night, they rest in dense cover in the early afternoon and around midnight. Shy and generally solitary, they have home ranges of 1-4 ha and forage in the forest by day and around the forest edge at night, following paths to feeding sites. They sometimes feed in small groups, and if disturbed they thump the ground with their hindfeet and dash for cover. **Reproduction** Females breed all year and give birth to a single young 28-30 days after mating. It suckles in the mother's pouch for 26-28 weeks and is weaned 9-10 weeks later. **Diet** Leaves, fruit, ferns, fungi, grass. **Habitat** Rainforests, wet sclerophyll forests, vine scrubs.

| FAMILY **MACROPODIDAE** | SPECIES *Thylogale billardierii* | SIZE **BODY TO 72 CM TAIL TO 48 CM** |

TASMANIAN PADEMELON

This stocky kangaroo has long, soft fur, a short, thick tail, rounded ears and a naked nose. The hindfeet have no first digit, the second and third are fused with a double claw for grooming, and the fourth is much longer than the others. **Behaviour** They feed at night and during the day in bad weather, rarely more than 100 m from the forest edge, following paths to feeding sites up to 2 km away, congregating in groups of 10 or more. They sleep in dense cover in home ranges of up to 170 ha. Males establish dominance hierarchies in the breeding season by fighting and ritualised aggression. **Reproduction** Females give birth to a single young mostly from April to June, 30 days after mating. It suckles in the mother's pouch for about 29 weeks and then at foot until about 10 months old. **Diet** Grasses, herbs, leaves, seedlings. **Habitat** Forests, scrubs.

FAMILY **MACROPODIDAE**   SPECIES *Setonix brachyurus*   SIZE **BODY TO 54 CM TAIL TO 31 CM**

QUOKKA

This small, robust wallaby has long, thick fur and a thick, sparsely-haired, scaly tail. The hindfeet have no first digit, the second and third are fused with a double claw for grooming, and the fourth is much longer than the others. **Behaviour** They shelter in dense vegetation and converge at night to feed around waterholes within a group territory occupied and defended by 25-150 adults. They have a bounding gait interspersed with short bouts of rapid hopping, and may climb trees to reach leaves. Males establish dominance hierarchies according to age, defend areas around their resting sites and may form long term bonds with females.
Reproduction Females breed all year (from January to August on Rottnest Island), giving birth to a single young 25-28 days after mating. It suckles in the mother's pouch for 26 weeks and then at foot for 2 months.
Diet Grasses, leaves, succulents. **Habitat** Sclerophyll forests, woodlands, heaths.

FAMILY **MACROPODIDAE**   SPECIES *Dendrolagus lumholtzi*   SIZE **BODY TO 65 CM TAIL TO 74 CM**

LUMHOLTZ'S TREE-KANGAROO

This arboreal kangaroo is pale creamy-brown, grey or rusty-brown with lighter flecks on the rump. It has a long tail, strong, curved claws and muscular forelimbs. The hindfeet have similar sized toes with granular soles, and the second and third toes are fused with a double claw for grooming. **Behaviour** They sleep crouched on a branch in the crown of a tree and feed at night in the mid-level of the canopy and understorey, alone or with 2-3 others, in a home range of 0.7-1.8 ha. They hop along branches, jump between trees and descend backwards to the ground, where they hop or move on all-fours. Males are aggressive and can inflict fatal wounds with their claws. **Reproduction** Females probably breed year round and give birth to a single young. It suckles in the mother's pouch for about 230 days and then at foot for up to 2 years.
Diet Leaves, fruit, flowers. **Habitat** Tropical rainforests.

FAMILY **MACROPODIDAE**   SPECIES *Macropus agilis*   SIZE **BODY TO 85 CM TAIL TO 84 CM**

AGILE WALLABY

This is the most commonly seen macropod along the tropical coast of Australia. It has dark stripes on the cheeks and forehead, whitish stripes along the cheeks and thighs, and a long, black-tipped tail. **Behaviour** They rest in the heat of the day in dense vegetation and live in groups of up to 10, congregating in larger mobs when food is short. In the breeding season dominant males monopolise females on heat and keep other males away. They are very alert and nervous, and when alarmed thump their hind feet before hopping away. **Reproduction** They breed all year and females mate soon after giving birth, although the embryo remains dormant until the pouch is empty. Gestation takes 29-31 days and the newborn stays in the pouch for 7-8 months, then suckles at foot until 10-12 months old.
Diet Grass, sedges, leaves, fruit and roots dug up with the forepaws.
Habitat Along creeks in open forests, adjacent grasslands and coastal sand dunes.

FAMILY **MACROPODIDAE**   SPECIES *Macropus rufogriseus*   SIZE **BODY TO 92 CM TAIL TO 88 CM**

RED-NECKED (BENNETT'S) WALLABY

This kangaroo is darker with a shaggier coat in Tasmania. The tail has a brushy tip. The hindfeet have no first digit, the second and third are fused with a double claw, and the fourth is much longer than the others. **Behaviour** They sleep by day in dense vegetation, emerge in the late afternoon and follow paths to feeding sites, often congregating in groups of 30 or more. They live in home ranges of 12-32 ha. In the breeding season, males range widely searching for females and establish dominance hierarchies by fighting and ritualised aggression. **Reproduction** Females breed all year (January to July in Tasmania) and give birth to 1-2 young, 29-30 days after mating. They suckle in the mother's pouch for 40-43 weeks, are then left in hiding while she feeds for 4 weeks, and suckle at foot until 12-17 months old. **Diet** Grass, herbs. **Habitat** Sclerophyll forests, woodlands, heaths.

FAMILY **MACROPODIDAE**   SPECIES *Wallabia bicolor*   SIZE **BODY TO 85 CM TAIL TO 86 CM**

SWAMP WALLABY

This stocky kangaroo has coarse fur, dark brown to black above, and red-brown to yellow-brown below. The cheeks and shoulders have a yellow, red-brown or black stripe. The hindfeet have no first digit, the second and third are fused with a double claw for grooming, and the fourth is much longer than the others. **Behaviour** They rest in thick undergrowth and usually feed after dusk or during the day in overcast weather, moving to open, grassy areas at night. They have home ranges around 2-6 ha and sometimes feed in small groups. **Reproduction** Females breed mainly between April and November and give birth to a single young 33-38 days after mating. It suckles in the mother's pouch for about 36 weeks, then at foot until about 15 months old. **Diet** Shrubs, seedlings, rushes, fungi, vines, ferns, grass. **Habitat** Rainforests, sclerophyll forests, woodlands, heaths with a dense understorey.

FAMILY **MACROPODIDAE**   SPECIES *Macropus robustus*   SIZE **BODY TO 1.1 M TAIL TO 90 CM**

COMMON WALLAROO (EURO)

Eastern animals (known as wallaroos) are dark-grey with coarse, shaggy fur. Some females are bluish-grey, and some males have a reddish band across the shoulders and neck. In central and western Australia they are known as euros, have shorter, reddish-brown fur and live in hot, arid areas. **Behaviour** They shelter among dense trees, in caves, or under rock ledges, and emerge in the late afternoon to graze. They are usually solitary and occupy small overlapping home ranges. Males establish dominance hierarchies, mark low vegetation with secretions from a chest gland and fight over females on heat, engaging in ritualised boxing matches. **Reproduction** Females breed all year and give birth to a single young about 34 days after mating. It suckles in the mother's pouch for about 34-37 weeks and then at foot until about 14 months old. **Diet** Grass, shrubs. **Habitat** Rocky sites from wet sclerophyll forests to arid tussock grasslands.

FAMILY **MACROPODIDAE**   SPECIES *Macropus giganteus*   SIZE **BODY TO 1.2 M TAIL TO 1.1 M**

EASTERN GREY KANGAROO

This large, robust marsupial varies from light silver-grey to dark grey flecked with light grey above. Females have a white chest. It has no first digit on the hindfoot, the second and third are fused with a double claw for grooming, and the fourth is much longer than the others. **Behaviour** They rest in the shade and feed from late afternoon to early morning, often in mobs of 10 or more, in home ranges of up to 5 sq km. Females congregate with female relatives and only mate with dominant males. Old males are solitary. They can swim if needed. **Reproduction** Females breed all year and give birth to a single young 33-38 days after mating, with a peak of births in summer. It suckles in the mother's pouch for about 11 months, then suckles at foot until 18 months old. **Diet** Grass, low shrubby vegetation. **Habitat** Dry sclerophyll forests, woodlands, low open scrub, with grassy areas.

FAMILY **MACROPODIDAE**   SPECIES *Macropus fuliginosus*   SIZE **BODY TO 1.2 M TAIL TO 1 M**

WESTERN GREY KANGAROO

This large, robust marsupial resembles the Eastern Grey Kangaroo. It has light to dark chocolate-brown fur, often flecked with grey above, dark brown to black paws, feet and tail tip, and buff patches on the legs and forearms. **Behaviour** They rest in the shade and feed from late afternoon to early morning. Mobs of 40-50 range over a large territory, with sub-groups of 2-4 animals in overlapping home ranges of up to 8 sq km. Females congregate with female relatives, form dominance hierarchies and will only mate with dominant males. Old males are usually solitary. When alarmed they make guttural coughs and thump their hindfeet before hopping away. **Reproduction** Females breed year round and give birth to a single young 30 days after mating. It suckles in the mother's pouch for about 42 weeks, then suckles at foot until 17 months old. **Diet** Grass, herbs, shrubs. **Habitat** Dry open forests, woodlands, open scrubs, heaths.

FAMILY **MACROPODIDAE**   SPECIES *Macropus rufus*   SIZE **BODY TO 1.4 M TAIL TO 1 M**

RED KANGAROO

Males of this large marsupial are more than twice the size of females and very powerfully built. They are reddish-brown above and paler below with a white stripe along the cheek. Eastern females are blue-grey. **Behaviour** They rest in the shade and feed from late afternoon to early morning, alone or in groups of 2-10, in a home range of around 8 sq km. Mobs of several hundred may gather to feed and drink in droughts. Males fight for dominance and exclusive mating rights. Young males range widely and old males are solitary. When alarmed they make a loud cough and thump their hindfeet before hopping away. **Reproduction** Females breed year round and give birth to a single young 33 days after mating. It suckles in the mother's pouch for about 8 months, then suckles at foot for another 3-4 months. **Diet** Grass, herbs, shrubs. **Habitat** Dry woodlands, scrub, grasslands, plains, deserts.

FAMILY **PTEROPIDIDAE**   SPECIES *Pteropus scapulatus*   SIZE **TO 24 CM**

LITTLE RED FLYING-FOX

This placental mammal has a wingspan of about 1 m, large eyes, simple ears, no tail, and claws on the first 2 fingers of the forelimbs. **Behaviour** Breeding camps of up to one million form in October/November. They hang from branches by their feet, wrapped in their wings, and adult males gather harems of 2-5 females. At dusk they fly off to feeding sites, travelling long distances, navigating by sight. Small single sex groups move to new camps in February. **Reproduction** Females mate from October to January and give birth to a single young in April or May. It suckles from a teat in the mother's armpit and clings to her until about one month old. It is then left at the roost until it can fly at 2 months. By October it has learned to forage and navigate. **Diet** Nectar, pollen, soft fruit, sap, manna. **Habitat** Rainforests, sclerophyll forests, woodlands, mangroves, paperbark swamps.

FAMILY **PTEROPIDIDAE**   SPECIES *Pteropus poliocephalus*   SIZE **TO 29 CM**

GREY-HEADED FLYING-FOX

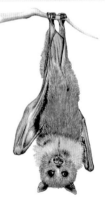

The largest Australian bat, it has a wingspan up to 1.3 m, large eyes, simple ears, no tail, and claws on the first 2 fingers of the forelimbs. **Behaviour** They navigate by sight, flying at dusk to foraging areas up to 50 km away, returning before dawn. Females form maternity camps in September and are joined by adult males in February. Large camps have hundreds of thousands of bats wrapped in their wings, hanging from branches . Males defend a small area and attract females to mate with. They disperse in winter. **Reproduction** They breed in March or April. A single young is born in September or October and suckles from a teat in the mother's armpit, clinging to her for 3-4 weeks. Young are then left behind while she forages. They can fly at 3-4 months and are weaned at 5-6 months. **Diet** Pollen, nectar, fruit, leaves. **Habitat** Sclerophyll forests, rainforests, paperbark swamps, mangroves.

FAMILY **MACRODERMATIDAE**   SPECIES *Macroderma gigas*   SIZE **TO 13 CM**

GHOST BAT

This predatory bat has a wingspan of about 50 cm, large ears joined above the head with a forked lobe over the aperture, no tail, large eyes and a large noseleaf above the snout. **Behaviour** They roost by day in deep caves, rock fissures and mines, hanging from the ceiling in colonies of up to 1500 in the breeding season. At dusk they fly to feeding sites up to 2 km away, using sight and echo-location to navigate and detect prey, swooping on small animals, enveloping them in their wings and biting them to death. **Reproduction** They breed in May. A single young is born in July/August and suckles from a teat in the mother's armpit for several months. It is carried for 4 weeks, then left in the roost until it can fly at 7 weeks. **Diet** Insects, small vertebrates. **Habitat** Rainforests, sclerophyll forests, arid woodlands.

FAMILY **VESPERTILIONIDAE**   SPECIES *Nyctophilus gouldi*   SIZE **BODY TO 7 CM TAIL TO 6 CM**

GOULD'S LONG-EARED BAT

This bat has small eyes, long, ribbed ears joined above the head with a triangular lobe over the aperture and a small noseleaf. The tail is enclosed in the tail-membrane. **Behaviour** They roost alone or in small groups in tree hollows and under loose bark, emerging after dusk to forage in the understorey. They use sight and echo-location to catch flying insects in their wings or tail membrane. Females form maternity colonies and mark their young with secretions from nose glands before leaving the roost.
Reproduction They mate from April to June. Females store the sperm, fertilise their ova in September/October, and give birth to 1-2 young in October-December. They suckle from teats in the mother's armpits, are carried for 3-5 days, then left in the roost until they can fly at 4 weeks. They are weaned at 6 weeks. **Diet** Insects, spiders. **Habitat** Sclerophyll forests, woodlands, subtropical rainforests.

FAMILY **VESPERTILIONIDAE**   SPECIES *Chalinolobus gouldi*   SIZE **BODY TO 6 CM TAIL TO 5 CM**

GOULD'S WATTLED BAT

This bat has a short muzzle with a loose flap hanging from the corner of the mouth and short ears with a small lobe partially covering the aperture. The tail is enclosed in the tail-membrane. **Behaviour** They roost in tree hollows, under bark, rock crevices and buildings. Males roost alone, females in colonies of 8-40 bats. At dusk they fly up to 15 km to feeding sites and hunt below the canopy, using good vision and echo-location to catch flying and crawling insects. They hibernate in cold conditions. **Reproduction** Females mate at the beginning of winter and store the sperm until they ovulate at the end of winter. Twins are born from September to late November. They suckle from teats in the mother's armpit, are carried until well-furred, then left at the roost while she forages, becoming independent at 6 weeks. **Diet** Insects. **Habitat** Most habitats from urban areas to deserts, tropical forests and alpine regions.

FAMILY **MURIDAE**   SPECIES *Hydromys chrysogaster*   SIZE **BODY TO 37 CM TAIL TO 33 CM**

WATER-RAT

Australia's largest rodent, it has soft, dense, water-repellent fur, a flattened head, long blunt muzzle, small eyes and ears and a thick tail used as a rudder. The hindfeet are large and webbed. **Behaviour** They forage from dusk to early morning, follow tracks along the water's edge to feeding sites, and sleep in a burrow in the riverbank or in a hollow log. Burrows have a concealed entrance, run parallel to the bank, and have one or more nest chambers. Males fight to establish dominance hierarchies and defend territories of some 2-10 ha. **Reproduction** They breed year-round, but most young are born from September to February. Females rear 1-5 litters annually of 3-4 young, born 34 days after mating. They suckle in the nest for one month and are independent at 2 months. **Diet** Fish, crustaceans, molluscs, frogs, birds, eggs, bats, insects. **Habitat** Waterways with good vegetative cover, to 1500 m.

| FAMILY **MURIDAE** | SPECIES *Mesembriomys gouldii* | SIZE **BODY TO 31 CM TAIL TO 41 CM** |

BLACK-FOOTED TREE-RAT

One of Australia's largest rodents, this arboreal rat has long, coarse, shaggy fur and a bushy-tipped tail.
Behaviour They live alone and shelter by day in a tree hollow, among palm fronds, in crevices and in buildings.
Several nests in different trees are used and other rats are kept away by grumbling and growling threats, or attacked if necessary. They are fast runners and agile climbers, often feeding on the ground, rushing up a tree if disturbed, and travelling 500 m or more from their nests to feeding sites. **Reproduction** They breed year-round with a peak in August and September, although few births occur in the wet season. Females give birth to up to 3 young 43-44 days after mating. If the mother leaves the nest the newborn are dragged clinging to the her teats until fully furred at 10-11 days old. They are weaned at about 28 days and are fully grown at 11-12 weeks. **Diet** Nuts, fruits, flowers, insects, molluscs. **Habitat** Open forests and tropical woodlands with a grassy or shrubby understorey.

| FAMILY **MURIDAE** | SPECIES *Rattus fuscipes* | SIZE **BODY TO 21 CM TAIL TO 19 CM** |

BUSH RAT

This rodent has dense soft fur and a sparsely-haired tail with overlapping scales. The soles of the hindfeet are pale, distinguishing it from the Swamp Rat which has black soles. **Behaviour** They shelter by day in rock crevices, beneath fallen timber or in burrows 2-3 m long. These are often built under logs or stones with a sloping, twisting tunnel leading to a vegetation-lined nest chamber about 40 cm deep. Adults live alone or with their young, and defend a home range of 0.1-0.4 ha, although males roam over large areas in spring looking for females. **Reproduction** They breed throughout the year with peaks in late spring and summer, and produce up to 4 litters of 4-5 young per year, 20-21 days after mating. They are weaned at 4-5 weeks and may live from 1 to 3 years. **Diet** Insects, fungi and other vegetation. **Habitat** Rainforests, heaths, sedgelands, wet sclerophyll forests, to 1800 m.

| FAMILY **MURIDAE** | SPECIES *Pseudomys novaehollandiae* | SIZE **BODY TO 95 MM TAIL TO 110 MM** |

NEW HOLLAND MOUSE

Easily confused with the House Mouse, but lacking its distinctive odour, this small rodent has larger ears and eyes and may have a dark stripe down the centre of the head. The feet are slender and covered with white hairs.
Behaviour Active mainly at night, they live in family groups, sharing a permanent nest in a deep burrow up to 5 m long, with a nest chamber and a vertical entrance shaft. They also build short, shallow burrows as refuges. They maintain separate home ranges, and up to 17 animals per hectare may be found in good conditions. **Reproduction** They breed from August to January, with up to 4 litters of 4-5 young produced per year, 32-39 days after mating. They are weaned at 3-4 weeks, and may live 18-24 months. **Diet** Seeds, flowers, fungi, moss, roots, insects. **Habitat** Dry coastal heaths, scrubs, woodlands, open forests.

FAMILY **MURIDAE** SPECIES *Notomys alexis* SIZE **BODY TO 11 CM TAIL TO 15 CM**

SPINIFEX HOPPING-MOUSE

This rodent has long hindlegs, a long tufted tail and a small throat pouch of unknown function. Males and some females have a naked glandular area on the chest. **Behaviour** Active at night, they shelter in burrows up to 1 m deep with several vertical shafts and a broad horizontal tunnel leading to a nest chamber. Up to 10 adults may share a burrow, and groups build adjacent burrows linked by runways, and cooperate in digging, rearing young and rejecting strangers. Secretions from the chest gland are probably used to scent-mark group members. They move slowly on four feet, but hop when moving fast. **Reproduction** They breed year round, with peaks in spring and after good rainfall, producing 3-4 young 32-34 days after mating. They are left in the nest while the mother forages and are weaned at 4 weeks. **Diet** Seeds, leaves, roots, insects. **Habitat** Arid spinifex and tussock grasslands, woodlands, shrublands, sand dunes.

FAMILY **CANIDAE** SPECIES *Canis familiaris* SIZE **BODY TO 98 CM TAIL TO 38 CM**

DINGO

A form of the domestic dog, the dingo is reddish-brown with white points, or black with sandy markings. It has a bushy tail with a scent gland at the base, erect ears, a narrower snout and longer canines than the domestic dog. **Behaviour** Active mainly around dawn and dusk, they shelter in a shady site. Females rear their young in a den in a cave, rock pile, hollow log, rabbit warren or wombat burrow. They form loose associations with a dominant male and female and 4-5 subordinates, distinguished by scent-marking. The pack cooperate to hunt large game. They howl to keep contact and to attract mates. **Reproduction** Females give birth to 2-9 pups from March to September, 63 days after mating. She suckles them for 3-4 months, then regurgitates water and provides food until they can hunt. Juveniles often follow their parents until about 12 months old. **Diet** Mammals, reptiles, birds, insects. **Habitat** Most habitats.

FAMILY **DELPHINIDAE** SPECIES *Delphinus delphis* SIZE **TO 2.4 M**

COMMON DOLPHIN

This torpedo-shaped marine mammal has an hourglass pattern on its flanks. It has a long slender beak, a slender, sickle-shaped dorsal fin, thin tapering flippers, and thin tail flukes with a slight notch in the edge. **Behaviour** They move in groups of 5-50 and congregate in herds of 3000 or more, following schools of migrating fish. Small groups scatter in the late afternoons to feed on organisms rising to the surface. They can dive to 280 m and stay underwater for 8 minutes or more. They use high pitched squeaks, yaps and whistles to communicate over long distances, and use echo-location to navigate and find prey in poor visibility. **Reproduction** They mate in spring and autumn at intervals of 1-3 years, producing a single calf 10-11 months later. It suckles for 1-3 years and may live to 22 years old. **Diet** Fish, cephalopods. **Habitat** Warm temperate, sub-tropical, tropical coastal and, deep oceanic waters.

| FAMILY **DELPHINIDAE** | SPECIES *Tursiops truncatus* | SIZE **TO 4 M** |

BOTTLENOSE DOLPHIN

This torpedo-shaped marine mammal has a blue-grey band from the base of its short beak to each eye. The lower jaw extends beyond the upper jaw and curves up slightly. The flippers are pointed, the dorsal fin is sickle-shaped and the tail flukes are thin with rounded tips and a notched edge. **Behaviour** They swim in pods of 5-20, forming part of a herd of several hundred with a home range of around 85 sq km, rising to breathe every 15-20 seconds. They communicate over long distances using squawks, squeaks, yaps and whistles, and can echo-locate to navigate and detect prey. **Reproduction** They mate from February to May and September to November at 2-3 year intervals, producing a single calf 12 months later. It suckles for 12-18 months and may live for 40 years. **Diet** Fish, squid, crustaceans and other marine organisms. **Habitat** Warm-temperate, subtropical and tropical coastal waters, bays, estuaries.

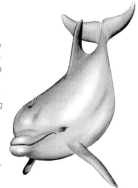

| FAMILY **DUGONGIDAE** | SPECIES *Dugong dugon* | SIZE **TO 3.3 M** |

DUGONG

The only herbivorous marine mammal, it has paddle-like fore-limbs, a horizontal tail-fluke, a broad, flat head, small eyes, small ear-openings, a large mouth with fleshy lips, and nostrils on top of the head. Males have a pair of tusk-like upper inci-sors. **Behaviour** They feed close to shore during day-light hours and travel about 25 km daily, diving repeatedly for food, staying underwater for up to 8.5 minutes, swimming at up to 22 km/h. They live alone or in small family groups, and sometimes congregate in herds of several hundred. They have good vision and hearing, and communicate with whistling and chirping sounds. **Reproduction** They mate from May to November at 3-6 year intervals, giving birth to a single young 12-14 months later. It rides on the mother's back when not suckling, stay-ing with her for about 2 years, and may live for 73 years. **Diet** Seagrasses, algae. **Habitat** Shallow tropical coastal waters and estuaries.

| FAMILY **OTARIIDAE** | SPECIES *Arctocephalus forsteri* | SIZE **MALE TO 2.5 M FEMALE TO 1.5 M** |

NEW ZEALAND FUR-SEAL

This marine mammal has a dog-like head, small, rolled ears, strong flippers and webbed hindlimbs. Bulls have a massive neck and a thick mane of coarse hair. Newborn are black. **Behaviour** They are powerful swimmers, but rest, moult and breed on land, moving with a slow, shuffling walk. Breeding colonies of up to 1300 form in October on exposed shores of offshore islands. The strongest bulls gather a harem of about 6 cows and defend a territo-ry by posturing, barking or fighting. In January the bulls disperse to other rocky beaches. **Reproduction** They give birth to a single pup from November to January and mate 8 days later. At 10 days old it is left with the other pups while the mother feeds at sea for 3-5 days. She leaves every 2-4 days until it is weaned at 9-10 months. **Diet** Squid, fish, octopus, rock lobster, crab, seabirds. **Habitat** Cool temperate coastal waters, rocky offshore islands.

FAMILY **OTARIIDAE**   SPECIES *Arctocephalus pusillus*   SIZE **MALE TO 2.3 M FEMALE TO 1.7 M**

AUSTRALIAN FUR-SEAL

This marine mammal has a dog-like head, small rolled ears, strong flippers and webbed hindlimbs. Bulls are dark grey-brown with a mane of long coarse hair. Cows are silver-grey with a creamy-yellow throat and chest.

Behaviour They are powerful swimmers and can dive to at least 200 m, but rest, moult and breed on land, moving with a slow, shuffling walk or a fast gallop. Bulls arrive at breeding grounds in late October and reoccupy territories by roaring, barking and fighting, acquiring a harem of 60 or more cows. Males disperse to feed at sea in January.

Reproduction They mate from October to late December,5-7 days after giving birth. Pups congregate and the cows go to sea after mating, returning weekly to suckle their pups for 8 months. They then accompany the mother at sea until weaned by 12 months. **Diet** Squid, fish, octopus, rock lobsters. **Habitat** Cool temperate coastal waters, rocky coastlines.

FAMILY **OTARIIDAE**   SPECIES *Hydrurga leptonyx*   SIZE **MALE TO 3 M FEMALE TO 3.6 M**

LEOPARD SEAL

This marine mammal has a reptilian-like head with wide gaping jaws and a narrow neck. It lacks an external ear and has distinctive 3-pronged cheek teeth. It has flippers for forelimbs and webbed hindlimbs. **Behaviour** Fast and powerful swimmers, they rest, moult and breed on land, heaving their whole body forward in a caterpillar-like motion. They are generally solitary, but form monogamous breeding pairs in summer on the edge of the Antarctic pack-ice. Young seals disperse north in winter, and some reach the coast of Australia between July and October. They have a vocal repertoire of gurgles, grunts, chirps and whistles, and a throaty alarm call.

Reproduction They mate from January to March and give birth to a single pup from September to January. It is suckled for about 4 weeks. **Diet** Krill, fish, cephalopods, seabirds, seal young. **Habitat** Pack ice, Antarctic coastline, subantarctic islands, cold to temperate coastal waters.

FAMILY **BALAENOPTERIDAE**   SPECIES *Megaptera novaeangliae*   SIZE **15 M**

HUMPBACK WHALE

This marine mammal has a hump back, barnacle-encrusted knobs on its jaw and hundreds of fringed sheets of baleen hanging from the roof of the mouth used to sieve krill. The flippers are up to 16 m long with knobs on their trailing edges. **Behaviour** They can swim at 20 km/h and dive for 30 minutes, often leaping out of the water and rolling in mid-air, using echo-location to navigate in murky waters. They leave summer feeding grounds in the Southern Ocean in May to calve and mate in tropical Australian waters, returning in November. They form social groups with up to 7 members and often fight over females.

Reproduction Females produce a single calf every 2-3 years, from June to October, and mate soon after. It suckles for 5-7 months from mammary glands beneath the mother's pectoral fins, and swims with her for 2-3 years. **Diet** Krill and other crustaceans. **Habitat** Coastal waters.

Birds

Birds are Australia's most conspicuous vertebrates, and among the 750 or so species are spectacular parrots and cockatoos, noisy and quarrelsome honeyeaters, amazing vocal mimics like the lyrebird, huge flightless emus and industrious bower birds who build elaborately-decorated structures to attract a mate.

The diversity of Australian birds is exemplified by the honeyeaters, and the 65 members of this family have colonised every corner of the continent. Nowhere else is there such a variation in form and colour as in Australia's parrots; and only here are cockatoos, nectar-feeding lorikeets and ground-feeding rosellas to be found.

Although birds are warm-blooded, they are more closely related to reptiles than mammals. They lay eggs with hard shells and their feathers are, in fact, modified scales. The hand and finger bones are fused together and anchor the primary flight feathers, while the secondary flight feathers are attached to the forearm. Perhaps the greatest modification has taken place in the bones themselves which are thin, hollow and reinforced inside with struts, making the skeleton both light and very strong.

These unique structural features have endowed the birds with the power of flight, enabling them to colonise almost every habitat on earth, from the frozen expanses of the Antarctic to the treeless deserts. Australia does, however, have a number of flightless birds, the ratites, a group that includes emus and cassowaries. Although unable to escape predators by taking to the air, they are powerful and formidable birds, quite capable of inflicting serious injuries if attacked.

Penguins have also lost the power of flight and have abandoned the skies for the sea. Their wings have evolved into flippers for rapid underwater swimming and their bones are denser than other birds. This, together with a layer of blubber prevents them from sinking too deep or floating on the surface.

FAMILY **CASUARIIDAE**   SPECIES *Casuarius casuarius*   SIZE **TO 1.75 M**

SOUTHERN CASSOWARY

This endangered flightless bird has a spike-like claw on its inner toe to 12 cm long, a pair of red wattles on its neck and a bony casque (helmet) on top of its head. Chicks are striped yellow and black, juveniles have smaller wattles and no casque.

Behaviour They live alone within a home range for most of the year. Females are larger and dominate males, stretching their necks, fluffing feathers and rumbling in threat. Males can be very aggressive when guarding their chicks, roaring loudly and kicking with both feet, sometimes inflicting serious wounds with their toe spike. **Breeding** They breed from June to October and lay 4 green eggs in a scrape in the ground, lined with vegetation, deep in the rainforest. Males incubate the eggs for about 2 months and care for the chicks for another 9 months. **Call** Rumbling; booming; roaring; hissing. **Diet** Fruit and some flowers, insects, snails. **Habitat** Tropical rainforests.

FAMILY **CASUARIIDAE**   SPECIES *Dromaius novaehollandiae*   SIZE **TO 1.9 M**

EMU

This flightless bird has vestigial wings about 20 cm long, brown eyes and a sparsely-feathered head and upper neck. Females develop thick black feathers over the head and neck in the breeding season. Chicks are dark brown with cream stripes. **Behaviour** They live in small groups or large flocks, staying in the same area or migrating to find food and water. Some make seasonal migrations, travelling hundreds of kilometres annually. They run with a swaying motion up to 48 km/h. Breeding pairs form in summer or autumn and stay together for about 5 months. **Breeding** They breed in winter and usually lay 7-11 green eggs in a scrape on the ground lined with vegetation. Males incubate the eggs for 8 weeks and care for the chicks for 6-7 months. **Call** Guttural grunts. Females emit a dull boom. **Diet** Leaves, grass, flowers, fruit, insects. **Habitat** From arid inland plains, tropical woodlands and heaths to coastal dunes.

FAMILY **MEGAPODIIDAE**   SPECIES *Alectura lathami*   SIZE **TO 75 CM**

AUSTRALIAN BRUSH-TURKEY

This mound-builder has a red head and neck with sparse hair-like feathers, bright yellow wattles, brown eyes and a laterally-flattened tail. Chicks are brown. **Behaviour** Generally ground-dwelling, they fly to escape danger and to roost in trees at night. In the breeding season the male builds a mound of decomposing leaf litter and soil up to 2 m high and 4 m wide, or adds to an existing mound, and chases away other males. He tests the temperature with his beak and adds or removes material to keep the mound at a constant 33° C. Each morning he struts to the top and emits deep booming calls. **Breeding** One or more females lay 18-24 eggs deep in the mound from August to December. The chicks dig their way out 50 days later and can fly and feed within hours. **Call** Grunting. Males boom at mound. **Diet** Fruit, insects, snails. **Habitat** Subtropical rainforests.

| FAMILY **MEGAPODIIDAE** | SPECIES *Leipoa ocellata* | SIZE **TO 60 CM** |

MALLEEFOWL

This mound-builder has a fine white line beneath its orange-brown eyes. Chicks are grey-brown, freckled with black and buff. **Behaviour** Generally ground-dwelling, they fly to escape danger and to roost in low trees at night. They mate for life and pairs live in a permanent territory of 40–70 ha. In autumn they build a mound of decomposing leaf litter, twigs, bark and sand to 1.5 m high and 5 m wide, or add to an existing one. The male defends the site and tests the temperature with his beak, maintaining a constant 33° C by opening the mound or adding warm sand. **Breeding** They breed from September to April. Females lay a single egg early each morning, deep in the mound, until 15–24 have been laid. The chicks dig their way out 7 weeks later and can fly and feed within hours. **Call** Grunts and booming territorial calls. **Diet** Seeds, buds, insects. **Habitat** Mallee.

| FAMILY **PHASIANIDAE** | SPECIES *Coturnix pectoralis* | SIZE **TO 19 CM** |

STUBBLE QUAIL

Females have an off-white throat, pale face and neck and a dusky-flecked breast. Males have a light chestnut throat and face, white stripes above the eyes and down the centre of the head, and a black patch on the breast. **Behaviour** Usually ground-dwelling, they hide in thick grass and are seldom seen, but fly off with a clatter of wings if disturbed. They are nomadic, travelling alone and following ripening grain, sometimes gathering in large numbers, feeding mainly at night. **Breeding** They breed mainly from August to February (year round in the north in good years), laying 7–14 eggs in a scrape on the ground lined with grass in dense cover. The female incubates the eggs and the chicks leave the nest on hatching 3 weeks later. Both parents care for them until they can fly at 6 weeks. **Call** Whistling 'cuck-ee-whit' and 'too-weep'. **Diet** Seeds, some invertebrates. **Habitat** Grasslands.

| FAMILY **SPHENISCIDAE** | SPECIES *Eudyptula minor* | SIZE **TO 33 CM** |

LITTLE PENGUIN

The only penguin to breed in Australia, this aquatic bird has a greyish face, a dark blue back, and a white trailing edge on its flippers. **Behaviour** They roost at night in burrows under tussocks and in crevices. Before dawn they converge on paths to the beach, plunge into the water and spend the day at sea. They swim at about 6 km/h, steering with their webbed feet, diving to 40 m deep for food. After dark they return to the roost, waddle up the beach and cliffs in groups, and regurgitate food into the chick's mouth. They moult after breeding and most disperse to sea for 2–3 months. **Breeding** They breed mainly in August and September and lay 1–3 eggs in a refurbished burrow or a new one. Both parents incubate the eggs for 35–42 days and share parental duties. The young fledge at 2 months. **Call** Yapping; braying. **Diet** Fish, squid. **Habitat** Coastal waters.

FAMILY **ANHINGIDAE** SPECIES *Anhinga melanogaster* SIZE **TO 90 CM**

DARTER

Males are glossy black with a white stripe below the eye and along the neck. Females are grey-brown above and pale grey below. Juveniles resemble females, but lack the neck stripe. **Behaviour** Their feathers are not waterproof and they spread their wings out to dry, squeezing out water with the bill and preening with oil. They hunt while partly submerged with only the neck above the surface, held in an S shape, ready to strike with their dagger-like bill. They also hunt underwater, diving frequently and staying submerged for up to 1 minute. To become airborne they leap from the water, and often soar on thermals. **Breeding** They breed mainly in spring and summer and lay 3-6 eggs at 2-3 day intervals in a rough platform nest in a tree over the water. Both parents incubate the eggs for 26-30 days. The young fledge at about 50 days. **Call** 'Kaah'; 'tjeeu'. **Diet** Fish, insects, frogs, turtles. **Habitat** Fresh and saline lakes and rivers.

FAMILY **PHALACROCORACIDAE** SPECIES *Phalacrocorax melanoleucos* SIZE **TO 63 CM**

LITTLE PIED CORMORANT

This darter is black above and white below, with a white line over the eye to its dusky-yellow bill. Breeding adults have a black forehead tuft, white frills on the side of the crown and an orange bill and chin. **Behaviour** They congregate in large flocks where food is plentiful, diving to catch fish and taking prey from the shallows. Their plumage is not waterproof and they rest on branches drying their wings, preening and shaking off the water. Colonies of a few to several hundred pairs form to breed around tree-lined rivers, lakes and wetlands. **Breeding** They breed in spring and summer in the south, and late summer to winter in the north. They lay 3-7 eggs in a platform nest in a tree, shrub or on the ground. Both parents incubate the eggs and feed the young on predigested food. **Call** Short croak. **Diet** Crustaceans, fish, frogs, water snails. **Habitat** Most aquatic habitats.

FAMILY **PHALACROCORACIDAE** SPECIES *Phalacrocorax carbo* SIZE **TO 92 CM**

GREAT CORMORANT

This darter is black with white or grey throat feathers and bare yellow skin on the face and throat. Breeding adults have white plumes on the upper neck and flanks, and an erectile crest on the head. **Behaviour** They usually roost in groups of around 10 birds and often fish alone, diving and staying submerged for 30 seconds or more. Breeding males display from the nest, waving their wings and exposing their white flank patches. Birds guarding the nest lower their crests, while those nearby raise their crests. **Breeding** They breed mostly in autumn and spring and lay 3-5 eggs in a nest of sticks and debris in a tree, shrub or on the ground. Both parents incubate the eggs for about 28 days and care for the young for a month after they fledge at 7 weeks. **Call** Croaks, grunts, hisses. **Diet** Fish, crustaceans, turtles, insects. **Habitat** Large fresh and saline lakes, rivers, bays, estuaries, wetlands.

| FAMILY **LARIDAE** | SPECIES *Larus novaehollandiae* | SIZE **TO 45 CM** |

SILVER GULL

This gull is white with a grey back and shoulders, black outer wing feathers with white tips and a scarlet red bill and feet. **Behaviour** They travel widely to exploit food sources and congregate in groups. Older birds dominate and drive the young from feeding areas, hunching, arching, running and squawking. At night they sleep on bare islands, sand spits and in parks. When breeding, they nest in small or large colonies on islands and spits with low vegetation. Males establish a small nesting territory and older birds form permanent pairs.
Breeding They breed mainly from August to April and lay 2-4 eggs in a shallow, cup-shaped nest on the ground or in a shrub. Both parents share incubation of 21-27 days and care for the young for about 6 weeks.
Call Harsh 'kwarr'. **Diet** Crustaceans, marine invertebrates, insects, worms. **Habitat** Coastal and inland waterways, parks, paddocks.

| FAMILY **LARIDAE** | SPECIES *Sterna bergii* | SIZE **TO 49 CM** |

CRESTED TERN

This tern is mid-grey above and white below with a black crown and a shaggy, erectable crest over the nape.
Behaviour They rest alone or in flocks of 50 or more on sand spits and reefs along coastal beaches and inlets. They fish in nearby waters, flying in patterns 5-15 m high, plunging for surface fish and submerging briefly before flying off. They often swim and float for hours during the day. Colonies of up to several thousand gather to breed on offshore islands. During courtship one bird carries a fish to the other, and they fly together, spiralling, twisting and turning in unison. **Breeding** They breed from September to December in the south, and March to June in the north. Females lay 1-2 eggs in a ground depression. Both parents share incubation of 25-26 days and care for the young, who fledge at 38-40 days. **Call** Rasping 'kirrik'.
Diet Small fish, eggs, baby turtles. **Habitat** Seashores, offshore islands.

| FAMILY **SCOLOPACIDAE** | SPECIES *Limosa lapponica* | SIZE **TO 45 CM** |

BAR-TAILED GODWIT

This non-breeding migrant is mid grey-brown above with light edges to the feathers. The underparts are creamy white with a grey-brown wash over the chest. In the weeks before leaving to breed the male becomes rich chestnut red. **Behaviour** They breed in Siberia and Alaska, and gather in thousands between Broome and Port Headland in April and May before migrating, and on their return in August and September. Returning birds travel around the coast, flying in close flocks, banking, rising and falling in unison. They roost together at night and feed in groups, walking over mudflats and wading in shallow water, probing frequently with the bill for buried animals. Non-breeders remain in Australia year-round. **Breeding** They breed in June and July and both parents incubate the usual clutch of 4 eggs for 20–21 days. **Call** Sharp 'kewit'; 'kip-kip-kip'. **Diet** Molluscs, crustaceans, marine worms and other invertebrates. **Habitat** Tidal flats, lagoons, coastal salt pans.

FAMILY **SCOLOPACIDAE** SPECIES *Numenius madagascariensis* SIZE **TO 66 CM**

EASTERN CURLEW

This large migratory wading bird is pale-brown streaked with dark-brown on the head, neck and breast, and mottled with dark-brown on the shoulders and back. It is paler below with a very long down-curved black bill with a pink base. **Behaviour** They arrive in northern Australia from far northeastern Asia in August and September, and migrate around the coast. They forage alone or in dispersed groups at low tide, probing the mud or sand for food with their long bill. At high tide they roost together on sandspits, rocky outcrops, salt marshes and among mangroves. In late March to early May they migrate back to their breeding grounds in Siberia and Manchuria, although some non-breeding birds remain in Australia. **Breeding** They breed in May and June and lay 4 eggs, incubated for 27-29 days. **Call** Mournful 'karr-er'. High-pitched 'ker-lee, ker-lee'. **Diet** Crustaceans, worms, molluscs. **Habitat** Estuaries, mud flats, mangroves, soft sandy beaches.

FAMILY **SCOLOPACIDAE** SPECIES *Calidris acuminata* SIZE **TO 22 CM**

SHARP-TAILED SANDPIPER

This migratory wading bird is mottled dark grey and grey-brown above with pale-edged feathers. It is white below with brown speckles and a pale brown wash over the breast. Immatures and breeding adults have rufous-pink breasts and bright rufous crowns. **Behaviour** They arrive in northern Australia from Siberia in August and September and migrate across the continent, congregating in large numbers in flooded areas. They shelter and roost in low herbage, tussock grasslands or on samphire flats in small groups or flocks of several hundred, and forage in shallow water, probing with the bill. They leave southern areas early in the year and move north to fatten up before migrating back to their breeding grounds in April and May. Some non-breeding birds remain in Australia. **Breeding** They breed in May and June and lay 4 eggs, incubated by the female. **Call** Soft 'pleep'; shrill 'wit-wit'. **Diet** Crustaceans, molluscs, insects, worms, aquatic plants. **Habitat** Estuaries, tidal flats, fresh and brackish lakes.

FAMILY **SCOLOPACIDAE** SPECIES *Calidris ferruginea* SIZE **TO 23 CM**

CURLEW SANDPIPER

This migratory wading bird is grey-brown above with a white eyebrow and a broad white wing stripe. The underparts are white with a grey wash over the breast. Breeding adults are dull red below. The bill is long, black and down-curving. **Behaviour** Large numbers arrive in northern Australia from the Arctic tundra in Siberia at the end of August and disperse along the coast and overland. Many return to the same area each year and congregate in flocks of tens or tens of thousands. They forage along the shore in groups, wading in water up to their bellies, probing and pecking in the sand and mud for food. Most leave Australia by the end of May and migrate back to their breeding grounds. Some non-breeding birds remain. **Breeding** They breed in June and July and lay 4 eggs. **Call** Soft twitters; loud trills. **Diet** Worms, molluscs, crustaceans, insects. **Habitat** Tidal flats, wetlands.

| FAMILY **JACANIDAE** | SPECIES *Irediparra gallinacea* | SIZE **TO 27 CM** |

COMB-CRESTED JACANA

This waterbird has a red, fleshy, forehead comb, yellow cheeks, and a black crown, hind neck and breast band. The belly is white. It has long legs and very long toes.

Behaviour They roost in a raft nest at night and forage alone or in pairs in the shallows or among floating plants. Their long legs hamper take off, but they can fly long distances. They run fast on land and walk on floating vegetation. If threatened, they dive and can remain submerged for up to 30 minutes with their nostrils above water. Adults with young feign a broken wing if disturbed. **Breeding** They breed from September to May and lay 3-4 eggs in a platform nest built on aquatic vegetation. Both parents share incubation of 4 weeks and care for the young for 2-3 weeks, carrying eggs and chicks under their wings to safety if the water level changes. **Call** Shrill trumpeting; squeaky 'pee-pee-pee'. **Diet** Aquatic plants, seeds, insects. **Habitat** Wetlands, lakes, lagoons.

| FAMILY **HAEMATOPODIDAE** | SPECIES *Haematopus longirostris* | SIZE **TO 52 CM** |

PIED OYSTERCATCHER

This oystercatcher is black with white underparts and a narrow wing stripe. It has scarlet eyes and eyerings and a long, orange-red, chisel-shaped bill. **Behaviour** They are noisy and sedentary and roost in small groups on sand bars, rock shelves or reefs at high tide, often standing on one leg. They forage alone or in dispersed pairs on sand flats at low tide, probing and pecking with the bill, hammering and stabbing to open molluscs. Pairs mate for life and defend a territory, although they may join flocks out of the breeding season. Adults with young feign an injury if disturbed. **Breeding** They breed from August to January and lay 2-3 eggs in a shallow scrape on the ground above the high tide line. Both parents share incubation of 28-32 days and feed the young until they fledge in 5-9 weeks. **Call** Clear 'he-eep'. Rapid 'pic-pic-pic' in display. **Diet** Molluscs, worms, crustaceans. **Habitat** Tidal flats, beaches, estuaries.

| FAMILY **HAEMATOPODIDAE** | SPECIES *Haematopus fuliginosus* | SIZE **TO 52 CM** |

SOOTY OYSTERCATCHER

This oystercatcher is black with scarlet eyes, orange eye-rings and a long, orange, chisel-shaped bill.

Behaviour They roost and nest in small groups on rocky headlands at high tide and forage alone, picking shellfish from the rocks and hammering them against a rock or prising them open with the bill. They usually move to offshore islands adjacent to their foraging grounds to breed, and the young stay with their parents for up to 9 months. Adults feign injury or pretend to brood elsewhere to divert threats from the nest. **Breeding** They breed from August to January and lay 2-4 eggs in a shallow scrape in the sand above high tide or in a rock depression. Both parents share incubation of 25-27 days and care for the young until they fledge at around 6 weeks. **Call** Loud 'he-eep'; pic-pic-pic' in display. **Diet** Mainly limpets, periwinkles, mussels. **Habitat** Rocky shores, stony beaches, coral reefs, estuaries, islands.

FAMILY **RECURVIROSTRIDAE**   SPECIES *Himantopus himantopus*   SIZE **TO 39 CM**

BLACK-WINGED STILT

This wader is white with a black back and nape, a long fine bill and spindly legs. **Behaviour** They gather in loose feeding flocks of several hundred outside the breeding season and forage in the mud and shallow water, probing and jabbing with their needle-like bill for food. They have a very small mouth and only tiny organisms can be eaten. They are quite nomadic, flying to new feeding grounds at night. Inland birds disperse to coastal areas in dry times. In the breeding season they nest in dispersed groups, and pairs defend a small territory. Family groups may also defend a feeding territory. **Breeding** They breed mainly from August to December and lay 4 eggs in a platform nest usually on a small island. Both parents share incubation of 22-25 days and care for the young for another month. **Call** Yelping. **Diet** Tiny molluscs, shrimps, diatoms, insects. **Habitat** Fresh and saline wetlands.

FAMILY **RECURVIROSTRIDAE**   SPECIES *Recurvirostra novaehollandiae*   SIZE **TO 48 CM**

RED-NECKED AVOCET

This wader has a long, black, upturned bill, a bright chestnut head and neck, a white eye-ring, white body and a dusky-black wing bar and wingtips. **Behaviour** They roost, fly and feed in compact flocks, sometimes with hundreds or thousands of birds, and move around following local rainfall. They wade in shallow water and soft mud, sweeping their partly open bill from side-to-side searching for food. They have half-webbed toes, swim well, and sometimes feed in deep water. Breeding pairs nest in dispersed groups, bowing, trampling, bill-dipping and preening in courtship displays. **Breeding** They breed mainly from August to December and lay 4 eggs in a ground depression lined with plant matter, beside shallow water. Both parents share incubation of 3-4 weeks and care for the young. **Call** Musical 'toot-toot'; yelps; wheezes. **Diet** Tiny crustaceans, worms, molluscs, insects, seeds. **Habitat** Fresh and saline marshes, lakes, mud flats.

FAMILY **CHARADRIIDAE**   SPECIES *Elseyornis melanops*   SIZE **TO 18 CM**

BLACK-FRONTED DOTTEREL

This small plover has a black forehead, black eye band and broad black 'V' on the chest. The upperparts are brown with pale streaks and a chestnut shoulder patch, the underparts are white. **Behaviour** They feed alone or in pairs, sometimes in loose flocks of up to 100 birds, and nest in solitary territories. They feed on the shoreline, running and pecking food from the surface without wading far. They are nomadic in inland areas, flying with deep, erratic wing-beats on long wings. Breeding adults feign injury to distract intruders from the nest. **Breeding** They breed from April to September in the south and September to December in the north, and lay 2-3 eggs in a shallow ground depression lined with mud pellets, shells, stones or twigs. Both parents share incubation of about 26 days. **Call** Contact 'tip' in flight; metallic 'pink'. **Diet** Insects, crustaceans, seeds. **Habitat** Wetlands, lakes, dams.

| FAMILY **CHARADRIIDAE** | SPECIES *Vanellus miles* | SIZE **TO 39 CM** |

MASKED LAPWING

This plover has yellow wattles over the face and small spurs on the shoulders. It is brown above and white below with a black crown and flight feathers.

Behaviour They roost and rest on one foot, often in shallow water, and forage on the ground in pairs or small groups with their shoulders hunched and head forward, stabbing with their bill. When not breeding they may travel widely and gather in flocks of several hundred. In the breeding season they stay in a local area and pairs establish territories in their traditional breeding grounds. **Breeding** They breed mainly from July to December in the south and November to June in the north. Females lay 3-4 eggs in a scrape on the ground. Both parents share incubation of about 28 days and care for the young who fledge in 3-4 weeks. **Call** Piercing 'ki-ki-ki-ki-ki-ki-ki'. **Diet** Insects, spiders, small crustaceans, worms. **Habitat** Wet grasslands, marshes, lakeshores.

| FAMILY **ANSERANATIDAE** | SPECIES *Anseranas semipalmata* | SIZE **TO 92 CM** |

MAGPIE GOOSE

This goose is distinguished by its long yellow legs, half-webbed feet, pied plumage and the knob on its head. **Behaviour** At the onset of the dry season family groups form loose flocks around swamps, flying out at dawn to feed on the plains. As the swamps dry up they move to more permanent wetlands. In the wet season they congregate in swamps, separate into breeding pairs (or trios with a male and 2 females), and build a floating platform from clumps of spike rush for resting and courtship. A nest is added before egg-laying. **Breeding** They breed mainly from March to May. Females lay 6-9 eggs and share incubation with the male. Hatchlings emerge 24-25 days later and are led away by both parents who help them to feed on shoots and seeds. They can fly at 11 weeks. **Call** Loud honking. **Diet** Bulbs, roots, seeds. **Habitat** Floodplains, wetlands.

| FAMILY **ANATIDAE** | SPECIES *Dendrocygna eytoni* | SIZE **TO 61 CM** |

PLUMED WHISTLING-DUCK

This duck is distinguished by the long, black-edged yellow plumes on its flanks. The feathers of the upper back have yellow edges. The wings are brown above and paler below. The eye is yellow-orange and the bill is pink mottled with black. **Behaviour** It walks gracefully with its head high and body upright, feeds mainly on land, swims rather clumsily and only dives to escape danger. It flies slowly and its wings make a whistling sound. By day they roost by the water, form large flocks in the dry season and range widely in the wet season. At night they fly off to graze on the plains. **Breeding** They breed in the wet season from February to April. Females lay 8-14 eggs in a scrape in the ground, lined with grass. Both parents incubate the eggs for 28 days and lead the hatchlings to water. **Call** Shrill whistle; twittering. **Diet** Sedges, spike rushes, seeds, grass, legumes, herbs. **Habitat** Wetlands.

FAMILY **ANATIDAE**   SPECIES *Cygnus atratus*   SIZE **TO 1.4 M**

BLACK SWAN

This large black swan has an orange and dark red bill with a white bar near the tip and white-tipped wings. Immatures are grey-brown with white wing feathers tipped with black. **Behaviour** They are often heard at night trumpeting to each other as they fly. They feed on water vegetation, up-ending as they drag plants from the water. They become flightless after moulting between September and February, and often gather in flocks of many hundreds on open lakes. When the lakes dry out, they fly long distances in extended V formations. Older birds pair for life and display for 20-25 minutes before copulating. **Breeding** They breed mainly from February to May in the north and May to September in the south. Females lay 4-6 eggs in a large mound of vegetation among reeds or on small islands, and both parents incubate the eggs for 39-43 days. The young fledge at 113-160 days. **Call** Loud trumpeting. **Diet** Aquatic plants, grasses. **Habitat** Rivers, estuaries, lakes, wetlands.

FAMILY **ANATIDAE**   SPECIES *Tadorna tadornoides*   SIZE **TO 72 CM**

AUSTRALIAN SHELDUCK

This duck has black primary wing feathers, white upper leading edges and glossy green trailing edges, showing as white and green patches on the sides when resting. Females have a white eye-ring, white base to the bill and a dark chestnut breast. **Behaviour** They congregate in summer to moult and feed on large lakes and estuaries, resting by the water's edge and flying off to feed in the late afternoon. In autumn they disperse to breeding grounds. Pairs bond for life and return to the same nest every year. **Breeding** They breed from June to October and lay 5-15 eggs in a nest in a tree hollow, on the ground, or in a rabbit hole. While the female incubates the eggs for 30-35 days, the male establishes a separate territory, up to 2 km away, where they will rear the young. The hatchlings are led to the male's territory and the family reunited. **Call** Low honking. **Diet** Plants, insects, invertebrates. **Habitat** Lowland freshwater and saline lakes, estuaries, flooded pastures.

FAMILY **ANATIDAE**   SPECIES *Chenonetta jubata*   SIZE **TO 59 CM**

AUSTRALIAN WOOD (MANED) DUCK

This duck has a dark head and pale body. Males have a short mane of black feathers, a mottled white and grey breast, pale grey flanks and a black belly. Females have a white line above and below the eye, mottled flanks and white belly. **Behaviour** They walk well and spend most of their time on land, resting by the water in small groups and usually foraging at night. They mate for life and copulate on the water, usually preceded by ritualised displays by the male. **Breeding** They breed in spring in the south and after heavy rain in the north. Females lay 9-12 eggs in a nest in a tree hollow and incubate them for 28 days. Both parents call to hatchlings to jump to the ground and then lead them to the water to be raised. They can fly at 7-8 weeks. **Call** Nasal 'mew'. **Diet** Green herbage, seeds, insects. **Habitat** Freshwater lakes and swamps, usually in open woodlands and savanna.

| FAMILY **ANATIDAE** | SPECIES *Anas superciliosa* | SIZE **TO 61 CM** |

PACIFIC BLACK DUCK

This duck has a white to buff head with 2 black stripes and a green patch on the wing. **Behaviour** Often seen in parks, they live by permanent lakes or migrate between ephemeral lakes in drought-prone areas. In the south they tend to head north in winter. In the north they move to the coast in the dry season. They feed in the early morning and evening on the water and adjacent pastures, and spend much of the day sitting on the ground. If disturbed they fly off in a compact flock. **Breeding** They breed from July to October in the south and January to April in the north. Females lay 7-13 eggs in a well-woven cup nest among grass or reeds, or in a scrape in the ground, covering them with down when leaving to feed. They hatch 26-30 days later. **Call** Raucus quack (female); soft warble (male). **Diet** Seeds, aquatic insects, crustaceans. **Habitat** Fresh and saline lakes.

| FAMILY **ANATIDAE** | SPECIES *Anas gracilis* | SIZE **TO 48 CM** |

GREY TEAL

This duck is mottled brown and dark brown. The side of the head, chin and throat are almost white, the lower secondary wing feathers are black with a green sheen and have a white band above and below. **Behaviour** Highly nomadic, they move around the continent between swamps and lagoons, congregating to breed after floods and dispersing widely in droughts. They feed in the water, up-ending and dredging for plant and animal material, and stripping seeds from waterside vegetation.
Breeding Breeding occurs when water levels are high enough to sustain their food supply, and several broods are reared in good years. Females lay 4-14 eggs in a nest on the ground, in a tree hollow, rabbit burrow or rock crevice, and incubate them for 24-26 days. Both parents care for the young. **Call** Quack (female); burp (male). **Diet** Seeds, insects, mussels, crustaceans. **Habitat** Freshwater and saline lakes and swamps.

| FAMILY **PODICIPEDIDAE** | SPECIES *Tachybaptus novaehollandiae* | SIZE **TO 27 CM** |

AUSTRALASIAN GREBE

Breeding adults have a glossy black head and neck, a black bill with a white tip, a chestnut-coloured stripe on the side of the neck and a pale yellow face spot. Non-breeding birds and juveniles have a white throat and a grey-brown bill. Juveniles have stripes on the side of the head. **Behaviour** Poor, fluttering flyers, they spend most of their time on the water, in small deep ponds with rushes to hide among. They gather in small groups or pairs and feed mostly at dawn and dusk, diving deeply and chasing surface prey. They also eat their feathers and feed them to their young. Territorial pairs form in the breeding season. **Breeding** They breed from September to March and lay 4-6 eggs in a floating nest attached to reeds. Both parents incubate the eggs for 21 days. **Call** Rattlings trills; sharp single notes. **Diet** Fish, crustaceans, aquatic snails and insects. **Habitat** Sheltered freshwater ponds.

FAMILY **PODICIPEDIDAE** SPECIES *Podiceps cristatus* SIZE **TO 50 CM**

GREAT CRESTED GREBE

Breeding adults have a black crest on each side of the crown and a rufous, black-tipped ruff around the neck. These are very small or absent in non-breeding birds. Juveniles have stripes on the head and neck. **Behaviour** They rarely fly except when migrating to join winter flocks and breeding colonies. They dive deeply for food and swim long distances under water, staying submerged for up to a minute. They also eat their feathers and feed them to their young. Breeding pairs have an elaborate courtship display, raising ruffs and tufts, head-shaking, wing-spreading and diving.
Breeding They breed from November to March and lay 3-7 eggs in a floating nest of water plants moored to reeds. Both parents incubate the eggs for 22-29 days. The young ride on one parent's back while the other fetches food. **Call** Loud rattling; trumpeting bark. **Diet** Fish, crustaceans, snails, insects, plant matter. **Habitat** Deep freshwater ponds and lakes.

FAMILY **PODICIPEDIDAE** SPECIES *Poliocephalus poliocephalus* SIZE **TO 31 CM**

HOARY-HEADED GREBE

Breeding adults have a black head with overlying narrow white plumes giving a striped appearance. In non-breeding birds the top of the head is dark grey, the sides of the head and throat are white.
Behaviour Highly nomadic, often flying long distances at night between ephemeral inland lakes and wetlands, they congregate on open water, roost in floating colonies and nest in groups, sometimes with up to 400 nests about 1 m apart. They fly fast and low, and dive for prey. Pairs form only for the breeding season, displaying both in the water and on the nest platform. **Breeding** They breed from November to January or after rain, and lay 5-6 eggs in a floating nest of algae and other water plants, moored to reeds. Both parents incubate the eggs. **Call** Usually silent; occasional soft 'churring' around nest. **Diet** Aquatic insects, zooplankton, crustaceans. **Habitat** Fresh and saline lakes and wetlands.

FAMILY **PELECANIDAE** SPECIES *Pelecanus conspicillatus* SIZE **TO 1.8 M**

AUSTRALIAN PELICAN

Australia's largest flying bird, the pelican has a wingspan of 3.5 m, and the world's longest bill at 47 cm, with an expandable pouch to hold fish. During courtship, the lower pouch turns scarlet with a dark blue stripe and the throat turns bright yellow. **Behaviour** They forage day and night, alone or in groups, driving fish into the shallows and catching them with their bills. They roost on mudbanks and islands, fluttering their pouch skin to keep cool. They sometimes migrate long distances, flying in loose V formation or in line, soaring up to 3000 m high. They nest in colonies on islands and the chicks gather in groups. **Breeding** They breed year round (mainly spring in the south) and lay 2-4 eggs in a loose platform nest on the ground. Both parents share incubation of 32-35 days and feed the chicks who fledge at 3 months. **Call** Grunting.
Diet Fish, crustaceans. **Habitat** Fresh and saline lakes, rivers, swamps.

| FAMILY **ARDEIDAE** | SPECIES *Egretta novaehollandiae* | SIZE **TO 69 CM** |

WHITEFACED HERON

This heron has grey plumage with darker flight feathers, a white face, a white stripe on the throat, long grey plumes on the back, and pale chestnut feathers on the lower neck. Juveniles have little white on the forehead and no plumes. **Behaviour** They feed in the shallows and on pastures, alone, in pairs or loose flocks, stalking prey or stirring up small animals from the mud with their feet. The sixth vertebra in their long, S-shaped neck has a hinge, allowing them to shoot the neck forward to catch prey. **Breeding** They breed in spring and summer in the south, or according to the food supply elsewhere. Females lay 3-7 eggs in a loose platform nest in a tree. Both parents share incubation of 24-26 days and feed the young who fledge at 40 days. **Call** Harsh croaks. **Diet** Fish, crustaceans, insects, other small animals. **Habitat** Fresh and saline shallow lakes, estuaries, wetlands.

| FAMILY **ARDEIDAE** | SPECIES *Ardea alba* | SIZE **TO 1.03 M** |

GREAT EGRET

The largest white heron, this egret is distinguished by its long bill, low flat forehead and prominent bend in its neck. It has a yellow bill, yellow facial skin, dark grey or black legs and yellow eyes. Breeding adults have long white plumes on the back extending beyond the tail, a black bill, red eyes and blue-green facial skin. **Behaviour** They hunt alone in shallow water up to 30 cm deep, using a wait-and-watch strategy, standing motionless for long periods, then slowly stalking prey. They often crouch slightly, stretching their neck to the side. Breeding colonies form in spring, often with other water birds. **Breeding** They breed in spring and summer and lay 3-6 eggs in a platform nest in a tree or reed bed. Both parents incubate the eggs for 25 days and feed the young. They fledge at 6 weeks. **Call** Harsh croaks. **Diet** Fish, crustaceans, insects, amphibians. **Habitat** Floodwaters, lakes, wetlands, mud-flats.

| FAMILY **ARDEIDAE** | SPECIES *Ardea ibis* | SIZE **TO 53 CM** |

CATTLE EGRET

This heron has white plumage, greenish-yellow facial skin, a pale yellow bill and yellow-olive feet. Breeding adults have rusty-brown plumage on the crown, neck and back, a red bill and reddish facial skin.

Behaviour They feed around the feet of cattle and buffalo in groups of 2-20, preferring wet pastures where they catch prey disturbed by the animals' feet. They perch on them to rest and pick parasites from their skin. Breeding colonies of tens or thousands of birds gather in trees and shrubs along waterways in spring. Males choose a nest site, defend it from rivals and display to attract females, raising their plumes and wings. **Breeding** They breed mainly in early summer and lay 3-6 eggs in a nest in a tree. Both parents share incubation of 22-26 days and care for the young who fledge at 25-30 days. **Call** Harsh croaks. **Diet** Insects, small aquatic animals. **Habitat** Pastures among stock, wetlands.

FAMILY **ARDEIDAE** SPECIES *Butorides striatus* SIZE **TO 51 CM**

STRIATED (MANGROVE) HERON

This heron has a glossy black crown and crest, a metallic sheen on its back, lemon-yellow facial skin, yellow eyes and brown to grey legs with yellow-orange lines behind. Breeding adults have a reddish face and legs.

Behaviour They roost alone in low branches at high tide, sometimes diving for prey and swimming back to eat it at the roost. At low tide they fly over tidal flats looking for food and stalk prey with a stealthy, hunched posture, suddenly dashing forward to catch their victim. Territorial and courtship displays include crest-raising, bowing, flapping the wings in flight and tail flicking. **Breeding** They breed from September to March, sometimes raising 2 broods in a season. Females lay 3-4 eggs in a platform nest in the fork of a mangrove tree. Both parents share incubation of 21-25 days and feed the young who fledge at 4 weeks. **Call** Squeaks; sharp calls. **Diet** Fish, crustaceans, molluscs, insects. **Habitat** Mangrove swamps.

FAMILY **ARDEIDAE** SPECIES *Nycticorax caledonicus* SIZE **TO 65 CM**

NANKEEN (RUFOUS) NIGHT HERON

This heron has rufous wings and upper-parts, a black bill and 2-3 slender white plumes on the crown.

Behaviour They camp in small or large groups in trees close to water. At dusk they fly off alone to forage in the shallows and around the shorelines, stalking prey or vibrating their bill in the water to attract fish. Colonies of thousands gather to breed. Males establish nesting territories no larger than a bill stab, and attract females with elaborate snap-stretch and wheezing song-and-dance displays. **Breeding** They breed mostly September to April, sometimes raising 2 broods of 2-3 eggs in a season, laid in a flimsy platform nest in a tree or shrub up to 25 m high, or in ground crevices on treeless islands. Both parents share incubation of about 3 weeks and feed the young who fledge at 42-49 days. **Call** Gutteral croaks. **Diet** Fish, crustaceans, amphibians, insects. **Habitat** Fresh and saline wetlands, dams, rivers, estuaries.

FAMILY **THRESKIORNITHIDAE** SPECIES *Threskiornis molucca* SIZE **TO 75 CM**

AUSTRALIAN WHITE IBIS

This bird has a long, slender, curved, black bill, a bald black head and upper neck, scarlet patches on the breast and under the wings, white plumage, and black wingtips. **Behaviour** Often seen scavenging in parks, they forage in shallow water, moving their bill from side-to-side, probing for prey. They roost in trees and gather in colonies of thousands to breed, flying in formation, flapping their wings in unison and soaring on thermals to 3000 m high. Flocks of males choose breeding sites and display from branches to establish a territory below, attracting females with deep bowing movements. **Breeding** They breed September to April and lay 1-5 eggs in a low platform nest. Both parents share incubation of 20-25 days and feed the young. They fledge in about 4 weeks. **Call** Harsh croaks. **Diet** Fish, crustaceans, frogs, insects, small invertebrates. **Habitat** Wetlands, irrigated pastures, shallow lakes, parks.

ANIMALS

FAMILY **THRESKIORNITHIDAE**   SPECIES *Threskiornis spinicollis*   SIZE **TO 75 CM**

STRAW-NECKED IBIS

These birds resemble vultures with bare black heads, upper necks and throats. Yellow, straw-like feathers extend from the neck to the upper breast. The wings, back and tail are black with a metallic sheen. **Behaviour** They roost in trees close to water and feed in pairs or flocks, foraging over the plains and wetlands. Colonies of up to 200 000 birds congregate to breed. They develop a red patch of skin behind the eye and on the breast while courting. Pairs bow and preen each other to reinforce their bond before establishing a nesting territory and chasing other birds away. **Breeding** They breed mainly in summer and lay 1-5 eggs in a platform nest on rushes, shrubs or on the ground. Both parents share incubation of 20-25 days and feed the young. They fledge in about 5 weeks. **Call** Drawn-out grunts. **Diet** Insects, molluscs, frogs, snakes. **Habitat** Swamps, lake margins, pastures, sea-shores.

FAMILY **THRESKIORNITHIDAE**   SPECIES *Platalea flavipes*   SIZE **TO 92 CM**

YELLOW-BILLED SPOONBILL

This bird has a long, yellow, spoon-shaped bill and grey facial skin bordered in black. The plumage is creamy-white with some black plumes on the wings. Breeding adults have spiny white plumes on the breast and a bluish face. **Behaviour** Highly nomadic, they feed in shallow water by day or night, walking slowly, stirring organisms from the bottom, sweeping their bill through the water and probing for prey. They return to the same site to breed each year and nest alone or in loose colonies. Males defend nest sites aggressively, bill-clapping, jumping and pushing with their feet. **Breeding** They breed September to April and lay 1-4 eggs in a large nest of sticks on the ground, in trees or shrubs. Both parents share incubation and feed the young. They fledge in about 7 weeks. **Call** Soft 'chhee'; bill-clapping. **Diet** Insects, crustaceans, fish, molluscs. **Habitat** Wetlands, dams, shallow lakes, river margins.

FAMILY **CICONIIDAE**   SPECIES *Ephippiorhynchus asiaticus*   SIZE **TO 1.3 M**

BLACK-NECKED STORK (JABIRU)

With a wingspan of 2.2 m, this is one of our largest birds. It has a thick, black bill about 30 cm long, a glossy, greenish-black head, neck and tail, and a broad black wing-stripe. The legs are red and the rest of the body is white. **Behaviour** They live alone or in family groups and forage independently in shallow water, probing with the bill, standing still or slowly stalking their prey, then running and jumping in long strides to catch it. Pairs stay together throughout the year. **Breeding** They breed February to June and lay 2-4 eggs in a bulky platform nest to 1.8 m wide on top of a large tree. Both parents share incubation and feed the young by regurgitation. They fledge in 100-115 days. **Call** No calls recorded, only bill-clattering. **Diet** Fish, with occasional reptiles, frogs, crabs and rodents. **Habitat** Lakes, swamps, rivers, mangroves.

FAMILY **GRUIDAE**   SPECIES *Grus rubicunda*   SIZE **TO 1.4 M**

BROLGA

This stately crane is pale grey with a bare head, grey on top and orange to scarlet on the back and face, with a hairy, black dewlap under the chin.
Behaviour They live in family groups with a dominant male and wander widely for food, soaring on thermals, roosting on water at night. Large flocks gather in permanent wetlands to breed, and engage in elaborate dances. One bird flies in and bows, wings outstretched to its mate, who bounces and bows in return. Soon the birds join the dance, lining up opposite each other, bowing and bouncing.
Breeding They breed September to February in the south and February to June in the north. Females lay 2 eggs in a platform nest on the ground, about 1.5 m across. Both parents incubate the eggs for 28-30 days and tend to the young for a year. **Call** Trumpeting; harsh croaks.
Diet Tubers, seeds, molluscs, insects. **Habitat** Wetlands, pastures.

FAMILY **RALLIDAE**   SPECIES *Porphyrio porphyrio*   SIZE **TO 48 CM**

PURPLE SWAMPHEN

This bird is black above with deep blue or turquoise underparts, white undertail feathers, a red bill and frontal shield, and very large feet. **Behaviour** Often seen grazing in parks, flicking their tail, they wade and clamber among dense reed beds by day, gripping reed stems with their feet, resting on roost platforms and grazing on wet pastures. They run fast, but rarely swim. In marginal or seasonal habitats they wander widely. On permanent waterways they live in territorial groups of 2 to 7 males, 1 to 2 females and some helpers. **Breeding** They breed mainly August to February in groups, sharing nesting, incubation and parenting. Females lay 3-8 eggs each on a platform of trampled reeds lined with grass. Incubation is 23-29 days and the chicks are reared in a nursery nest. **Call** Harsh screech, often at night. **Diet** Reed stems, herbs, seeds, fruit, small animals. **Habitat** Swamps, lakes, ponds, streams.

FAMILY **RALLIDAE**   SPECIES *Gallinula tenebrosa*   SIZE **TO 38 CM**

DUSKY MOORHEN

This moorhen is sooty, washed-brown to grey above with white lines on each side of the tail, a red frontal shield on the forehead, red upper legs and green feet that turn red when breeding. **Behaviour** They form sedentary groups of 2-7 birds with 1-3 females per group and defend a group territory in the breeding season. They feed by day in the water or on land and roost at night on platforms in reeds and shrubs up to 2 m above water. **Breeding** They breed August to March in groups, sharing nesting, incubation and parenting. Females lay 5-9 eggs each in a platform nest among rushes or at the base of a waterside tree. Incubation is 19-24 days. Hatchlings are taken to a nursery nest over deeper water and fed for about 9 weeks.
Call Raucous crowing; shrill notes. **Diet** Plant matter, insects, fish, molluscs, worms. **Habitat** Swamps, lakes, waterways.

| FAMILY **RALLIDAE** | SPECIES *Fulica atra* | SIZE **TO 39 CM** |

EURASIAN COOT

This bird is dark slate-grey with a white frontal shield and bill, and red eyes. **Behaviour** Highly nomadic, they can fly long distances, travelling at night looking for food and breeding sites, often gathering in floating flocks of several hundred. They feed mainly in deep, open water, diving to 7 m and staying submerged for up to 15 seconds. They sleep on the water, display on open water to attract a breeding partner, and aggressively defend a territory. **Breeding** They breed mainly August to March and lay 4-15 eggs in a loose, cup-shaped nest about 30 cm wide, hidden among plants or floating on the water. Both parents share nest-building and incubate the eggs for 21-26 days. **Call** Loud 'kyok'; shrill notes. **Diet** Algae, shoots, seeds, invertebrates, amphibians, fish. **Habitat** Swamps, open lakes, ponds.

| FAMILY **COLUMBIDAE** | SPECIES *Columba livia* | SIZE **TO 36 CM** |

FERAL PIGEON

This pigeon has many breeds and colour patterns. The basic form is blue-grey with a purple and green display sheen on the neck, and black wings with a chequered pattern or 2 black bars. **Behaviour** Descended from the wild rock pigeon and introduced from Europe, they live in all urban areas and nest in loose colonies. Males display during courtship, facing the female, spreading the wings and tail slightly, and bowing while cooing softly. **Breeding** They breed year round and lay 2 eggs in a loose stick nest on a ledge, in a rock hole or tree hollow. Both parents share incubation of 17-19 days and feed the young on a cheese-like secretion of the throat pouch and regurgitated food. They fledge in 30-35 days. **Call** Moaning 'cooo'; 'co-roo-coo-coo' in display. **Diet** Seeds, shoots, berries, worms, insects, food scraps. **Habitat** Urban areas, grain fields, cliffs, inland rivers.

| FAMILY **COLUMBIDAE** | SPECIES *Ocyphaps lophotes* | SIZE **TO 34 CM** |

CRESTED PIGEON

This pigeon has a long, slender, erect, black crest, a grey body, brown wings with black bars on the shoulders, and an iridescent green and purple patch edged with white below. It has a red eye and eye-ring.

Behaviour Usually seen in groups of 5 or 6, they roost in trees and often perch on roadside fences and wires. They forage on the ground and run when approached, or fly off with rapid whistling wing-beats. Courtship displays include bowing and tail-spreading by the male, and flying steeply up from a perch with a loud clap before gliding straight down. **Breeding** They breed mostly in spring and early summer, and lay 2 eggs in a frail stick nest in a low, dense shrub. Both parents share incubation of 18-20 days. The young fledge in 20-25 days. **Call** Low 'coo'; sharp 'whoop'. **Diet** Seeds, green herbage, insects. **Habitat** Lightly-wooded grasslands, watercourses, parks.

FAMILY **COLUMBIDAE**   SPECIES *Geopelia placida*   SIZE **TO 23 CM**

PEACEFUL DOVE

The forehead, throat and breast of this dove are blue-grey. The back, crown and wings are grey-brown with black bars and streaks. The belly is pinkish.
Behaviour Usually seen in pairs or small groups, they roost in trees and shrubs, forage on the ground and sun-bathe on dusty ground with one wing raised. Large groups often congregate around waterholes and feeding sites. They bob their heads when running and take off with whirring wings, usually flying only short distances. Males bow, fan their tail and coo in display to females, and rise in a steep, clapping display flight. **Breeding** They breed year round and lay 2 eggs in a frail stick nest on a horizontal limb of a tree or in a shrub, 1-12 m high. Both parents share incubation of 13 days. The young fledge in about 16 days. **Call** High 'goola-goo' and 'doo-a-luk'; soft cooing. **Diet** Seeds. **Habitat** Woodlands, rainforest margins.

FAMILY **COLUMBIDAE**   SPECIES *Leucosarcia melanoleuca*   SIZE **TO 45 CM**

WONGA PIGEON

This pigeon is slate-grey with a white forehead, a broad white 'V' on the chest and a white belly spotted with black. **Behaviour** Solitary and sedentary, they spend the day foraging on the ground and roost in trees at night. They stay in the same territory year round, are more often heard than seen, and sometimes congregate where food is plentiful. Males display to females by rhythmically raising the tail and wings, spreading the tail and swinging the head from side-to-side. The distinctive white 'V' on the chest becomes very obvious during this process. **Breeding** They breed mostly from October to January and lay 2 eggs in a sparse, stick, platform nest in a tall, open tree, vine, or tree fern. Both parents incubate the eggs for 17-18 days. The young fledge in 18-19 days. **Call** Monotonously repeated 'coo'. **Diet** Seeds, fruit, invertebrates. **Habitat** Wet sclerophyll forests, rainforests.

FAMILY **COLUMBIDAE**   SPECIES *Phaps chalcoptera*   SIZE **TO 36 CM**

COMMON BRONZEWING

This pigeon has a purple-brown nape, a white line below the eye, brown back with pale-edged feathers, and a bronze metallic sheen on the wings. Males have a cream forehead and a pink-brown breast. Females have a grey forehead and grey-buff breast. **Behaviour** They live in pairs and gather in small flocks where food is plentiful, foraging on the ground by day and roosting at night in trees and shrubs. Generally shy and sedentary, they walk through the scrub and fly to cross open areas or escape danger, taking off with a clatter of wings. Courtship by the male includes head-bobbing, partly spreading the tail and twisting the wings to expose their bronze colour. **Breeding** They breed year round and lay 2 eggs in a saucer-shaped nest in a tree fork or thicket 1-10 m high. Both parents share incubation of 14-16 days. **Call** Soft, repeated 'oom'. **Diet** Seeds. **Habitat** Forests, woodlands, mallee, heaths.

FAMILY **COLUMBIDAE**	SPECIES *Ptilinopus superbus*	SIZE **TO 24 CM**

SUPERB FRUIT-DOVE

Males have a purple crown, a blue-grey throat and chest, an orange collar and nape, a black breast band, a white belly and tail tip, a green back spotted with black, and green-barred sides. Females have a dull blue crown and lack the black breast band and orange neck. **Behaviour** They occur singly or in pairs, although larger number sometimes gather where food is plentiful. Some populations are sedentary while others travel long distances looking for food. Courtship by the male includes bowing and gazing at the female while moving his head from side-to-side and edging towards her. **Breeding** They breed from June to February in the north and November to December elsewhere. Females lay a single egg in a flimsy platform nest in a tree, shrub, palm or vine thicket. Both parents share incubation of 14 days and the young fledge in 7 days. **Call** Loud 'coo-coo'; low 'oom'. **Diet** Fruit. **Habitat** Rainforests, mangroves, wet sclerophyll forests, scrubs.

FAMILY **CACATUIDAE**	SPECIES *Calyptorhynchus banksii*	SIZE **TO 66 CM**

RED-TAILED BLACK COCKATOO

This large parrot has a rounded crest and large, powerful bill. Males are black with a broad red band on the tail. Females are brown-black spotted with yellow on the head, neck and shoulders, with yellow bars on the underparts and orange-yellow bars on the tail. **Behaviour** They live in pairs, family groups or in flocks of up to 200, and usually feed high up in the trees, coming to the ground only to drink. They are highly nomadic and often return seasonally to some areas. They fly slowly with sluggish wingbeats, calling loudly to each other. **Breeding** They breed from March to October and lay 1 or rarely 2 eggs in a nest lined with wood chips in a tree hollow. The female incubates the egg for about 4 weeks and is fed by the male. Both parents feed the young which fledges in 10-12 weeks. **Call** Harsh, grating 'kree' or 'krarr'. **Diet** Seeds. **Habitat** Open forests, woodlands.

FAMILY **CACATUIDAE**	SPECIES *Calyptorhynchus funereus*	SIZE **TO 65 CM**

YELLOW-TAILED BLACK COCKATOO

This large parrot has dusky-black feathers edged with pale yellow, yellow cheek patches and a broad yellow band on the tail. **Behaviour** They live in family parties of up to 20 birds, or in flocks of a hundred or more, and wander between the coast and adjacent ranges looking for food. They fly slowly over the trees and patrol the mountain ranges, calling to each other with their loud, mournful cries. They use their sharp, powerful bill to open tough seed-bearing cones and dig into the bark looking for larvae to eat. **Breeding** They breed from March to August and lay 2 eggs in a high tree hollow. The female incubates the eggs for 4 weeks and is fed by the male. Only one chick survives to fledge about 3 months later. It is fed by both parents and becomes independent just before the next breeding season. **Call** Loud wailing 'kee-ah'. **Diet** Seeds, wood-boring larvae. **Habitat** Sclerophyll forests, heaths, pine plantations.

FAMILY **CACATUIDAE** SPECIES *Callocephalon fimbriatum* SIZE **TO 35 CM**

GANG-GANG COCKATOO

This parrot is grey with pale edges to the feathers. Males have a scarlet head and whispy crest. Females have a grey head and crest and salmon-pink or green-yellow edges to the feathers on their underparts.

Behaviour They live in pairs or family groups in the breeding season and gather in flocks of up to 100 birds at other times, feeding quietly in trees and shrubs, biting off whole clusters of fruit and returning every day until the food is exhausted. Sociable and quite tame, they will often allow you to come very close when feeding. They breed in the mountain forests and usually move to the lowlands in winter.

Breeding They breed from October to January and lay 2 or rarely 3 eggs in a tree hollow at great height. Both parents share incubation of about 30 days and feed the young for 11-13 weeks. **Call** Creaky-door screech. **Diet** Seeds, fruit. **Habitat** Forests, woodlands, parks.

FAMILY **CACATUIDAE** SPECIES *Probosciger aterrimus* SIZE **TO 64 CM**

PALM COCKATOO

This large parrot is very dark-grey or black with crimson cheek patches, a huge bill and a large crest raised in display and when calling.

Behaviour They live alone or in family parties and congregate in groups of up to 7 in a large tree just after sunrise. Before flying off to feed one bird hangs head-down with its wings outstretched and tail raised. They feed in woodland trees and on the ground, returning to the rainforest in mid-morning and retiring to roost just before dusk. **Breeding** They breed in October and November and lay a single egg in a tree hollow lined with crushed twigs. The female incubates the egg for 31-35 days and both parents feed the young who fledge at 14-16 weeks and become independent 6 weeks later. **Call** Disyllabic whistle at perch; harsh alarm screech; loud wailing flight call. **Diet** Seeds, fruit, leaf buds, insects, larvae. **Habitat** Rainforests, woodlands.

FAMILY **CACATUIDAE** SPECIES *Eulophus roseicapillus* SIZE **TO 36 CM**

GALAH

This cockatoo has grey and pink feathers and a white crown. Males have a brown iris, females a red iris.

Behaviour Often seen flying and foraging in flocks of up to 1000 birds, they gather in communal roosts at night and fly up to 15 km looking for food. Breeding pairs return to the same nesting hollow each year and defend the tree, marked by biting off an area of bark and regularly wiping their face and bill over the bare patch. **Breeding** They breed mostly from August to November and lay 2-6 eggs in a tree hollow lined with leafy twigs. Both parents share incubation of 30 days and care for the young. They fledge at about 8 weeks and join a creche of up to 100 young birds. They fend for themselves 6-8 weeks later and travel in flocks of immatures until they breed at 3-4 years. **Call** Screeching. **Diet** Seeds, green shoots. **Habitat** Woodlands, grasslands, open shrublands, parks.

FAMILY **CACATUIDAE**	SPECIES *Cacatua sanguinea*	SIZE **TO 42 CM**

LITTLE CORELLA

This cockatoo is white with a strong yellow wash under the wings and tail. It has a white, erectable crest, bare bluish skin around the eyes, and dull red feathers between the eye and bill. **Behaviour** They feed on the ground and are often seen in noisy flocks, sometimes comprising thousands of birds. They roost at midday and at night along watercourses and often strip the leaves from the trees. Breeding pairs are silent and secretive with well-established nest-building and bonding rituals. They probably mate for life and return to the same tree hollow each year, chewing out the inside to line the nest. **Breeding** They breed from June to October and at the end of the wet season in the north. The female lays 2-3 eggs, incubated by both parents for about 25 days. **Call** Raucous screeches. **Diet** Seeds. **Habitat** Semi-arid and monsoonal woodlands, shrublands, tree-lined watercourses, farmlands.

FAMILY **CACATUIDAE**	SPECIES *Cacatua leadbeateri*	SIZE **TO 36 CM**

MAJOR MITCHELL'S (PINK) COCKATOO

This beautiful cockatoo has a white back and salmon pink head, neck and underparts. It has a narrow, white-tipped scarlet crest with a central yellow band. **Behaviour** They feed on the ground or in trees and shrubs, usually in pairs or small groups, and fly off if disturbed. In the late afternoon and early morning they drink at waterholes. In the breeding season males display to females by strutting along a branch and bobbing the head up and down with the crest raised. They chase other birds from an area several kilometres around their nest site. **Breeding** They breed from May to December and lay 2-4 eggs in a nest in a tree hollow lined with wood dust and bark strips. Both parents incubate the eggs for 26-30 days and feed the young who fledge at 6-8 weeks. **Call** Two-note quavering screech. **Diet** Seeds, fruit, roots. **Habitat** Mallee and mulga shrublands; pine and sheoak stands.

FAMILY **CACATUIDAE**	SPECIES *Cacatua galerita*	SIZE **TO 50 CM**

SULPHUR-CRESTED COCKATOO

This familiar cockatoo has white feathers and a narrow, sulphur-yellow, forward-pointing crest. **Behaviour** They congregate in large flocks, small groups or pairs, and feed on the ground and in trees, using their powerful bill to dig insects from the bark and seeds from the ground. Feeding flocks post sentry birds in trees who screech if an intruder approaches. Each flock has its own roosting site and returns to the same feeding area every morning until the food is exhausted. **Breeding** They breed from August to January in the south and May to September in the north. They nest in a tree hollow or cliff hole and lay 2-3 eggs, incubated by both parents for about 30 days. The young fledge in 6-10 weeks and stay with their parents until mature. **Call** Loud, raucous screech. **Diet** Seeds, roots, berries, insects. **Habitat** Open forests, woodlands, wet sclerophyll forests, rainforests, mangroves, parks.

FAMILY **CACATUIDAE**   SPECIES *Nymphicus hollandicus*   SIZE **TO 32 CM**

COCKATIEL

This cockatoo is grey with white shoulder patches and an orange ear patch. Males have a yellow forehead, crest, cheeks and throat. Females have a grey face tinged with yellow and a grey crest. **Behaviour** They gather in groups, sometimes comprising several hundred birds, roost together in trees and on overhead wires, and forage mainly on the ground. Large numbers migrate south in summer and north in winter. They become nomadic in dry conditions and travel long distances searching for water. **Breeding** They breed from August to December in the south and April to August in the north. They nest in a tree hollow near water and lay 2-8 eggs, incubated by both parents for 18-20 days. The young are fed by regurgitation and fledge in 4-5 weeks.
Call Warbling 'queel-queel'. **Diet** Seeds. **Habitat** Most habitats; prefers open, lightly timbered areas; avoids forests and treeless deserts.

FAMILY **PSITTACIDAE**   SPECIES *Trichoglossus haematodus*   SIZE **TO 32 CM**

RAINBOW LORIKEET

This gaudy parrot has a violet-blue head, a coral-red or yellow-green collar, a bright red bill, orange-yellow breast, deep-blue abdomen and green upperparts.
Behaviour Pairs or flocks of up to 50 birds feed in the outer foliage of flowering trees, often upside down, gathering nectar and pollen with their brush-tipped tongues. At night they congregate in set roosts in tall trees on the coast or hills, in flocks of up to several hundred. In the early morning they fly from their roosts and disperse to feed, sometimes travelling 50 km or more. **Breeding** They breed mainly from August to January in the south and year round in the north. They nest in a tree hollow near water and lay 2-3 eggs, incubated by the female for 25-26 days. Both parents care for the young who fledge in 8 weeks. **Call** Screeching; chattering. **Diet** Nectar, pollen, fruit, insects. **Habitat** Forests, woodlands, heaths.

FAMILY **PSITTACIDAE**   SPECIES *Trichoglossus chlorolepidotus*   SIZE **TO 23 CM**

SCALY-BREASTED LORIKEET

This parrot is generally green with orange-red underwings. Yellow feathers edged with green on the back of the neck, throat and breast give it a scaly appearance.
Behaviour Often seen in mixed flocks with rainbow lorikeets, they chatter and screech incessantly while feeding, often hanging upside down, gathering nectar and pollen with their brush-tipped tongues. If disturbed they fly off screeching and move around to feed on flowering eucalypts, banksias and grevilleas, often travelling long distances from their nesting site. **Breeding** They breed mainly from August to January in the south and May to February in the north. They nest in a tree hollow high above ground and lay 2-3 eggs, incubated by the female for 25-26 days. Both parents care for the young who fledge in 6-8 weeks. **Call** Screeching; chattering. **Diet** Nectar, pollen, fruit, seeds. **Habitat** Lowland forests, woodlands, heaths.

| FAMILY **PSITTACIDAE** | SPECIES *Alisterus scapularis* | SIZE **TO 43 CM** |

KING PARROT

This distinctive parrot has a green back, blue rump, bluish-black tail and scarlet underparts. Males have a scarlet head and neck. Females have a light-green head and neck. **Behaviour** They are often seen in small groups or pairs feeding in the outer foliage or foraging on the ground, walking with an awkward waddle. They roost in communal camps, travelling back and forth in groups high above the forest soon after sunrise and before sunset. They fly fast with deliberate, rather laboured wing beats, and weave through the trees with great manoeuvrability. **Breeding** They breed from September to January and lay 3-5 eggs in a large, deep tree hollow. The female incubates the eggs for about 20 days and both parents care for the young who fledge at 5-7 weeks. **Call** Shrill 'crassak-crassak' in flight; piping whistle at perch. **Diet** Seeds, fruit, nuts, nectar, blossom, leaf buds. **Habitat** Forests, woodlands.

| FAMILY **PSITTACIDAE** | SPECIES *Platycercus caledonicus* | SIZE **TO 36 CM** |

GREEN ROSELLA

This large rosella has blackish-green feathers on the back edged with dark green, a bright-yellow head and underparts, blue cheeks and throat, and a scarlet brow. **Behaviour** Often seen in parks, they feed quietly in the trees usually between early and mid-morning and late afternoon. They are sedentary, mate for life and often form feeding flocks of 3-4 pairs. They display to their mates and social group by drooping wings, fluffing feathers, shaking the tail and bowing slightly while continually chattering. **Breeding** They breed from September to January and lay 4-6 eggs in a high tree hollow. The female incubates the eggs for 20-22 days. The young fledge at 5 weeks and stay with the parents for a month before joining juvenile flocks. **Call** Musical chattering; bell-like whistle. **Diet** Fruit, seeds, nectar. **Habitat** Sclerophyll forests, temperate rainforests, woodlands, parks.

| FAMILY **PSITTACIDAE** | SPECIES *Platycercus elegans* | SIZE **TO 36 CM** |

CRIMSON ROSELLA

On the east coast this rosella has a crimson head, rump and underparts. In the Murray Valley it has a yellow neck, back and underparts. In the Mt Lofty Ranges the yellow is replaced by varying amounts of orange.

Behaviour They forage quietly in groups of up to 30 on the ground and outer foliage, flying from their roost in the early morning and taking dew from the leaves. They pair for life and tend to stay around their breeding grounds year round. **Breeding** They breed from Sept ember to January and lay 4-8 eggs in a tree hollow 5-20 m high. The female incubates the eggs for 19-21 days and is fed by the male. Both parents feed the young who fledge at 5 weeks and stay with the parents for a month before joining a flock of juveniles. **Call** Harsh screeching. Bell-like whistle. Musical chattering. **Diet** Seeds, fruit, nectar, lerps. **Habitat** Sclerophyll forests, woodlands, rainforests, parks.

FAMILY **PSITTACIDAE** SPECIES *Platycercus adscitus* SIZE **TO 32 CM**

WHITE-CHEEKED ROSELLA

There are 2 principal forms of this rosella. Both have white cheeks. The southeastern form has a scarlet head and yellow-green body. The notheastern form has a pale head and bluish body. The two forms interbreed in the Queensland/New South Wales border region.
Behaviour Rarely travelling far, they band together in family groups or flocks of 20-30, and search silently on the ground for seeds, or forage noisily in trees. Groups disband in the breeding season and pairs establish a nesting territory. **Breeding** They breed from June to February and lay 3-9 eggs in a tree hollow 2-15 m high. The female incubates the eggs for 19-20 days and both parents care for the young who fledge at 5-6 weeks and stay with the parents until the next breeding season. **Call** High-pitched harsh 'chut-chit'. Piping whistle. Musical chattering. **Diet** Seeds, fruit, nectar, insect larvae. **Habitat** Open forests, woodlands, parks.

FAMILY **PSITTACIDAE** SPECIES *Barnardius zonarius* SIZE **TO 38 CM**

AUSTRALIAN RINGNECK

This parrot is distinguished by its yellow collar and generally greenish plumage. Eastern birds have a blue back and a red band above the bill. The western race has a black head, blue cheeks and green belly.
Behaviour They form permanent pairs and stay close to their birthplace, chattering quietly while feeding in trees, and foraging silently on the ground. They shelter in the midday heat and roost at night in the crowns of trees, singly, in pairs, or in small family groups outside the breeding season. **Breeding** They breed from July to February, and February to June in northwestern Queensland. They nest in a tree hollow 1-15 m high and lay 2-6 eggs, incubated for 19-20 days by the female. Both parents feed the young who fledge at about 5 weeks. **Call** Ringing 'kwink-kwink'; clattering 'chuk-chuk-chuk'. **Diet** Seeds, fruit, leaf buds, insects. **Habitat** Forests, woodlands, mallee, floodplains.

FAMILY **PSITTACIDAE** SPECIES *Pezoporus wallicus* SIZE **TO 31 CM**

GROUND PARROT

This rare parrot is bright green with yellow and black bars and spots, and black streaks on the forehead.
Behaviour Solitary, sedentary and largely nocturnal, they are difficult to see on the ground. During the day they roost in squats beneath tussocky vegetation and call for 30-40 minutes at dusk and dawn. At night they forage in the undergrowth, running and clambering through dense vegetation, taking flight only if disturbed, and crashing back into cover after 50 m or so. **Breeding** They breed from September to December and lay 3-4 eggs in a shallow, cup-shaped nest of chewed stalks and leaves in a scrape in the ground, hidden beneath vegetation. The eggs are incubated for 21 days. The young leave the nest at 20 days to shelter in nearby vegetation and can fly at 30 days. **Call** Bell-like 'tee-tee-stit'. **Diet** Flowers, green shoots, seeds. **Habitat** Swampy heaths, sedgelands.

| FAMILY **PSITTACIDAE** | SPECIES *Psephotus haematonotus* | SIZE **TO 27 CM** |

RED-RUMPED PARROT

Males are green with a red rump, a yellow shoulder patch and abdomen. Females are dull olive-green with a green rump. **Behaviour** They are sedentary, pair for life and congregate in family groups to form loose foraging flocks of up to 100 birds outside the breeding season. They leave the roost soon after sunrise, fly off to drink, and move to feeding sites where they forage mostly on the ground and rest at midday in shrubs and trees. Mated birds often preen each other, and flocks will allow humans to come close before taking flight. **Breeding** They breed from August to January and lay 2-7 eggs in a tree hollow 2-12 m high. The female incubates the eggs for 20 days and the young fledge in 4-5 weeks. **Call** High-pitched 2-syllable whistle. **Diet** Seeds, flowers, shoots, leaves. **Habitat** Sparsely-timbered grasslands, open plains, mallee, farmlands.

| FAMILY **PSITTACIDAE** | SPECIES *Melopsittacus undulatus* | SIZE **TO 18 CM** |

BUDGERIGAR

This small parrot is bright green with a yellow throat and forehead, and blue-tipped feathers on the cheeks. **Behaviour** Flocks of up to 100 feed, fly and roost together, coordinating take-offs, landings and mid-air manoeuvres. They forage on the ground, moving together in a line and climbing grass tussocks looking for food. They usually change roosts each night and leave for feeding areas at sunrise. Towards sunset they rise in a display flight, calling and swirling over trees before roosting. In southern areas they arrive in spring and head north after breeding. **Breeding** They breed mainly from August to January in the south and June to September in the north. They nest in a tree hollow, often communally, and lay 4-8 eggs, incubated by the female for 18-20 days. The young fledge in 5 weeks. **Call** Warbling 'chirrup'. **Diet** Seeds. **Habitat** Grasslands, mallee, mulga, tree-lined watercourses.

| FAMILY **PSITTACIDAE** | SPECIES *Polytelis alexandrae* | SIZE **TO 48 CM** |

PRINCESS (ALEXANDRA'S) PARROT

This is one of Australia's most elusive parrots, and is con-sidered to be vulnerable. Females are smaller and duller with a shorter, greener tail. **Behaviour** They are nomadic, roaming the inland looking for food. A pair or small flock of around 20 birds will appear at irregular intervals at a tree-lined watercourse, breed, and disperse. They often nest in the same tree and spend most of the day searching for food on or close to the ground. If dis-turbed they fly to a nearby tree, and may mob predators. **Breeding** They breed mostly from September to January and nest in a tree hollow, usually near water. The male feeds the female who lays and incubates 4-6 eggs, for about 20 days, and feeds the young. The young fledge in 5-6 weeks, breed at 2 years, and may live for 20-30 years. **Call** Loud rattling contact call in flight; soft twittering and cackling at other times. **Diet** Seeds, flowers, leaves. **Habitat** Arid woodlands, scrublands, sandy deserts.

FAMILY **CUCULIDAE** | SPECIES *Cuculus pallidus* | SIZE **TO 33 CM**

PALLID CUCKOO

This cuckoo is grey above and paler below with a yellow eye-ring, dark eye-stripe and white bars on the tail and wings. Juveniles are streaked dark-brown and white. **Behaviour** Solitary and nomadic, they move north and inland in winter, and some migrate across southern Australia, returning to breed in spring. They feed from a perch, diving to the ground for prey, raising their tail on landing. After leaving the nest, the loud squawks of the young sometimes induce other birds to feed them. **Breeding** They breed from September to January and lay a single egg in an open cup nest of a honeyeater, miner, woodswallow, thornbill, robin, whistler or flycatcher. The nestling ejects the host's eggs or young from the nest. Several nests may be parasitised by the same female each year. **Call** Hoarse whistling 'too-too-too'. **Diet** Insects. **Habitat** Open forests, woodlands, farmlands.

FAMILY **CUCULIDAE** | SPECIES *Eudynamys scolopacea* | SIZE **TO 46 CM**

COMMON KOEL

Males are glossy blue-black with a long tail and red eyes. Females are dark-brown with pale brown stripes below and white spots on their backs and wings. **Behaviour** They migrate from Indonesia and New Guinea to Australia in September to breed, returning in March or April. They are usually seen alone, in pairs or courting groups of one female and several males. **Breeding** They breed mainly from September to March and lay a single egg in the nest of a figbird, magpie-lark, friarbird, oriole, red wattlebird, large honeyeater or other species with similar eggs. The egg hatches 13-14 days later and the other nestlings are ejected or starve as the young koel eats all the food brought by its foster parents. It is fully feathered and ready to fly in 2 months. **Call** Shrill, repetitive 'ko-el'. **Diet** Fruit. **Habitat** Rainforests, monsoon forests, open forests, dense woodlands, paperbark swamps, mangroves.

FAMILY **CUCULIDAE** | SPECIES *Cacomantis flabelliformis* | SIZE **TO 27 CM**

FAN-TAILED CUCKOO

This cuckoo is dark grey above and light to medium cinnamon-brown below. It has a yellow eye-ring and a notched, wedge-shaped tail barred black and white below. **Behaviour** Females are secretive, and males are usually seen alone or rarely in groups of 2-4. Tasmanian birds migrate to the mainland in winter and those in the southeast migrate north. They feed from a perch, flying out to glean insects from the foliage or on the ground, hopping along and pouncing on their prey, returning to the perch to eat. **Breeding** They breed from August to January and lay a single egg in the domed nest of a thornbill, scrubwren, fairywren or other species with similar eggs. The egg hatches 14-15 days later, the hatchling ejects the other eggs and fledges in 16-17 days. **Call** Descending trill; plaintive 'chiree'. **Diet** Insects. **Habitat** Rainforests, sclerophyll forests, woodlands, heaths.

| FAMILY **CENTROPODIDAE** | SPECIES *Centropus phasianinus* | SIZE **TO 75 CM** |

PHEASANT COUCAL

This ground-dweller is brown, barred with rufous, black and cream above, with a long, pheasant-like-tail. Breeding adults have a sooty-black head, back and underparts. **Behaviour** They hunt in the undergrowth, and fly clumsily for a short distance if startled. They are mainly sedentary, but wander locally, sometimes climbing in a series of leaps to the top of a tree and gliding from tree-to-tree. **Breeding** They breed mainly from October to March and lay 2-5 eggs in a nest of twigs and leaves in dense vegetation, trampled into a platform with the surrounding plants pulled down to form a canopy. Both parents share incubation of 15 days. The young fledge in 12-15 days. Two clutches may be reared in a season. **Call** Low, repetitive 'oop'. **Diet** Small reptiles, frogs, rodents, bandicoots, birds, eggs, crabs, large insects. **Habitat** Woodlands with dense undergrowth, salt marshes, canefields.

| FAMILY **ACCIPITRIDAE** | SPECIES *Haliastur sphenurus* | SIZE **TO 59 CM** |

WHISTLING KITE

This hawk is light brown with pale streaks, dark wings with pale linings, and a long, rounded tail. **Behaviour** They hunt alone or in small groups. In drier inland areas they congregate where prey is abundant and move to new areas when food is scarce. In coastal areas they scavenge along the tide line and dive into the water to scoop up fish with their feet. They fly with slow wing beats and soar with down-curved wing-tips. Pairs return to the same nest every year and tolerate others nesting in the same tree. **Breeding** They breed when food is abundant, mainly in the dry season, or in late winter and spring in the south. Females lay 2-4 eggs in a stick nest 60-70 cm wide, high up in a large tree, usually near water. The female incubates the eggs and the young fledge in about 6 weeks. **Call** Shrill, descending 'seeo' whistle, followed by ascending 'si-si-si-si'. **Diet** Small reptiles, mammals, birds, fish, crustaceans, insects, carrion. **Habitat** Open woodlands.

| FAMILY **ACCIPITRIDAE** | SPECIES *Haliastur indus* | SIZE **TO 51 CM** |

BRAHMINY KITE

This hawk has a white head, chestnut body, a short square tail and wingspan of 1.2 m. **Behaviour** They are solitary and patrol a stretch of shoreline, scavenging marine animals cast up by the tide. Small animals are caught and eaten at a perch high up in a tree. They glide on coastal breezes looking for food, flying in tight circles below 50 m with their wings held straight out. Courtship may last several months before nesting. Breeding pairs soar over their nest site, and often clasp their feet together in mid-air before whirling down. **Breeding** They breed in the dry season in the tropics, and in late winter to spring further south. Females lay 1-2 eggs in a platform nest 40-60 cm wide, built in a tree high up, and incubate the eggs. The young fledge in 50-55 days. **Call** Plaintive 'pee-ah-ah'. **Diet** Marine animals, frogs, crabs, snakes, insects. **Habitat** Coastal mudflats, mangroves, rocky shores, beaches, offshore islands, large rivers.

FAMILY **ACCIPITRIDAE**   SPECIES *Milvus migrans*   SIZE **TO 55 CM**

BLACK KITE

This hawk has a long forked tail and a wingspan of about 1.3 m. It is dark brown with black flight feathers and pale shoulder bars. **Behaviour** They congregate in small groups, perching in trees near waterholes, resting with their wings spread and beaks open. They fly with slow wing beats and soar to great heights, sometimes spiralling up in a column comprising hundreds or thousands of birds, especially during locust plagues. They scavenge carrion and refuse around rubbish dumps, but also dive onto live animals and patrol bushfires looking for prey that may be flushed. **Breeding** They breed mainly from August to November, and lay 2-3 eggs in a rough platform nest in the fork of a tree branch. The female incubates the eggs and the male brings food. The young fledge in 38-42 days. **Call** Plaintive 'swee-err'; whistled 'see-ee-ee'. **Diet** Carrion, insects, small vertebrates. **Habitat** Woodlands, savanna, farmlands, rubbish tips.

FAMILY **ACCIPITRIDAE**   SPECIES *Haliaeetus leucogaster*   SIZE **TO 85 CM**

WHITE-BELLIED SEA-EAGLE

This eagle is white with ash-grey feathers on its wings, on its back, and on the base of its tail. **Behaviour** They form permanent pairs and occupy the same home range year round, using the same nest each year, roosting together and often performing aerial duets in the morning and evening. They spend most of the day soaring and patrolling waterways looking for food. They also hunt from perches and dive to catch fish. **Breeding** They breed from May to October and lay 2 eggs several days apart in a stick nest to 4 m deep in a tree or on the ground. The female incubates the eggs for about 6 weeks, relieved periodically by the male. The first chick takes the food and the second usually starves to death. The young fledge in about 10 weeks. **Call** Goose-like honking. **Diet** Fish, sea snakes, turtles, birds, small mammals. **Habitat** Coast, islands, large rivers, inland lakes.

FAMILY **ACCIPITRIDAE**   SPECIES *Aquila audax*   SIZE **TO 1 M**

WEDGE-TAILED EAGLE

The largest raptor in Australia, this eagle has a wingspan of 2.5 m and has a long, wedge-shaped tail. It is smoky black with brown on the wings. **Behaviour** They form permanent pairs and live in the same home range all year, patrolling the treetops at dawn and dusk. They do aerobatic displays prior to breeding, diving and looping together, and use the same nest each year. They hunt from an exposed perch or soar and circle on thermals looking for prey. Groups gather around carrion taking it in turns to feed. **Breeding** They breed from April to September and lay 1-3 eggs in a platform nest to 2.5 m wide, built in a tree fork or on a cliff. The female incubates the eggs for about 45 days while the male brings food. The young fledge in 70-90 days. Only one chick usually survives. **Call** Screeches; whistles. **Diet** Small mammals, birds, reptiles, carrion. **Habitat** Forests, woodlands, plains.

ANIMALS

| FAMILY **ACCIPITRIDAE** | SPECIES *Circus assimilis* | SIZE TO 60 CM |

SPOTTED HARRIER

This raptor has blue-grey upperparts, a chestnut chest, belly and face with numerous white spots, prominent black wingtips, and a barred, slightly wedge-shaped tail. **Behaviour** Solitary and nomadic, they rest and roost on the ground and methodically patrol the countryside looking for prey, hunting by hedge-hopping, usually flying no more than 5 m high, with long glides and slow wing beats. They pair temporarily and display by flying high and descending in slow spirals and side-slips, sometimes dropping with half-closed wings. **Breeding** They breed mainly from July to October and lay 2-4 eggs in a bulky stick nest in a low tree. Both parents incubate the eggs for 32-34 days and feed the young who fledge in 4-6 weeks. If food is short the dominant chick may peck the others to death. **Call** Whistled 'seep'; rapid 'kit-kit-kit'. **Diet** Small mammals, ground-dwelling birds, reptiles, large insects. **Habitat** Grassy plains, croplands.

| FAMILY **FALCONIDAE** | SPECIES *Falco berigora* | SIZE TO 50 CM |

BROWN FALCON

This raptor is brown above with dark marks below the eye, dark thighs, and pale bars under the wings and tail. The underparts are whitish with dark streaks or dark brown. The legs have tough scales to protect it from snake bites. **Behaviour** Usually seen alone or in pairs, perching on posts and wires, or hovering looking for prey, they drop onto victims and chase prey on the wing. Flocks gather at bushfires to catch fleeing animals and follow farm machinery looking for prey. Courtship displays include rapid circling and aerial manoeuvres. **Breeding** They breed mainly from June to November and lay 2-5 eggs in an abandoned nest, in a tree hollow, or in a large stick nest. The female does most of the incubation of about 30 days while the male hunts. The young fledge at 40-50 days. **Call** Loud cackling. **Diet** Small mammals, birds, reptiles, insects, carrion. **Habitat** Open forests, woodlands.

| FAMILY **FALCONIDAE** | SPECIES *Falco peregrinus* | SIZE TO 50 CM |

PEREGRINE FALCON

This compact, heavily-built falcon is blue-grey above with dark bars. The head is black and the underparts are cream with dark bars on the belly. **Behaviour** One of the fastest raptors, they swoop on prey at great speed, catching their victim with their talons or stunning it by striking with the feet. They attack birds flying in the open and sometimes take swans and other large birds. They roost on cliffs and on high, exposed branches and mate for life, occupying a territory of around 20-50 sq km. Pairs sometimes hunt cooperatively. **Breeding** They breed from August to December and lay 2-4 eggs in a recess in a cliff, in a tree hollow, or in an abandoned nest. Females do most of the incubation of about 30 days. The young fledge in 5-6 weeks. **Call** Harsh chattering; long shrieks. **Diet** Birds, small mammals. **Habitat** Most habitats, especially cliffs and rocky outcrops.

FAMILY **FALCONIDAE**   SPECIES *Falco cenchroides*   SIZE **TO 35 CM**

NANKEEN (AUSTRALIAN) KESTREL

Males are pale rufous above with a grey head and tail and whitish underparts with dark streaks. Females and juveniles have a pale rufous head and tail. **Behaviour** Often seen perching on posts and wires or hovering over paddocks, they search for prey on the ground, hovering 10-20 m high over one spot and dropping in steps before diving head-first onto the victim. Flocks congregate where there are insect and mice plagues. Old established pairs occupy a territory year-round, while the young are nomadic, moving north in winter and south in summer. **Breeding** They breed from July to December and lay 3-7 eggs in a tree hollow, on a cliff ledge or recess, or in an abandoned nest. The female incubates the eggs for 26-28 days while the male hunts. The young fledge in 26-33 days. **Call** Shrill twittering. **Diet** Large insects, small mammals, birds, reptiles. **Habitat** Open woodlands, farmland.

FAMILY **STRIGIDAE**   SPECIES *Ninox novaeseelandiae*   SIZE **TO 30 CM**

SOUTHERN BOOBOOK

This small owl is brown above, streaked and spotted with white, and dull white below, mottled with brown. It has a dark facial disc edged with white. **Behaviour** They live in pairs and roost by day, often alone, in dense foliage or sometimes in a cave, using a number of sites in a territory of up to 10 ha. Their location is often betrayed by the calls of other birds attempting to mob them. When disturbed they turn side-on and sit up tall and slender hoping to escape detection. They feed mostly just after dusk and before dawn. **Breeding** They breed from August to January and lay 2-4 eggs in a tree hollow 3-25 m high. The female incubates the eggs for 26-33 days. Both parents feed the young who fledge in 5-6 weeks. **Call** High 2-syllable 'coo-book' or 'mo-poke'; aggressive screams. **Diet** Small mammals, birds, invertebrates. **Habitat** Open forests, woodlands, farmland.

FAMILY **TYTONIDAE**   SPECIES *Tyto alba*   SIZE **TO 40 CM**

BARN OWL

This owl has a heart-shaped mask with a brown border, a white facial disc and chestnut marks around the eyes. It is grey washed with gold above, with fine black spots, white with dusky flecks below. **Behaviour** They live singly or in pairs and are nomadic, congregating where food is abundant and roosting by day in dense foliage, caves, buildings or tree hollows. When hunting they fly silently, close to the ground, or listen from a low perch, gliding or dropping on their prey. **Breeding** Breeding depends on food abundance but is mainly in autumn and spring. They nest in a tree hollow or cave and lay 3-7 eggs, incubated for 33-35 days by the female. Both parents feed the young who fledge in 7-10 weeks. **Call** Rasping screech. **Diet** Small mammals, birds, reptiles, flying insects. **Habitat** Open woodlands, scrubs, grassy plains.

FAMILY **TYTONIDAE**   SPECIES *Tyto novaehollandiae*   SIZE **TO 55 CM**

MASKED OWL

This owl has a round, dark-bordered mask, an off-white or chestnut facial disc and dark chestnut marks around the eyes. It is blackish-brown, speckled white and washed with rufous above, and is pale-rufous below. **Behaviour** They mate for life and stay in the same territory all year. Pairs roost separately by day in tree hollows, rock crevices and caves and meet in the evening to hunt. When hunting they fly silently, close to the ground, and listen from a perch or on the ground. Large prey is shredded and consumed on the spot. Smaller prey is carried back to the roost. **Breeding** They breed at any time of year and lay 2-3 eggs in a tree hollow or cave. The female incubates the eggs for 35 days and both parents feed the young until they fledge in 10-12 weeks. **Call** Long rasping screech. **Diet** Small mammals, reptiles, birds, insects. **Habitat** Eucalypt forests, woodlands, caves.

FAMILY **PODARGIDAE**   SPECIES *Podargus strigoides*   SIZE **TO 53 CM**

TAWNY FROGMOUTH

This nightjar-like bird has grey plumes around its bill, a flat crown, orange eyes, pale-grey eyebrows, and is grey to reddish-brown above, streaked with black. **Behaviour** They pair for life, live in the same territory all year and roost together in a tree where they closely resemble a branch. If threatened they fluff their feathers, open their large orange eyes and snap their yellow-mouthed bill with a loud clap. They hunt after dusk and before dawn, diving on prey from a low branch or chasing flying insects. **Breeding** They breed from August to December and lay 1-3 eggs in a flimsy platform nest, 10-30 cm across, in a tree fork, stump, or in an abandoned nest. Both parents share incubation of 28-32 days and feed the young who fledge in 25-35 days. **Call** Soft, deep booms. **Diet** Large invertebrates, frogs, mice, small birds. **Habitat** Open forests, woodlands, gardens.

FAMILY **AEGOTHELIDAE**   SPECIES *Aegotheles cristatus*   SIZE **TO 25 CM**

AUSTRALIAN OWLET-NIGHTJAR

Australia's only owlet-nightjar, it is grey above, speckled and barred with white or rufous, and white below speckled with grey or washed with pale rufous. Black stripes above and below the eye join at the crown. **Behaviour** Rarely seen, they mate for life, and pairs roost alone by day in tree hollows and rock crevices. They live in a territory of 50-100 ha year-round and meet to hunt in the first hours after dusk and before dawn, flying low through the trees to catch insects, or listening from a perch and planing down on prey. **Breeding** They breed from August to December and lay 2-5 eggs in a rough, dish-shaped nest in a small hollow or crevice up to 5 m high. Both parents share incubation of 25-27 days and feed the young who fledge in 20-30 days. **Call** Loud, rattling 'chirr-churr'. **Diet** Insects and small invertebrates. **Habitat** Sclerophyll forests, woodlands.

FAMILY **ALCEDINIDAE**   SPECIES *Alcedo azurea*   SIZE **TO 19 CM**

AZURE KINGFISHER

This kingfisher has a long black bill with a rufous spot before the eye and a white mark on the side of the neck. Northern birds have a rufous-brown belly, southern birds have a cinnamon-brown belly. **Behaviour** Alone or in dispersed pairs, they hunt by day from a low perch over water and dive for prey, moving systematically between perches with a zig-zag flight pattern and fast glides. Pairs occupy a permanent territory of 200-500 m of waterfront, and males chase females in zig-zag display flights along the waterway. **Breeding** They breed from September to January and lay 4-7 eggs in a loose nest of fish bones, scales and the remains of crustaceans, at the end of a tunnel about 1 m long dug into a stream bank. Both parents share incubation of 20-22 days. The young fledge in 3-4 weeks. **Call** Shrill 'peee-peee'. **Diet** Fish, crustaceans, frogs, insects. **Habitat** Wetlands, mangroves, tree-lined waterways.

FAMILY **HALCYONIDAE**   SPECIES *Dacelo novaeguineae*   SIZE **TO 47 CM**

LAUGHING KOOKABURRA

The largest Australian kingfisher, the kookaburra has a massive bill, a brown stripe through the eyes and over the crown, off-white head and underparts. It is mottled light blue on the wings and has brown bars on the tail. **Behaviour** Family members live in the same territory year-round and reinforce the boundaries at the beginning of the breeding season, calling together and awaiting the response of neighbours. Young stay with their parents for up to 4 years helping to raise the offspring. They hunt from a perch, staring at the ground and fluttering down to catch prey. **Breeding** They breed from September to January and lay 1-4 eggs in a nest in a tree hollow or termite mound. The female and family helpers incubate the eggs and care for the young who fledge in about 5 weeks. **Call** Raucous laughing. **Diet** Reptiles, rodents, birds, insects, other invertebrates. **Habitat** Sclerophyll forests, woodlands, parks.

FAMILY **HALCYONIDAE**   SPECIES *Todiramphus sanctus*   SIZE **TO 23 CM**

SACRED KINGFISHER

Widely encountered, this kingfisher is distinguished by its green head and back, black band through the eye and around the head, and buff spot in front of the eye. **Behaviour** Usually solitary, they form pairs in the breeding season and live in family groups until autumn. In southern Australia they migrate north in the winter. They hunt from a low perch, sitting motionless, occasionally bobbing the head, and plunging onto their prey. **Breeding** They breed from June to October and lay 3-6 eggs in a nest at the end of a burrow dug into a termite mound or stream bank, or in a tree hollow. Both parents share incubation of 16-17 days and rear the young who fledge in about 4 weeks. Two broods are often raised in a season. **Call** Loud 'ek-ek-ek-ek'; harsh churring alarm call. **Diet** Small reptiles, fish, crustaceans, invertebrates. **Habitat** Open forests, woodlands, mangroves, tree-lined watercourses.

| FAMILY **MEROPIDAE** | SPECIES *Merops ornatus* | SIZE **TO 26 CM** |

RAINBOW BEE-EATER

This bee-eater has a golden-rufous crown, a black eye-stripe edged with blue, a black band on its yellow throat, and very long central tail feathers.
Behaviour They live in groups of 20-40, roosting in a small shrubby tree at night, and migrating to far northern Australia in winter. They hunt from a perch, or rarely from the ground, making complex aerial manoeuvres to catch insects, and squeezing out bee-stings before eating the bees. **Breeding** They breed from November to January in the south and at the beginning of the dry season in the north. Females lay 3-7 eggs in a nest at the end of a tunnel to 1 m long, dug into a bank, or on bare, flat ground. Group members help to dig tunnels, incubate the eggs for 21-25 days and rear the young, who fledge in about 4 weeks. **Call** High-pitched chittering. **Diet** Bees, other flying insects. **Habitat** Woodlands, savannah, farmland.

| FAMILY **CORACIIDAE** | SPECIES *Eurystomus orientalis* | SIZE **TO 30 CM** |

DOLLARBIRD

The only roller to reach Australia, the dollarbird has conspicuous, dollar-like, pale-blue patches on each wing, visible in flight. The wings are greenish-blue, the tail and throat blue and the upperparts brown.
Behaviour They migrate from New Guinea and adjacent islands to Australia in spring and summer to breed, returning in March or April, flying by day and night at up to 2500 m high. Breeding adults gather in groups and display to each other, twisting and rolling in aerial acrobatics. Males establish a territory and court a female. They often perch conspicuously, sitting motionless high up in tall trees on the lookout for flying insects. **Breeding** They breed usually from October to January and lay 3-5 eggs in a shallow cavity in a tall tree. Both parents incubate the eggs and feed the young. **Call** Harsh 'kak-kak-kak'. **Diet** Flying beetles, bugs, moths, mantids, cicadas. **Habitat** Rainforest margins, open woodlands.

| FAMILY **PITTIDAE** | SPECIES *Pitta versicolor* | SIZE **TO 20 CM** |

NOISY PITTA

This dumpy pitta has a black head, a broad chestnut stripe above the eyes joining behind the crown, a black throat and black stripe down the upper belly that becomes crimson on the lower belly. **Behaviour** Usually alone or in dispersed pairs, they are generally silent and hard to see on the rainforest floor. They become noisy when breeding, uttering loud territorial whistles from a perch up to 10 m high. They forage on the ground and crack snail shells open on a stone or piece of wood. **Breeding** They breed from October to January and sometimes August to March. A large domed nest with a circular side entrance is built between buttress roots or on a stump or cleft in a tree trunk. Both parents incubate the 3-4 eggs for around 17 days. **Call** Melodious 'walk-to-work' territorial whistle; single high 'keow'. **Diet** Insects, snails, other small animals, fruit. **Habitat** Rainforests, mangroves.

FAMILY **MENURIDAE**   SPECIES *Menura novaehollandiae*   SIZE **TO 1 M**

SUPERB LYREBIRD

Males are dark brown above and grey-brown below with long, filamentous tail feathers. Females are smaller with shorter, plain grey tail feathers. **Behaviour** They fly only to escape or when roosting in trees at night. They are usually solitary with foraging territories of 2-3 ha. In the breeding season males display from mounds, spreading their lyre-shaped tails, mimicking sounds of the forest while stamping and prancing to attract a female. They sometimes mate with several females. Family groups of 4-5 forage together after breeding, raking the ground with their powerful feet. **Breeding** They breed from May to October and lay a single egg in a dome nest in a tree fern, among rocks or on a tree stump. The female builds the nest and incubates the eggs for about 6 weeks. The young fledge 6 weeks later. **Call** Loud high 'chuck' in alarm; territorial resounding 'chonk-chonk'; mimicked calls. **Diet** Insects, worms, other invertebrates. **Habitat** Rainforests, wet sclerophyll forests.

FAMILY **HIRUNDINIDAE**   SPECIES *Hirundo neoxena*   SIZE **TO 16 CM**

WELCOME SWALLOW

This swallow is metallic blue-black above with dusky wings, a rufous-red throat and forehead, and a forked tail. It is dull white below. **Behaviour** They breed in single pairs or small groups, often returning to the same nest with the same partner in spring. After breeding they gather in flocks of 100 or more. Flocks roost together at night and forage in pairs from perches to catch small flying insects, often over water. Southern populations move north in autumn. **Breeding** They breed from August to December and often raise 2-3 broods per season. The female lays 4-6 eggs in a cup-shaped nest of mud and vegetation plastered to a wall or tree hollow. Both parents share incubation of about 15 days and feed the young who fledge in about 28 days. **Call** Twittering and warbling. **Diet** Insects. **Habitat** Open areas, preferably near water.

FAMILY **HIRUNDINIDAE**   SPECIES *Petrochelidon nigricans*   SIZE **TO 13 CM**

TREE MARTIN

This swallow-like bird is glossy blue-black above with a buff forehead, dull-white underparts streaked grey on the throat, and a shallowly-forked tail. **Behaviour** When not breeding they gather in large flocks in open areas, perching side-by-side on wires and fences. They forage on the wing, catching flying insects above the treetops or over water, and rest or roost communally in trees or dense rushes. At dusk they circle slowly over the treetops in ever-growing numbers, and as the light fails they dive down together to roost. Breeding pairs nest side-by-side or share a tree hollow with several nest chambers. **Breeding** They breed from July to January and lay 3-5 eggs in a nest in a tree hollow or cliff, lined with leaves. They often use the same nest each year. Both parents share incubation of 15-16 days and feed the young. **Call** Twittering song. **Diet** Insects. **Habitat** Open forests, woodlands.

| FAMILY **DICRURIDAE** | SPECIES *Grallina cyanoleuca* | SIZE **TO 30 CM** |

AUSTRALIAN MAGPIE-LARK

This conspicuous bird is black and white with a white bill. Males have a black face and throat, a white eyebrow and a small white bar below the eye. Females have a white face and throat. **Behaviour** Established pairs live in a permanent territory of 8-10 ha, but young birds roam widely in flocks, sometimes with thousands of birds, shifting with the seasons and roosting together at night. They forage on the ground in open areas, often in muddy shallows, and walk with a bobbing head, sometimes approaching picnickers. **Breeding** They breed mostly from August to December, sometimes rearing 2 broods in a season. Females lay 3-5 eggs in a bowl-shaped, mud nest, plastered to a branch, building or pole, 4-20 m high. Both parents share incubation of 17-18 days and feed the young who fledge in 18-23 days. **Call** Strident 'pee-wee'; piping calls. **Diet** Insects, larvae, worms, molluscs, seeds. **Habitat** Open areas, usually near water.

| FAMILY **DICRURIDAE** | SPECIES *Dicrurus bracteatus* | SIZE **TO 32 CM** |

SPANGLED DRONGO

This glossy black bird has a heavy, bristled bill, tapering wings and a distinctive forked tail. **Behaviour** Seen alone, in pairs, or sometimes in small flocks, they forage for insects from set perches through the middle strata of the forest, flying fast and erratically, banking, weaving and hovering, gleaning insects from the foliage and in flight. Northwestern populations are sedentary, while some eastern populations are nomadic or partly migratory, many moving north to New Guinea in winter and returning to breed in spring. **Breeding** They breed from September to March and lay 3-5 eggs in a shallow, saucer-shaped nest of vine tendrils, plant stems and fibres in a horizontal fork of a densely-foliaged tree up to 25 m high. Both parents incubate the eggs and feed the young. **Call** Metallic chattering, cackling, hissing; rasping. **Diet** Insects, fruit, small birds. **Habitat** Rainforests, vine scrubs, mangroves, parks, gardens.

| FAMILY **DICRURIDAE** | SPECIES *Rhipidura albiscapa* | SIZE **TO 17 CM** |

GREY FANTAIL

This common fantail is mid-grey above and cream below with a white eyebrow, throat and ear mark, white wing bars and outer tail feathers. **Behaviour** Usually alone or in breeding pairs, they are constantly active, flitting about the outer foliage, hovering, spiralling up and down tree trunks, twisting and turning in mid-air, picking up small insects as they go, with the tail usually fanned out. Southern populations migrate north after nesting; those in arid inland areas are nomadic, and northern birds stay in the same area year-round. **Breeding** They breed from August to January, sometimes raising 2-3 broods in a season. The female lays 2-4 eggs in a small, tailed, cup-shaped nest in a horizontal tree fork to 6 m high. Both parents share incubation of 13-14 days and rear the young who fledge in 10-12 days. **Call** Ascending, twangy, whistled song. Sharp 'chip' call. **Diet** Insects. **Habitat** Forests, woodlands, mangroves, riverine vegetation, parks, gardens.

FAMILY **DICRURIDAE** SPECIES *Rhipidura leucophrys* SIZE **TO 21 CM**

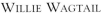

WILLIE WAGTAIL

This familiar wagtail is glossy black above with a white eyebrow, faint white flecks on the cheeks, black throat and white underparts. **Behaviour** Usually alone or in pairs, they forage conspicuously in open areas, perching on exposed stumps and in low, open trees, hawking insects in flight, zig-zagging and hopping over the ground looking for prey. Before taking off and after landing they flash their wings and fan their tail. When stationary they sway and wag their tail constantly. They are quite bold around humans and will nest close to houses. **Breeding** They breed from August to January, raising up to 4 broods per season. Females lay 2-4 eggs in a small, neat, cup-shaped nest placed on a branch 1-20 m high. Both parents share incubation of about 14 days and care for the young who fledge in about 14 days. **Call** Musical chattering 'sweet-pretty-creature'; metallic, hissing 'chik-a-chik-a-chik'. **Diet** Insects. **Habitat** Lightly-timbered and open areas.

FAMILY **DICRURIDAE** SPECIES *Rhipidura rufifrons* SIZE **TO 16 CM**

RUFOUS FANTAIL

This fantail is brown above with a rufous-orange lower back, tail-base and eyebrow. It has a white throat, a black band on the chest and white underparts. **Behaviour** Usually alone or in pairs, they forage in the shrubby understorey, making short, sallying flights from perches, tumbling, diving and twisting among the foliage, fluttering close enough to flush out and dis-lodge insects. They are constantly active, fidgeting the wings and body, wagging and fanning the tail. Southeastern populations migrate north in winter. **Breeding** They breed from October to February, some-times raising 2 broods in a season. The female lays 2-3 eggs in a neat, tailed, cup-shaped nest placed in a horizontal fork of a tree or shrub, 1-10 m high. Both parents share incubation of 14-15 days and care for the young who fledge in about 10 days. **Call** Sharp 'chip' call; short, tinny sequence of notes. **Diet** Insects, spiders. **Habitat** Rainforests, monsoon forests, dense wet sclero-phyll forests, mangroves.

FAMILY **MOTACILLIDAE** SPECIES *Anthus australis* SIZE **TO 18 CM**

AUSTRALIAN (RICHARD'S) PIPIT

This lark-like bird is mottled brown with pale stripes above and below the eye. It has whitish underparts with dark streaks on the breast. **Behaviour** They eat, sleep and nest on the ground, wagging the tail, darting around, gleaning insects from the vegetation and rock crevices. They often perch on low vantage points and fly to the top of a shrub or post if alarmed. Loose groups of up to 100 wander locally and break into pairs to breed, often with close territories. Many Tasmanian birds move to the mainland in winter, and alpine populations move to the lowlands. **Breeding** They breed from August to January and lay 2-4 eggs in a shallow ground depression lined with plant material, often beneath vegetation. The female incubates the eggs for 13-14 days and both parents feed the young who fledge in 13-14 days. **Call** Chirrups; repeated trilled 'peer' in flight. **Diet** Insects, seeds. **Habitat** Open country, clearings, beaches.

65

FAMILY **CAMPEPHAGIDAE**   SPECIES *Coracina novaehollandiae*   SIZE **TO 34 CM**

BLACK-FACED CUCKOO-SHRIKE

Named for its cuckoo-like form and shrike-like bill, this bird is light-grey above with a black face and flight feathers. The underparts are grey, grading to white on the belly. **Behaviour** Pairs and family groups gather in loose flocks of 6-100 birds after breeding and roam widely looking for food, generally heading north. They capture insects by diving from open perches, flying from tree to tree, sometimes dropping to the ground and hovering over prey. Flocks disperse in spring and pairs return to the same territory of 5 ha or more each year to breed. **Breeding** They breed from August to February and lay 2-3 eggs in a small, shallow, saucer-shaped nest placed near the end of a branch 8-20 m high. Both parents share incubation and raise the young who fledge in about 25 days. **Call** Trilling 'kereer-kereer-kereer'; rolling 'churrriink'. **Diet** Insects, fruit, seeds, nestling birds. **Habitat** Open forests, woodlands, heaths, parks, gardens.

FAMILY **PETROICIDAE**   SPECIES *Microeca fascinans*   SIZE **TO 14 CM**

JACKY WINTER

This flycatcher is grey-brown above and pale-grey to white below with a short black bill, a black line through the eye and a whitish eyebrow. **Behaviour** Established pairs occupy the same territory year-round, singing incessantly in the breeding season. They hunt from a perch, catching flying insects and picking invertebrates from the ground and tree trunks, often flying 30-50 m from the oerch, and hovering over the ground or beside foliage. They sometimes follow large animals and humans, catching insects flushed out by their passage. **Breeding** They breed from July to February and lay 2 eggs in a tiny, frail, saucer-shaped nest on a large bare branch to 22 m high. Both parents share incubation of 17-18 days and feed the young, who fledge in about 18 days. **Call** Rapidly-repeated jingling 'winter-winter-winter'. **Diet** Insects and other invertebrates. **Habitat** Dry sclerophyll forests, woodlands, mallee scrub, parks, gardens.

FAMILY **PETROICIDAE**   SPECIES *Petroica boodang*   SIZE **TO 13 CM**

SCARLET ROBIN

Males have a scarlet breast, a black throat, head and back, a white forehead patch and a broad white stripe on the wing. Females are grey-brown above with a buff-white forehead patch, a dull-red breast, white belly and undertail. **Behaviour** They live alone or in established pairs in a permanent territory, breeding in scrubby areas and moving to more open sites in autumn and winter. They forage from a perch, catching insects in flight and on the ground, or picking them from the leaves and bark. **Breeding** They breed from July to January and may raise 3 broods in a season. The female usually lays 3 eggs in a cup-shaped nest in a tree fork or hollow stump up to 20 m high, and incubates them for 15-17 days. Both parents feed the young who fledge in 15-17 days. **Call** Sweet, rippling, whistled trill. **Diet** Insects and other small invertebrates. **Habitat** Sclerophyll forests, woodlands, parks, gardens.

FAMILY **PETROICIDAE**   SPECIES *Petroica goodenovii*   SIZE **TO 11 CM**

REDCAPPED ROBIN

Males have a scarlet cap and breast, a black throat and back, a white wing bar, and white underparts. Females have a reddish-brown forehead, russet-brown back, darker wings and tail, creamy-white underparts, and a brownish chest. **Behaviour** They live alone or sometimes in established pairs and stay in a permanent territory or wander locally outside the breeding season, particularly in the west and southern interior. They flit from perch-to-perch when feeding, hawking flying insects and diving to the ground for prey. **Breeding** They breed from July to January, sometimes raising 2 broods in a season. The female lays 2-3 eggs in a compact, cup-shaped nest in a tree fork a few metres high, and incubates them for about 14 days. Both parents feed the young who fledge in about 14 days. **Call** Rattling trill 'tit-tit-trrr-it'. **Diet** Insects and other small invertebrates. **Habitat** Dry scrub and woodlands, especially mallee and mulga.

FAMILY **PETROICIDAE**   SPECIES *Eopsaltria australis*   SIZE **TO 15 CM**

EASTERN YELLOW ROBIN

This common robin is grey washed with olive above, grading to citrine or bright yellow on the rump. The underparts are yellow. **Behaviour** They live in permanent territorial pairs, breeding in dense, shrubby areas, often joining mixed flocks of small insectivorous birds to forage in open woodlands in winter. They hunt from a perch, flitting quietly between low branches, sitting sideways, catching prey on the ground, in the foliage or rarely in flight. **Breeding** They breed from July to January, raising up to 3 broods per season. The female lays 2-3 eggs in a cup-shaped nest usually placed in an upright tree fork up to 5 m high, and incubates them for 15-16 days. Both parents feed the young who fledge in 10-14 days. **Call** Bell-like piping; harsh 'chip-chip'; trilled whistles. **Diet** Spiders, ants, grasshoppers, wasps and other insects. **Habitat** Rainforests, sclerophyll forests, woodlands, mallee and acacia scrub, parks, gardens.

FAMILY **PACHYCEPHALIDAE**   SPECIES *Pachycephala pectoralis*   SIZE **TO 17 CM**

GOLDEN WHISTLER

Males have a black head and collar, a white throat, yellow neck and underparts, an olive-green back and black wing feathers edged with yellow-green. Females are brownish-grey, washed with olive over the back, with a white, yellow or buff undertail. **Behaviour** Usually silent and unobtrusive, they forage alone or in pairs, gleaning insects from the vegetation, probing in the leaf litter and sometimes catching insects in flight. They are attracted by humans making loud kissing sounds. In winter, southeastern populations migrate north. **Breeding** They breed from September to January and lay 2-3 eggs in a rough, cup-shaped nest in the upright fork of a shrub to 5 m high. Both parents share incubation of 14-17 days and feed the young who fledge in 10-13 days. **Call** Melodious whistling sometimes with whip-crack ending. **Diet** Insects, larvae, berries. **Habitat** Rainforests, sclerophyll forests, dense woodlands, mallee scrub, parks, gardens.

| FAMILY **PACHYCEPHALIDAE** | SPECIES *Colluricincla harmonica* | SIZE **TO 24 CM** |

GREY SHRIKE-THRUSH

Males vary from mid-brown to grey above, with a dark eye-ring, a white stripe from bill to eye and light-grey underparts. Females have a white eye-ring and grey streaks on the throat and breast. **Behaviour** Established pairs live in a permanent territory of 2-10 ha and sometimes wander locally in winter. Others travel more widely. They forage in trees and on the ground, hopping on branches, gleaning insects from the vegetation, pulling off bark and picking insects from the leaf litter and logs. **Breeding** They breed from July to February and lay 3-4 eggs in a bowl-shaped nest placed in a hollow log, stump, crevice, rock ledge, tree fork, or on the ground. Both parents share nest-building, incubation of 16-18 days and care for the young. **Call** Melodious whistled 'pip-pip-pip-pip-ho-ee'. **Diet** Insects, spiders, lizards, small mammals, frogs, nestlings, eggs. **Habitat** Forests, woodlands, scrubs, parks, gardens.

| FAMILY **CINCLOSOMATIDAE** | SPECIES *Psophodes olivaceus* | SIZE **TO 30 CM** |

EASTERN WHIPBIRD

More often heard than seen, this elusive bird has a black head and crest, dark olive-green back, a long broad tail tipped white, large white patches on the sides of the cheeks and throat, and a mottled-white belly. **Behaviour** Established pairs live in permanent territories of 5-10 ha. They forage mostly on the ground in the dense undergrowth up to 30 m apart, scratching in the leaf litter and calling frequently to keep in contact. **Breeding** They breed from July to January and may raise 2 broods in a season. The female lays 2-3 eggs in a loose, cup-shaped nest in a low shrub or dense undergrowth, to 2 m high, and incubates them for 17-18 days. Both parents feed the young who fledge in 10-11 days. **Call** Loud whipcrack by male, followed by female's 'choo-choo'. **Diet** Insects, larvae. **Habitat** Dense undershrubs in rainforests, wet sclerophyll forests, coastal heaths.

| FAMILY **CINCLOSOMATIDAE** | SPECIES *Cinclosoma punctatum* | SIZE **TO 28 CM** |

SPOTTED QUAIL-THRUSH

Males are brown-grey above with black spots, a black face, white eyebrow and black throat with white patches. Females have a white throat with dull orange patches. **Behaviour** Shy and elusive, they live in pairs or small family groups and forage alone, crouching and running erratically, picking insects from the ground and calling to keep in contact. If flushed they fly low and direct with whirring wings for up to 50 m. Pairs hold a permanent breeding territory. **Breeding** They breed from July to February and raise up to 3 broods in a season. The female lays 2-3 eggs in a ground depression beside a tree, boulder or grass tuft, loosely lined with vegetation. She incubates the eggs and both parents feed the young who fledge in about 19 days. **Call** Thin, high-pitched whistle; loud double whistle. **Diet** Insects, lizards, seeds. **Habitat** Sclerophyll forests and woodlands. Prefers rocky ridges with abundant leaf litter.

FAMILY **POMATOSTOMIDAE**　　　SPECIES *Pomatostomus temporalis*　　　SIZE **TO 29 CM**

GREY-CROWNED BABBLER

Australia's largest babbler, this bird has a grey crown, a large white eyebrow, dark eye-stripe, white throat and breast grading to a rufous-brown belly. **Behaviour** They mate for life and live in groups comprising a breeding pair and up to 10 family members in a permanent territory of around 12 ha. Groups perch and forage together, bounding on the ground, probing in the leaf litter and gleaning insects from the bark and foliage. They roost together in a nest at night and cooperate in nest-building and feeding the young. **Breeding** They breed from July to February, sometimes raising 2 broods in a season. The female lays 2-3 eggs in a bulky domed nest in a tree fork about 4 m high, and incubates them for 18-23 days. The young fledge in about 21 days. **Call** Loud 'wa-oo'; chattering 'chuk'; cat-like meowing. **Diet** Insects, spiders, lizards, seeds. **Habitat** Open forests, woodlands.

FAMILY **MALURIDAE**　　　SPECIES *Malurus cyaneus*　　　SIZE **TO 15 CM**

SUPERB FAIRY-WREN

Outside the breeding season they are grey-brown above and greyish-white below. Breeding males have a bright blue crown, cheeks and upper back, a blue-black chest and tail. **Behaviour** Groups comprising an adult pair, young of the year, and often several sub-adult males occupy an exclusive territory. Song battles between neighbouring males are common. By day they forage on the ground and in shrubs, rest side-by-side, and huddle together on a branch at night. **Breeding** They breed from August to March and lay 3-4 eggs in a small spherical nest with a side entrance, loosely made of grass, lined with feathers and placed in a dense shrub. The female incubates the eggs for 13-15 days. Group members help to raise the young who fledge in 12-13 days. Up to 4 broods may be raised in a season. **Call** Musical trill; staccato 'prip-prip'. **Diet** Insects, fruit. **Habitat** Open forests, woodlands, parks, gardens.

FAMILY **CLIMACTERIDAE**　　　SPECIES *Cormobates leucophaeus*　　　SIZE **TO 17 CM**

WHITE-THROATED TREECREEPER

This treecreeper is deep olive-brown above with a white throat and breast patch, grading to creamy-yellow on the belly. Females have a rusty orange spot on the lower cheek. **Behaviour** They forage alone by day, climbing methodically up and around a tree, probing under branches and digging into the bark with their bill looking for insects. They then fly down to the base of the next tree and start again. Pairs maintain an exclusive year-round territory and sleep clinging to a tree trunk, in a hollow, or beneath the bark. **Breeding** They breed from August to December and lay 2-3 eggs in a nest in a tree hollow or behind bark. The female incubates the eggs for 22-23 days and both parents feed the young who fledge in 26 days. **Call** Repeated piping whistle descending or rising in pitch. **Diet** Insects, spiders. **Habitat** Rainforests, sclerophyll forests, woodlands.

FAMILY **MELIPHAGIDAE** SPECIES *Anthochaera carunculata* SIZE **TO 35 CM**

RED WATTLEBIRD

This large honeyeater has dark pink lobes on its
grey-white cheeks. The back is grey-brown
streaked white, the underparts pale brown-
grey streaked white with a yellow belly. **Behaviour** Noisy
and aggressive, they congregate in loose, nomadic groups
of 5-100 birds after breeding, and roam on established flight paths to
flowering trees where they chase away other honeyeaters. Nectar and
pollen is lapped up with the brush-tipped tongue, insects are taken in flight
or gleaned from the leaves and bark. **Breeding** They breed from July to
December and lay 2-3 eggs in a small, rough, cup-shaped nest 3-20 m high
in the outer foliage. Incubation is about 15 days and both parents raise the
young who fledge at about 15 days. **Call** Harsh 'yak-yak-yak' or coughing
'chork-chock'. **Diet** Nectar, pollen, insects, honeydew, fruit, seeds.
Habitat Sclerophyll forests, woodlands, mallee scrub, parks, gardens.

FAMILY **MELIPHAGIDAE** SPECIES *Anthochaera chrysoptera* SIZE **TO 32 CM**

LITTLE WATTLEBIRD

This large honeyeater has inconspicuous wattles and is brownish-grey with fine white streaks and spots, and grey-white
cheeks. **Behaviour** They usually live in groups of up to 30
birds and vigorously defend individual territories around food
sources. Feeding colonies are constantly noisy with frequent
squabbling as they glean insects from the foliage and nectar from the flowers,
and swoop from tree-to-tree. In some areas they are nomadic or locally migratory. Courting pairs often sing duets. **Breeding** They breed mainly from July
to November, raising up to 3 broods in a season. Females lay 1-2 eggs in a
rough, cup-shaped nest in the outer branches of a tree or shrub, and incubate
them for about 16 days. The male helps to feed the young for several weeks
after fledging at about 16 days old. **Call** Squawking 'crock-chaawk' by
male; high-pitched twittering by female. **Diet** Nectar, manna, insects,
fruit, seeds. **Habitat** Forests, woodlands, tall heaths, parks, gardens.

FAMILY **MELIPHAGIDAE** SPECIES *Philemon corniculatus* SIZE **TO 34 CM**

NOISY FRIARBIRD

This large honeyeater has a bare head with black skin, a
grey-brown eyebrow, a triangle of silver-grey feathers on the
chin, and a small knob at the base of the bill.
Behaviour They are noisy and aggressive birds. In the south,
they migrate north in loose groups of 30-40 in autumn and
return in early spring alone or in pairs. In the north they are nomadic. They
congregate in flowering trees and each bird noisily defends its feeding branches. They pick fruit, glean insects from the bark and foliage, and probe flowers
with their brush-tipped tongue, often hanging upside down; and catch flying
insects. **Breeding** They breed from July to February and lay 2-3 eggs in a
large, open, cup-shaped nest in the outer branches. The female incubates the
eggs and both parents attend the young. **Call** Raucous cackling 'four-o'clock',
'tabacco-tabacco'; chuckling cackles. **Diet** Nectar, lerps, honeydew, fruit, seeds,
insects. **Habitat** Wet and dry sclerophyll forests, woodlands, parks, gardens.

FAMILY **MELIPHAGIDAE**   SPECIES *Entomyzon cyanotis*   SIZE **TO 30 CM**

BLUE-FACED HONEYEATER

Distinguished by a large patch of light blue skin around the eye, it has a black head and neck, a dark grey chin and throat, an olive-yellow back and white underparts. **Behaviour** They live in communal groups of 2-10 and feed close together in the upper foliage, chirping and following each other from tree to tree, often diving to bathe and drink. They hop on branches, cling to trunks, probe under bark for insects and catch flying insects. After breeding communal groups wander locally and often shift north in winter. **Breeding** They breed from June to January and lay 2-3 eggs in a deep, untidy, cup-shaped nest in the fork or branch of a tree, sometimes refurbishing deserted nests of grey-crowned babblers. The female incubates the eggs and both parents raise the young. **Call** Loud metallic 'tink'; harsh mewing; piping whistle. **Diet** Insects, fruit, nectar. **Habitat** Open forests, woodlands, mangroves, parks, gardens.

FAMILY **MELIPHAGIDAE**   SPECIES *Manorina melanophrys*   SIZE **TO 19 CM**

BELL MINER

This honeyeater is olive-green with a black forehead, an orange-yellow bill and an orange patch behind the eye. **Behaviour** They live in colonies with a territory of up to 2 ha, comprising several groups, each with a mated pair and up to 8 others. They feed in the lower and middle layers of the forest, hopping and fluttering, gleaning lerps and other insects from the foliage and trunks, and chasing away other birds. **Breeding** They breed from June to February in the south and April to June in the north. Females lay 1-3 eggs in a loose, cup-shaped nest suspended by the rim and bound by cobwebs to a branch, and incubate them for 15 days. Group members help to feed the young until they are about 4 weeks old. **Call** Aggressive sharp 'jak-jak-jak' and 'kwee-kwee-kwee'; single, repeated, bell-like 'tink' contact call. **Diet** Insects, nectar, fruits. **Habitat** Sclerophyll forests, usually near water.

FAMILY **MELIPHAGIDAE**   SPECIES *Manorina melanocephala*   SIZE **TO 29 CM**

NOISY MINER

This honeyeater has a black crown and face with a light-grey forehead, yellow skin behind the eye, a yellow bill, grey back, and white underparts mottled grey on the breast. **Behaviour** They live in territorial groups of 6-30 birds, within a loose colony of several hundred, uniting to mob predators and attack other birds in their territory. They feed, bathe and sleep together. Groups have boisterous social displays and greeting ceremonies. They feed in the trees, hopping and fluttering around, and on the ground. **Breeding** They breed mainly from June to December and lay 2-4 eggs in a flimsy, cup-shaped nest in outer branches up to 20 m high. The female incubates the eggs for 15-16 days. Male group members help to feed the young who fledge in about 16 days. **Call** Harsh alarm calls; repeated territorial 'teu-teu-teu-teu'; whistling song. **Diet** Insects, honeydew, fruit, nectar. **Habitat** Open forests, woodlands, urban areas.

FAMILY **MELIPHAGIDAE**   SPECIES *Manorina flavigula*   SIZE **TO 28 CM**

YELLOW-THROATED MINER

This honeyeater is distinguished by the yellow wash on the sides of the neck and forehead, and yellow skin at the sides of the chin and behind the eye.

Behaviour They breed in small, close-knit colonies comprising several communal groups of a pair plus helpers. In well-watered places they stay in the same area year-round, while those in drier areas wander locally after breeding, coalescing in flocks of 50 or more birds. They forage on the bark and foliage and search among the leaf litter for insects. **Breeding** They breed from July to December and lay 3-4 eggs in a bulky, cup-shaped nest bound with cobwebs to the outer branches of a low tree. Group members feed the young, continuing even after they have fledged and left the nest. **Call** Repeated territorial 'teu-teu-teu-teu'; whistling song. **Diet** Insects, other invertebrates, fruit, seeds, nectar. **Habitat** Dry open forests, woodlands, mallee scrub, parks, gardens.

FAMILY **MELIPHAGIDAE**   SPECIES *Meliphaga lewinii*   SIZE **TO 22 CM**

LEWIN'S HONEYEATER

This honeyeater is mid to dark olive-green with a creamy-yellow, crescent-shaped patch behind the ear, and a yellow line running under the eye to the bill. **Behaviour** They forage alone or in loose pairs in the mid to upper layers of the rainforest, gathering to feed in groups around profusely-flowering or fruiting trees, often spiralling up the trunk, picking insects from the bark, or hovering to glean insects from the foliage. Individuals and pairs occupy the same territory most of the year, and spend much time chasing other birds from their feeding sites. **Breeding** They breed from August to January and lay 2-3 eggs in a cup-shaped nest suspended by the rim, in foliage 2-6 m high. Incubation takes 14-15 days and the young fledge in 14-15 days. **Call** Loud staccato chatter. **Diet** Insects, fruit, nectar. **Habitat** Rainforests, wet sclerophyll forests, woodlands, heaths, parks, gardens.

FAMILY **MELIPHAGIDAE**   SPECIES *Lichenostomus chrysops*   SIZE **TO 17 CM**

YELLOW-FACED HONEYEATER

This honeyeater is grey-brown with a yellow stripe below the eye ending in a white tuft, bordered by black lines. It has a small white patch over the eye. **Behaviour** They migrate in flocks of up to 100 or more birds each autumn from breeding grounds in southeastern Australia, travelling north along established flyways, following the flowering of trees and shrubs. They forage for insects on the branches and in the foliage, and take nectar from the flowers. In spring they return south. The flocks break up into breeding pairs who establish nesting territories. **Breeding** They breed from July to March and lay 2-3 eggs in a small, cup-shaped nest in the outer branches of a tree or shrub, up to 7 m high. Incubation takes about 14 days and the young fledge in about 13 days. **Call** Ringing 'chickup-chickup-chickup'. **Diet** Insects, nectar, fruit. **Habitat** Forests, woodlands, mangroves, heaths, parks, gardens.

FAMILY **MELIPHAGIDAE**   SPECIES *Lichenostomus leucotis*   SIZE **TO 21 CM**

WHITE-EARED HONEYEATER

This common honeyeater is olive-green above and yellow-ish below. It has a grey crown, a black face, throat and upper breast, and a white ear patch. **Behaviour** Rarely gathering in groups, established males or pairs live in large, well-spaced territories year-round, although in alpine regions they overwinter in the lowlands. They feed in shrubs and in the lower canopy, hopping along branches, gleaning insects and sugary secretions from the foliage and probing for insects in the bark. They poke a hole in the base of flowers to suck out the nectar. **Breeding** They breed mostly from August to December and lay 2-3 eggs in a cup-shaped nest bound with cobwebs, suspended by the rim from a small shrub 2-3 m high. Incubation is about 14 days and the young fledge in 14-15 days. **Call** Loud resounding 'chock-up, chock-up'. **Diet** Insects, other invertebrates, manna, hon-eydew, nectar, fruit. **Habitat** Sclerophyll forests, woodlands, mallee scrub, coastal heaths, parks, gardens.

FAMILY **MELIPHAGIDAE**   SPECIES *Phylidonyris novaehollandiae*   SIZE **TO 18 CM**

NEW HOLLAND HONEYEATER

Distinguished by its black head with a white streak behind the eye, a white ear patch and white 'beard', it is streaked black and white with a yellow wing patch. **Behaviour** Usually seen in pairs or small flocks, they are highly nomadic, following flowering shrubs. In good sites 5-10 birds may be found per hectare, each with a small feeding terri-tory marked by morning and afternoon song flights. Pairs often nest in loose communal groups and disperse when food becomes scarce. **Breeding** They breed any time with peaks from July to December and March to May, and raise 2-3 broods in a season. The female lays 1-3 eggs in a cup-shaped nest in a shrub or tree 1-5 m high, and incubates them for 14-15 days. Both parents feed the young who fledge in 10-14 days. **Call** Harsh notes; rapid shrill whistling. **Diet** Nectar, manna, honeydew, insects. **Habitat** Sclerophyll forests and woodlands with a dense understorey, heaths, parks, gardens.

FAMILY **MELIPHAGIDAE**   SPECIES *Acanthorhynchus tenuirostris*   SIZE **TO 16 CM**

EASTERN SPINEBILL

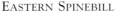

This honeyeater has a long curved bill for probing flowers. Males have a glossy black head and wings, a russet collar and a chestnut patch on the throat. Females are duller with a greyish crown. **Behaviour** They forage in low flow-ering shrubs, alone or in loose groups, often hovering beside flowers to sip their nectar, and occasionally snatching insects from the air. Most populations stay in the same area year round, but in the southern moun-tains they disperse to the lowlands after breeding. **Breeding** They breed from August to March and usually raise 2 broods in a season. The female lays 2-3 eggs in a cup-shaped nest, attached by its rim to a bushy tree or shrub 1-5 m high, and incubates them for about 14 days with occasional help from the male. Both parents feed the young. **Call** Rapid piping 'pi-pi-dee, pi-pi-dee'. **Diet** Nectar, insects. **Habitat** Wet sclerophyll forests, rainforests, woodlands, heaths, parks, gardens.

FAMILY **MELIPHAGIDAE** · SPECIES *Myzomela sanguinolenta* · SIZE **TO 11 CM**

SCARLET HONEYEATER

Males have a scarlet head, breast and rump, black wings and tail. Females are pale to olive-brown above with a red wash on the chin and off-white underparts. **Behaviour** They congregate in loose flocks in tall flowering trees and shrubs, constantly flitting around, hanging head-down and hovering to probe flowers, sometimes snatching flying insects. Northern populations stay in the same area year-round, elsewhere they wander up and down the coast and ranges looking for food, sometimes travelling long distances. **Breeding** They breed from July to January and often raise 2 broods in a season. The female lays 2 eggs in a flimsy, cup-shaped nest attached by the rim to a horizontal fork in a tree, 1-15 m high, and incubates the eggs for about 12 days. Both parents feed the young. **Call** Bell-like tinkering by male; squeaks by female. **Diet** Nectar, insects, fruit. **Habitat** Sclerophyll forests, rainforests, woodlands, heaths, parks, gardens.

FAMILY **NECTARINIIDAE** · SPECIES *Nectarinia jugularis* · SIZE **TO 13 CM**

YELLOW-BELLIED SUNBIRD

This common tropical bird has a long, slender, curved bill, and an olive-green back. Males have a metallic blue-black bib and yellow underparts. Females have a yellow bib. **Behaviour** Although usually seen in pairs, groups of 8-10 males gather before the main breeding season, chattering and chasing each other, then suddenly perching in a line with their bills pointing up for a few minutes or longer. Established pairs hold a permanent territory, defended by the male, while the female builds or renovates the nest. **Breeding** They breed mainly from July to March and raise up to 3 broods in a season. The female lays 2-3 eggs in a long, spindle-shaped nest with a hooded side entrance, hung from a tree or under eaves. She incubates the eggs and feeds the young for 6-8 days until the male comes to help. **Call** High-pitched 'tzit-tzit-tzit'; hissing trill. **Diet** Nectar, insects, spiders. **Habitat** Rainforest margins, mangroves, parks, gardens.

FAMILY **DICAEIDAE** · SPECIES *Dicaeum hirundinaceum* · SIZE **TO 11 CM**

MISTLETOEBIRD

Males are glossy blue-back above with a scarlet throat and undertail, a grey-white breast and belly with a broad black central streak. Females are brownish-grey above and off-white below with a pale-scarlet undertail. **Behaviour** Usually alone or in pairs, they forage in the upper canopy, feeding almost exclusively on mistletoe fruit, flying fast and erratically over the tree-tops. They are the main disseminator of the seeds, which stick to branches and germinate. The young are fed on insects for the first few days. **Breeding** They breed mainly from October to March and lay 3 eggs in a purse-shaped nest with a narrow side entrance, suspended in the outer foliage of a tree or shrub to 10 m high. The female incubates the eggs and both parents feed the young who fledge in about 15 days. **Call** High-pitched 'szit' in flight; whistled 'witu-witu, tzee zit, tsew-wit-zit' from perch. **Diet** Fruit, insects. **Habitat** Rainforests, sclerophyll forests, woodlands.

FAMILY **PARDALOTIDAE**   SPECIES *Pardalotus punctatus*   SIZE **TO 10 CM**

SPOTTED PARDALOTE

This tiny pardalote has a spotted crown and back, a white eyebrow, a yellowish throat and a cream belly. Males have a bright-yellow throat. **Behaviour** They gather in loose nomadic feeding flocks of 10-100 birds and move quickly through the crowns of eucalypt trees looking for food. In southern areas they move to the warmer lowlands or head north in winter, often travelling as far as central Queensland. Flocks return to breed in early spring and disperse in pairs to previously occupied territories, chasing off intruders with long, twisting flights. **Breeding** They breed from August to January and lay 3-6 eggs in a loose dome nest at the end of a tunnel, dug into a creek bank, cliff, sand pile or wall. Both parents incubate the eggs for 14-16 days and feed the young. **Call** High-pitched 'sa-weet', 'be-bee' or 'wee-eee'. **Diet** Lerps, insects, manna. **Habitat** Sclerophyll forests, woodlands, wetter mallee scrub.

FAMILY **PARDALOTIDAE**   SPECIES *Pardalotus striatus*   SIZE **TO 12 CM**

STRIATED PARDALOTE

This small pardalote has a black crown with or without white streaks, a yellow and white stripe over the eye, a grey-brown back and a red or yellow spot on the wings. **Behaviour** They form loose flocks of 100 or more birds, heading north or to warmer lowlands in winter. They feed in the crowns of eucalypt trees, running like a mouse, picking food from the foliage. Flocks return to breed, and disperse into pairs or groups of 3-6 to nest, defending only the immediate vicinity of the nest. **Breeding** They breed from June to January and lay 3-5 eggs in a cup-shaped nest placed in a tree hollow or at the end of a tunnel, dug into a cliff, creek bank or building. Both parents share incubation and feed the young, often helped by other group members. **Call** Loud, sharp, double or triple notes. **Diet** Lerps, insects and other invertebrates. **Habitat** Open forests, woodlands.

FAMILY **PARDALOTIDAE**   SPECIES *Sericornis frontalis*   SIZE **TO 14 CM**

WHITE-BROWED SCRUBWREN

This scrubwren is dark olive-brown above and dirty yellow below. It has a white stripe above and below the eye, a white throat with faint dark streaks (spotted black in western birds). **Behaviour** They live in groups with a breeding pair, immatures and often several additional adults, and occupy the same territory of 1-5 ha year-round. They feed under cover as a loose party, constantly chattering, hopping on the ground and sometimes among low branches, making short, low, dipping flights between feeding areas. **Breeding** They breed from July to January and lay 2-3 eggs in a coarse, dome-shaped nest with a side entrance, hidden in the undergrowth on or near the ground. The female probably incubates the eggs, and group members help to feed the young. **Call** Repeated soft whistle; harsh 'chur'in alarm. **Diet** Insects, spiders, seeds. **Habitat** Coastal heath, mallee scrub, mangrove fringes, dense shrubs along creeks.

ANIMALS

FAMILY **PARDALOTIDAE**   SPECIES *Smicrornis brevirostris*   SIZE **TO 9 CM**

WEEBILL

The shortest bird in Australia, the weebill is dull olive-brown to bright olive-yellow above with a whitish stripe above the eye and sometimes a rufous spot in front of the eye. The undersides are yellow, sometimes with sparse dark streaks. **Behaviour** They feed in the outer foliage, hopping, flitting, gleaning insects from the leaves and hovering to catch flying insects. Pairs or loose parties of up to 10 birds forage together within a permanent territory, communicating with sharp buzzing notes and singing sporadically. **Breeding** They breed from August to February and lay 2-3 eggs in a dome-shaped nest bound with cobwebs, placed in a leafy branch 1-10 m high. The female incubates the eggs for about 12 days and group members help to feed the young who fledge in 10 days. Two or more broods are raised each year. **Call** Sharp repeated 'chiz'; whistled song 'weebill-weebill-weebee'. **Diet** Insects. **Habitat** Open forests, woodlands.

FAMILY **PARDALOTIDAE**   SPECIES *Gerygone mouki*   SIZE **TO 11 CM**

BROWN GERYGONE

This small warbler is deep olive-brown above with a white stripe on the side of the forehead. The underside is cream to soft grey, sometimes with a red-brown wash on the side of the belly. **Behaviour** They live singly, in pairs or loose groups of 3-4 birds, gleaning insects from the foliage, sometimes hovering to catch insects in flight and often joining other birds to forage in the rainforest edges. They stay in the same area throughout the year. **Breeding** They breed from September to February and lay 2-3 eggs in a slender domed nest with a long tail and hooded side-entrance, bound with cobwebs, hanging 1-15 m high from a branchlet or vine. The female probably incubates the eggs for 16-19 days. Both parents feed the young who fledge in 15-16 days. **Call** Soft twittering 'did-dle-it-did-dit'. **Diet** Insects. **Habitat** Subtropical rainforests.

FAMILY **PARDALOTIDAE**   SPECIES *Acanthiza pusilla*   SIZE **TO 11 CM**

BROWN THORNBILL

This small bird has a black, thorn-like bill and is rich olive-brown to brownish-grey above, with a pale crescent above its red eye. The throat and chest are light-grey streaked with black. The rump is cinnamon-brown. **Behaviour** Established pairs occupy permanent territories of up to 5 ha and expel the young when they are a few months old. Outside the breeding season they forage by day with other birds in the middle and upper layers of the understorey, flitting from shrub to shrub, probing flowers with the bill, gleaning insects from the leaves and bark. **Breeding** They breed from June to December and lay 2-3 eggs in an untidy domed nest, bound with cobwebs and placed in low vegetation. The female incubates the eggs for 17-21 days. The young fledge in about 15 days. **Call** Whistles, trills and warbles; harsh 'churr' in alarm. **Diet** Insects, seeds, nectar. **Habitat** Forests and woodlands with sufficient understorey.

FAMILY **PARDALOTIDAE**   SPECIES *Acanthiza lineata*   SIZE **TO 10 CM**

STRIATED THORNBILL

This forest-dweller has a black, thorn-like bill, white streaks on its crown and dark striations on its white chest. It is olive-brown above and light yellowish-brown below. **Behaviour** They live in groups of around 25 birds in a year-round territory of about 6 ha, feeding, roosting and nesting in eucalypt trees, foraging in the canopy and calling constantly. Breeding groups of a single female and up to 3 males occupy a smaller territory. **Breeding** They breed from July to December and lay 3 eggs in a dome-shaped nest of bark strips, grass and cobwebs with a spout-like entrance, suspended from a branch 5-10 m high. The female incubates the eggs for 15-17 days. Both parents and helper males feed the young. **Call** Persistent buzzing 'tizz'. Soft, high-pitched trill. **Diet** Leaf beetles, weevils, bugs, caterpillars, spiders. **Habitat** Wet and dry sclerophyll forests.

FAMILY **ZOSTEROPIDAE**   SPECIES *Zosterops lateralis*   SIZE **TO 13 CM**

SILVEREYE

Named for its white eye-ring, this small bird is olive-green above with a grey back, a greenish-yellow throat, pale buff flanks and a pale-grey chest and belly. **Behaviour** They form permanent pairs and are busy feeders, hopping on the ground, jumping between branches, catching insects, sipping nectar, gathering seeds and hanging upside down to pick fruit. Most southern populations gather in flocks and migrate north each autumn and return in late winter, although older pairs remain in the same territory. **Breeding** They breed from August to February, raising 2 broods per season. The female lays 2-4 eggs in a small, cup-shaped nest suspended from a small outer branch 1-5 m high. Both parents share incubation of 10-13 days and feed the young who fledge in 9-12 days. **Call** Pleasant trilled warbling song. Repeated whistled 'peee-oow' contact call. **Diet** Insects, nectar, seeds, fruit. **Habitat** Forests, woodlands, heaths, parks, gardens.

FAMILY **PASSERIDAE**   SPECIES *Taeniopygia guttata*   SIZE **TO 12 CM**

ZEBRA FINCH

Males have rusty cheeks, a black chest bar, fine black bars on the throat, and russet flanks spotted white. Females have grey cheeks and buff underparts. **Behaviour** They mate permanently and live in close-knit flocks of 10-100 year-round, roosting in communal nests, feeding together in the morning, pecking seeds and insects from the ground and vegetation. They stay in the same area, close to water, and gather in the late afternoon to drink, bathe and preen each other. Up to 12 breeding pairs will nest in the same shrub in poor habitats. **Breeding** They breed most months and lay 4-5 eggs in a flask-shaped nest with a side tunnel in a low tree, shrub or on the ground. Both parents share incubation of 12-14 days and feed the young who fledge in about 3 weeks. They can breed at 9-10 weeks. **Call** Nasal, twangy 'tiah'; harsh, nasal, trilling song. **Diet** Seeds, insects. **Habitat** Dry, wooded grasslands, farmlands.

Family **PASSERIDAE** Species *Neochmia temporalis* Size **to 12 cm**

RED-BROWED FINCH

This common finch is olive-green above with a grey head, crimson rump, eyebrow and sides of the bill. The underparts are pale-grey. **Behaviour** They live in close-knit flocks year-round, and mate permanently. Pairs sleep at night in a roost nest, often with several others. Flock members call constantly in flight and while feeding, and drink frequently. They forage for seeds on the ground, balance on stalks to peck at seed heads, and glean insects from the foliage. Several breeding pairs may nest in the same shrub. **Breeding** They breed from August to January in the south and December to April in the north. Females lay 4-8 eggs in a flask-shaped nest with a side tunnel, in a thorny shrub. Both parents share incubation of 13-14 days and feed the young who fledge in 15-17 days. **Call** High-pitched, piercing, 'sseee-see'. **Diet** Seeds, fruit, insects. **Habitat** Grassy clearings in forests, parks, gardens.

Family **ORIOLIDAE** Species *Oriolus sagittatus* Size **to 28 cm**

OLIVE-BACKED ORIOLE

This common woodland bird is rich olive-green above with faint black streaks, and white below with short black streaks. It has a red eye, brick-red bill and grey wings. **Behaviour** They live and feed in the upper foliage, singly and in dispersed pairs, gleaning insects from the outer foliage and twigs. Large numbers gather to feed on caterpillar-infested crops. Breeding pairs stay together throughout the year, singing regularly to each other. Southeastern populations migrate north in autumn, flying fast and silently. Other populations are locally nomadic when not breeding. **Breeding** They breed from September to January and lay 2-4 eggs in a deep, cup-shaped nest suspended by the rim from a tree fork. The female incubates the eggs for 17-18 days and both parents feed the young who fledge in 15-17 days. **Call** Rolling 'olly-olly-olly-o-loi'; mimics other calls. **Diet** Fruit, insects. **Habitat** Rainforests, open forests, woodlands, mallee scrub, parks, gardens.

Family **ORIOLIDAE** Species *Sphecotheres vieilloti* Size **to 29 cm**

AUSTRALASIAN FIGBIRD

Males have a black head, pinkish facial skin, an olive-green back and a yellow or greenish-yellow belly. Females have bluish facial skin, brownish upperparts, a cream throat and breast streaked brown. **Behaviour** They live in noisy and active flocks of 20-50 birds after breeding, travelling locally, following food sources, gathering in fruiting trees and shrubs. They concentrate on a single tree until it is virtually stripped, hanging upside down to reach the last fruit. They breed in small groups and nest in adjoining trees. **Breeding** They breed from September to January and lay 2-3 eggs in a flimsy, saucer-shaped nest of vine tendrils and twigs suspended by its rim from a tree fork. Both parents share incubation of about 18 days and care for the young who fledge in about 17 days. **Call** Loud, descending 'tchiew'. **Diet** Figs and other fruit, some insects. **Habitat** Rainforests, wet sclerophyll forests, parks, gardens.

FAMILY **PTILONORHYNCHIDAE**   SPECIES *Ailuroedus crassirostris*   SIZE **TO 32 CM**

GREEN CATBIRD

This bowerbird is emerald-green with white and buff speckles on the head and nape, and white streaks and spots below. **Behaviour** They pair for life and occupy a permanent territory, marked by loud wailing calls at dawn and dusk. They roost in separate trees at night and hop and flit through the forest by day, eating mostly figs and other fruit. When breeding, the male defends an area of 15-20 m around the nest. Groups of up to 15 sometimes wander locally after breeding. **Breeding** They breed from September to January and lay 1-3 eggs in a deep, cup-shaped nest placed in an upright fork in dense foliage or in the crown of a tree fern. The female incubates the eggs for 23-24 days and both parents feed the young who fledge in about 3 weeks. **Call** Nasal, cat-like wail; sharp 'chik' when feeding. **Diet** Fruit, insects, eggs, nestling birds, frogs, shoots, flowers. **Habitat** Rainforests.

FAMILY **PTILONORHYNCHIDAE**   SPECIES *Sericulus chrysocephalus*   SIZE **TO 28 CM**

REGENT BOWERBIRD

Males are black and gold with a pale bill. Females are greyish or fawn mottled brown, with a black bill, crown and throat. **Behaviour** They live in the forest canopy and often gather in loose flocks of 10-30 or more, wandering locally into more open areas. In the breeding season males construct an avenue of upright twigs in the undergrowth, paint them with the yellow juice of crushed leaves and saliva and adorn the central runway with red and black berries, shells and other objects. The male displays from the bower when a female approaches, prancing, twisting and turning. Females nest alone after mating. **Breeding** They breed from October to January and lay 2-3 eggs in a loose, saucer-shaped nest of twigs placed in a dense tangle of vines 3-25 m high. The female incubates the eggs for about 18 days and rears the young. **Call** Chattering; harsh squawk. **Diet** Fruit, insects, spiders. **Habitat** Rainforests.

FAMILY **PTILONORHYNCHIDAE**   SPECIES *Ptilonorhynchus violaceus*   SIZE **TO 33 CM**

SATIN BOWERBIRD

Males are glossy bluish-black. Females are dull grey-green with brown wings and tail, buff-white underparts with dark crescents. **Behaviour** Young birds live in flocks until they have full adult plumage at 7 years. Mature males may join roving flocks but return to the same territory to breed. Each has a bower of thin woven sticks forming 2 north-south walls, usually blackened with charcoal and saliva. Blue objects are arranged at each end. If a female enters the bower he displays by prancing and bounding. They mate in the bower and she nests alone. **Breeding** They breed from September to January and lay 1-3 eggs in a saucer-shaped nest in a tree or shrub 2-35 m high. Females incubate the eggs for 21-22 days and raise the young who fledge in 19-22 days. They are independent at 8-9 weeks. **Call** Hissing; chattering; mimicry. **Diet** Fruit, shoots, insects. **Habitat** Rainforests, adjoining forests and woodlands.

| FAMILY **ARTAMIDAE** | SPECIES *Artamus personatus* | SIZE **TO 20 CM** |

MASKED WOODSWALLOW

Males have a black face and throat edged white, pale grey underparts, bluish-grey back and a pale-blue bill tipped black. Females have a dusky face and throat.
Behaviour They gather in large flocks, often with white-browed woodswallows, fluttering and circling high in the sky for long periods, catching insects, calling constantly to keep in contact. They suddenly swoop into trees to rest or glean insects and nectar. Flocks make long, nomadic flights north in autumn and move south in spring to breed. They often cram their nests together and sometimes depart before all the young are raised, leaving them to starve. **Breeding** They breed from August to December and lay 2-3 eggs in a shallow, bowl-shaped nest placed in a shrub, or on a stump or fence post, 1-2 m high. Both parents share incubation of about 12 days and feed the young. **Call** Descending 'chirrup'; chattering; soft twittering. **Diet** Insects, nectar. **Habitat** Open woodlands.

| FAMILY **ARTAMIDAE** | SPECIES *Cracticus torquatus* | SIZE **TO 30 CM** |

GREY BUTCHERBIRD

This familiar woodland bird has a black head with a prominent white collar, grey back, black wings with a narrow white streak, a white-tipped tail and white to greyish underparts. **Behaviour** Established pairs live in permanent territories and usually nest in the same site. They feed alone, hunting from a perch 1-10 m high and diving on prey. Large items are impaled on the bill and carried back to the perch to be torn apart and eaten. They are bold but wary, and often visit gardens looking for food. **Breeding** They breed from July to January and lay 3-5 eggs in a cup-shaped nest placed in a vertical tree fork 3-19 m high. The female incubates the eggs for 24-26 days and both parents feed the young who fledge in about 4 weeks. **Call** Piping whistles; ringing 'caws' in alarm or aggression. **Diet** Insects, small birds, reptiles, mice, fruit, seeds. **Habitat** Open forests, woodlands, parks, gardens.

| FAMILY **ARTAMIDAE** | SPECIES *Cracticus nigrogularis* | SIZE **TO 36 CM** |

PIED BUTCHERBIRD

This large black and white bird has a wide, white collar, a black throat, a white bar on the wing and white tips on the outer tail feathers. **Behaviour** Established pairs hold a permanent territory and often live in family groups of 3-5 with their young of several years. At dawn they announce their territory by sustained singing which continues sporadically throughout the day in the breeding season. They hunt in open areas, often in pairs, with one bird backing the other, and pounce or spiral down on their prey from a post or other perch, sometimes chasing small birds in flight. **Breeding** They breed from August to December and lay 3-5 eggs in a cup-shaped nest in an upright tree fork over 5 m high. The female incubates the eggs for 21 days and both parents feed the young who fledge in about 30 days. **Call** Pure, melodic, flute-like song. **Diet** Insects, mice, small birds, and reptiles. **Habitat** Open woodlands.

FAMILY **ARTAMIDAE** SPECIES *Gymnorhina tibicen* SIZE **TO 44 CM**

AUSTRALIAN MAGPIE

This butcherbird has a wide white collar (extending to the tail in the west and south), a white tail with a black tip, white shoulders and wing bands.
Behaviour Groups of 3-24, comprising mostly females with a dominant male, defend a permanent territory of up to 40 ha. Groups with marginal territories rarely nest successfully. Immatures and non-breeding adults form loose mobile flocks, sometimes with hundreds of birds. They feed in open areas most of the day, probing and jabbing for food on the ground. **Breeding** They breed from June to December and lay 1-6 eggs in a rough basket of sticks in the outer branches, 5-20 m high. The female incubates the eggs for 20 days and feeds the young who fledge in 4 weeks. Fledglings follow adults, cawing for food.
Call Flute-like carolling song; loud cawing. **Diet** Insects and other invertebrates. **Habitat** Open forests, woodlands, farmlands, parks, gardens.

FAMILY **ARTAMIDAE** SPECIES *Strepera graculina* SIZE **TO 48 CM**

PIED CURRAWONG

This large scavenger has a black body with a white, crescent-shaped patch on the wing, a white-tipped tail, yellow eyes and a robust bill with a hooked tip.
Behaviour They wander nomadically when not breeding, often in flocks of 100 or more, migrating to the lowlands in winter, often dispersing to feed by day and returning to a communal roost at dusk. Breeding pairs defend a territory until the end of summer. They feed on the ground and in trees, pecking, jabbing and poking into crevices, often walking with one wing drooped. **Breeding** They breed from August to January and lay 3 eggs in a rough, cup-shaped nest placed in a tree fork 7-25 m high. The female incubates the eggs for about 3 weeks and both parents feed the young who fledge in about 30 days.
Call Loud, ringing, yodelling calls. **Diet** Insects, carrion, small birds, lizards, snails, berries. **Habitat** Sclerophyll forests, woodlands, parks, gardens.

FAMILY **CORVIDAE** SPECIES *Corvus coronoides* SIZE **TO 54 CM**

AUSTRALIAN RAVEN

The largest member of the crow family, it has black plumage with a purple and green sheen, long throat feathers, a white eye and large bill. **Behaviour** Established pairs live in a permanent territory of about 100 ha, patrolling and calling from the boundaries every morning, and storing food in crevices. Young birds join nomadic flocks of 30 or more until they breed at 3-4 years old. In summer they feed mainly on insects; at other times they eat mainly carrion. **Breeding** They breed from July to September and lay 4-5 eggs in a large basket of sticks placed in a tree fork more than 10 m high. The female incubates the eggs for 20 days while fed by the male, and both parents feed the young who fledge in about 43 days. **Call** Long, falling and fading wail 'aah-aah-aahhaah'. **Diet** Insects, carrion. **Habitat** Open areas with large trees and fresh water, pastures, parks, gardens.

Reptiles

Australia could well be called the land of reptiles. With some 760 native species the reptiles are as diverse and widespread as the birds, although they are much less conspicuous.

Snakes often invoke fear, but of our 130 species, most are completely harmless, and encounters with snakes are uncommon. Australia does, however, have eight of the world's ten deadliest snakes, and although they are not aggressive, they will bite if harassed or threatened. Some venomous snakes have fangs at the back of the jaw and can only inject venom into small animals, while in others the venom is not very toxic or the amount injected too small to seriously affect a human. The following descriptions indicate how dangerous the venomous snakes are.

Unlike mammals and birds, reptiles do not maintain a constant body temperature, and are referred to as 'cold bloodied' or 'ectothermic'. This drastically reduces the amount of food they need, and when it is too cold to function they simply close down their metabolism and enter a state of torpor, enabling them to survive for long periods without food or water. In cool conditions reptiles are sluggish and spend time warming themselves in the morning sun. They are particularly vulnerable to predators at this time, and to give themselves time to escape, most lizards are able to shed all or part of their tail as a sacrifice. Some, like the frilled lizard, rely on aggressive displays, backed up by biting or tail swiping.

All have tough, scaly skin which must be shed to allow them to grow. Their skin is also impermeable and helps them conserve water, and in the case of the crocodiles and turtles forms a tough, body armour.

Australia's reptiles have developed interesting adaptations to cope with drought and heat. Water is obtained from food, and in the case of the Thorny Devil, from night-time dew and moist sand. Burrows provide the best shelter, and most desert-dwelling reptiles dig a burrow or take over the burrow of another animal.

FAMILY **ELAPIDAE**   SPECIES *Demansia psammophis*   SIZE **TO 1 M**

YELLOW-FACED WHIP SNAKE

This slender snake has a long whip-like tail, a narrow head barely distinct from its neck, large eyes and a dark, comma-like mark between the eye and mouth. The belly is grey-green to yellowish. In the north-east they usually have a reddish flush on the back, and in SA and WA they have a dark, net-like pattern above. **Behaviour** This ground-dwelling snake is active by day and can catch prey moving at more than 10 km/h. It shelters under debris, low vegetation and in crevices, often sharing shelters in winter and returning to the same area every year to breed. It will not hesitate to bite if caught. **Reproduction** They breed in late winter and spring, and females lay 3-9 eggs in early summer in deep soil cracks or rock crevices, sometimes communally. **Diet** Small lizards, frogs and reptile eggs. **Habitat** Rainforest margins, sclerophyll forests, woodlands, heathlands and hummock grasslands.

VENOMOUS. ONLY LARGE INDIVIDUALS MAY BE HARMFUL.

FAMILY **ELAPIDAE**   SPECIES *Pseudonaja affinis*   SIZE **TO 2 M**

DUGITE

A slender snake with a narrow head indistinct from its neck. It has large eyes with a round pupil encircled by a narrow golden ring. The belly is pale grey or pale brown with orange or brownish blotches. **Behaviour** This fast-moving, shy, ground-dwelling snake is active by day and on warm nights, and subdues its prey using both constriction and venom. It shelters beneath logs, rocks, surface debris, in hollow logs and abandoned burrows. If confronted or provoked, it rises up in a double curve, hisses and will strike fast and accurately.
Reproduction They breed in early spring and females lay 13-31 eggs in a rocky crevice or a disused burrow in late spring to early summer. Hatchlings emerge in February. **Diet** Mammals, especially house mice, birds, lizards, frogs and snakes. **Habitat** Sclerophyll forests, woodlands, shrublands and heathlands on coastal dunes, plains, slopes and ranges, including arid areas.

DANGEROUSLY VENOMOUS

FAMILY **ELAPIDAE**   SPECIES *Pseudechis porphyriacus*   SIZE **TO 2.7 M**

RED-BELLIED BLACK SNAKE

This robust snake has a broad, flattened head just distinct from its neck and small eyes. It is iridescent purplish-black above, bright red to deep pink on the lower sides, cream on the belly and black beneath the tail. **Behaviour** Active by day and on warm nights, this ground-dwelling snake hibernates in cold weather and shelters in abandoned burrows, hollow logs, under rocks and dense vegetation. If provoked it rises up, flattens its neck and hisses loudly, but is reluctant to bite. Rival males wrestle in the breeding season, and pregnant females may share a burrow and bask together by a creek. **Reproduction** They breed in spring and females give birth to 5-40 (average 12) live young, about 22 cm long, from January to March. They become sexually mature between 19 and 31 months. **Diet** Mostly frogs, also reptiles, mammals and fish. **Habitat** Sclerophyll forests, woodlands, shrublands and rainforests, often around waterways.

DANGEROUSLY VENOMOUS

FAMILY **ELAPIDAE**   SPECIES *Pseudechis guttatus*   SIZE **TO 1.9 M**

BLUE-BELLIED BLACK SNAKE

This robust snake has a dark, flattened head just distinct from its neck and small eyes. It is shiny bluish to brownish-black above, varying through grey to pale brown or cream, sometimes with pale spots. The belly is bluish-black.

Behaviour This shy, ground-dwelling snake is active by day and on warm nights, sheltering in abandoned burrows, among rocks, soil cracks, dense vegetation and rubbish dumps, usually staying close to its shelter, and retreating if disturbed. If provoked it can be very aggressive, rising slightly, flattening its neck, arching its forebody, and hissing loudly. It swings from side to side before striking, but often doesn't bite. Rival males wrestle in the breeding season, and may bite each other. **Reproduction** They breed in spring and females lay 6-16 soft-shelled eggs in December. The eggs hatch 2-3 months later. **Diet** Frogs, reptiles and small mammals. **Habitat** Dry sclerophyll forests and woodlands, often around lakes and flood plains.

DANGEROUSLY VENOMOUS

FAMILY **ELAPIDAE**   SPECIES *Pseudonaja textilis*   SIZE **TO 2.2 M**

EASTERN BROWN SNAKE

This slender snake has a narrow head indistinct from its neck, large eyes and a pink mouth lining. It is yellow to light brown, reddish-brown or almost black above with a cream or orange belly. Juveniles usually have a black head and black bands. **Behaviour** This swift and aggressive snake is active by day, and on warm nights, sheltering under debris, in rock crevices, soil cracks and hollow logs, and hibernating in cold weather. It may tolerate being accidentally stepped on, but if provoked it hisses, flattens its neck, rises into a double S-shape, and strikes very quickly, occasionally chasing its aggressor and striking repeatedly. **Reproduction** They breed in spring and early summer, and females lay 8-35 soft-shelled eggs from October to December. The eggs hatch 7-8 weeks later. **Diet** Small mammals and reptiles, some frogs, birds and eggs. **Habitat** All non-arid habitats except rainforests and alpine areas.

DANGEROUSLY VENOMOUS

FAMILY **ELAPIDAE**   SPECIES *Pseudonaja nuchalis*   SIZE **TO 1.5 M**

WESTERN BROWN SNAKE

This slender snake has a narrow head indistinct from its neck, large eyes and a bluish-black mouth lining. It varies from light brown to orange-brown, olive or almost blac¬k above with a cream belly with dark blotches. Some have dark bands, herring-bone patterns and V-shaped marks. **Behaviour** This shy, swift, snake is active by day and on warm nights, sheltering under debris, large flat rocks, in soil cracks, hollow logs and abandoned burrows. It is reluctant to bite and tries to avoid humans, but if provoked it rises into an S-shape, hisses and may strike rapidly before attempting to escape. Rival males wrestle in the breeding season. **Reproduction** They breed in spring and early summer in the south, year round in the north. Females lay 9-38 eggs that hatch about 2 months later. **Diet** Small mammals, frogs, reptiles and their eggs. **Habitat** Dry sclerophyll forests, woodlands, arid scrubs, spinifex dune fields and sandplains.

DANGEROUSLY VENOMOUS

FAMILY **ELAPIDAE**   SPECIES *Pseudechis australis*   SIZE **TO 3 M**

KING BROWN SNAKE

This robust snake has a flattened head just distinct from its neck and small eyes. It is reddish-brown to dark brown above, often with a dark net pattern, and cream to white below, sometimes with orange blotches. **Behaviour** This ground-dwelling snake is active by day in cool weather, and at night in hot weather. It shelters in abandoned burrows, beneath logs, rocks, in rock crevices and soil cracks, staying close to its shelter or travelling along familiar routes looking for food. It tries to flee if disturbed, but if provoked flattens its neck and forebody into a horizontal curve, hisses, and may strike towards the opposite side, biting a number of times. **Reproduction** Females lay 4-19 large, soft-shelled eggs in a sticky mass from December to February. Hatchlings emerge about 2 months later. **Diet** Reptiles, frogs, birds, eggs, and small mammals. **Habitat** Most habitats including woodlands, monsoon forests, grasslands, shrublands and deserts.

DANGEROUSLY VENOMOUS

FAMILY **ELAPIDAE**   SPECIES *Austrelaps ramsayi*   SIZE **TO 1.2 M**

HIGHLAND COPPERHEAD

This robust snake has a narrow head barely distinct from its neck and prominent black and white bars on the upper lips. It is generally dark brown to grey or black above with a coppery head and a light grey to creamy-yellow belly. **Behaviour** This shy, ground-dwelling snake is active by day and on warm nights, and hibernates in winter. It hunts around waterways and shelters under rotting timber, in dense vegetation, deep burrows and below rocks. It avoids humans and is reluctant to bite, but if provoked it rises in a low curve, flattens its neck, hisses and often flicks from side to side or thrashes menacingly. **Reproduction** They breed in autumn and spring, and most breed every second year. Females give birth to 3-32 live young from late January to March. **Diet** Frogs, reptiles, small mammals and some insects. **Habitat** Around waterways in sclerophyll forests, woodlands, heaths and tussock grasslands in cool highland areas.

DANGEROUSLY VENOMOUS

FAMILY **ELAPIDAE**   SPECIES *Austrelaps superbus*   SIZE **TO 1.7 M**

LOWLAND COPPERHEAD

This robust snake has a narrow head barely distinct from its neck and obscure white bars on the upper lips. It is brown, grey to almost black, above, sometimes with a dark narrow stripe along the spine, and a cream, pink or orange belly. **Behaviour** This shy, ground-dwelling snake is active by day and warm nights, sheltering under rotting logs, large rocks, in abandoned burrows and dense grass, hibernating in winter. Large numbers often gather around marshes where prey is abundant. It avoids humans and is reluctant to bite, but if provoked it rises in a low curve, flattens its neck, hisses and often flicks from side to side or thrashes menacingly. **Reproduction** They breed every second year, mating in autumn, spring, and on warm winter days, producing 9-45 live young from January to March. **Diet** Frogs, reptiles, small mammals and birds. **Habitat** Near waterways in forests, woodlands, heathlands, shrublands and tussock grasslands in cool lowland areas.

DANGEROUSLY VENOMOUS

FAMILY **ELAPIDAE**   SPECIES *Furina ornata*   SIZE **TO 70 CM**

ORANGE-NAPED SNAKE

This slender snake has a slightly flattened head barely distinct from its neck, small eyes, pale cream lips and a broad, bright orange or yellow band across the back of the neck. It is pale-orange to reddish-brown above with a black net-like pattern, and a pale cream belly. **Behaviour** This ground-dwelling, nocturnal snake shelters in deep cracks in the ground, in abandoned burrows, beneath logs, in dead vegetation and sometimes under rocks. It hunts by probing into confined spaces with its slender head and forebody looking for sheltering lizards, subduing its victims by constriction as well as venom. If threatened or disturbed it rises high off the ground, thrashes around menacingly and usually strikes with its mouth closed, biting only if severely provoked. **Reproduction** Females lay 1-6 soft-shelled eggs in summer, sometimes producing 2 clutches per year. **Diet** Skinks and other reptiles. **Habitat** Open woodlands, shrublands and hummock grasslands, with deep cracking soils.

VENOMOUS,
BUT NOT DANGEROUS.

FAMILY **ELAPIDAE**   SPECIES *Notechis scutatus*   SIZE **TO 2 M**

EASTERN TIGER SNAKE

This robust snake has a blunt head, only slightly distinct from its neck, and small eyes. It is light grey to olive or blackish-brown above, darker in cold area, usually with narrow yellowish bands, giving it a tiger-like appearance. The belly is cream, olive-green to grey. **Behaviour** It is active by day and on warm nights, sheltering under rotting timber, rocks, in abandoned burrows and dense vegetation. In floods it climbs into low trees to reach birds' nests. It flees if disturbed, but if provoked it rises in a low, open curve, swings sideways, inflates and deflates its body, hisses, and strikes wildly. Its venom is among the most toxic of all the land snakes. **Reproduction** They breed from autumn to spring, producing around 15-30 live young from January to April. **Diet** Frogs, lizards, birds, small mammals and fish. **Habitat** Rainforests, sclerophyll forests, woodlands and heathlands, preferring swamps and flood plains.

DANGEROUSLY VENOMOUS

FAMILY **ELAPIDAE**   SPECIES *Notechis ater*   SIZE **TO 2.5 M**

BLACK TIGER SNAKE

This robust snake has a blunt head, barely distinct from its neck, and small eyes. It is black or very dark brown above with faint paler or darker bands. The belly is pale to dark grey or almost black. **Behaviour** It is active by day and on warm evenings, sheltering in abandoned burrows, among tussock grasses, in dense vegetation, beneath rocks and fallen timber, sometimes climbing trees to bask or hunt. It flees if disturbed, but if provoked it rises in a low, open curve, inflates and deflates its body while hissing loudly, striking out and biting strongly and quickly, injecting some of the most toxic venom of all the land snakes. **Reproduction** They breed from autumn to early summer, producing around 10-20 live young in mid to late summer. **Diet** Frogs, tadpoles, lizards, birds, small mammals and fish. **Habitat** Sclerophyll forests, woodlands, shrublands, coastal heaths and sand dunes.

DANGEROUSLY VENOMOUS

FAMILY **ELAPIDAE**   SPECIES *Acanthophis antarcticus*   SIZE **TO 1.1 M**

COMMON DEATH ADDER

This robust, viper-like snake has a broad triangular head, small eyes with a vertical pupil and a thin tail with a small, curved spur at the tip. It is pale grey to rich reddish-brown above, often with cross-bands, and a cream or grey belly. The tip of the tail  is usually white or cream. **Behaviour** This sluggish, ground-dwelling snake moves silently, and is most active on warm after-noons and nights. It hides beneath vegetation or half buries itself, and wriggles the tip of its tail in front of its snout to lure small animals within striking range. It usually tolerates being stepped on momentarily, but if threatened it flicks from side to side, and may strike repeatedly.
Reproduction They breed in spring and sometimes in autumn, usually every second year, producing 2-33 live young from December to April. **Diet** Small mammals, birds, lizards and frogs. **Habitat** Rainforests, wet sclerophyll   DANGEROUSLY VENOMOUS
forests, woodlands, shrublands and coastal heaths.

FAMILY **ELAPIDAE**   SPECIES *Acanthophis praelongus*   SIZE **TO 70 CM**

NORTHERN DEATH ADDER

This robust, viper-like snake is smaller than the Common Death Adder and has rough head scales usually protrud-ing above the eye. It varies from grey to brownish-red, usually with distinct cross-bands. **Behaviour** It moves  around on warm afternoons and nights, climbing around dry leaf litter to avoid making a noise, but spends most of the day half buried in spinifex hummocks or beneath trees or shrubs, with the tip of its tail held up close to its head. When prey approaches it wriggles the tip of its tail, luring the animal into striking range. It usually tolerates being momentarily stepped on, but if strongly provoked it flattens its body into a tense coil, flicks from side to side and strikes fast and often repeatedly. **Reproduction** Females give birth to up to 20 live young around February or March, usually every second year. **Diet** Lizards, small mammals and birds. **Habitat** Woodlands and grasslands in rocky areas.   DANGEROUSLY VENOMOUS

FAMILY **ELAPIDAE**   SPECIES *Acanthophis pyrrhus*   SIZE **TO 75 CM**

DESERT DEATH ADDER

This robust snake has a broad triangular head and a thin tail ending in a small, soft spine. It is reddish-brown above with lighter cross-bands and rough scales. The belly is cream or reddish. **Behaviour** It shelters in hum-mock grasses and abandoned burrows, emerging at night and on warm afternoons. Prey is ambushed while the snake lies partly concealed beneath vegetation or half buried in loose sand. The snake wriggles the tip of its tail above its snout to lure an animal within striking distance. In warm weather it stalks lizards in open areas. It may tolerate being momentarily stepped on, but if provoked it flattens its body into a rigid coil, flicks from side to side, and may strike repeatedly.
Reproduction They breed in spring and produce some 8-13 live young in sum-mer. **Diet** Mainly skinks and dragons. **Habitat** Arid hills, sandy ridges, stony flats and rocky outcrops with hummock grasslands and sparse, low trees.   DANGEROUSLY VENOMOUS

| FAMILY **ELAPIDAE** | SPECIES *Oxyuranus microlepidotus* | SIZE **TO 3 M** |

INLAND TAIPAN

This large snake has a long, narrow head distinct from its neck, and is pale yellowish-grey to olive or rich brown above with thin diagonal lines. The head and neck are usually glossy black in winter, fading to brown in summer. The belly is cream to yellow, sometimes with orange blotches. **Behaviour** This snake is active by day and on warm nights, searching for prey around cracks and crevices. It shelters in rat burrows, deep soil cracks, sink holes and in rocky crevices. It usually flees if approached, but rears up in a low curve if threatened, striking fast and accurately. It has the most potent venom of all the land snakes. **Reproduction** They breed from August to December and females lay 9-20 eggs that hatch after about 10 weeks. **Diet** Small to medium-sized mammals. **Habitat** Flood plains with deep cracking soil, gibber plains, sand dunes and rocky outcrops in arid to semi-arid drainage areas.

DANGEROUSLY VENOMOUS

| FAMILY **ELAPIDAE** | SPECIES *Oxyuranus scutellatus* | SIZE **TO 4 M** |

MAINLAND TAIPAN

This large, slender snake has a long, narrow, pale head distinct from its neck, and is yellow-brown, reddish-brown to almost black above. The belly is cream with scattered orange spots. **Behaviour** This semi-nomadic snake is active by day and on warm nights, sheltering in abandoned burrows, hollow logs and beneath surface litter. It is shy, swift and very alert with keen eyesight, and captures large prey by striking rapidly and releasing quickly to avoid retaliation and potential injury, following its victim until it succumbs to the venom. If threatened it coils itself loosely, raises its head and forebody slightly, and will deliver one or more accurate, stabbing bites. **Reproduction** They breed from July to December, and females lay 3-20 large, soft-shelled eggs from October to February. Hatchlings emerge 60-84 days later. **Diet** Small to medium-sized mammals and birds. **Habitat** Woodlands, dry sclerophyll forests, monsoon forests and sugarcane fields.

DANGEROUSLY VENOMOUS

| FAMILY **ELAPIDAE** | SPECIES *Tropidechis carinatus* | SIZE **TO 1.2 M** |

ROUGH-SCALED SNAKE

This robust snake has a broad, glossy, triangular head distinct from its neck, and rough scales with projecting ridges. It is matt yellowish-brown, greenish to almost black above, usually with narrow, dark, cross-bands. The belly is cream, olive or grey, usually with dark blotches. **Behaviour** This ground-dwelling and arboreal snake is active mainly at night, sheltering in tree hollows, among dense foliage, in large epiphytic ferns, under fallen timber and in soil cracks. It is shy and nervous, but becomes very aggressive when provoked, raising its neck and forebody in an upright S-shape, hissing before striking with several fast bites. **Reproduction** They breed in spring and summer, and females give birth to 5-18 live young in late summer and autumn. **Diet** Small mammals, frogs, birds and reptiles. **Habitat** Rainforests and wet sclerophyll forests along the coast and ranges, close to swamps and creeks with dense vegetation.

DANGEROUSLY VENOMOUS

FAMILY **ELAPIDAE**   SPECIES *Rhinoplacephalus nigrescens*   SIZE **TO 1 M**

EASTERN SMALL-EYED SNAKE

This small snake has a broad, flattened head just distinct from its neck, and small, beady eyes. It is glossy, steely bluish-black above and cream to bright pink below, often with dark blotches or flecks. **Behaviour** This secretive, ground-dwelling snake, forages at night in hollows, among ground litter and other sites looking for sleeping lizards and other animals. It shelters under rocks, logs, in rocky crevices, beneath ground litter or bark, and in termite mounds. If provoked it flattens its body into stiff, open coils, hisses loudly and thrashes about wildly It may strike, although this snake usually avoids biting humans. **Reproduction** They breed in late autumn, winter and spring, and females give birth to 2-8 live young in February or March in the south, and from October to February in the north. **Diet** Lizards, frogs and lizard eggs. **Habitat** Coastal heaths, woodlands, wet sclerophyll forests and rainforests, favouring rocky outcrops.

VENOMOUS.
POTENTIALLY DANGEROUS.

FAMILY **ELAPIDAE**   SPECIES *Vermicella annulata*   SIZE **TO 1. M**

BANDY-BANDY

This slender burrowing snake has a narrow, flattened head indistinct from its neck, very small eyes, a white band between the eye and the nostril and bluish-black and white bands around the body. **Behaviour** It is active at night, sheltering in a burrow dug under rocks or logs, in soil cracks and termite mounds. It may stay in its shelter for up to 3 months after feeding, emerging only to mate or if forced out by heavy rain. Although venomous, it rarely bites humans. When alarmed it flattens its body and con- torts itself into one or more vertical loops, raising itself high above the ground, interspersed with bouts of thrashing around. **Reproduction** Females lay 2-13 eggs in February or March. **Diet** Mostly blind snakes and burrowing skinks. **Habitat** Rainforests, sclerophyll forests to savanna woodlands, mallee and mulga shrublands, and dry spinifex sandhills.

VENOMOUS
BUT NOT DANGEROUS.

FAMILY **HYDROPHIIDAE**   SPECIES *Pelamis platurus*   SIZE **TO 1.1 M**

YELLOW-BELLIED SEA SNAKE

This sea snake has a large narrow head distinct from its neck, and a flattened, paddle-shaped tail. A wide black to dark bluish-brown stripe runs along the spine, contrasting with the cream, yellow or pale brown sides and belly. The tail is yellow with black bars or spots. The head is bluish-black above with yellow lips and chin. The nostrils have valves allowing it to submerge. **Behaviour** It drifts around the oceans carried by winds and currents, and feeds among surface slicks of seaweed where small fish shelter. If approached by a swimmer it usually dives, but beached snakes and those in shallow coastal waters may bite, and have an extremely toxic venom. **Reproduction** Females often congregate to breed in the warmer months and give birth to 1-6 live young, 5-6 months later. **Diet** Fish. **Habitat** Open seas above 20° C, usually more than 100 m deep, sometimes in estuaries and coastal waters.

DANGEROUSLY VENOMOUS

FAMILY **ACROCHORDIDAE** SPECIES *Acrochordus arafurae* SIZE **TO 2.5 M**

ARAFURA FILESNAKE

This robust, freshwater snake has a flattened body, loose skin and tiny file-like scales. The head is just distinct from the neck. It has small eyes with vertical pupils and valved nostrils. It is grey to dark brown above with a broad dark band along the back, and blotches or cross-bands extending onto the whitish belly. **Behaviour** It rests by day close to the banks of waterways, hiding in the shadows. It moves slowly, ambushing fish, probing in their hiding places or grasping underwater roots with its prehensile tail so that it can seize large, passing fish. It strikes with remarkable speed, biting and constricting its prey. They disperse widely in the wet season floods, and congregate in large numbers in the dry season as the pools shrink. **Reproduction** They breed from May to August, producing 6-30 live young from February to April. **Diet** Fish. **Habitat** Freshwater lagoons, slow-moving rivers, estuaries and the sea.

NON-VENOMOUS

FAMILY **COLUBRIDAE** SPECIES *Boiga irregularis* SIZE **TO 2 M**

BROWN TREE SNAKE

This slender snake has a broad head distinct from its neck, large eyes with vertical pupils and a prehensile tail. It is pale to reddish-brown above with dark blotches, sometimes forming narrow cross-bands. The belly is salmon pink or cream. **Behaviour** Predominantly tree-dwelling and rock inhabiting, it also hunts on the ground at night, sheltering in tree hollows, rock crevices and termite mounds by day. It stalks and ambushes prey, biting as well as constricting its victims. If threatened it curls into S-shaped loops and strikes repeatedly and savagely. It is rear-fanged and unable to bite humans effectively. **Reproduction** They breed in spring and early summer. Females lay 4-12 eggs in humid leaf litter, tree hollows, or rocky crevices, and often stay nearby to protect their eggs. **Diet** Small mammals, birds and their eggs, lizards and frogs. **Habitat** Rainforests, mangroves, sclerophyll forests, paperbark swamps and coastal heaths.

VENOMOUS
BUT NOT DANGEROUS.

FAMILY **COLUBRIDAE** SPECIES *Dendrelaphis punctulatus* SIZE **TO 2 M**

GREEN TREE SNAKE

This slender snake has a narrow head barely distinct from its neck, large eyes, and a prehensile tail. It is grey to olive-green above, varying to dark brown, black or blue in the north. The belly is yellow, sometimes white, olive, green or bluish. **Behaviour** Fast and alert, it is predominantly tree-dwelling, but also hunts on the ground by day, sheltering among foliage, in tree hollows, rock crevices and caves. If cornered, it inflates its neck and upper body, displaying the blue skin between its scales, hisses, and bites if provoked. It may also emit a strong-smelling odour from its anal glands. **Reproduction** Females lay 5-14 eggs from December to February, beneath bark, leaf litter, in rocky crevices and hollow tree stumps. Hatchlings emerge in about 11 weeks. **Diet** Mostly frogs, some lizards, small mammals, stranded tadpoles and fish. **Habitat** Rainforests, vine thickets, sclerophyll forests, woodlands, coastal heaths and along inland rivers.

NON-VENOMOUS

FAMILY **PYTHONIDAE** SPECIES *Morelia spilota* SIZE **TO 4 M**

CARPET (DIAMOND) PYTHON

This large snake has a triangular head distinct from its neck, vertical pupils and heat-sensitive pits in the lips to detect warm-blooded prey. Coastal NSW forms are dark olive with a cream diamond-shaped pattern (Diamond Python). Others are pale to dark brown with blackish blotches, sometimes with cross-bands (Carpet Python). **Behaviour** Arboreal, terrestrial and rock inhabiting, it is active by day in cool weather and by night in warm weather, sheltering in tree hollows, animal burrows, caves and rock crevices, beneath leaf litter, and in roof spaces of buildings. It ambushes prey and constricts its victims, often waiting beside a trail for weeks. Diamond Pythons are usually passive when approached, while Carpet Pythons may hiss and strike. **Reproduction** They breed in spring. Females lay 7-54 eggs in a nest from November to January and coil around the eggs to incubate them. Hatchlings emerge in summer. **Diet** Mammals, some reptiles and birds. **Habitat** Rainforests, forests, woodlands and shrublands.

NON-VENOMOUS

FAMILY **PYTHONIDAE** SPECIES *Chondropython viridis* SIZE **TO 2 M**

GREEN PYTHON

This snake has a large head distinct from its neck, vertical pupils and heat sensitive pits in the lips to detect warm-blooded prey. It is emerald-green above with scattered white scales on the sides and a white or yellow line along the spine crossed by light blue bars. Juveniles are bright-yellow, occasionally orange, brick-red or deep-blue. **Behaviour** This nocturnal, arboreal snake lives mainly in the forest canopy, resting draped over branches, in tree hollows and in large epiphytic ferns. It ambushes prey, moving slowly through the branches or concealing itself. Juveniles vibrate the bright blue tip of their tail to lure prey close to their resting site. The victim is grasped by biting and suffocated by constriction. **Reproduction** Females lay 10-26 eggs in a tree hollow, and coil around the eggs to incubate them. Hatchlings emerge 7 to 9 weeks later. **Diet** Reptiles, small mammals, some birds. **Habitat** Rainforests, monsoon forests and bamboo thickets.

NON-VENOMOUS

FAMILY **PYTHONIDAE** SPECIES *Aspidites melanocephalus* SIZE **TO 2.5 M**

BLACK-HEADED PYTHON

This snake has a narrow head indistinct from its neck and small dark eyes with obscure pupils. The head, neck and throat are glossy jet black. The body is light to dark brown above, patterned with darker cross bands. The belly is cream to yellow, sometimes with dark blotches. **Behaviour** This ground-dwelling snake forages at night, probing crevices and holes for prey which it kills by constriction. It shelters in caves, crevices, hollow logs, soil cracks, termite mounds, grass hummocks and in abandoned burrows, sometimes digging its own burrow. When threatened it raises its head and hisses, but rarely bites. **Reproduction** They breed from July to September, and females lay 5-12 soft-shelled eggs in a sticky clump in October or November, coiling around the clutch for 9-13 weeks to incubate the eggs and protect them from predators. **Diet** Reptiles, rarely small mammals and birds. **Habitat** Wet sclerophyll forests, woodlands, shrublands and grasslands.

NON-VENOMOUS

| FAMILY **PYGOPODIDAE** | SPECIES *Lialis burtonis* | SIZE **TO 62 CM** |

BURTON'S LEGLESS LIZARD

This snake-like lizard has a wedge-shaped snout, small eyes with vertical pupils and conspicuous ear openings. It has a broad tongue, lacks forelimbs and has small triangular flaps instead of hind limbs. It varies from pale grey or cream to brown or almost black above, often with a cream stripe along the side of the head and neck. **Behaviour** A ground-dweller, it is active both day and night, but most frequently after dusk and in the early morning, sheltering under rocks, logs, among leaf litter, in hummock grasses and abandoned burrows. It moves like a snake, stalking prey, or hiding until a small lizard comes close enough to catch. If attacked it readily sacrifices its tail and grows a new one. **Reproduction** They breed in spring, and females lay 2-3 soft-shelled eggs under logs, rocks or in the nests of sugar ants. **Diet** Small reptiles. **Habitat** Most habitats from deserts to rainforest margins.

| FAMILY **PYGOPODIDAE** | SPECIES *Pygopus lepidopodus* | SIZE **TO 84 CM** |

COMMON SCALY FOOT

This legless lizard has a blunt snout, conspicuous ear openings and a broad tongue. It lacks forelimbs and has paddle-shaped flaps instead of hind limbs. It varies from grey to reddish-brown above, sometimes with rows of black dashes or blotches along the sides. **Behaviour** It is active on warm mornings and warm nights, hibernating in cold weather and sheltering under low vegetation, fallen timber, leaf litter and in dense grasses and shrubs. It forages in open areas and climbs into dense shrubs and hummock grasses. If threatened it mimics a snake, rising off the ground, flattening its neck, flicking its tongue in and out, and sometimes striking. **Reproduction** They breed in spring and females lay 2 soft-shelled eggs in summer beneath a log or rock. Hatchlings emerge in March and April. **Diet** Spiders, scorpions, insects and some native fruits. **Habitat** Dry sclerophyll forests, the margins of wet sclerophyll forests, semi-arid mallee woodlands, coastal heaths and sand dunes.

| FAMILY **CROCODYLIDAE** | SPECIES *Crocodylus johnstoni* | SIZE **TO 3.2 M** |

FRESHWATER CROCODILE

This fierce, amphibious predator has bony body armour, a long, slender and smooth snout, valves in the nostrils and throat to keep water out while submerged, webbed feet, and short, strong limbs. The powerful jaws have sharp, intermeshing teeth. **Behaviour** It basks in shallow water or on riverside banks and forages on warm evenings and nights, using sensory pits in the snout to detect animals moving in the water. It ambushes small animals and sometimes stalks large prey, galloping at up to 18 km/h over short distances. It submerges if disturbed, and rarely threatens humans. **Reproduction** They breed early in the dry season, laying 4-21 eggs some 6 weeks later in a moist hole dug into a sandbank. Hatchlings emerge 2-3 months later and call to attract a female who digs them out. **Diet** Insects, fish, frogs, crustaceans, small reptiles, birds, mammals and carrion. **Habitat** Permanent freshwater rivers, swamps, billabongs and some tidal estuaries.

FAMILY **CROCODYLIDAE**   SPECIES *Crocodylus porosus*   SIZE **TO 6.2 M**

ESTUARINE (SALTWATER) CROCODILE

The world's largest and most dangerous reptile, it differs from the Freshwater Crocodile by its shorter, broader, granular snout and heavier body armour. **Behaviour** It usually basks by day and hunts at night close to the water's edge with only its nostrils above water, striking remarkably fast, driving itself out of the water with its powerful tail. Large animals are dragged into deep water and rolled over until they drown. Females are very aggressive when nesting. **Reproduction** They breed early in the wet season and the female lays 30-70 eggs inside a mound of plant matter and mud close to the water. She guards the nest until the eggs hatch about 3 months later, digs them out, carries them in her mouth to the water and protects them for 2-3 months. **Diet** Any small or large animal, including insects. **Habitat** Mainly tropical estuaries in the dry season; freshwater swamps and billabongs in the wet season.

FAMILY **VARANIDAE**   SPECIES *Varanus varius*   SIZE **TO 2.25 M**

LACE MONITOR

This large monitor has a long, slender tail, vertically flattened at the end, with a double ridge on top. It is dark bluish-black above, scattered with white or yellow flecks, spots or blotches, sometimes forming cross-bands. **Behaviour** It is active by day, foraging in trees and on the ground, and often scavenges around picnic areas. It shelters in tree hollows, rabbit warrens and shallow burrows beneath rocks or logs, becoming inactive in winter. If alarmed it dashes up a tree. If cornered it inflates its throat pouch, hisses and may rear up and lash out with its tail. Rival males stand up and wrestle in the breeding season. **Reproduction** Females lay 6-20 soft-shelled eggs in early summer in a hole beneath a log or in a termite mound. The brightly banded hatchlings emerge in late winter or early spring. **Diet** Nesting birds, eggs, small mammals, reptiles, insects and carrion. **Habitat** Woodlands, wet sclerophyll forests and rainforests.

FAMILY **VARANIDAE**   SPECIES *Varanus giganteus*   SIZE **TO 2.5 M**

PERENTIE

Australia's largest lizard, this monitor has a long neck and a slender tail flattened vertically. It is brown above with bands of black-edged cream or yellow spots, forming a net-like pattern on the head and neck. **Behaviour** It shelters in a deep burrow or beneath a boulder, emerging in the early morning, digging small animals from their burrows and hunting in open country. It can run fast on all-fours or on its hind limbs, and readily climbs trees. If disturbed it lies flat, but when cornered it rears up, distends its neck pouch and makes a loud, rattling hiss. If provoked it lunges, bites, and lashes out with its powerful tail. **Reproduction** They breed in spring and females lay 6-13 soft-shelled eggs in January in a termite mound or in a long burrow under a rock. Brightly-coloured young emerge the following spring. **Diet** Reptiles, mammals, birds, eggs and carrion. **Habitat** Woodlands, shrublands and sand plains with hummock grasses.

| FAMILY **VARANIDAE** | SPECIES *Varanus gouldii* | SIZE **TO 1.7 M** |

GOULD'S GOANNA

This large lizard is yellow to almost black above with narrow yellow bands, dark-centred spots and a dark stripe behind the eye. The tail is flattened vertically with a double raised ridge towards the end.
Behaviour It shelters in a burrow beneath low vegetation with a large terminal chamber and a vertical escape shaft. It emerges in the early morning, basks in the sun, forages among grass and leaf litter, chases prey, digs animals from their burrows, and some-times climbs trees and shrubs. If disturbed it flees or climbs a tree. If cornered it rears up, inflates its neck pouch, flicks its tongue, hisses, thrashes its tail, lunges and may bite. **Reproduction** They breed in spring and females lay 3-11 soft-shelled eggs in early summer in a deep burrow, hollow log or termite mound. Brightly-coloured hatchlings emerge the following spring. **Diet** Small animals, insects, eggs and carrion. **Habitat** Most open habitats from deserts to tropical woodlands.

| FAMILY **VARANIDAE** | SPECIES *Varanus indicus* | SIZE **TO 1.4 M** |

MANGROVE MONITOR

This large monitor lizard is dark purplish-brown to black above, covered with small cream or yellow flecks and has a vertically flattened tail.
Behaviour It is a good climber and a powerful swim-mer. It shelters by night in tree hollows, emerging in the morning to forage in forest streams and tidal mangroves, digging up turtle eggs and preying on fish and small animals. It prefers areas with dense vegetation and is often seen basking on branches above the water. When alarmed it slips quietly into the water or climbs high up in a tree. **Reproduction** Females lay around 8 soft-shelled eggs from August to March in a burrow concealed beneath rotting wood or ground litter. **Diet** Fish, crustaceans, insects, small mammals, birds, marine tur-tle eggs, juvenile crocodiles and other reptiles. **Habitat** Mangroves, monsoon vine forests and tidal waterways, often near fruit bat colonies.

| FAMILY **VARANIDAE** | SPECIES *Varanus mertensi* | SIZE **TO 1.25 M** |

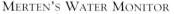

MERTEN'S WATER MONITOR

This lizard has a vertically flattened tail with a ridge along the top. It is olive-grey to dark brown or black above, scattered with small pale spots, and white to yellowish below.
Behaviour It lives among trees close to water and is active by day, foraging in the water and among tree roots lining the bank. It swims fast with its limbs against its sides, and can walk on the bottom, stay-ing submerged for 30 minutes. It basks on overhanging branches and on partly submerged timber and rocks, dropping into the water if threatened. If cornered, it stands on its hindlegs, inflates its throat pouch, arches its back and hisses loudly. **Reproduction** Females lay 3-14 soft-shelled eggs in the dry season at the end of a sealed burrow. Hatchlings emerge 182-281 days later. **Diet** Fish, frogs and carrion, with some crustaceans, insects, lizards, turtle eggs and small mammals. **Habitat** Beside permanent waterways, swamps and lagoons.

FAMILY **AGAMIDAE**	SPECIES *Moloch horridus*	SIZE **TO 19 CM**

THORNY DEVIL

This lizard has short limbs, a broad head, and is covered in large conical spines. It is pale grey-brown to fawn or reddish-brown above,
becoming paler in hot conditions, and chang-
ing colour to match its background.
Behaviour Slow-moving, it shelters under low
vegetation and in shallow burrows, avoids the midday heat, and
is inactive in the hottest and coldest months. It emerges in the
early morning to collect dew from plants and throw damp sand
over itself. Moisture travels by capillary action along its skin to
the corner of its mouth. It stands beside ant trails, flicking
up ants with its tongue. If threatened it drops its head and
exposes the spined lump on its neck to the aggressor.
Reproduction Females lay 3-10 soft-shelled eggs in spring in a sloping burrow in
soft sand. The hatchlings emerge in late summer and dig their way out of the burrow.
Diet Ants. **Habitat** Deserts, arid scrublands, hummock grasslands and mallee woodlands.

FAMILY **AGAMIDAE**	SPECIES *Chlamydosaurus kingii*	SIZE **TO 90 CM**

FRILLED LIZARD

This powerful dragon varies from grey to almost black, brown or brick-
red above, often with darker brown cross-
bands on the tail. It has a loose, yellow to
black, erectable, neck frill, up to 25 cm
across. **Behaviour** Mostly arboreal, it shelters
in hollows and crevices and emerges in the morning to forage in trees and on the ground, especially after rain. It
often perches on tree trunks and fence posts, and runs on
its hind legs with its tail held out. If threatened it rears up,
opens its mouth wide, erects its frill, rocks, hisses, and may
jump or lash out with its tail. **Reproduction** They breed in
spring and females lay 4-23 soft-shelled eggs in early summer
in a burrow in soft soil in a sunny site. The hatchlings emerge 2-3
months later. **Diet** Mainly arthropods with some small lizards, mice, and plant matter.
Habitat Dry sclerophyll forests, monsoonal woodlands and semi-arid grassy woodlands.

FAMILY **AGAMIDAE**	SPECIES *Ctenophorus pictus*	SIZE **TO 19 CM**

PAINTED DRAGON

This dragon has a small crest and a ridge of erectable scales along
the spine. Breeding males have a blue stripe down the spine, pale
orange or yellow flushes on the head and a bright blue flush on
the throat and flanks. Otherwise they are bluish-grey to reddish-
brown with pale bands or rows of spots. Females are usually rusty-
brown. **Behaviour** This fast-moving dragon shelters in a burrow dug beneath
low vegetation, or in an abandoned burrow, sometimes sharing with another
dragon. It is active by day, often perching on branches and logs, and
foraging in leaf litter. It raises its crest when agitated, freezes if
threatened and dashes to its burrow or into cover if alarmed.
Reproduction They breed in spring and females lay 2-6 soft-
shelled eggs in a burrow. Hatchlings emerge about 15 weeks later.
Diet Ants, other small insects and some plant matter. **Habitat** Arid
and semi-arid woodlands, shrublands, hummock grasslands and around salt lakes.

| FAMILY **AGAMIDAE** | SPECIES *Hypsilurus boydii* | SIZE **TO 37 CM** |

BOYD'S FOREST DRAGON

This lizard has long hind limbs, a wedge-shaped head bearing a crest of long white spines that continue to the tail, and a drooping yellow throat pouch with a row of large, flat spines. The back is chocolate to purplish-brown or pale grey, becoming black on the sides, often tinged with green. **Behaviour** This slow, inoffensive dragon, is well camouflaged and sleeps on exposed branches in warm weather or in hollows or dense vegetation in the cooler months. It is active by day, perching on tree trunks, basking on the ground and foraging among leaf litter. It freezes if disturbed, or moves slowly out of sight, and deters other dragons from its territory by displaying its colourful throat pouch. **Reproduction** Females lay clutches of 1-5 soft-shelled eggs from July to November in a shallow burrow. Hatchlings emerge 60-100 days later. **Diet** Fruits and invertebrates with the occasional mouse or bird. **Habitat** Rainforests.

| FAMILY **AGAMIDAE** | SPECIES *Physignathus lesueurii* | SIZE **TO 90 CM** |

EASTERN WATER DRAGON

This lizard has long limbs, a vertically flattened tail and raised spines along the back. The northern form is dark to light brown above and males have an orange chest. Southern animals are grey-blue with yellow, orange and blue streaks on the throat. **Behaviour** It is active by day and basks, rests and sleeps on overhanging riverside branches, rocks and logs. If disturbed it jumps into the water, where it swims like a snake with its limbs against its sides, and can stay submerged for 90 minutes. In cold weather it hibernates in a sealed burrow beneath a rock or log. **Reproduction** Females lay 6-20 soft-shelled eggs in late spring and early summer under cover or at the end of a sealed burrow. Hatchlings emerge about 80-100 days later. **Diet** Insects, worms, frogs, mice, lizards, aquatic organisms, flowers and fruit. **Habitat** Waterways and rocky sites by beaches.

| FAMILY **AGAMIDAE** | SPECIES *Pogona barbata* | SIZE **TO 60 CM** |

EASTERN BEARDED DRAGON

This robust, spiny dragon has a triangular head with a loose, beard-like throat pouch. It is dark to yellowish-brown or pale grey above with a row of pale blotches on each side of the back, sometimes forming 2 stripes. **Behaviour** It is well-camouflaged and is often seen foraging on roadside verges and basking on fence posts. It sleeps at night on a branch or beneath a log, rock or in a burrow. It becomes torpid in winter and stays in a burrow plugged loosely with soil. When approached it freezes, and if threatened it stands up, inflates its body and 'beard', and gapes widely, showing its bright yellow mouth lining. **Reproduction** They breed in spring and females lay up to 3 clutches of 6-35 soft-shelled eggs from September to December in a short, sealed burrow. Hatchlings emerge 9-12 weeks later. **Diet** Insects with some small lizards, flowers and fruits. **Habitat** Dry woodlands and dry sclerophyll forests.

FAMILY **AGAMIDAE**   SPECIES *Tympanocryptis diemensis*   SIZE **TO 23 CM**

MOUNTAIN DRAGON

Tasmania's only dragon, this lizard has a blunt head with a blue mouth lining, is pale grey to brick-red above with raised spines at the base of the tail and 4 rows of spines along the back. Each side has a row of pale semi-circles above a pale line on the flanks and tail. It is white or cream below. **Behaviour** It is well camouflaged, shelters at night among low vegetation, and is often seen in pairs during the day perching on rocks and logs or foraging in the leaf litter. Rather than pursuing prey it usually ambushes passing insects, remaining motionless until its victim comes within range. **Reproduction** Females lay 2-8 soft-shelled eggs from late November to December beneath rocks, logs or in a burrow. Hatchlings emerge in March or April. **Diet** Mainly ants with some small arthropods. **Habitat** Sclerophyll forests, woodlands, heaths and low scrubs on sandy plateaus, stony ranges and rocky outcrops.

FAMILY **AGAMIDAE**   SPECIES *Amphibolurus muricatus*   SIZE **TO 36 CM**

JACKY LIZARD

This robust dragon has spines on the side of its neck. It is pale grey to dark brown above with pale stripes from the neck to the tail, dark bands on the tail, and usually a dark brown bar behind the eye and dark bands across the head. **Behaviour** Well camouflaged, it basks in low bushes, on tree trunks, rocks and logs, and ambushes prey, waiting until its victim comes within range. At night it shelters in tree hollows, beneath bark, fallen timber, under low vegetation or rocks. It freezes if disturbed or races to cover on its hind legs. If cornered it gapes widely, showing its bright yellow-orange mouth lining. **Reproduction** They breed in spring and females lay 3-12 soft-shelled eggs from November to January beneath logs, rocks, or in a hole dug in sandy soil. Hatchlings emerge from January to March. **Diet** Insects with some flowers and fruit. **Habitat** Dry sclerophyll forests, rocky ridges, heaths and sand dunes.

FAMILY **GEKKONIDAE**   SPECIES *Gehyra dubia*   SIZE **TO 15 CM**

HOUSE GECKO

This lizard has a flattened body, a slender tail and clawed digits with large pads at the tips, giving it great climbing agility. It is pale grey to pale brown above with irregular bands of paler spots, and becomes paler at night. The underside is white to pinkish. **Behaviour** It shelters by day in tree hollows, beneath loose bark and in rock crevices and emerges at night to forage, frequently entering houses hunting for insects. It is swift and agile and can leap between branches and walk on ceilings. It discards its tail if attacked and grows a new one. **Reproduction** Females lay 2 brittle-shelled eggs beneath the bark of tree stumps from October to January in the south, and in August in the north. Hatchlings emerge 10-21 weeks later. **Diet** Insects, spiders and sap licked from the trunks of wattle trees. **Habitat** Dry sclerophyll forests, savanna woodlands and rocky outcrops.

| FAMILY **GEKKONIDAE** | SPECIES *Heteronotia binoei* | SIZE **TO 10 CM** |

BYNOE'S GECKO

This slender lizard has clawed feet and a long, tapering tail. Its skin is finely granular above and varies from pale grey through dull yellowish-brown to bright reddish-brown or almost black, usually with bands of light and dark spots. The underside is whitish to pale pinkish-brown. **Behaviour** It shelters in rock crevices, soil cracks, under logs and among ground litter, emerging at dusk to forage in open areas. Adult males occupy and defend an exclusive home range about 10 m wide, It discards its tail if attacked and grows a new one. **Reproduction** Females lay 2 brittle-shelled eggs beneath bark, under logs, or in cracks and crevices from October to early January. Hatchlings emerge from late February to March. Several all-female populations in central and western Australia lay unfertilised eggs that hatch into female clones of themselves. **Diet** Insects, spiders and other geckos. **Habitat** Most habitats from wet coastal forests to central deserts, excluding alpine areas and rainforests.

| FAMILY **GEKKONIDAE** | SPECIES *Oedura lesueurii* | SIZE **TO 13 CM** |

LESUEUR'S VELVET GECKO

This lizard has a flattened body, a long, flattened tail, and long digits tipped with pads and small retractable claws. Its skin is finely granular to velvety above, pale grey to brown with a pale, dark-edged, zigzag band along the spine and many small, dark-edged spots or blotches on the sides and limbs. The belly is whitish. **Behaviour** It shelters in caves, beneath rock slabs and exfoliating rocks, moving to deeper, cooler crevices in summer. In some areas it shelters in beehives, coexisting with the bees. It forages at night on open rock faces, among ground litter and around the edges of low vegetation. It discards its tail if attacked and grows a new one. **Reproduction** Females lay 2 parchment-shelled eggs from December to January. Hatchlings emerge about 2 months later. **Diet** Insects and spiders. **Habitat** Dry sclerophyll forests and heaths near the coast and ranges, on rocky hills and outcrops in well-watered areas.

| FAMILY **GEKKONIDAE** | SPECIES *Nephrurus asper* | SIZE **TO 15 CM** |

SPINY KNOB-TAILED GECKO

This lizard has a short, knobbly tail and a large head with large eyes and vertical pupils. The long, slender limbs have clawed digits bearing small spines below. It is pale grey to olive or reddish-brown above with fine dark bands. It is smooth, pale brown or whitish below. **Behaviour** It shelters in shallow scrapes beneath rocks and logs or in abandoned burrows. At night it forages in open spaces, stalking and chasing prey, or ambushes prey from its shelter. It walks with a slow, jerky, swaying motion. When alarmed it inflates its body, does push-ups with its forelimbs, twitches its tail from side to side, makes a loud, wheezing bark and may leap and bite. **Reproduction** Females lay up to 5 clutches of 1-2 soft-shelled eggs in mid to late summer, in a moist, sealed hole. Hatchlings emerge about 4 months later. **Diet** Ants, spiders, other arthropods, geckos and skinks. **Habitat** Open forests, woodlands and sandy heaths.

FAMILY **GEKKONIDAE**  SPECIES *Underwoodisaurus milii* SIZE **TO 15 CM**

BARKING GECKO

This plump lizard has a short, swollen tail, constricted at the base, and long, clawed digits. It is deep purplish-brown to reddish-brown above, with 2-3 curved lines of pale spots across the shoulders, neck and side of the head. The tail is black with 5-6 white cross bands while regenerated tails are uniformly brown. **Behaviour** It is slow-moving and shelters under ground litter, peeling bark or rock overhangs, in crevices and animal burrows, often sharing with others. It hunts at night in open areas close to its shelter. If threatened it inflates its body, does push-ups with its back arched and tail waving slowly, and may leap at its attacker, uttering a loud, wheezing bark, and will readily sacrifice its tail. **Reproduction** They breed in spring and early summer, and females lay 2 soft-shelled eggs beneath a rock or in a deep crevice. **Diet** Spiders, scorpions, crawling insects and lizards. **Habitat** Sclerophyll forests, woodlands, heaths, arid and semi-arid shrublands.

FAMILY **GEKKONIDAE** SPECIES *Phyllurus platurus* SIZE **TO 17 CM**

SOUTHERN LEAF-TAILED GECKO

This lizard has a flattened body, a large triangular head, a broad leaf or heart-shaped tail constricted at the base and spindly limbs with clawed digits. The skin is granular and spiny, pale grey to rich reddish-brown above, covered with dark brown and black speckles and blotches. **Behaviour** It shelters with other geckos in deep rock crevices and forages at night in sandstone caves, penetrating deep, narrow crevices, and often enters garages and stone cellars. If alarmed it makes a loud, long, rasping bark, gapes widely and may wave its tail from side to side. If attacked it readily sheds its tail, regenerating a broader, flatter, spineless tail. **Reproduction** They breed in May and females lay 2 soft-shelled eggs in a deep rock crevice in November and December. Hatchlings emerge from January to April. **Diet** Spiders, cockroaches, flies and other arthropods, and juvenile Lesueur's Velvet Geckos. **Habitat** Sclerophyll forests and heaths in sandstone areas.

FAMILY **SCINCIDAE**  SPECIES *Bassiana platynota* SIZE **TO 20 CM**

RED-THROATED SKINK

This lizard has a fragile tail and short limbs with 5 digits. It is pale silvery-grey to brown above with a bronze head, a red throat (brighter in breeding males and juveniles), a broad dark stripe from the snout to the tail, and a whitish belly. **Behaviour** Shy, fast and sun-loving, it forages among dense ground cover and on rocky sandstone ridges and dashes into cover at the least hint of disturbance. It shelters at night under rock slabs, in crevices, cracks in fallen timber, under logs and beneath leaf litter. It basks on the ground or on fallen timber or rocks near its shelter site. **Reproduction** They breed from late August to mid October and females lay 3-10 eggs in late December or January. Hatchlings emerge in February and March. **Diet** Mainly ants, other small insects, worms and skink eggs. **Habitat** Dry sclerophyll forests, woodlands, heaths and tussock grasslands with rocky outcrops.

| FAMILY **SCINCIDAE** | SPECIES *Egernia whitii* | SIZE **TO 31 CM** |

WHITE'S SKINK

This lizard has short limbs with 5 digits and creamy-white rings around its eyes. It is pale to dark brown above, usually with 2 dark stripes along the back enclosing small white to cream spots, and a pale stripe running from the nostril, below the eye to the eardrum. It is pale grey to white below. **Behaviour** It is active by day, and shelters at night in a shallow depression, in hollow logs, rock crevices, abandoned burrows or in a complex burrow system dug beneath a large rock or log, often shared with others. Small piles of scats mark the shelter site and their home range. It forages close to its shelter and dashes into cover if disturbed. **Reproduction** They breed in spring and females give birth to 2-5 live young from late January to early March. **Diet** Spiders, ants, other arthropods, flowers and berries. **Habitat** Dry sclerophyll forests, woodlands, tussock grasslands and heaths.

| FAMILY **SCINCIDAE** | SPECIES *Cryptoblepharus virgatus* | SIZE **TO 10 CM** |

EASTERN SNAKE-EYED SKINK

This lizard has a flattened body, long limbs with 5 digits and snake-like eyes without a moveable eyelid. It is coppery-brown, silvery-grey to black above, with cream and black stripes running above the eye to the tail. The top of the head is coppery-brown flecked with black. The belly is white or pale metallic-blue. **Behaviour** It shelters beneath loose bark, flat stones, in crevices and holes, often with others, foraging by day among trees and rocks, and sometimes on the ground. It moves fast and stops suddenly, making it difficult to catch. If attacked it sheds its tail and regenerates a new one. **Reproduction** They breed in spring and summer and females lay 2-3 soft-shelled eggs from October to late January in deep rock crevices and holes in rotting tree trunks. **Diet** Flies, cockroaches, ants and their larvae, spiders and other small invertebrates. **Habitat** Sclerophyll forests, woodlands, mangroves, heaths, rocky outcrops and urban areas.

| FAMILY **SCINCIDAE** | SPECIES *Ctenotus robustus* | SIZE **TO 37 CM** |

STRIPED SKINK

This lizard has a long tail and striped or mottled limbs with 5 digits. It is pale to dark brown or olive-brown above with a broad, black, white-edged stripe along the spine and prominent stripes along the sides, often mottled. Some populations have no patterning and are a uniform fawn-brown above. The belly is whitish. **Behaviour** It is active by day and shelters in short shallow burrows dug beneath rock slabs, or under ground debris. It forages among ground litter, under rocks and logs, and ambushes any prey that comes close to its shelter. It dashes to cover at the slightest hint of disturbance. If attacked it readily sacrifices its tail and regenerates a new one. **Reproduction** They breed in spring in the south and in the dry season in the north. Females lay 2-9 soft-shelled eggs. **Diet** Insects, small skinks. **Habitat** Open woodlands, shrublands, hummock grasslands, mallee, coastal heaths and sclerophyll forests.

FAMILY **SCINCIDAE** SPECIES *Lampropholis guichenoti* SIZE **TO 10 CM**

COMMON GARDEN SUNSKINK

This lizard has a coppery-brown head and neck and a fragile tail. It is grey, olive-brown or coppery-brown above with pale flecks and usually has a pale-edged dark stripe along each side. The belly is white to grey. **Behaviour** Common in suburban gardens, it shelters at night under rocks, logs and ground debris, often with others, and is usually seen basking or foraging on the ground. It is nomadic, moving to a new area every few weeks. Local populations can become very dense and groups of up to 18, each grasping another with its mouth, form writhing balls in the mating season, sometimes staying entwined for a few minutes. **Reproduction** They breed in spring and females lay 1-6 eggs in a communal egg-laying site. Hatchlings emerge from late summer to early autumn. **Diet** Worms, small insects and other arthropods. **Habitat** Sclerophyll forests, open woodlands, coastal heaths, rainforest margins and moist tussock grasslands.

FAMILY **SCINCIDAE** SPECIES *Ctenotus taeniolatus* SIZE **TO 20 CM**

COPPER-TAILED SKINK

This skink has a distinctive pattern of contrasting stripes and a long, coppery tail. It is rich brown above with a series of dark and pale stripes along the back and sides, and a black line along the side of the tail to the tip. The limbs are reddish with black streaks, and it is whitish below. **Behaviour** It shelters in crevices, under rock slabs or logs or in a burrow dug beneath a rock or low shrub. It forages by day in open areas and around low shrubs, and often basks on flat rocks. It dashes to cover at the least hint of disturbance, and if attacked will readily sacrifice its tail and grow a new one. **Reproduction** They breed in spring and early summer, and females lay 2-7 soft-shelled eggs in a burrow beneath a rock. Hatchlings emerge in early autumn. **Diet** Worms, insects and other arthropods. **Habitat** Dry sclerophyll forests, woodlands and heaths.

FAMILY **SCINCIDAE** SPECIES *Eulamprus quoyii* SIZE **TO 30 CM**

EASTERN WATER SKINK

This skink has a long tail, slightly flattened from the side and long limbs with 5 digits. It is metallic-brown to coppery or grey-brown above, usually with small black flecks and a narrow, pale yellow stripe along each side. The underside is white to yellow, often with dark lines from the throat to the belly. **Behaviour** It shelters in crevices, holes or burrows and forages by day among waterside vegetation, on rocky ridges, around the roots of large riverside trees, and in intertidal zones where freshwater seeps out among rocks. It can be approached, but if startled it runs to cover or plunges into the water and swims quickly to the opposite bank. **Reproduction** They breed in spring and females give birth to 2-9 live young in summer. **Diet** Worms, tadpoles, small frogs, water beetles, aquatic larvae, snails, smaller lizards and berries. **Habitat** Along permanent waterways in rainforests, sclerophyll forests, woodlands and heaths.

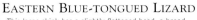

| FAMILY **SCINCIDAE** | SPECIES *Tiliqua scincoides* | SIZE **TO 60 CM** |

EASTERN BLUE-TONGUED LIZARD

This large skink has a slightly flattened head, a broad, bright blue tongue, short limbs with 5 digits and a short, thick tail. It varies from yellow, brown, pale grey to black above with paler bands on the back tail and a dark stripe from the eye to the eardrum. The under-side is white to grey or yellow. **Behaviour** Slow-moving and shy, it is most active in the early morning, late afternoon, and on warm nights, and is often seen basking on roads. It enters parks and gardens and shelters in abandoned burrows, beneath fallen logs, in crevices and hollows. If cornered it gapes widely, sticks out its bright blue tongue, inflates its body and hisses. **Reproduction** They breed in spring and females give birth to 5-25 live young in summer. **Diet** Snails, mice, carrion, insects, flowers, leaves, fruit and fungi. **Habitat** Most habitats excluding rainforests.

| FAMILY **SCINCIDAE** | SPECIES *Trachydosaurus rugosus* | SIZE **TO 39 CM** |

SHINGLEBACK LIZARD

This robust skink has a triangular head, a wide, greyish-blue tongue, a short blunt tail used to store fat and short limbs with 5 digits. It is yel-lowish-brown to black above, usually with 5-7 pale yellow, orange or grey bands. The belly is cream with grey to brown stripes or blotches. **Behaviour** It shel-ters at night in abandoned burrows, beneath ground debris and under low vegetation in a home range of around 4000 sq m, and is often seen basking on roads. Monogamous pairs re-form each year for the 6-8 week breeding season. It is generally inoffensive, but if cornered it inflates its body, displays its blue tongue, hisses loudly and may bite. **Reproduction** They breed in spring, and females give birth to 1-3 live young in late sum-mer or early autumn. **Diet** Flowers and green plant matter, some insects, snails and carrion. **Habitat** Dry sclerophyll forests and woodlands to hummock grasslands and shrublands.

| FAMILY **SCINCIDAE** | SPECIES *Egernia major* | SIZE **TO 75 CM** |

LAND MULLET

Australia's largest skink, this lizard is powerfully built with a shiny body, fish-like head and stumpy limbs with 5 digits (although most adults lack some toes). It is a dark brown to black above with a pale rim around the eye, and white, yellow to orange-brown below. Juveniles have cream or bluish-white spots on the flanks. **Behaviour** It is active by day and hibernates in winter, sheltering in hollow logs and in extensive bur-rows dug beneath logs or dense vegetation. Small colonies often live together and bask on the forest floor or on logs, before forag-ing independently around dense vegetation. Although slow-moving, it can move very fast if disturbed, making a noisy dash to its bur-row. When startled or threatened it makes snorting and hissing sounds. **Reproduction** Females bear 2-9 live young in late summer. **Diet** Fungi, fallen fruits and other plant matter; some insects, snails, slugs and mice. **Habitat** Rainforest margins and wet sclerophyll forests.

FAMILY **CHELONIIDAE**   SPECIES *Chelonia mydas*   SIZE **TO 1.5 M**

GREEN TURTLE

This turtle has strong, unwebbed, paddle-shaped limbs and is olive-green above with reddish-brown to black markings, and cream below. Hatchlings are shiny black above and white below. **Behaviour** It spends its life at sea, resting under rock over-hangs and in underwater caves, surfacing every 30 minutes or so to breathe. Young turtles float on weed rafts until they are 30-40 cm long, then settle in shallow-water feeding areas for the rest of their lives, returning to their original nesting beach every few years to breed. **Reproduction** Females lay one or more clutches of some 110 soft-shelled eggs on coastal islands at any time of year, burying them above the high water mark. The hatchlings emerge at night, 7-10 weeks later, and dash to the water. **Diet** Seagrass, seaweed and jellyfish. Young turtles eat fish, crustaceans, plankton and jellyfish. **Habitat** Shallow tropical and warm temperate coastal waters.

FAMILY **CHELONIIDAE**   SPECIES *Caretta caretta*   SIZE **TO 1.5 M**

LOGGERHEAD TURTLE

This endangered turtle is dark reddish-brown above, some-times with darker speckles, and white to yellowish below. Hatchlings are reddish-brown above and dark brown below. It lacks the beak-like upper jaw of other sea turtles. **Behaviour** It forages in deep water around coral reefs and bays staying submerged for up to 30 minutes. Young turtles ride the ocean currents until they are about 30-40 cm long, then settle in a feeding area for the rest of their lives, returning every few years to the waters around their original nesting beach to breed. **Reproduction** Females lay several clutches of about 100 soft-shelled eggs between October and May, burying them above the high water mark. The hatchlings emerge at night, about 2 months later, and dash to the water. **Diet** Fish, molluscs, crustaceans, sponges and jellyfish. Young turtles eat plankton. **Habitat** Tropical and warm temperate waters.

FAMILY **CHELONIIDAE**   SPECIES *Natator depressus*   SIZE **TO 1.2 M**

FLATBACK TURTLE

This sea turtle has a heart-shaped shell with upturned edges and strong, unwebbed, paddle-shaped limbs. It is grey to pale grey-green or olive above and creamy-yellow below. Hatchlings are olive-green with black-edged plates. **Behaviour** It spends its life at sea, floating on the surface when resting, and can stay submerged for 30 minutes. Young turtles live in shallow coastal waters and eventually settle in a shallow-water feeding area for the rest of their lives. Adults return to the waters around their original nesting beach every few years to breed. **Reproduction** Females lay several clutches of about 50 soft-shelled eggs at any time of year on the mainland and continental islands, burying them on the beach above the high water mark. The hatchlings emerge at night, about 6 weeks later, and dash to the water. **Diet** Brown algae, cuttlefish, soft corals, sea pens and sea cucumbers. The young feed on plankton. **Habitat** Shallow tropical coastal waters.

FAMILY **CHELONIIDAE**   SPECIES *Eretmochelys imbricata*   SIZE **TO 1 M**

HAWKSBILL TURTLE

This sea turtle has a beak-like upper jaw and strong, unwebbed, paddle-shaped limbs. It is olive-green or brown above with patches of reddish-brown, and dark brown or black and cream below.
Behaviour It forages around coral reefs, prising molluscs and other marine creatures from rocks with its beaked jaw. Young turtles drift with ocean currents for several years. When they are around 30 cm long they settle in a shallow-water feeding area for the rest of their lives. Adults return to the waters around their nesting beach every few years to breed. **Reproduction** Females lay 2-4 clutches of about 50 soft-shelled eggs in summer, mainly on Great Barrier Reef and Torres Strait islands, burying them on the beach above the high water mark. The hatchlings emerge at night about 8 weeks later and dash to the water. **Diet** Fish, crustaceans, molluscs, sponges, anemones, marine algae, jellyfish. Young feed on plankton. **Habitat** Tropical and warm temperate coastal waters.

FAMILY **CHELIDAE**   SPECIES *Chelodina longicollis*   SIZE **TO 30 CM**

EASTERN LONG-NECKED TURTLE

This freshwater turtle has a long neck and webbed feet. It is fawn to black above with black-edged plates and cream below. Hatchlings are black with orange markings.
Behaviour It searches for prey in shallow water, keeping its neck bent close to its shell and striking with its mouth open. If alarmed it emits a foul-smelling milky fluid from glands in its legs. In droughts it buries itself in mud or under leaf litter, and may travel up to 2 km looking for a new waterhole. Southern turtles hibernate in winter buried in the mud. **Reproduction** Females lay 8-24 brittle-shelled eggs from late spring to early winter, buried in moist soil in a swamp or stream bank. The hatchlings dig their way out at night 3-6 months later and dash to the water. **Diet** Fish, molluscs, tadpoles, frogs, snails, crustaceans and carrion. **Habitat** Swamps, billabongs, slow-moving rivers and oxbow lakes.

FAMILY **CHELIDAE**   SPECIES *Elseya latisternum*   SIZE **TO 28 CM**

SAW-SHELLED TURTLE

This freshwater turtle has soft, spines on the back of its long neck and webbed feet. It is brown to dark brown above and whitish below with a pale line along the side of its head. **Behaviour** This slow-moving, river-dwelling turtle feeds in the water and will snap at any passing object. If threatened it retracts its head and emits a foul-smelling fluid from glands in its legs. It is generally shy and placid, but may bite savagely in self defence if handled. **Reproduction** Females lay several clutches of 9-17 brittle-shelled eggs from September to January in a hole dug into moist soil high up in the river bank. The hatchlings dig their way out at night about 2 months later and dash to the water. **Diet** Fish, molluscs, crustaceans, tadpoles, frogs, aquatic insects, water weeds and fallen fruit. **Habitat** Rivers and creeks.

Frogs

Frogs are the only native amphibians in Australia, and there are many colourful and unusual examples among our 200 species. Frogs are more likely to be heard than seen, and the repertoire of thousands of males calling to attract a mate can create a deafening chorus on damp summer evenings.

Many of our frogs have adapted their life cycles, behaviour and physiology to cope with extended droughts and short wet seasons. An occasional inflow of water, either from the sky or from temporary waterways, is usually sufficient to support a frog population. Desert-dwelling frogs cope with droughts by hiding in soil cracks or burying themselves beneath drying ponds. There, in a small chamber up to 50 cm underground, they enclose themselves in a cocoon made by shedding several layers of skin to form a waterproof sack, leaving only their nostrils exposed. With a bladder full or water they can survive for many months underground, slowing down their metabolism and digging themselves out when surface water penetrates their burial chamber.

Most frogs, however, prefer warm, moist habitats, and in the coastal forests many have taken to the trees. Tree frogs have grooved discs or pads on the tips of their fingers and toes that allow them to 'stick' onto leaves and other smooth, vertical surfaces. In the dry season they hide in moist leaf bases to prevent dehydration.

Frogs are carnivores and eat virtually any small animal that fits into their mouth. Most are, however, unable to swallow anything larger than insects, other arthropods and earthworms. Larger frogs occasionally eat small reptiles and other frogs.

Frogs absorb water through the skin on the underside of their body and never need to drink. Most also have the ability to change colour slightly within a few hours or days to absorb or reflect heat or to match their surroundings and avoid being seen by predators.

FAMILY **MYOBATRACHIDAE**　　SPECIES *Crinia signifera*　　SIZE **TO 3 CM**

EASTERN FROGLET

This frog has a horizontal pupil, fringed toes without webbing and a small white spot at the base of each arm. It is often light grey or brown above with black blotches. Some have black sides, a V-shaped bar between the eyes or stripes on the back. The belly is mottled whitish, varying to marbled black and white. Males have a dark throat and chest. **Behaviour** It shelters beneath rocks, logs, vegetation and in soil cracks around ponds and slow-flowing streams, emerging to breed after rain. Males call day or night while floating among vegetation in shallow water, producing a repetitive 'creek' or a chorus of 'creek-creek'. **Reproduction** They breed year round. females lay up to 275 eggs in jelly-like clumps of 1-30, attached to submerged vegetation. The tadpoles metamorphose into froglets at 7 weeks old and 3 cm long. **Diet** Beetles, ants and other small arthropods. **Habitat** Most habitats from coastal wetlands to forests and alpine meadows.

FAMILY **MYOBATRACHIDAE**　　SPECIES *Limnodynastes convexiusculus*　　SIZE **TO 55 MM**

MARBLED GRASS FROG

This stout, tropical frog has a horizontal pupil and no visible webbing on the hands and feet. It is grey, brown or dark olive above, marbled with dark blotches, and the skin has many low, flat glands, giving it a lumpy feel. **Behaviour** It lives on the ground and has an unusual humpback posture. In the dry season it retreats to permanent swamps or lives underground, digging a burrow or taking over an existing hole. After the first major rains of the wet season males congregate around low-lying swamps, often in large numbers, and call from hiding places in the grass and ground litter, making a repeated high-pitched 'pung' call. **Reproduction** They breed from October to March, and females lay their eggs in a foamy raft under dense vegetation or in a small puddle. The tadpoles are washed into nearby ponds and swamps by the rain. **Diet** Insects and spiders. **Habitat** Lowland coastal scrubs and savanna woodlands.

FAMILY **MYOBATRACHIDAE**　　SPECIES *Limnodynastes dumerilii*　　SIZE **TO 7 CM**

EASTERN BANJO FROG

This stout frog has short hindlegs and partially webbed toes. The hindfeet have a spade-like pad for digging. There are 5 subspecies varying in size, colour and mating call. All have a pale cream stripe beneath the eye to the shoulder and a pale ridge at the corner of the mouth. **Behaviour** It is active most of the year, foraging in open areas on wet nights and hiding by day in a burrow dug into the bank of a pond. Males call from floating vegetation or from an air pocket in the flooded burrow. The banjo-like 'plonk' or 'kuk-kuk' is repeated at intervals, often in chorus at slightly different pitches. A gland on the calf produces a toxin that may deter predators. **Reproduction** They breed in warm weather. females lay up to 4000 eggs in a floating, frothy mass, usually attached to vegetation. The tadpoles develop slowly and metamorphose into young frogs in February. In cold areas they may take up to 15 months to develop. **Diet** Insects and other arthropods. **Habitat** Most habitats including heaths, forests, woodlands and grasslands.

FAMILY **MYOBATRACHIDAE**   SPECIES *Limnodynastes ornatus*   SIZE **TO 5 CM**

ORNATE BURROWING FROG

This globular frog has lozenge-shaped pupils, one quarter webbed toes and a spade-shaped pad for digging on the hindfoot. It is white below and blotched yellowish-brown or dark grey above with a large pale brown patch on the head. Some have a cream stripe down the back. **Behaviour** It shelters in a burrow, digging backwards into soft sand, and stays underground in dry periods, emerging after heavy rain to feed and breed. Males gather around ponds and make a repetitive 'unk' call while floating with outstretched limbs to attract females. On warm wet nights it often forages around river flood plains and roads. **Reproduction** Females lay a floating foam mass of some 1500 eggs in the northern wet season or in spring and summer. The tadpoles metamorphose into froglets at 3-4 weeks old before the pond dries out. **Diet** Ants, beetles, spiders and other arthropods. **Habitat** Rainforests, wet sclerophyll forests, inland woodlands and grasslands.

FAMILY **MYOBATRACHIDAE**   SPECIES *Limnodynastes tasmaniensis*   SIZE **TO 5 CM**

SPOTTED GRASS FROG

This small frog has a round to lozenge-shaped pupil and a golden iris. The toes are fringed and slightly webbed at the base. A pale yellow, russet or bright red stripe runs down the back. **Behaviour** Often seen around dams and ditches, it rests by day beneath logs, rocks or debris near the edge of waterways. On wet nights, at any time of year, males congregate around water in low-lying areas and call while floating, or from grassy vegetation on the bank. **Reproduction** They breed after rain and females lay around 1400 eggs in a floating foam mass created by forcing bubbles into the egg mass with their paddle-like hands. Some southern females cannot synchronise their hand movements well enough to create foam. The tadpoles metamorphose into froglets at 3-5 months old. **Diet** Arthropods, some small snakes. **Habitat** Most habitats from the dry interior to the wet coas. They readily colonise disturbed sites.

FAMILY **MYOBATRACHIDAE**   SPECIES *Notaden bennettii*   SIZE **TO 5 CM**

CRUCIFIX TOAD

This distinctive frog of semi-arid areas has a horizontal pupil, a globular body and short limbs. The toes are slightly webbed with a large, spade-shaped pad on hindfeet for digging. The back is warty with a cross-shaped pattern. Juveniles are bright yellow or emerald green. **Behaviour** It lives in a deep burrow most of the year and emerges after heavy summer rain. Males call while floating in temporary pools, making a series of long, owl-like "whooos". It is a poor jumper, but can run with remarkable speed, and may be seen squatting beside ant trails. It inflates its vocal sacs if threatened and can secrete a sticky, yellow, poisonous fluid from glands on its back. This dries into a strong, elastic mass, entangling and irritating an attacker. **Reproduction** They breed in temporary pools after summer rains. Females lay about 500 eggs in a floating oval mass. They hatch 2-3 days later, and the tadpoles metamorphose into young frogs at 28-30 days old. **Diet** Mainly small black ants and termites. **Habitat** Open woodlands, mallee, black-soil flood plains.

FAMILY **MYOBATRACHIDAE** SPECIES *Pseudophryne corroboree* SIZE **TO 3 CM**

CORROBOREE FROG

This small endangered frog has a horizontal pupil and short limbs with unwebbed toes. It is black and yellow above, and marbled black and white or black and yellow below. Northern frogs are sometimes lime or green.

Behaviour It shelters by day beneath logs and leaf litter and hibernates in winter, and generally crawls around on all-fours. Males dig shallow burrows 5-10 cm apart in thick moss beside shallow pools in summer and make short, harsh, squelching calls to attract females to their burrow. **Reproduction** Females breed in summer, laying 12-50 eggs in a jelly-like mass in the male's burrow. Hatchlings emerge 4-5 weeks later and the tadpoles feed on the yolk until the burrow floods. Then they swim to the nearest pool and metamorphose into froglets in December or January. **Diet** Ants and other small arthropods. **Habitat** Alpine heaths, snow gum woodlands, wet sclerophyll forests, and sphagnum bogs above 1000 m.

FAMILY **HYLIDAE** SPECIES *Cyclorana australis* SIZE **TO 10 CM**

NORTHERN WATER-HOLDING FROG

This large frog has horizontal pupils, toes webbed at the base and spade-shaped pads on the hindfeet for digging. It is grey to sandy brown or dull pink above with a dark stripe from the snout to the shoulder. Some have bright green patches, and juveniles are often emerald green. The underside is white with brown flecks. **Behaviour** It shelters from the desert heat in a deep burrow with its bladder full of water, enclosed in a waterproof cocoon, and emerges at night after heavy rain. Males gather around waterholes and make loud, deep, 'wok' or honking calls to attract females. **Reproduction** Females lay up to 7000 eggs early in the wet season in small pools attached to plants. The tadpoles metamorphose into froglets before they are one month old and the pond dries out. **Diet** Any animal it can swallow, including its own species. **Habitat** Coastal flood plains to inland woodlands and monsoon forests.

FAMILY **HYLIDAE** SPECIES *Cyclorana brevipes* SIZE **TO 45 MM**

SHORT-FOOTED FROG

This stout frog of arid areas has a horizontal pupil, partially-webbed toes and a spade-shaped pad on the soles of the hindfeet for digging. **Behaviour** To survive dry conditions it buries itself deep underground and can live without water in a chamber at the base of its burrow for at least a year. Once buried it sheds a number of layers of skin to create a water-resistant cocoon around itself, leaving only the nostrils exposed. When water penetrates its underground chamber it eats the cocoon wrapping and digs itself out. Thousands congregate around temporary waterholes to feed and mate, producing long, loud, moaning calls that can be heard for several hundred metres. **Reproduction** They breed in the wet season and females lay long strings of eggs in temporary ponds. The eggs hatch and develop rapidly before the waterhole dries up. The tadpoles metamorphose into young frogs at about 25 days old. **Diet** Insects and other arthropods. **Habitat** Mainly savanna woodlands.

FAMILY **HYLIDAE**　　　SPECIES *Litoria caerulea*　　　SIZE **TO 10 CM**

GREEN TREE FROG

This large frog has a horizontal pupil, large pads on its fingers and toes and partial webbing. It is bright pale green to dark olive-green above, often spotted, sometimes with a white stripe down the side. The belly is pale cream. **Behaviour** It is often found around houses, and can climb up windows, gripping with the pads on its fingers and toes. It is a powerful jumper, and often pounces on insects around outdoor lights. Males call to attract females from rocks beside waterways and from hollow tree limbs or drainpipes which amplify their rasping 'wark' or deep 'crawk' calls.
Reproduction Females lay up to 3000 eggs in the northern wet season or in summer, squirting large clumps up to half a metre away onto a pond where they sink to the bottom. The tadpoles metamorphose into froglets at about 38 days old. **Diet** Any small animal it can swallow. **Habitat** Coastal and inland waterways.

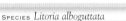

FAMILY **HYLIDAE**　　　SPECIES *Litoria alboguttata*　　　SIZE **TO 7 CM**

STRIPED BURROWING FROG

This slender frog has a horizontal pupil and grooved discs on its toes and fingertips. The toes are half-webbed, and the hindfeet have a hard, spade-shaped pad for digging. **Behaviour** It is active both day and night, and can climb smooth, vertical surfaces, gripping with the discs on its toes and fingertips. To avoid dehydration it burrows into the ground and forms a waterproof cocoon around itself by shedding several layers of skin, leaving only its nostrils exposed. When rain penetrates its burrow the frog eats its cocoon and digs its way out. Males congregate around temporary pools after heavy summer rain and make loud, rapid, quacking calls to attract females. **Reproduction** They breed after good rain and females lay a sheet of eggs over submerged rocks or on the bottom of a pond. The eggs hatch into tadpoles in less than 36 hours. **Diet** Insects and other arthropods. **Habitat** Woodlands, cleared areas, flood plains, dams, waterholes.

FAMILY **HYLIDAE**　　　SPECIES *Litoria fallax*　　　SIZE **TO 25 MM**

EASTERN DWARF TREE FROG

This tiny, elongated frog has a horizontal pupil and moderate discs on the tips of the fingers and toes. The toes are partially-webbed and there is a small hard pad on the inside edge of the hindfoot. It changes colour to match its background. **Behaviour** This climbing frog is active both day and night, and is often seen resting on plants growing in swamps, dams and lagoons. It also travels well away from water, and shelters in the leaf bases of banana plants, pandans, pineapples and bromeliads. In southern areas they are active mostly in the warmer months when males call from vegetation fringing still waterways, making repeated squeaky 'reeek, reeek, reeek' calls. **Reproduction** Females lay clumps of around 250 eggs in still water among submerged plants. The tadpoles metamorphose into froglets at about 4 months old. **Diet** Small insects and other arthropods. **Habitat** Various habitats around waterways.

ANIMALS

| FAMILY **HYLIDAE** | SPECIES *Litoria gracilenta* | SIZE **TO 45 MM** |

DAINTY GREEN TREE FROG

This climbing frog has a horizontal pupil and a golden-yellow or reddish iris. It has bright yellow feet with large flattened discs on the tips of the toes and fingers which are almost fully webbed. **Behaviour** It is often found in boxes of bananas and is also known as the Banana Frog. It is active at night and is usually seen on roads, among low vegetation after rain, and sometimes around houses. It rests by day in dense streamside vegetation, flattening itself against the foliage, holding its limbs tight against its body, showing as much leaf-green colour as possible. After spring and summer rainfall, males call from floating vegetation, reeds, or from trees or shrubs, making long 'waaa' or 'weee' calls. **Reproduction** They breed in spring and summer and females lay their eggs in still water. The tadpoles metamorphose into young frogs at about 16 weeks old. **Diet** Insects and other arthropods. **Habitat** Moist forests and woodlands.

| FAMILY **HYLIDAE** | SPECIES *Litoria infrafrenata* | SIZE **TO 14 CM** |

GIANT TREE FROG

The world's largest tree frog, this species has a horizontal pupil, large pads on the tips of its digits, partially webbed fingers and completely webbed toes. It is bright green above, changing to brown depending on the temperature and background, with a white stripe along the lower lip to the shoulder, and along the edge of the hindleg to the toes. It is whitish below. **Behaviour** It forages on wet and humid nights, often around houses, climbing smooth vertical surfaces using the gripping pads on its fingers and toes. After summer rainstorms males gather around ponds, often perching on trees, and set up a deafening chorus of barking calls to attract females. When distressed it makes a cat-like miaowing call. **Reproduction** Females lay some 430 eggs in summer in still water. The tadpoles metamorphose into froglets at about 2 months old. **Diet** Mainly insects and other arthropods. **Habitat** From rainforests to seasonally dry monsoon woodlands.

| FAMILY **HYLIDAE** | SPECIES *Litoria lesueuri* | SIZE **TO 7 CM** |

LESUEUR'S FROG

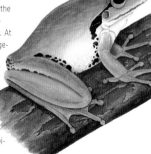

This frog has a horizontal pupil, webbed toes and very small discs on the tips of the fingers and toes. Males are smaller and become bright yellowish-bronze in the breeding season. **Behaviour** Predominantly ground-dwelling, it rests by day beneath rocks and in crevices. At night it roams widely, looking for food among leaf litter and in low vegetation along waterways. It is very agile and escapes predators by making fast, powerful leaps. In the breeding season males find and defend territories 1-2 m apart around waterways. The call is a purring trill. **Reproduction** They breed in all but the coldest months, and mate on the bottom of a quiet creek. The eggs are laid in clumps of about 500 and stick to rocks or pebbles in flowing water. In the far north females lay their eggs in a shallow nest dug into a sandy creek bank. **Diet** Arthropods and small vertebrates. **Habitat** Most habitats from heaths to tropical rainforests.

| FAMILY **HYLIDAE** | SPECIES *Litoria nasuta* | SIZE **TO 5 CM** |

ROCKET FROG

This streamlined frog has a pointed snout, a horizontal pupil, partially webbed toes and small discs on the tips of the fingers and toes. The back has small warts and folds, forming longitudinal ridges. **Behaviour** A ground-dweller, it forages in the leaf litter in open forests and around waterways. If threatened it jumps with remarkable speed, covering up to 4 m in one hop. Males call from vegetation around waterways, their 'yap yap' calls often creating a raucous chorus after heavy summer rain. **Reproduction** In the north they breed in temporary soaks and waterholes during the wet season, and in permanent swamps in the dry season. Southern populations breed in summer. Females lay 50-100 eggs in a thin film of jelly that floats on the surface of still water. The tadpoles take around 31 days to metamorphose into young frogs. **Diet** Insects and spiders. **Habitat** Most habitats surrounding flooded grasslands, coastal swamps, streams and ponds.

| FAMILY **HYLIDAE** | SPECIES *Litoria rothii* | SIZE **TO 55 MM** |

RED-EYED TREE FROG

This tropical frog has a horizontal pupil and the top half of its iris is rusty-red. It has large discs on the tips of its partially-webbed fingers and toes. The skin is rough above with low, rounded warts, and granular below. In direct hot sunlight it changes to a pale putty colour. **Behaviour** It is active at night and avoids dehydration by hiding among vegetation, under bark and in tree hollows. It forages on the ground on humid nights, often far from water and around houses, relying on puddles, ditches and claypans to breed. On the coast it frequents trees and shrubs along waterways. Males call throughout the summer from perches close to water, making loud chuckling or cackling calls. **Reproduction** They breed in the wet season in semi-permanent swamps, and females lay 500 eggs. The tadpoles metamorphose into young frogs at around 65 days old. **Diet** Insects and other arthropods. **Habitat** Most habitats, usually around larger river systems in inland areas.

| FAMILY **HYLIDAE** | SPECIES *Litoria rubella* | SIZE **TO 35 MM** |

NAKED TREE FROG

This, widespread, short-legged frog has a horizontal pupil and large discs on the tips of its partially-webbed fingers and toes. In hot, dry conditions it becomes white to prevent overheating. **Behaviour** Often seen clinging to a window on summer nights, it forages mostly on the ground and sometimes basks in the sun. In arid areas it stays close to permanent water. Groups often squeeze into rock crevices to prevent dehydration, or huddle in damp soil under rocks or in tree hollows. Breeding males congregate beside still or slow-moving water, their loud, high-pitched buzzing calls creating a deafening chorus. **Reproduction** They breed at any time of year in the north and after summer rains elsewhere. Females lay 300-750 eggs in a thin film on the surface of still water. The tadpoles metamorphose into young frogs in only 14 days, and leave the water before losing their tails. **Diet** Arthropods. **Habitat** Most habitats from wet coastal forests to the central deserts.

Fishes

Australian waters are home to around 3500 of the world's 23 000 fish species. They have adapted to habitats in the deep oceans, the shallow tropical waters of the Great Barrier Reef and temporary pools in the arid interior. Fishes have evolved into a vast array of shapes and colours. Some look more like seaweed than a fish, while others look like snakes. Yet all fishes are cold-blooded, possess gills, fins and a backbone.

The gills are fine, frilly filaments on each side of the mouth usually protected by gill covers behind the eyes. The filaments are enmeshed with minute blood vessels that extract oxygen from the water as it flows into the mouth and over the gills. Some fast-swimming, open-water fish such as tuna, mackerels and some sharks must keep moving to force enough water over their gills, but most other fishes are able to pump water over their gills by flapping their gill covers and swallowing.

All fishes reproduce sexually, and many Australian fishes change sex as they grow older. At spawning time many fishes congregate in huge shoals. Females release clouds of eggs and males squirt sperm into the surrounding water. The eggs sink to the bottom or drift with the wind and water currents on the surface. Most are eaten by other sea creatures, but the huge numbers produced ensure that enough survive to form the next generation. Some fishes lay a small number of large eggs in a burrow or nest and guard them until they hatch.

Water is drawn out of marine fishes by a process called osmosis, and seeps into the bodies of freshwater fishes, causing either dehydration or salt loss. To counter-act water loss and the build up of salt, marine fishes constantly drink sea water, produce concentrated urine and excrete salt through their gills. Freshwater fishes, on the other hand, avoid the loss of salt by producing very weak urine. They also absorb salts from the water as it flows over their gills.

FAMILY **HETERODONTIDAE**   SPECIES *Heterodontus portusjacksoni*   SIZE **TO 1.6 M**

PORT JACKSON SHARK

This shark has a squarish blunt head with a small, low mouth, a crest above each eye, 2 triangular dorsal fins tipped with a large, venomous spine, and a slender tail. It is grey to brown with a dark band over the head and a dark, harness-like pattern on the body. **Behaviour** Docile and active at night, they are often seen on the seabed, swimming slowly or pushing themselves along with their large pectoral fins. They congregate in large caves and under ledges during the day, and migrate to breeding areas in spring, travelling up to 850 km. **Reproduction** Females deposit about 15 large eggs with spiral-flanged casings in winter, wedged between rocks or buried in the sand and mud. After 8-10 months the young, about 20 cm long, emerge and fend for themselves. **Diet** Sea urchins, crabs, lobsters, abalones, periwinkles. **Habitat** Coastal waters around reefs, rocky estuaries to about 250 m deep.

FAMILY **STEGOSTOMATIDAE**   SPECIES *Stegostoma fasciatum*   SIZE **TO 3.5 M**

ZEBRA SHARK

Juveniles have a strong zebra-like pattern of black and white bands, while adults are yellowish with a spotted, leopard-like pattern, hence the alternative common name of Leopard Shark. It has a small mouth, a very long tail and hard ridges along its sides. **Behaviour** This non-aggressive shark is often seen resting on the sandy seabed during the day. It is active mostly at night, moving slowly around the sea bottom searching for food, usually alone, although large numbers congregate in some areas to breed. **Reproduction** Females attach their large egg cases to the sea floor with bundles of hairy fibres. They are golden-brown, about 18 cm long and 9 cm wide, and become almost black with age. Hatchlings are about 20 cm long. **Diet** Sea snails, small fish, bivalves, crustaceans. **Habitat** Coastal waters around coral reefs and offshore atolls in tropical and some temperate waters.

FAMILY **ODONTASPIDIDAE**   SPECIES *Carcharias taurus*   SIZE **TO 3.6 M**

GREY NURSE SHARK

This stout shark has a conical, bluntly-pointed snout, long, slender, pointed teeth, small eyes, 2 large dorsal fins, 2 similar-sized anal fins and a large tail fin with a pronounced upper lobe. It is grey to brownish-grey, paler below, often with scattered brownish blotches or spots on the sides. **Behaviour** It is harmless unless provoked and is usually seen by day in small resident groups around reefs and sometimes off surf beaches catching fish. At night it probably feeds alone. It is usually slow-moving, but can take off at great speed with a loud clap of its tail. It swallows air for buoyancy and hangs motionless just above the sea bed. **Reproduction** Females have 2 uteri and give birth to 2 young per year, about 1 m long. One siblings eats the other in the uterus. **Diet** Fish and other marine creatures. **Habitat** Tropical, subtropical and temperate coastal waters to about 200 m deep.

| FAMILY **LAMNIDAE** | SPECIES *Carcharodon carcharias* | SIZE **TO 6.4 M** |

GREAT WHITE SHARK

The largest shark, this species has a heavy, streamlined body tapering to the snout and tail with a very large mouth containing broad, triangular, serrated teeth. It has long pectoral fins, the first dorsal fin is centrally placed, very large and triangular, the second is small and close to the tail. It is pale to dark grey or blue-grey above and white below. **Behaviour** Very dangerous and unpredictable, this shark hunts alone, mainly in offshore waters, sometimes entering shallow bays, using its acute senses of smell and hearing to detect prey. Groups sometimes gather around abundant food supplies. It can swim very fast, but must keep moving at 3.5 km/h, 24 hours a day, to extract enough oxygen from the water. **Reproduction** Females produce up to 10 pups to 1.4 m long. The young feed on eggs and other embryos within the mother before birth. **Diet** Fish and other marine animals. **Habitat** Cooler waters, often around coasts.

| FAMILY **CARCHARINIDAE** | SPECIES *Carcharinus amblyrhynchos* | SIZE **TO 2.6 M** |

GREY REEF SHARK

This shark has a streamlined body and a broad, rounded snout, pointed from the side, long pectoral fins and a long, notched tail fin with black edges. **Behaviour** They swim towards low-frequency vibrations such as those made by a struggling fish and are attracted by divers entering the water. They can be very aggressive and will attack if cornered, provoked or threatened. Warning displays include arching the back, dropping the pectoral fins and swimming with an exaggerated sway. They attack with lightning speed, biting once or twice before swimming away. They are more active at night and patrol the edges of the reefs where they drop away into deeper water, threatening intruders. Schools sometimes form during the day and swim close to the bottom. **Reproduction** Females bear 1-6 live young, 45-60 cm long, after 12 months gestation. **Diet** Fish, squid, crustaceans. **Habitat** Tropical and subtropical coastal waters around the edges of coral reefs.

| FAMILY **CARCHARHINIDAE** | SPECIES *Prionace glauca* | SIZE **TO 3.8 M** |

BLUE SHARK

This streamlined shark has a long, slender body, a long snout, large eyes and very long, wing-shaped pectoral fins. It is deep indigo blue above, fading to white below. The tail fin has a much longer upper lobe, notched near the tip. **Behaviour** They are inoffensive and will not attack unless provoked. Generally solitary and sluggish, they are usually seen cruising on the surface, but are able to swim at up to 40 km/h if excited or feeding. They are long-distance travellers, riding the ocean currents migrating up to 6000 km. Females have skin three times as thick as males to protect them during aggressive mating behaviour, and many bear the scars of bites inflicted while mating. **Reproduction** Females bear litters of 25-50 pups, 40-51 cm long, 9-12 months after mating. **Diet** Mainly squid and schooling fish. **Habitat** Deep temperate and tropical waters.

FAMILY **SPHYRNIDAE**   SPECIES *Sphyrna zygaena*   SIZE **TO 4 M**

SMOOTH HAMMERHEAD

This shark's flattened hammer-shaped head acts like a wing, providing extra lift and manoeuvrability. The eyes are on the on the outer edges of the head and the nostrils on the corners, giving heightened directional sensitivity. The head is rounded at the front and deeply indented around the nostrils, distinguishing it from other hammerhead sharks.

Behaviour This shark is not considered dangerous and sometimes congregates in large schools. Primarily oceanic, it also comes inshore and is encountered mostly in shallow bays and around reefs. It swims close to the surface and is often seen with its dorsal and caudal fins exposed. It detects prey using vision, smell and electro-receptors in its head, swimming fast, using its large, flattened head to twist and turn in pursuit of fast-moving prey. **Reproduction** Females produce about 30 live young around 55 cm long at birth. **Diet** Small fish. **Habitat** Coastal and offshore waters to about 275 m deep.

FAMILY **UROLOPHIDAE**   SPECIES *Urolophus paucimaculatus*   SIZE **TO 40 CM**

SPARSELY-SPOTTED STINGAREE

This ray has a small dorsal fin, a short, deep tail fin, and a cylindrical tail bearing one or two venomous spines. It is flat, slightly broader than long with raised side-viewing eyes with large openings just behind. The mouth is on the underside, slightly arched with large nostrils in front of its corners and 5 pairs of gill slits behind.

It is pale grey or brown above, usually with several dark-edged white spots. **Behaviour** It is fast-moving, swimming as fast backwards as forward, and is active mostly at night. It often swims over shallow sandbanks just above the sea floor and buries itself when resting. It will attack if stepped on or provoked, striking with lightning speed, inflicting a deep, painful wound with its venomous spine. **Reproduction** Females bear 1-2 live young in spring or early summer, 10-12 months after mating. **Diet** Marine invertebrates. **Habitat** Muddy and sandy sites in bays and estuaries, reefs and seagrass beds.

FAMILY **MURAENIDAE**   SPECIES *Gymnothorax prasinus*   SIZE **TO 1 M**

GREEN MORAY

This eel has a muscular, laterally flattened body, scaleless thick skin covered by yellowish mucus, lacks pelvic and pectoral fins and has a continuous fin along its back. It has a pair of tube-like nostrils and needle-like teeth. The mouth opens and closes constantly to pump water for respiration. It is brown or yellow, but becomes green in shallow water due to algal growth. It hides by day in rocky crevices, sometimes with other morays, with its head exposed. It forages at night, probing crevices in reefs, relying largely on its sense of smell to locate prey. If disturbed it can become aggressive and inflict a severe bite. **Reproduction** Females lay numerous small eggs that hatch into filmy larvae and become tiny glass eels before settling as juveniles at about 40 mm long. **Diet** Crustaceans, fish, cephalopods. **Habitat** Most habitats from rocky estuaries to offshore reefs, to 30 m deep.

| FAMILY **PLOTOSIDAE** | SPECIES *Plotosus lineatus* | SIZE **TO 35 CM** |

STRIPED CATFISH

This bottom-feeder has an elongated body with an eel-like tail, smooth slimy skin and venomous spines heading the dorsal and pectoral fins. The head is slightly flattened and has a small mouth with thick fleshy lips and 5 pairs of long, sensitive, fleshy, whisker-like barbels. **Behaviour** They are nocturnal bottom feeders and sense water movements of prey with their barbels. Tiny juveniles swim in tightly-packed groups and seem to collectively mimic branches, coconuts and other objects to escape detection. Schools become less defined as they become older, but re-form quickly if threatened. Adults are seen alone or in small groups and hide in crevices by day. The venomous spines inflict extremely painful wounds. **Reproduction** Females lay thousands of eggs in shallow-water gravel nests up to 2 m wide. One parent stays at the nest until the tiny larvae emerge 2-7 days later. **Diet** Fish, invertebrates, algae. **Habitat** Coastal waters and estuaries.

| FAMILY **ANTENNARIIDAE** | SPECIES *Antennarius striatus* | SIZE **TO 20 CM** |

STRIPED ANGLERFISH

This fish has a greatly enlarged third dorsal spine and a modified first dorsal spine. This arises from the snout tip and extends in front of the head, and has a rod-like section tipped with 2-7 pinkish-white thick, worm-like pieces that unfold to lure prey. This fish is highly variable in colour, usually striped, and may be yellow, orange, black or white, changing to match its surroundings. The skin is covered with tiny spines. **Behaviour** They usually remain motionless on the bottom, often next to a sponge, changing colour to match it perfectly. Passing fish are lured within range by wriggling their worm-like bait. They strike with great speed, sucking small prey into the mouth in milliseconds. The stomach expands to accommodate any prey that fits through the throat. **Reproduction** Females lay numerous eggs in a mucus raft. **Diet** Fish. **Habitat** Shallow rocky estuaries to 200 m or more deep.

| FAMILY **MELANOTAENIIDAE** | SPECIES *Melanotaenia splendida* | SIZE **TO 20 CM** |

RAINBOW FISH

This colourful freshwater fish is found in most inland waterways, from the desert to the coast. Desert sub-species are smaller, growing to about 8 cm. It has a deep, thin body, and varies through shades of red, blue, green and yellow, according to the mood of the fish and the water turbidity. During spawning the male has a bright pink belly. **Behaviour** They school in mid-water and are often seen in the shallows catching insects falling onto the surface. They can jump out of the water and make their way to the top of waterfalls. **Reproduction** They breed year-round and spawning is often triggered by monsoonal rains. Pairs swim side-by-side among aquatic vegetation, and as the eggs are shed and fertilised they are scattered over the plants. Females lay 50-100 eggs each day. They hatch in about 7 days and mature in a few months. **Diet** Algae, aquatic plants, invertebrates. **Habitat** Streams, lakes, rivers.

| FAMILY **MORIDAE** | SPECIES *Lotella rhacina* | SIZE **TO 66 CM** |

LARGE-TOOTH BEARDY

This fish has a slightly flattened body with tiny, smooth-edged scales. It has a broad head with a prominent barbel on the chin. It has a distinctive rounded tail fin and long-based fins running along the back and underside. It varies in colour from reddish-brown to yellowish-grey with distinct white margins on the edges of the fins.
Behaviour They are often seen at night swimming beneath rock overhangs and around the entrances of underwater caves. They feed after dark and sometimes venture well away from the reefs looking for food. During the day they hide in the gloomy depths of caves and beneath rock overhangs. **Diet** Mostly small fish and cephalopods. **Habitat** Coastal bays to offshore reefs, usually in caves, in waters 10-90 m deep.

| FAMILY **MONOCENTRIDIDAE** | SPECIES *Cleidopus gloriamaris* | SIZE **TO 25 CM** |

PINEAPPLEFISH

The body of this fish is covered with plate-like scales armed with curving spines outlined in black, and resembles the skin of a pineapple. It varies in colour from pale-yellow to yellow-orange. Its fin spines are lockable in an outward position, or folded into grooves. It has a prominent red light-organ on the sides of its lower jaw containing phosphorescent bacteria living symbiotically on a patch of skin. The light-organ is blue-green in young fish. **Behaviour** This non-aggressive fish shelters in caves or beneath rock ledges in reefs, either alone or in a small group. It is active at night and hunts alone using the greenish light produced by its light organs to locate prey over open sand. It often ventures a long way from its daytime shelter, but returns before dark. **Diet** Shrimps and other crustaceans. **Habitat** Shallow rocky estuaries and offshore to at least 250 m deep.

| FAMILY **ZEIDAE** | SPECIES *Zeus faber* | SIZE **TO 66 CM** |

JOHN DORY

This widespread fish is green to olive-grey or silvery-bronze with a large dark eye-spot mark edged by a pale ring centrally on each side. It has an oval, flattened body with a large oblique mouth. The jaws expand into a long suction tube used to target small fish. The dorsal fin has long extended spines. The ventral fins are small and paddle-like. Juveniles have very large dorsal and ventral fins. **Behaviour** A solitary hunter, it cunningly approaches its prey then shoots out its tubular mouth to engulf small creatures. This fish sometimes pursues its victims into very shallow water. **Diet** Fish, squid, crustaceans.
Habitat Mostly in waters 60-400 m deep, sometimes in shallow estuaries.

FAMILY **SYGNATHIDAE** · SPECIES *Phycodurus eques* · SIZE **TO 25 CM**

LEAFY SEADRAGON

This spectacular fish is encased in bony plates, and has many large spines and elaborate leaf-like appendages at the ends of bony stalks. It has large pectoral and dorsal fins and a long, tubular snout ending in a small, toothless mouth. It varies from orange-brown to yellowish-green or burgundy-red, depending on the depth. **Behaviour** It is almost indistinguishable from a piece of loose weed, which allows it to approach prey without being seen and suck small crustaceans up with its tube-like snout. It lives around reefs dominated by kelp and weed, floating slowly over sandbanks. Males migrate to shallow parts of the reef when they are carrying eggs. **Reproduction** Breeding occurs in early summer and the male incubates about 250 eggs in the skin under his tail during November and December. Hatchlings are about 25 mm long. **Diet** Mysids and other small crustaceans. **Habitat** Shallow coastal bays to about 30 m deep.

FAMILY **SYGNATHIDAE** · SPECIES *Hippocampus whitei* · SIZE **TO 20 CM**

WHITE'S SEAHORSE

Protected by bony plates, this spectacular fish has a long tubular snout ending in a small toothless mouth, a pointed head with a knob-like crown. It varies from greyish-brown to yellow, depending on its surroundings. Males are darker and often finely-spotted with scribbled facial markings. **Behaviour** They hide among seagrasses and sponges, holding on with their prehensile tail, or move slowly, fins whirring, sucking up unwary prey with their long snout. They usually occur in pairs, and may form small groups in the summer breeding season, with peaks of mating near the full moon. Males grow a sack-like pouch on their underbelly a few days before mating. **Reproduction** Females lay about 50 eggs in the male's pouch. They are fertilised and fed by a fluid secreted by the pouch lining. Some 25 days later the young are ejected and attach to floating weed. **Diet** Small crustaceans. **Habitat** Seagrass beds, sheltered bays to about 25 m deep.

FAMILY **AULOSTOMIDAE** · SPECIES *Aulostomus chinensis* · SIZE **TO 90 CM**

TRUMPETFISH

This fish has a long, slightly compressed tubular snout ending in a small, flap-like mouth, a fleshy barbel on the chin and a slightly compressed, elongated body, with small fins placed well back. It varies in colour. Juveniles are dull greyish-brown with banded or striped patterns, and adults are often bright yellow or reddish.
Behaviour A cunning daytime predator, it ambushes prey, resting motionless behind coral or riding behind or on the back of a larger, usually harmless fish. When a small creature comes close it streaks out from cover to strike, sucking in its prey with its tube-like mouth. It sleeps at night, resting vertically among sea whips. Juveniles inhabit seagrass and soft coral areas while adults prefer shallow reef flats and drop-offs.
Reproduction Females transfer their eggs to the male who fertilises and carries them in a pouch. **Diet** Fish, crustaceans. **Habitat** Near rocky and coral reefs to 122 m deep.

| FAMILY **TRIGLIDAE** | SPECIES *Chelidonichthys kumu* | SIZE **TO 50 CM** |

RED GURNARD

The pectoral fins of this bottom-dweller have an irides-cent blue margin and blue spots on a greenish-yellow background (greenish-grey in juveniles). The lower few rays of the fins are not connected to the membrane. The large head is armoured with bony plates. **Behaviour** They hide by day partly buried in the sand and become active around dusk, using their large lower pectoral fin rays, which are studded with taste buds, to walk along the bottom and probe for prey. The colourful fins are also used for display and to startle potential predators. When handled they pro-duce grunting or chirping sounds and turn bright red. Juveniles are often found on the sand along coastal beaches. Adults usually prefer deeper water. **Diet** Fish, crustaceans, cephalopods. **Habitat** Shallow coastal estuaries and deep water to 200 m.

| FAMILY **SCORPAENIDAE** | SPECIES *Synanceja horrida* | SIZE **TO 47 CM** |

ESTUARINE STONEFISH

This dangerous fish has warty projections on its body. It is usually brownish-grey to reddish-brown and resem-bles a stone. It has 13 sturdy dorsal fin spines each with a pair of venom sacs, covered by loose skin except for the tips. **Behaviour** This bottom-dwelling fish has caused many fatalities, although antivenom is available. It lies partly buried in the sand, coral rubble or mud with only its mouth slit exposed, and is almost impossible to detect. If stepped on, the spine tips can puncture the soles of sandshoes and penetrate the skin releasing highly toxic and extremely painful venom (pain is relieved by the application of heat). They ambush prey, lying in wait for fish or crabs to come close enough to seize and swallow, and can survive many hours out of water. They hop across the bottom using their pectoral fins. **Diet** Fish, crus-taceans. **Habitat** Coastal foreshores and estuaries with a muddy bottom.

| FAMILY **SCORPAENIDAE** | SPECIES *Pterois volitans* | SIZE **TO 38 CM** |

RED FIREFISH

This spectacular fish has very long dorsal spines and long, broad, filamentous, unbranched pectoral rays that resemble butterfly wings. The dorsal and anal fins are tipped with ven-omous spines, covered with skin that slides back when the spine pierces its victim. It varies in colour, depending on its surroundings, from completely black to white with reddish-brown to black bands. It has spots on the dorsal, anal and tail fins. **Behaviour** Venom from this fish is dangerous and extremely painful (relieved by the application of heat). It lives in caves and crevices around reefs, and is often seen in pairs in shallow water over coral reefs. It ambushes prey while resting on the bottom and defends itself by pumping venom from its spines into its victim. It deters predators by swimming slowly with its long pectoral fins spread out. **Diet** Fish. **Habitat** Shallow estuaries to deep offshore reefs.

119

| FAMILY **CENTROPOMIDAE** | SPECIES *Lates calcarifer* | SIZE **TO 1.8 M** |

BARRAMUNDI

This large-scaled fish is silvery-grey with a deeply-notched dorsal fin, humped back, large mouth and glassy eyes. **Behaviour** Young fish may live in freshwater habitats until they become sexually mature at the end of their third year. All are male, and migrate to estuaries and coastal shallows where they fertilise eggs for the next 2 years. At 6 years old they change sex and begin laying eggs. **Reproduction** Females lay millions of eggs between September and March. They are swept into mangroves and estuaries and hatch within 24 hours. The young develop rapidly and remain in coastal shallows or migrate to nearby swamps and floodplains. **Diet** Fish and crustaceans. Juveniles also eat aquatic insects. **Habitat** Estuaries and freshwater rivers.

| FAMILY **TOXOTIDAE** | SPECIES *Toxotes jaculatrix* | SIZE **TO 20 CM** |

BANDED ARCHERFISH

This amazing fish has a pointed snout, a laterally compressed body and 4 dorsal spines when held erect. It is silvery white with black bars or large spots on its back. **Behaviour** It is usually seen in schools patrolling the shoreline looking for prey, swimming just below the surface. It brings down insects resting on riverside banks or hovering above the water up to 2 m away with drops of water squirted with great force and accuracy. It forms a tube by pressing its tongue against a groove in the roof of its mouth and clamps its gill covers shut, forcing drops of water out in rapid succession like pellets from an airgun. It has excellent binocular vision to determine range and positions itself directly beneath its target to compensate for the effects of light refraction. **Diet** Insects, crustaceans, water snails. **Habitat** Brackish mangrove estuaries, rivers and creeks.

| FAMILY **GOBIIDAE** | SPECIES *Periophthalmus argentilineatus* | SIZE **TO 27 CM** |

MUDSKIPPER

This unusual fish can live out of the water for considerable periods. It has protruding eyes that can rotate in all directions, and a large, sail-like dorsal fin. **Behaviour** An aggressive predator, it is often seen resting on muddy banks, energetically posturing with its dorsal fins to keep others away. When the tide goes out the mudskipper leaves the water and moves across the mud, swinging its pectoral fins forward while supporting itself on its pelvic fins. Oxygen is extracted from water carried in its gill chambers as well as through its skin and mouth-lining. To avoid the rising tide it can climb onto mangrove roots. When alarmed it skips quickly away, flicking its tail, and hides in a mud crater. It also swims just below the surface with its eyes exposed. **Diet** Invertebrates including spiders, insects, worms, crabs, molluscs. **Habitat** Brackish mangrove estuaries.

FAMILY **CHAETODONTIDAE**   SPECIES *Chelmon rostratus*   SIZE **TO 20 CM**

BEAKED CORALFISH

This butterflyfish has a very long beak-like snout with slender, brush-like teeth, a steep forehead profile, a laterally compressed body and a single dorsal fin with stout spines when erect. It is distinctively patterned with broad, black-edged orange bands and a black eye-spot at the base of the dorsal fin. **Behaviour** It shelters among the coral at night and is often seen during the day in pairs swimming closely together looking for food near the bottom. It uses its long snout to pick prey from crevices in the reef and from the substrate. Juveniles are secretive and live in shallow waters in protected bays, whereas adults live on coastal reefs and lagoons with mixed soft and hard coral. It erects its fin spines to deter predators. **Diet** Worms and small invertebrates. **Habitat** Clear waters around coastal reefs, lagoons, bays and estuaries to about 15 m deep.

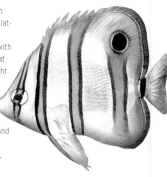

FAMILY **POMACANTHIDAE**   SPECIES *Pomacanthus xanthometopon*   SIZE **TO 38 CM**

YELLOWMASK ANGELFISH

This fish has a spine on its cheek, blue scribble markings on its head, a yellow mask, yellow to orange chest and pectoral fins, a black spot at the base of the dorsal fin and a bright yellow tail fin. Juveniles are almost black with about 15 pale vertical bars. **Behaviour** They shelter at night beneath boulders, in caves and coral crevices, and are usually seen alone during the day on outer reefs. They are territorial and search around the bottom for food and dash to cover if disturbed. Males drive rivals from their territory in the breeding season and display to attract passing females. **Reproduction** Mating pairs spiral slowly to the surface at dusk, shed eggs and sperm at the apex of their ascent, then swim back to the bottom. The eggs are less than 1 mm across and hatch 15-20 hours later. Juveniles live secretly among reefs. **Diet** Sponges and small invertebrates. **Habitat** Coral reefs.

FAMILY **POMACENTHIDAE**   SPECIES *Amphiprion percula*   SIZE **TO 11 CM**

CLOWN ANEMONEFISH

This damselfish is compressed laterally with a small mouth and 2 spines on the anal fin. It is bright orange with 3 white bands edged with black. **Behaviour** They are active by day around shallow reef crests and slopes where sea anemones proliferate, hiding from predators among the anemones' tentacles, protected from their deadly stinging cells by a layer of mucus acquired by gradually increasing contact with the anemone. They are usually found in small groups with a single dominant female, her monogamous partner and up to 3 non-breeding males. When the female dies the largest male changes sex. **Reproduction** Females lay up to 1000 eggs in a nest on a rock under the anemone. The male cares for them until they hatch 6-7 days later and swim to the surface. At 8-12 days they find a host anemone. **Diet** Algae and plankton. **Habitat** Coral reefs to 15 m.

FAMILY **APOGONIDAE**	SPECIES *Apogon properuptus*	SIZE **TO 85 MM**

ORANGE-LINED CARDINALFISH

This small cardinalfish has a laterally compressed body, large eyes and mouth, 2 separate angular dorsal fins and 2 spines on its anal fin. It is distinguished by its broad orange to yellow-orange stripes.

Behaviour They sleep by day in small groups deep in coral caverns, among boulders, rocks and beneath ledges. At night they drift out into open water above the reef and disperse to feed.
Reproduction The female lays a mass of several hundred eggs into the water, the male fertilises them and sucks the cluster of eggs into his mouth and keeps them there until they hatch several days later. Ocean currents carry the larvae until they eventually settle on new reefs.
Diet Fish, crustaceans, small invertebrates. **Habitat** Clear coastal and outer reefs to 30 m deep.

FAMILY **LABRIDAE**	SPECIES *Achoerodus viridus*	SIZE **TO 1.2 M**

EASTERN BLUE GROPER

This large member of the wrasse family has a long body with a single, long-based dorsal fin, thick fleshy lips and small eyes. Males are grey or blue, females reddish brown. Small juveniles are green and change to brown, with blue and orange stripes radiating from the eyes, becoming scribbles in adults.
Behaviour These diurnal bottom-feeders probe the sand for food, gulping up mouthfuls, crushing shells at the back of the throat and spitting out debris. They shelter at night in caves and beneath ledges. Large adults roam over offshore reefs and shallows. Small juveniles live mostly in seagrass beds in large estuaries, moving out to rock-reefs as they grow. Fully developed males are territorial and dominate a group of females, driving rivals away. If the male dies, the largest female changes sex and colour, and becomes the dominant male. **Diet** Small fish, invertebrates. **Habitat** Estuaries and offshore reefs to about 40 m deep

FAMILY **LABRIDAE**	SPECIES *Choerodon fasciatus*	SIZE **TO 30 CM**

HARLEQUIN TUSKFISH

A member of the wrasse family, this fish has a long body with a single, long-based dorsal fin, and derives its name from its large, protruding canine-like teeth. Adults have red bands outlined in blue over the body and head, while juveniles have light-brown bands and false eye-spots on the fins. **Behaviour** Active by day, adults swim over the rubble bottom around inner reefs, probing for food, crushing crabs and molluscs with their strong jaws and large teeth. They shelter at night in small, loose aggregations in large caves or beneath rock overhangs. They are strongly territorial with a dominant adult male controlling a group of females and fending off rivals. When the male dies the largest female changes sex and dominates the group. Small juveniles are secretive and stay close to reef walls and the ceilings of caves. **Diet** Small fish, crustaceans and other invertebrates. **Habitat** Coastal reefs to about 40 m deep.

FAMILY **SCARIDAE**   SPECIES *Scarus ghobban*   SIZE **TO 1 M**

BLUE-BARRED PARROTFISH

The teeth of this fish are fused to form a beak-like structure, which is used to scrape algae from the reef, hence its common name. Males have broad blue scale margins and blue bands on the head. Females are yellowish with blue bars and spots on the sides. **Behaviour** They congregate in schools, juveniles in lagoons and adults in deeper water off the reef edge, feeding over sand and coral. Rock and coral ingested as they scrape the reef are ground to powder and pass out as fine white sand, contributing significantly to the sediment. At dusk they retire to shelter in crevices and under ledges. Adult females change sex and colour as they age. **Reproduction** A number of females spawn together near the surface and their eggs are fertilised simultaneously by a male. Larvae float with the ocean currents and juveniles may drift for hundreds of kilometres. **Diet** Algae, sea grasses. **Habitat** Coral reefs to 50 m or more.

FAMILY **ACANTHURIDAE**   SPECIES *Acanthurus lineatus*   SIZE **TO 38 CM**

LINED SURGEONFISH

This fish is distinguished by its numerous yellow to orange, blue and white lines. It has a very laterally compressed body, a small mouth with many small teeth, tiny scales and leathery skin. The tail fin is the shape of a crescent moon with a sharp, scalpel-like venomous, moveable spine on each side of the body at the tail base. **Behaviour** It is found in gutters and channels on shallow outer reefs, scraping algae from rock or coral. Small or large colonies often occur, occupying adjacent territories of 6-8 sq m on the bottom. Adults occupy the central areas with juveniles around the periphery. They attack other algal-feeding intruders, using their spines in territorial defence, and can inflict a painful wound if mishandled. **Reproduction** Larvae drift with the currents, often to subtropical areas where they stay for several months. **Diet** Alage. **Habitat** Shallow coastal and outer reefs with wave action, to about 6 m deep.

FAMILY **TETRAODONTIDAE**   SPECIES *Canthigaster valentini*   SIZE **TO 11 CM**

SADDLED PUFFER

The skin and organs of this fish contain nerve poisons that are highly toxic to humans and other fish mimic pufferfish to deter predators. It has a small, beak-like mouth with fused teeth divided in the front, and 4 black bands across its back, the middle 2 tapering towards a stripe on the belly. Adults become spotted with many thin lines on the snout and chin. Males have iridescent green lines radiating behind the eyes. **Behaviour** Often seen openly over shallow to moderately deep reefs in pairs, they are territorial and males defend the area, biting intruders. If threatened it inflates its body to almost balloon-like proportions to deter predators. Out of the water this puffing-up process creates a croaking sound, and they are also known as toadfish. Juveniles hide in the coral, often among sea urchins. **Diet** Algae, worms, small invertebrates. **Habitat** Coastal and offshore coral reefs to about 20 m deep.

Marine Invertebrates

The diversity of marine invertebrate life is immense, from single-celled protozoans to intelligent animals such as squids and octopuses. Sponges are simple multi-celled animals in which different types of cells cooperate to form the complete creature. If separated, each cell can survive and reaggregate to form new individuals.

Corals, sea jellies and sea anemones are more complex colonial animals, armed with stinging tentacles fringing a mouth leading to a gut cavity lined with digestive tissue. They all belong to the phylum Cnidaria and include so many strange and beautiful animals that it is difficult to believe that they are related.

Worms have specialised organs controlling reproduction, movement, excretion and coordination. Many marine worms bury themselves in the sand or mud, while others resemble feathers or fans attached to coral or rocks. Some move by the synchronised beating of tiny hair-like structures while others have muscular segments giving them great flexibilty.

The segmented body plan has allowed the arthropods to dominate life on earth, and they are well represented in marine habitats by the crustaceans. All crustaceans have an external skeleton with appendages for feeding, sensing their surroundings, movement, respiration and mating. They range in size from tiny water fleas to crabs weighing up to 17 kg.

Molluscs are even more varied in body form. They include limpets, oysters, slugs, clams, squids and octopuses. All have soft, fleshy bodies, and most breathe through gills and have an external shell, although some groups have an internal shell.

Echinoderms, like molluscs, do not have segmented bodies. They include sea stars, sea urchins and sea cucumbers. All have a hydraulic system of water-filled canals to move the hundreds of tiny tube-feet that propel the animal along.

PHYLUM **PORIFERA**   SIZE **TO 2 M**

SPONGES

Sponges are the simplest and most ancient multi-celled animals. Australia has more than 5000 species, varying from thin encrustations to whips, fans or massive volcano shapes. They may be drab or vibrantly-coloured, soft or brittle. **Features** Sponges grow permanently attached to the sea bed or other submerged structures. They lack identifiable organs and are essentially a labyrinth of canals and chambers made of soft protein, often strengthened by sharp, microscopic spicules. These house masses of minute cells working in groups to carry out the basic functions of life, such as feeding, breathing and reproduction. **Feeding** Water drawn in through pores is pumped through the canals by special cells beating their whip-like tails in unison, and filtered to extract nutrients and oxygen. **Reproduction** Sponges reproduce by budding and fragmentation, or sexually by releasing both eggs and sperm. The eggs hatch into tiny swimming larvae that eventually settle on a surface and grow into a sponge. **Habitat** Deep oceans to shallow rock pools, creeks, rivers.

Vasiform sponge

PHYLUM **CNIDARIA**   CLASS **ANTHOZOA**

CORALS

Corals are an extraordinary group of animals that appear to be more like rocks than living creatures. Many take on amazing shapes and vibrant colours, creating mounds, plates, branches and crusts in dazzling reds, yellows and blues. Corals take dissolved calcium carbonate from the water and produce stony deposits around them, creating the frameworks of coral reefs found in warm tropical seas around the world. **Features** Corals are modular organisms based on a single tiny polyp that divides to replicate itself over and over again, creating a colony comprising hundreds of polyps united by common tissue connections. Young polyps build on the old, hard skeleton, of dead polyps, forming shapes that are determined by the genetic make-up of the original polyp. Thousands of polyps may live in one colony, and colonies may mass together to form a huge structure covering the sea floor.

Daisy coral

Most corals have millions of tiny single-celled plants (zooxanthellae) in their tissues. They produce food by photosynthesis, and some is absorbed by the coral, limiting it to shallow water where enough sunlight penetrates. Corals can be distinguished by their skeletons. Reefs are actually built by hard corals which have a white, limestone skeleton. Soft corals have tiny crystalline structures in their tissues and form tough, but fleshy structures. The beautiful fans and whips are known as gorgonian corals. They have a flexible skeleton of proteins, minerals and limestone. **Feeding** Most corals feed at night. They catch tiny floating animals from the surrounding waters by extending tentacles armed with stinging cells. When touched, the cells fire barbed darts that paralyse and hold the prey until the polyp's tentacles transfer it to its mouth. Food is broken down in the polyp's stomach and helps to nourish the whole colony. **Reproduction** Coral colonies can reproduce from broken fragments, or sexually by participating in mass synchronised spawnings. These happen in the week following a full moon in late spring or early summer. Most corals are hermaphrodites and produce tiny pink, red or orange spheres containing bundles of eggs and sperm. Fertilisation takes place on the surface where the bundles break up to release the eggs and sperm. Fertilised eggs become tiny larvae and float with the currents for a few days before settling in a suitable site to grow. **Habitat** Warm coastal waters to 60 m deep.

Gorgonian fan

Brain coral

| PHYLUM **CNIDARIA** | CLASS **HYDROZOA** | SPECIES *Physalia physalis* | SIZE **TO 3 M** |

PORTUGUESE MAN-O'-WAR

Also known as the 'bluebottle' this marine stinger floats around the oceans in large groups, and is often found washed up on beaches in eastern Australia. Some individuals are blown to the left and others to the right, ensuring that not all end up ashore. **Features** This animal is actually a colony of 4 types of polyps (zooids). A blue, air-filled bladder to 15 cm long keeps the animal afloat. Hanging below are feeding zooids with sucker-like mouths, male and female reproductive zooids, and long, thin, fishing tentacles armed with stinging cells that remain potent long after the animal has been washed up. **Feeding** Small animals are stunned by stinging cells and pulled to the feeding zooids where they are digested. **Reproduction** Large groups congregate, generally in autumn, and release eggs or sperm into the water. Fertilized eggs develop into small floating larvae. They form an adult bluebottle by budding. **Habitat** Tropical and subtropical marine waters.

| PHYLUM **CNIDARIA** | ORDER **CUBOMEDUSAE** | SPECIES *Chironex fleckeri* | SIZE **TO 3 M** |

SEA WASP

This box jellyfish is one of Australia's most dangerous marine animals and has caused many human deaths. **Features** Adults have a transparent, pale-blue, cube-shaped bell to 35 cm across with up to 15 tentacles extending from each corner bearing millions of stinging cells. Each side of the bell has a niche containing 3 eyes and a balance organ. Usually solitary, they actively hunt prey, swimming with jet-like propulsion at up to 7 km/h. **Feeding** Small marine animals, stunned by stinging cells, are lifted to the mouth by a feeding appendage. **Reproduction** Before dying in late summer, adults release millions of eggs or sperm into river mouths. They hatch into small, free-swimming larvae, and eventually settle beneath rocks in creeks. Here they metamorphose into small polyps. These feed and bud into new polyps, and in November each buds off a baby sea wasp. They swim to coastal waters and grow into adults. **Habitat** Shallow tropical coastal waters, creeks, estuaries.

| PHYLUM **CNIDARIA** | ORDER **ACTINIARIA** | SPECIES *Actinia tenebrosa* | SIZE **TO 4 CM** |

WARATAH ANEMONE

Usually seen at low tide, this common sea anemone looks like a dark red, jelly-like blob attached to a rock. **Features** It comprises a jelly-like column containing a gastric cavity and reproductive organs. The column has a central mouth surrounded by up to 200 feeding tentacles, and when exposed to the air the tentacles and mouth contract into the cavity. The base of the column sticks firmly to a rock, but the anemone can move imperceptibly slowly towards food or to attack and devour unrelated anemones. Small iridescent blue bumps beneath the tentacles contain stinging cells. **Feeding** Crustaceans, worms, fish and other small animals are trapped by the tentacles, stunned by the stinging cells and pulled to the mouth. **Reproduction** Young anemones develop in the gastric cavity. Miniature adults are ejected through the mouth and often settle close to their parents. **Habitat** Rocky crevices and the undersurfaces of rocks in the intertidal zone in tropical and temperate waters.

PHYLUM **ANNELIDA**   FAMILY **ONUPHIDAE**   SPECIES *Australonuphis teres*   SIZE **TO 3 M**

KING WORM

Prized by anglers as bait, this large, muscular bristleworm lives in the sand at the low-water mark and pops its head out when it detects food. **Features** It lives in burrows beneath the sand, secreting mucus to support the walls. Each segment has a pair of paddle-like structures with tiny bristles. The large front segments are modified for digging. Smaller lower segments bear comb-like gills, and grip the sand during locomotion.
Feeding This voracious carnivore has a ring of sensitive tentacles around its mouth enabling it to detect pipis, other burrowing animals and rotting flesh. To feed, the worm pushes its muscular throat through its mouth, turning it inside out to expose its strong, horny jaws. **Reproduction** Separate sexes synchronise the release of eggs or sperm into the overlying water where fertilization occurs. Microscopic larvae swim freely before settling on the sand to become juvenile worms. **Habitat** Low tide zone on sandy beaches.

PHYLUM **ARTHROPODA**   FAMILY **RHYNCHOCINETIDAE**   SPECIES *Rhynchocinetes durbanensis*   SIZE **TO 5 CM**

DURBAN DANCING SHRIMP

This colourful crustacean is common on the Great Barrier Reef. It has a humpback and is transparent with red and white spots and bars. **Features** It has 5 pairs of legs, a pair of feeding limbs, 2 pairs of sensitive antennae, bulging eyes on stalks, and a hinged beak between its eyes that can move up and down independently of its head. The abdomen bears short swimmerets and a tail fan used for locomotion. It congregates in large numbers in deep crevices and rocky caves by day, and emerges to feed at night. It moves across the seabed with a dancing motion, hence its common name. It has a hard outer skeleton and grows by periodically shedding its shell. **Feeding** It feeds on small food particles gleaned from the seabed. **Reproduction** Females carry their eggs under their tail until they hatch into miniature adults and settle among the coral. **Habitat** Subtidal areas on coral reefs.

PHYLUM **ARTHROPODA**   FAMILY **MYCTIRIDAE**   SPECIES *Mictyris longicarpus*   SIZE **TO 3 CM**

LIGHT BLUE SOLDIER CRAB

This globular crab has a dark patch on the joints of its legs. **Features** Vast numbers of these small crabs swarm on beaches and mud flats at low tide, moving together like an army. Unlike other crabs they move forward instead of sideways. As the tide comes in or if threatened they spiral into the damp sand, digging on one side while walking backwards on the other side. **Feeding** They feed on minute organisms and fine organic matter, sifted from the mud or sand by their bristly mouthparts. Non-organic matter is discarded as round pellets that litter the surface at low tide. **Reproduction** After mating females carry fertilized eggs beneath the abdomen. They hatch into tiny larvae and swim away into open water. A few weeks later the larvae moult into miniature adults and settle in a suitable habitat. **Habitat** Low tide zone on sandy beaches and mud flats.

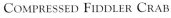

| PHYLUM **ARTHROPODA** | FAMILY **OCYPODIDAE** | SPECIES *Uca coarctata* | SIZE **TO 3 CM** |

COMPRESSED FIDDLER CRAB

Males have a grossly enlarged, orange right-hand claw and one small feeding claw. Females have two small feeding claws. The eyes are raised on long, thin stalks. **Features** They live in a burrow, high up on creek banks and sloping mudflats, emerging to feed at low tide. Males wave their large claw as a courtship display and use it to fight other males for their burrows after mating. **Feeding** They scrape up the surface sediment with their small feeding claws, transfer it to the mouth where organic matter is sifted out, and spit out pellets of clean sand. **Reproduction** Females time egg release to coincide with the spring tide. They mate in the male's burrow and the female incubates the eggs below her abdomen for 2 weeks while sealed in the burrow. They hatch into free-swimming larvae and are swept out to sea where they grow and moult for a few weeks before washing inshore. **Habitat** Tidal creeks and rivers, mangroves.

| PHYLUM **ARTHROPODA** | FAMILY **PAGURIDAE** | SPECIES *Pagurus sinuatus* | SIZE **TO 10 CM** |

RED HERMIT CRAB

This common crab has a red body and hairy claws and takes over an abandoned snail shell to protect it from preda-tors. **Features** Hermit crabs have one pair of claws and 4 pairs of legs. They lack an external skeleton and have a soft and delicate abdomen that twists spirally to fit into the borrowed shell. The abdomen is equipped with hook-like appendages to hold it in the shell, which it drags around using its walking legs. They move to a larger shell to grow, and carefully inspect shells before moving. Fights over empty shells are common. Large gill chambers hold water, allowing the crab to wander far from water. **Feeding** Predominantly a scav-enger, it eats food scraps and preys on crabs and other small animals. **Reproduction** Females lay eggs in the water. They hatch into small larvae that drift and feed on plankton, moulting into young adults before settling in a suitable site. **Habitat** Intertidal rocky shores, beaches, mangroves, estuaries and seagrass beds.

| PHYLUM **MOLLUSCA** | FAMILY **TRIDACNIDAE** | SPECIES *Tridacna maxima* | SIZE **TO 35 CM** |

GIANT CLAM

This two-shelled aquatic mollusc is common in shallow parts of the reef, exposing its vividly-coloured, blue, green or brown mantle to the sun. **Features** The large fleshy mantle is fused together and water is taken in or out via 2 tubes (siphons). It attaches to coral by a thread-like tuft. If threatened it clos-es its shell and can expel a powerful jet of water through its exhalent siphon. Algae (zooxanthellae) are farmed in the mantle tissue and provide food by photosynthesis. Special organs focus light on pockets of algae to increase their effectiveness. **Feeding** Plankton is filtered from the water and carbohydrates are produced by the algae. **Reproduction** They are hermaphrodites and release first sperm and then eggs into the water. Fertilised eggs hatch into free swimming, shelled larvae. They begin to settle on the seabed about 2 weeks later and transform into miniature adults. **Habitat** Sandy sites on coral reefs in shallow tropical waters.

PHYLUM **MOLLUSCA**   FAMILY **DONACIDAE**   SPECIES *Plebidonax deltoides*   SIZE **TO 6 CM**

PIPI

This aquatic mollusc is common on exposed sandy beaches and is often used as bait. Its smooth, hinged shell, is white, yellow or light pink outside and purple inside. **Features** It lives just below the sand and when exposed by receding waves quickly burrows back in with its muscular foot. Its fleshy mantle is enclosed in the shell, while two small tubes (siphons) are usually exposed. One takes water, sand and mud into the shell while a smaller one passes waste products out. **Feeding** Plankton and small food particles are filtered from mud and sand by the gills and carried by tiny, beating hairs and fleshy appendages to the mouth. **Reproduction** Males and females release sperm and eggs into the water over a long period. Fertilised eggs hatch into minute, free-swimming, plankton-feeding larvae. They disperse along the coast before settling and transforming into miniature adults. **Habitat** Sandy beaches in the intertidal and subtidal zones.

PHYLUM **MOLLUSCA**   FAMILY **CONIDAE**   SPECIES *Conus textile*   SIZE **TO 13 CM**

TEXTILE CONE-SHELL

This dangerous marine snail has highly potent venom and should be handled with great care. **Features** A carnivorous gastropod, it lives in shallow water and hides under stones or burrows into the sand with its tube-like proboscis protruding from the narrow end of its shell. It crawls slowly along the seabed using its flat, fleshy, muscular foot, waving its proboscis around to detect prey. **Feeding** It eats other molluscs, paralysing them almost instantly with a powerful neurotoxin delivered by long, slender, barbed darts These are modified teeth, filled with poison and fired from the proboscis when prey comes within reach. **Reproduction** Females deposit capsules containing around 600 eggs under rocks on the sea bed. They hatch into microscopic, free-swimming, shelled larvae and feed on plankton before settling and transforming into miniature adults. **Habitat** Shallow coastal waters, reefs, rock pools, rubble-strewn sandy seabeds.

PHYLUM **MOLLUSCA**   FAMILY **NAUTILIDAE**   SPECIES *Nautilus pompilius*   SIZE **TO 20 CM**

CHAMBERED NAUTILUS

Almost unchanged for 550 million years, this mollusc is a cephalopod with an external shell. **Features** The spiralled shell contains up to 30 chambers connected by a tube called a siphuncle, used to pump gas into the chambers to alter the shell's buoyancy. The animal lives in the outer chamber and has about 90 small suckerless tentacles beneath a tough hood attaching it to the shell. It has eyes without lenses and moves by forcing a jet of water out of a funnel, or pulls iself along with its tentacles. It lives in deep water and rises at night to feed. **Feeding** It feeds on small fish, crustaceans and carrion detected by smell. **Reproduction** The male transfers a packet of sperm to the female using 4 of its tentacles. Females lay oblong eggs about 4 cm long. They hatch into miniature shelled nautiluses and become sexually mature at 15-20 years. **Habitat** Tropical waters off reef edges to 500m deep.

129

PHYLUM **MOLLUSCA**   FAMILY **OCTOPODIDAE**   SPECIES *Hapalochlaena lunulata*   SIZE **TO 20 CM**

GREATER BLUE-RINGED OCTOPUS

This dangerous cephalopod produces powerful venom in its salivary glands that can kill a human in minutes.

Features It hides in crevices and shells, emerging to feed or mate, crawling along using its 8 long arms, or propelling itself with water squirted from a tube at the base of the arms. It changes colour according to its mood or surroundings, and when threatened its blue markings become vividly iridescent. It has excellent vision and the suckers on its arms are sensitive to taste and touch.

Feeding It hunts fish, crustaceans and other marine animals, bites them with its beak-like jaws and injects venom. **Reproduction** Males transfer packets of sperm to females using a modified arm. The female lays 60-100 eggs and carries them under her arms until they hatch into free-swimming larvae about 50 days later. She dies from starvation after hatching her young, who mature at 4 months. **Habitat** Rock pools in shallow tropical waters.

PHYLUM **MOLLUSCA**   FAMILY **LOLIGINIDAE**   SPECIES *Sepioteuthis lessoniana*   SIZE **TO 36 CM**

BIGFIN REEF SQUID

This squid is often seen close to the beach and around lights at night. **Features** They have an internal, plastic-like shell, 8 arms lined with suckers and 2 longer feeding tentacles around the mouth. They live in schools and can swim very fast by squirting water from a moveable tube at the base of the arms. They have excellent vision and change colour to match their surroundings or indicate their mood. If threatened they eject a blob of purple ink to distract predators. **Feeding** They hunt for fish, crustaceans and other marine animals at night, using their tentacles to seize prey and pull it to their beak-like jaws. **Reproduction** Males transfer packets of eggs to the female with a modified arm. Females lay clutches of finger-like egg capsules containing 10 large eggs in crevices in the coral or on the seabed. They hatch 15-30 days later into miniature adults, grow rapidly and die after spawning. **Habitat** Coastal waters around coral reefs and seagrasses.

PHYLUM **MOLLUSCA**   FAMILY **SEPIDAE**   SPECIES *Sepia apama*   SIZE **TO 1.5 M**

GIANT CUTTLEFISH

This cephalopod is the world's largest cuttlefish. **Features** Usually solitary, it moves by crawling, swimming or by squirting water from a funnel at the base of its arms. It has an internal cuttlebone about 60 cm long, 2 retractable feeding tentacles and 8 arms lined with suckers. It has excellent vision, changes colour to match its surroundings, and generates spectacular colour displays to indicate its mood. If threatened it ejects ink to distract predators. **Feeding** Fish and crustaceans are seized with the feeding tentacles and crushed by its beak-like jaws. **Reproduction** In autumn thousands congregate to mate in rocky shallows. Males display to establish dominance, pulsing with vivid colours. They interlock arms while mating and the male deposits a sperm capsule into a pouch below the female's mouth with a modified arm. She lays about 200 golf ball-size eggs in rock crevices. They hatch into miniature adults in spring. Adults die after spawning at 2-3 years old. **Habitat** Coastal waters, oceans and estuaries.

PHYLUM **MOLLUSCA**   FAMILY **CALIPHYLLIDAE**   SPECIES *Cyerce nigricans*   SIZE **TO 4 CM**

SARCOGLOSSAN SEA SLUG

This brightly-coloured mollusc is only distantly related to the land slug. It has no shell and is often seen on reefs at low tide. **Features** Like other gastropods it crawls on the substrate using its flat, fleshy, muscular foot. It has sensory tentacles on its head and a rasp-like tongue called a radula. The leaf-like body projections contain branches of the slug's gut. They also contain noxious chemicals that deter predatory fish. **Feeding** It grazes on algae and has a modified radula equipped with a row of dagger-like teeth which it uses to pierce algal cells and suck out their nutritious contents. **Reproduction** Females produce ribbon-like masses of eggs in the form of flattened spirals and attach them to submerged rocks or coral. The eggs hatch into free-swimming larvae before settling and transforming into minia-ture adults. **Habitat** Shallow coastal waters, rock pools, reef flats.

PHYLUM **MOLLUSCA**   FAMILY **CHROMODORIDIDAE**   SPECIES *Chromodoris elisabethina*   SIZE **TO 5 CM**

ELISABETH'S CHROMIODORIS

This brightly-coloured sea slug has naked external gills and is one of many nudibranchs in Australian waters. **Features** Like other gastropods it has a fleshy mantle, a rasp-like tongue (the radula), and moves using its fleshy foot, but lacks a shell. The head has short, sensory tentacles and the posterior end has exposed gill plumes. They are generally solitary, cannot see or hear, and use chemoreceptors on the tentacles to find a mate or food. Noxious chemicals ingested with the food are stored in their skin and deter predators. **Feeding** It is carnivorous and feeds on encrusting sponges, using its radula to scrape off the sponge and ingest it. **Reproduction** They are her-maphrodites, and mate by passing sperm to another nudibranch through a common opening in the side of the body. Eggs are laid in masses and hatch into free-swimming larvae. They eventually metamorphose into miniature adults. **Habitat** Shallow tropical coastal waters.

PHYLUM **ECHINODERMATA**   FAMILY **GONIASTERIDAE**   SPECIES *Pentagonaster dubeni*   SIZE **TO 8 CM**

BISCUIT SEA STAR

This distinctive sea star is glossy orange, red or yellow with smooth, rounded plates. **Features** It has hollow arms con-taining identical sets of respiratory, digestive and sex organs. A groove beneath each arm is edged with tiny, flexible, hydraulic, suckered tube feet, enabling it to creep over the seabed. Sensory cells on the suckers detect food and predators, and a simple eye-spot on the tip of each arm detects light intensi-ty. **Feeding** Shrimps, snails and other small creatures are cap-tured by the tube feet and passed to the mouth at the centre of the underside of the body. The stomach can be turned inside out through the mouth to digest large prey. **Reproduction** They can reproduce by tearing themselves into two parts and regenerating new arms, or sexually by releasing millions of eggs and sperm into the water. Fertilised eggs hatch into plankton-feeding lar-vae and eventually metamorphose into miniature adults. **Habitat** Rock pools, and among boulders in the intertidal zone and deeper coastal waters.

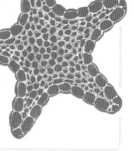

PHYLUM **ECHINODERMATA**   FAMILY **OPHIODERMATIDAE**   SPECIES *Ophiarachnella ramsayi*   SIZE **TO 12 CM**

RAMSAY'S BRITTLE STAR

This common echinoderm has coloured arm bands varying from bright pink and greenish black to greenish brown and grey.

Features Brittle stars have a rounded central disc containing the major organs and 5 long, snake-like arms. The flexible arms have tiny vertebrae. They are shed if the animal is attacked, but regenerate rapidly. They lack eyes but can sense light. Tiny tube feet beneath the arms have chemical receptors at the tips. Solitary and nocturnal, this species hides under rocks in pockets of sand or gravel. The arms are covered in short spines and propel the animal rapidly along with a rowing or snake-like motion. **Feeding** Detritus and small animals are detected by receptors on the tube feet and passed to the mouth by the arms. **Reproduction** They reproduce sexually by releasing millions of eggs and sperm into the water. Fertilised eggs hatch into plankton-feeding, armed larvae and eventually metamorphose into adults. **Habitat** Rock pools and shallow waters to 70 m.

PHYLUM **ECHINODERMATA**   FAMILY **HIMEROMETRIDAE**   SPECIES *Himerometra robustipinna*   SIZE **TO 30 CM**

ROBUST FEATHER STAR

The arms of this delicate, flower-like echinoderm are bright crimson above and pale-grey below. **Features** It has a cup-shaped body with a central disc surrounded by more than 50 branched feathery arms bearing tiny tube feet and coated with a sticky mucus. It often rests in exposed places by day with its arms curled up. It feeds at night, positioned in a water current, clinging to a coral head with strong, grasping claws beneath the body disc. It waves its arms to create a large net that traps passing food particles. It can crawl using its arms or swim short distances. **Feeding** Tube feet on the feathery arms grasp plankton and pass them along a groove to the mouth on the upper side of the disc. **Reproduction** Reproductive organs in the arms shed eggs or sperm into the water. The fertilised eggs hatch into tiny, plankton-feeding larvae and eventually metamorphose into the adult form. **Habitat** Tropical coastal waters around reefs to about 60 m.

PHYLUM **ECHINODERMATA**   FAMILY **ACANTHASTERIDAE**   SPECIES *Acanthaster planci*   SIZE **TO 70 CM**

CROWN-OF-THORNS STARFISH

This venomous echinoderm has destroyed large areas of coral on the Great Barrier Reef.

Features It hides under coral ledges and emerges at night to feed. It has up to 23 arms, each with hundreds of tiny, hydraulic tube feet lining a groove on the underside. The upper surface is covered with long spines coated with toxic mucus. Its mouth is under the body and the major organs are in the arms which are tipped with light-sensitive eye-spots. Chemical receptors on the tube feet detect other feeding sea stars, and large groups often gather around them. **Feeding** It settles on a coral colony, turns its stomach out through its mouth and slowly digests the coral polyps. **Reproduction** Millions of eggs and sperm are released into the water. The eggs hatch into free-swimming, plankton-eating larvae and eventually metamorphose into adults. **Habitat** Tropical coastal waters around coral reefs.

PHYLUM **ECHINODERMATA**   FAMILY **ECHINIDAE**   SPECIES *Tripneustes gratilla*   SIZE **TO 15 CM**

HAIRY SEA URCHIN

This echinoderm often covers itself with shells, pebbles or seaweed. It is brown to purple with short white spines sometimes tipped with orange, and hundreds of long, white or pale brown tube feet protruding through pores in the body wall. **Features** The mouth is on the underside and the anus on top. Apart from its vital organs the body is filled with fluid, allowing room for massive expansion of the gonads in the breeding season. It pulls itself around using its manoeuvrable spines and tube feet. **Feeding** They eat seaweed, algae scraped from rocks and small animals including molluscs. The tube feet transfer food to the mouth. **Reproduction** Clouds of sperm and eggs are released into the water. Fertilised eggs hatch into tiny gelatinous larvae with long, swimming arms. They feed on plankton for several weeks then settle on new reefs and transform into miniature adults. **Habitat** Intertidal rock pools, coastal waters to 75 m.

PHYLUM **ECHINODERMATA**   FAMILY **HOLOTHURIDAE**   SPECIES *Bohadschia argus*   SIZE **TO 40 CM**

LEOPARD SEA CUCUMBER

This sausage-shaped echinoderm is common on lagoon floors. Its leathery, flexible body is adorned with brown to reddish spots and is often partly buried in the sand. **Features** They rest by day and feed at night moving slowly along the seabed using rows of tube feet beneath the body and rythmic body contractions. If threatened they eject fine sticky threads from their anus. These entangle and immobilise a crab or small fish. **Feeding** Feeding tentacles surrounding the mouth are wiped over the sediment to pick up food particles and transfer them to the mouth. **Reproduction** Mass spawnings occur in spring when separate sexes rise to the top of the reef and release clouds of eggs and sperm into the currents. Fertilised eggs hatch into tiny, plankton-feeding larvae. They swim for several weeks, then settle on the bottom and metamorphose into miniature adults. **Habitat** Tropical coastal waters to 20 m.

PHYLUM **CHORDATA**   CLASS **ASCIDIACEAE**   SPECIES *Polycarpa aurata*   SIZE **TO 15 CM**

INK SPOT SEA SQUIRT

This reef animal is thought to be an ancester of the vertebrates although it has no backbone. It is stained with irregular white, yellow and blue blotches. **Features** It lives permanently attached to a rock or reef and has a sac-like body with 2 openings (siphons) that move water in and out of the body. A tough, leathery coat protects its delicate, sieve-like internal filtering system. Minute hairs inside the siphons beat regularly to push water in and out, and if threatened, muscles in the body wall contract to squirt water out. **Feeding** Plankton and small food particles are filtered out by thousands of gill slits lining the body cavity. **Reproduction** It has both male and female sex organs, although they mature at different times to avoid self-fertilisation. Sperm and eggs are released into the water and fertilised eggs hatch into free-swimming, tadpole-like larvae. They eventually attach to a surface with sticky glands at the front, absorb their tails and metamorphose into juveniles. **Habitat** Reefs and rocky coasts, 3-20 m deep.

Land Invertebrates

Animal life began with the invertebrates some 4 billion years ago, and today there are millions of invertebrate species. The majority remain undescribed, making this one of the least explored frontiers of biological science.

Worms are generally considered to be slimy, limbless, creatures, yet these fascinating invertebrates are so diverse that biologists have grouped them into 11 different phyla. Most Australians are familiar with leeches, but few are aware of the elegant velvet worms, found in rotting logs and leaf litter. These remarkable creatures have been around for more than 500 million years and share features with both segmented worms and arthropods.

More than 100,000 species of mollusc have been described. Most have an external shell to protect their soft body, and the majority live in water. Among the land molluscs, the most familiar are the snails and slugs. They belong to the class Gastropodia and are found in habitats as diverse as shady rainforests and arid deserts. Gastropods have a flat, fleshy, muscular foot, and well-formed heads bearing sensory tentacles, eyes and a rasp-like tongue. Most land snails and all land slugs have lungs and breathe through a small pore in their side. They are also active mainly at night when it is cooler and more humid.

Three-quarters of the known living animal species are arthropods, and they dominate life on the land. They include insects, millipedes, crustaceans, spiders, scorpions, ticks and lice. Their success is partly due to their segmented body plan, although in various groups the segments have fused into one body part, such as the head of a fly which has 6 segments fused into one. The limbs of these segments form sensory antennae and mouthparts. Specialised limbs underpin most arthropod activities, and insects have greatly enhanced their success by developing wings.

PHYLUM **MOLLUSCA**   FAMILY **ATHORACOPHORIDAE**   SPECIES *Triboniophorus graeffei*   SIZE **TO 14 CM**

RED TRIANGLE SLUG

Australia's largest land slug, this mollusc has rough skin with a red or red-outlined triangle on its back. The body may be white, yellow, grey, green, orange or red. **Features** Land slugs breathe through a small pore in their fleshy mantle, marked in this species by the red triangle on its back. They are active mainly at night when it is cool and moist, and crawl along by rhythmic muscular contraction of their flat foot, helped by a layer of mucus that glues them to the substrate. The head bears a pair of tentacles sensitive to light and smell, and a rasplike tongue called a radula used to macerate food. **Feeding** They graze on algae, fungi and lichen growing on tree trunks (particularly eucalypts) and rocks, leaving zigzag feeding tracks. **Reproduction** They are hermaphroditic, having both male and female sex organs. Mating slugs exchange sperm through their protruding genitalia. A few days later about 30 eggs are laid into a hole in the ground. They hatch into tiny slugs. **Habitat** Forests, woodlands, heaths, parks, gardens.

PHYLUM **ANNELIDA**   FAMILY **HAEMADIPSIDAE**   SPECIES *Chtonobdella limbata*   SIZE **TO 5 CM**

AUSTRALIAN LAND LEECH

This blood-sucking segmented worm is commonly encountered by bushwalkers. It is brown to black with a yellow to orange stripe. **Features** Leeches have a slimy body with 34 segments and a powerful sucker at each end. They live in moist sites on the ground or foliage and move with a looping motion, attaching their front and back suckers alternately to the surface. Sense organs on the head and body detect smell, light intensity, temperature and vibration. **Feeding** They feed on blood, slicing into the host with their jaws and secreting an anticoagulant and a histamine to dilate the blood vessels before sucking out the blood. They can store enough blood to survive for several months. **Reproduction** They are hermaphrodites and intertwine their bodies to mate, each depositing sperm into a saddle-like structure (the clitellum) on the other leech. Fertilised eggs are contained in a tough cocoon and either buried or attached to a rock, log or leaf. Miniature adults emerge several weeks later. **Habitat** Forests and woodlands.

PHYLUM **ONCHYOPHORA**   FAMILY **PERIPATOPSIDAE**   SIZE **TO 3 CM**

VELVET WORM

Velvet worms have remained almost unchanged for more than 500 million years and share features with segmented worms and arthropods. **Features**, They hide by day in rotting logs, leaf litter and other moist sites and emerge at night to feed, moving on pairs of short, unjointed, clawed legs. They have velvety skin and a soft, segmented body. The head bears a pair of mobile sensory antennae, 2 simple-lensed eyes, and a mouth with sharp, slashing jaws. **Feeding** They are carnivorous and trap small invertebrates by shooting sticky threads from projections on each side of the head. The threads set hard, immobilising the prey, which is macerated, mixed with saliva and sucked into the worm's mouth. **Reproduction** They have separate sexes and males deposit packets of sperm in the female. In some species the males have spikes, pits and other structures on their heads to hold the sperm packets. Some species give birth to live young, others lay shelled eggs. Newborn are miniature adults. **Habitat** Wet forests.

PHYLUM **ARTHROPODA**   FAMILY **LIBELLULIDAE**   SPECIES *Orthretrum villosovittatum*   SIZE **TO 6 CM**

TROPICAL DRAGONFLY

Often seen resting with their gauzy wings spread horizontally, or circling over ponds and creeks, dragonflies are the aerial gymnasts of the insect world. Males are usually more brightly coloured and the different sexes can spot each other from as far away as 40 m. **Features** They fly backwards and forwards, dash in circular territorial flight patterns and swoop on prey at up to 50 km/h. They have large compound eyes and their short spiny legs form a cage for holding prey. **Feeding** Small insects are seized with the legs and eaten in flight. **Reproduction** During courtship the male clasps the female's head with his tail claspers while in flight. The female inserts her tail into the male's sperm pouch and lays strings of fertilised eggs into water. They hatch into aquatic larvae and feed on small animals. Nymphs leave the water about one year later, climb a plant stem and moult into the adult form. **Habitat** Freshwater pools and creeks.

PHYLUM **ARTHROPODA**   FAMILY **BLATTIDAE**   SPECIES *Polyzosteria mitchelli*   SIZE **TO 6 CM**

STRIPED COCKROACH

This giant, wingless, native cockroach is often seen in heathlands and emits a pungent odour to deter predators. **Features** Although most cockroaches are nocturnal, this species is active by day and often basks in the sunlight on trees and shrubs. It has a flattened body protected above by a tough shield with overlapping segments. The head bears long, sensitive antennae, a pair of compound eyes, and chewing mouthparts with strong, toothed mandibles. The 6 spiky legs are built for running and bear sensors that detect air vibrations and light. **Feeding** They probably feed on organic matter in the leaf litter. **Reproduction** Females lay 12-40 eggs in an egg capsule that protrudes from the end of her abdomen and is carried around before being deposited in ground litter or on a tree trunk. Wingless nymphs emerge from the capsule and resemble miniature adults. They develop slowly, moulting 6-12 times to reach adult size. **Habitat** Heaths, woodlands, forests, caves.

PHYLUM **ARTHROPODA**   FAMILY **RHINOTERMITIDAE**   SPECIES *Coptotermes lacteus*   SIZE **3-12 MM**

MILK TERMITE

These termites usually build conical mounds to 2 m high with clay walls, and are commonly seen in eucalypt forests. **Features** They are active in the dark and live in colonies established by a winged pair who find a suitable site, shed their wings and lay their first eggs. The eggs hatch into sterile workers who enlarge the nest into a mound and feed the king and queen. The queen lives in the centre of the mound and is attended by workers while larger soldier termites protect the colony. Conditions are controlled by opening and closing ventilation channels on the outside of the mound and bringing moist material in. **Feeding** Workers collect mostly weathered wood and partially digest it to feed the colony. **Reproduction** The queen is the colony's only reproductive female and lays up to 2000 eggs per day for many years. They hatch into nymphs who moult 7 times to become workers, soldiers or, at certain times of year, winged males and females who fly off to start new colonies. **Habitat** Forests and woodlands.

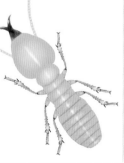

| PHYLUM **ARTHROPODA** | FAMILY **MANTIDAE** | SPECIES *Orthodera ministralis* | SIZE **TO 6 CM** |

PRAYING MANTID

This common mantid has a triangular head, a wide, flattened thorax and bulging eyes. It is one of about 160 species in Australia, so-called because they hold their forelegs in a prayer-like pose while waiting for prey. **Features** Their large eyes give them all-round vision. They have 2 pairs of wings and rows of hooked spines on the forelegs that face towards each other when the legs are folded. They are well camouflaged and hide motionless in the vegetation waiting to ambush prey. **Feeding** When an insect comes within range its spiny forelegs spring out and snap shut, impaling the victim on the spines. **Reproduction** A male approaches a female cautiously from behind, and may be decapitated by her while mating, although he still transfers a packet of sperm to her before dying. She lays 100-400 eggs into a foam case stuck to a branch or leaf. The foam hardens and wingless nymphs emerge from the egg case a few weeks later. They catch tiny insects and moult several times into winged adults. **Habitat** Heaths, forests, woodlands, parks, gardens.

| PHYLUM **ARTHROPODA** | FAMILY **ACRIDIDAE** | SPECIES *Petasida ephippigera* | SIZE **TO 5 CM** |

LEICHHARDT'S GRASSHOPPER

This strikingly coloured grasshopper is restricted to escarpment country in Arnhem Land, and is one of about 700 species in Australia. It stores plant toxins in its body and the bold red and blue markings are a warning to predators. **Features** Grasshoppers have powerful hindlegs and can leap 30 times their own length. They are active during the day and have 2 pairs of wings and relatively short antennae. Their hearing organs are located on the first segment of the abdomen. **Feeding** They eat mainly grass, supplemented with leaves and other vegetation. **Reproduction** Males produce clicking calls to attract females by rubbing a row of pegs on their hind legs against a scraper on the edge of their upper wings. Females dig a deep hole using spade-like plates at the tip of the abdomen and deposit masses of eggs inside a frothy coating that sets hard. Nymphs hatch in warm weather after rain and moult 5 times to become adults. **Habitat** Savanna grasslands and woodlands.

| PHYLUM **ARTHROPODA** | FAMILY **PHASMATIDAE** | SPECIES *Didymuria violescens* | SIZE **TO 13 CM** |

SPUR-LEGGED STICK INSECT

Plagues of this insect sometimes occur, defoliating whole eucalypt forests. When numbers are high the nymphs take on a pattern of black and yellow markings. **Features** Stick insects mimic twigs and sway slowly, making them very difficult to spot. They generally rest by day and feed at night, alone or in small numbers. They have a small head with compound eyes, a long thorax and long, spindly legs, often with strong spines. About half of Australia's 150 species have wings, although most females have short wings and are flightless. The forewings are short, the hindwings fan-like and usually hidden beneath drab wing covers. **Feeding** They eat a variety of leaves. **Reproduction** Females produce a scent to help males find them. If no male arrives, they may lay unfertilised eggs, producing female clones. The seed-like eggs are dropped to the ground and often remain dormant for months or years. Tiny nymphs emerge and moult 5-8 times to become adults. **Habitat** Forests, woodlands.

PHYLUM **ARTHROPODA**　　FAMILY **SCUTELLERIDAE**　SPECIES *Tectocoris diophthalmus*　SIZE **TO 2 CM**

COTTON HARLEQUIN BUG

This colourful shield bug is often found on hibiscus and cotton plants. Males are usually iridescent red, green and blue, while females are orange-yellow with dark spots.

Features Part of the thorax, called the scutellum, entirely covers the wings of shield bugs and looks like a single dome. They have 2 pairs of wings held flat over the back at rest. If disturbed they spray foul-smelling defensive secretions from their anal glands. Like other true bugs, their mouthparts are adapted for piercing tissue and sucking fluids, and bear sharp, slender tubes enclosed in a sheath when not in use. **Feeding** They suck sugary sap from young shoots of plants mostly belonging to the Malvaceae family. **Reproduction** To mate, the male mounts the female and then turns round to continue end-to-end. Females lay clusters of 50-500 eggs around a stem, and guard them until they hatch weeks or months later. Nymphs emerge and moult several times to reach maturity. **Habitat** Heaths, woodlands, parks, gardens.

PHYLUM **ARTHROPODA**　　FAMILY **CICADIDAE**　SPECIES *Cyclochila australasiae*　SIZE **TO 85 MM**

GREEN GROCER CICADA

This common cicada varies in colour from green to yellow, blue and brown, and its shrill song is a familiar sound of summer nights. **Features** Like the other true bugs it has piercing and sucking mouthparts, large, prominent, compound eyes and 4 wings. Males produce a shrill, distinct, sometimes ear-splitting call to attract females by vibrating drum-like membranes on each side of the body. These click like a tin lid 600 times a minute and the sound is amplified by the cicada's hollow abdomen. **Feeding** Nymphs feed on the sap of tree roots while underground. Adults feed on the sap of branches in the canopy. **Reproduction** Females lay eggs into slits cut into branches of their host tree with a spear-like egg-laying organ. Nymphs hatch a few weeks later, fall to the ground and use their front legs to burrow into the soil. They live underground for 2-4 years, emerge in early summer, climb the nearest tree and moult to become a winged adult. **Habitat** Forests, woodlands, heaths.

PHYLUM **ARTHROPODA**　　FAMILY **CARABIDAE**　SPECIES *Mecynognathus damelii*　SIZE **TO 75 MM**

GROUND BEETLE

Beetles belong to the largest order of insects on earth, the Coleoptera. Australia has more than 28,000 species and this is the continent's largest ground beetle. **Features** Most beetles shelter by day under stones and other objects and come out at night to feed. The forewings are modified into hard covers (elytra), held over the abdomen and meet in a straight line along the centre. This ground beetle lacks hindwings and is flightless. Like other ground beetles it is very active and has long, slender legs enabling it to run down small animals. **Feeding** Both adults and larvae capture ground-dwelling insects, slaters, worms and other small animals. Victims are torn apart with the beetle's powerful jaws. **Reproduction** The eggs hatch into predatory larvae with well-developed mouthparts. They moult several times and pupate in the soil, eventually emerging as adults. **Habitat** Open forests, rainforests.

| PHYLUM **ARTHROPODA** | ORDER **DIPTERA** | FAMILY **CULICIDAE** | SIZE **TO 6 MM** |

MOSQUITOES

These blood-sucking insects carry a number of disease organisms, including dengue fever, Ross River fever and encephalitis. There are around 275 species in Australia. **Features** They have long, piercing and sucking mouthparts, a single pair of long, narrow wings and large compound eyes. Males have feathery antennae. **Feeding** Males feed on sap and nectar, females feed on blood to produce eggs. They are attracted by exhaled carbon dioxide and some species are drawn to the odours of different body parts. Anticoagulants in the saliva cause itching and swelling. **Reproduction** Males are attracted to the whine of a female's wingbeats. They mate in flight and lay their eggs on water, although in arid areas the eggs may lay dormant for years. The aquatic larvae eat plant and animal particles and breathe through a siphon at the tip of the abdomen. They moult over 2-4 weeks and transform into swimming pupae. Adults emerge 2 days later. **Habitat** Most habitats.

| PHYLUM **ARTHROPODA** | ORDER **DIPTERA** | FAMILY **TABANIDAE** | SIZE **TO 3 CM** |

MARCH FLIES

Also known as horse flies, Australia has some 245 species of these stockily built insects. Most are bloodsuckers and many inflict humans with painful bites, although they do not carry diseases in Australia. **Features** Their rasping, needle-like mouthparts are adapted to piercing thick animal hides. They have a single pair of wings and large compound eyes, larger and iridescent-green in males. **Feeding** Males feed on nectar, while females need blood proteins to produce eggs. They are attracted to exhaled carbon dioxide, body heat and odours, and often to dark colours. Anticoagulants in the saliva produce an allergic reaction. **Reproduction** They mate in flight and females lay their eggs in damp sites or among floating vegetation. They often hatch in population waves, particularly in spring and summer. The larvae are aquatic with sharp mandibles, and feed on the larvae of other insects before turning into pupae. Adults emerge in warm weather. **Habitat** Freshwater creeks, intertidal estuaries, mangroves.

| PHYLUM **ARTHROPODA** | FAMILY **PAPILIONIDAE** | SPECIES *Ornithoptera priamus* | SIZE **TO 18 CM** |

CAIRNS BIRDWING BUTTERFLY

Australia's largest butterfly, the males are green, yellow and black, the larger females black, yellow and white. The caterpillars are dark-brown with red-banded fleshy spines. **Features** They fly by day and hold their wings erect when feeding. Males tend to stay in the canopy and may set up territories around larval food plants, ready to mate with newly-emerging females. Females spend most of their time close to the ground looking for plants to lay their eggs on. **Feeding** Adults suck up nectar with their coiled, straw-like proboscis. Caterpillars feed on native aristolochia vine leaves. **Reproduction** They mate tail-to-tail, and females lay eggs singly beneath the leaves of aristolochia vines. They hatch 5-10 days later and the caterpillars feed for about 2 weeks. When fully grown they pupate and the adult butterfly emerges one month later. It has a lifespan of 4-5 weeks. **Habitat** Tropical rainforests, parks, gardens.

139

PHYLUM **ARTHROPODA**   FAMILY **PAPILIONIDAE**   SPECIES *Papilio ulysses*   SIZE **TO 12 CM**

ULYSSES BUTTERFLY

One of Australia's most spectacular butterflies, its wings are iridescent blue and black above, and brown below with paler markings. The hindwings have a long, black, clubbed tail. Males have 6 brown elliptical marks on the forewings. The caterpillars are dark green with blue and white markings. **Features** Like other butterflies, they have overlapping scales on their wings, large compound eyes, and slender, club-tipped antennae. They soar above the canopy and males swoop down to investigate blue objects, while females search for the pink euodia flowers. **Feeding** Adults feed on nectar with their straw-like proboscis. The caterpillars eat euodia leaves. **Reproduction** Females lay their eggs singly beneath euodia leaves. They hatch about a week later and the caterpillars feed on the leaves, moulting 4-5 times over the next 2 weeks until fully grown, when they turn into pupae. The adult butterfly emerges from the pupa about one month later. **Habitat** Tropical rainforests, parks, gardens.

PHYLUM **ARTHROPODA**   FAMILY **NYMPHALIDAE**   SPECIES *Danaus plexippus*   SIZE **TO 12 CM**

WANDERER BUTTERFLY

This butterfly followed the introduction of its food plants from America to Australia in the 1870s. Adults have orange wings with black veins, black margins and white spots. Caterpillars are black with white and yellow bands. **Features** These butter-flies are tough and long-lived. Toxic chemicals from the food plants accumulate in their tissues and deter predators. In southern areas they hibernate in winter, often in large aggregations, or move to warmer areas. **Feeding** Adults feed on nectar. Caterpillars eat milkweeds leaves. **Reproduction** Females are attracted by chemicals produced by scent glands at the tip of the male's abdomen. Pairs spiral in courtship flights and alight to mate. The eggs are laid on young milkweed shoots and hatch about a week later. The caterpillars moult several times until fully grown at 3-4 cm and transform into pale-green pupae. Adults emerge about a month later. **Habitat** Forests, woodlands, parks, gardens.

PHYLUM **ARTHROPODA**   FAMILY **LYCAENIDAE**   SPECIES *Acrodipsas illidgei*   SIZE **TO 3 CM**

ILLIDGE'S ANT BLUE BUTTERFLY

Like other lycaenid butterflies this remarkable species uses ants to rear its caterpillars. Its mangrove habitat is, however, threatened by development and the butterfly is listed as vulnerable. Females have iridescent blue areas on their wings, while the males have brown wings. The caterpillars are white. **Features** Adults perch with their wings closed and only fly for brief periods each year. The caterpillars produce chemicals that mimic the odour of their host ants and are treated as the ants' own larvae. The caterpillars may also produce sugary secretions to feed the ants. **Feeding** Caterpillars feed on ant eggs and larvae. **Reproduction** Eggs are laid in early summer in small clusters on the trunks of grey man-groves and associated casuarina trees colonised by the host ant species. The ants carry newly hatched caterpillars to their nest in the branches of the tree. Emerging adult butterflies avoid being eaten by shed-ding disposable scales to distract the ants as they flee the nest. **Habitat** Mangrove communities.

PHYLUM **ARTHROPODA**   FAMILY **SATURNIIDAE**   SPECIES *Opodipthera eucalypti*   SIZE **TO 15 CM**

EMPEROR GUM MOTH

This large moth is covered with soft hairs and has broad yellow-brown or orange-brown wings. The forewings have pale pink eyespots and the hindwings have striking orange eyespots. Males have feathery antennae. The caterpillar is bluish-green with a yellow stripe and tufts of red bristles.

Features Like other moths the forewings and hindwings are joined in flight by tiny hook-like structures. They fly at night and rest with their wings spread widely, revealing the bright eyespots to deter preda-tors. **Feeding** Adults have degenerate mouthparts and cannot feed. Caterpillars eat the young leaves of various gum trees and some introduced species. **Reproduction** Females lay eggs on the leaves of food plants. They hatch 7-10 days later and the caterpillar moults several times until fully grown at 6-8 cm. It attaches to the bark and transforms into a pupa. The adult emerges in spring or summer up to 5 years later and lives for about 2 weeks. **Habitat** Forests, woodlands, parks, gardens.

PHYLUM **ARTHROPODA**   FAMILY **FORMICIDAE**   SPECIES *Myrmecia pyriformis*   SIZE **TO 3 CM**

BULL ANT

These aggressive ants are among the largest in the world and can inflict a painful sting. **Features** Ants live in social communities comprising a fertile, egg-laying queen and various castes of wingless, sterile, female workers. Worker castes include nest-builders, nursery work-ers, foragers and soldiers with large heads. Bull ants live in underground nests, and if disturbed, soldiers rush out, bite intrud-ers with their powerful toothed jaws and stab them with their tail sting. **Feeding** Adults eat nectar, sap and honeydew and feed the larvae on insects. Workers leave scent trails to guide other ants to food sources. **Reproduction** The queen is the colony's only reproductive female. Her eggs hatch into legless larvae who are fed by workers until they pupate and transform into the various worker castes. In late summer, winged males and females are produced. They fly off and form mating swarms with other winged ants. The males die after mating while the females shed their wings, lay their eggs and begin new colonies. **Habitat** Forests, woodlands, heaths.

PHYLUM **ARTHROPODA**   FAMILY **FORMICIDAE**   SPECIES *Melophorus bagoti*   SIZE **TO 2 CM**

HONEY POT ANT

These remarkable ants are sought after by desert Aborigines who dig them up and squeeze out the honey. **Features** They live in underground nests with a queen and different castes of sterile workers. They forage during the day, particularly after rain, when plants are producing new leaves and flowers. Storage workers live in deep underground galleries and have long, slender abdomens. Soldier ants protect the colony, spraying formic acid from the tip of their abdomens at intruders. **Feeding** Foraging workers bring honeydew and nectar back to the nest and feed it to storage workers whose abdomens swell up to the size of peas. They hang from the roofs of the galleries. Other ants eat the honey when food is scarce. **Reproduction** The queen's eggs hatch into larvae who are attended by workers until they pupate and emerge as the various worker castes. Once a year winged fertile males and young queens emerge and fly off to join winged ants from other colonies to mate and start new colonies. **Habitat** Arid inland habitats.

PHYLUM **ARTHROPODA**   FAMILY **IXODIDAE**   SPECIES *Ixodes holocyclus*   SIZE **TO 12 MM**

PARALYSIS TICK

Bandicoots are the principal natural hosts of this blood-sucking arachnid, although it also attacks humans, sometimes causing sickness and, very rarely, death. **Features** They lack wings and antennae, have simple eyes, 4 pairs of legs, and mouthparts with a barbed feeding tube. They are attracted to animals by exhaled carbon dioxide. **Feeding** They feed on the blood of many animals, including marsupials and humans, injecting a paralysing toxin with their saliva. They attach for about a week, and are most toxic as adults in spring when they become enormously engorged with blood. **Reproduction** Females lay up to 3000 eggs on the ground. Around January they hatch into tiny, 6-legged larvae, climb nearby vegetation, attach to a passing animal, feed and drop to the ground. They moult into 8-legged nymphal ticks the size of pinheads, repeat the feeding and moulting cycle around July, and emerge as adults. Adult females have a final blood meal in spring before laying their eggs. **Habitat** Forests, woodlands, heaths, parks, gardens.

PHYLUM **ARTHROPODA**   **URODACIDAE** FAMILY   SPECIES *Urodacus yaschenkoi*   SIZE **TO 12 CM**

DESERT SCORPION

Scorpions, like spiders and ticks, are arachnids. Australia has some 30 species, all are brownish or reddish in colour and fluoresce under ultraviolet light. Their venom is not deadly to humans, although some can deliver a painful sting. **Features** Scorpions have simple eyes, 4 pairs of legs and 2 large claws to seize prey. The end segments of the abdomen form a tail tipped with a stinger linked to poison glands. Desert scorpions shelter by day in a deep spiral burrow with a crescent-shaped entrance and hunt at night. They have poor vision and detect prey by vibration and scent. The sting is used in self-defence or to subdue powerful prey. **Feeding** Mostly insects, spiders and other arthropods. **Reproduction** Mating pairs dance with their claws interlocked. The male drops a sperm packet and manoeuvres the female so that it enters her genital opening. Females give birth to live young who ride on her back beneath the tail for several days. They may live for 10 years. **Habitat** Open sandy woodlands and shrublands.

PHYLUM **ARTHROPODA**   FAMILY **HEXATHELIDAE**   SPECIES *Atrax robustus*   SIZE **TO 3 CM**

SYDNEY FUNNELWEB SPIDER

Male funnelwebs are the world's most venomous spiders. Australia has around 40 funnelweb species, and bites from some, including the Sydney funnelweb, may be lethal. **Features** They live in a burrow with a silken tube at the opening and trip-lines radiating from the entrance. At night the spider waits until a small animal disturbs the lines, rushes out, seizes the victim, paralyses it with venom and drags it back into the burrow to be devoured. **Feeding** They eat any small animal including insects, slugs, small lizards and frogs. **Reproduction** Males search for females from January to March. When a female's nest is found, the male squirts sperm onto a silk pad, sucks it up with a pair of short, leg-like structures (palps), and to avoid being eaten, vibrates the trip-lines in a distinctive pattern. He then lifts the female and squeezes the sperm into her abdomen. In spring she lays about 100 eggs in a silk sac at the end of her burrow. Spiderlings emerge in summer and disperse in autumn. **Habitat** Forests, woodlands, heaths, parks, gardens.

PHYLUM **ARTHROPODA**   FAMILY **THERIDIIDAE**   SPECIES *Latrodectus hasseltii*   SIZE **TO 15 MM**

REDBACK SPIDER

The female redback's bite is potentially lethal. Males are harmless, about 3 mm long, cream with brown markings. Females have a black or brown abdomen with a red stripe.
Features Timid and reclusive, redbacks bite only if handled. They build untidy webs in cool, dry places such as tree stumps, in empty containers and under houses. Stout, sticky trap lines run from the web to the ground. When touched the line recoils, suspending the victim in mid-air.
Feeding They feed on small arthropods and occasionally small reptiles or frogs. Larger animals are paralysed and wrapped in silk before being eaten. **Reproduction** They mate in summer and to avoid being devoured before he can insert his sperm, the male allows the female to begin digesting his abdomen. Females lay several batches of 3-10 egg sacs in their web, each holding about 250 eggs. Tiny green spiderlings emerge about 2 weeks later, spin a long silk thread and drift away on the breeze. **Habitat** Forests, woodlands, heaths, urban areas.

PHYLUM **ARTHROPODA**   FAMILY **SPARASSIDAE**   SPECIES *Holconia immanis*   SIZE **TO 47 MM**

GIANT HUNTSMAN SPIDER

With a legspan of up to 16 cm this intimidating spider often enters houses, but is quite inoffensive. It is grey to brownish-grey and hairy all over with a dark line on its bulbous abdomen. **Features** Huntsmen have 8 large eyes and 2 sets of jaws, each with 2 leg-like structures, called palps, used to taste and manipulate food, and in males to transfer sperm to the female. The giant huntsman has a flattened body and legs that spread out in a crab-like fashion, allowing it to scurry sideways to hide in crevices and under loose bark. It hunts at night, generally ambushing passing prey. Adults hibernate in winter. **Feeding** They feed on arthropods and occasionally small reptiles and frogs.
Reproduction The male inserts sperm into the female with his palps. She lays up to 200 eggs in an oval egg sac placed under bark or a rock and guards them until they hatch about 3 weeks later. Pale spiderlings emerge and stay with her for several weeks before dispersing. **Habitat** Forests, woodlands, heaths, urban areas.

PHYLUM **ARTHROPODA**   FAMILY **ARANEIDAE**   SPECIES *Argiope aetherea*   SIZE **TO 15 MM**

ST ANDREW'S CROSS SPIDER

This common, harmless, orb-weaving spider constructs a large wheel-shaped web with a zigzag silken cross at the centre. Females are vividly patterned in silver, yellow and black, while males are tiny and dull-cream coloured.
Features Every few days this spider creates a new web of radiating silken spokes overlaid with a spiral of sticky threads suspended between buildings, shrubs or trees. The spider clings motionless to the centre of the web, its legs held in pairs, awaiting its prey. **Feeding** Flying insects trapped by the sticky threads are paralysed with poison and wrapped in silk before being sucked dry. **Reproduction** The male cautiously strums a female's web to signal his presence, hoping not to be devoured. If she is receptive a duet of vibrating threads ensues before mating. Eggs are laid in a pear-shaped sac of greenish silk, suspended by golden threads among the vegetation. They hatch in winter or early spring and the tiny spiderlings disperse by drifting on silken threads. **Habitat** Forests, woodlands, heaths, urban areas.

Rainforests

Although rainforests cover less than half a per cent of the Australian landmass, they support about half of the plant species and one-third of the birds and mammals.

Rainforests occur in strips and patches along the eastern edge of the continent and are generally categorised into three main types. Tropical rainforests of north Queensland are the quintessential form, packed with vines, palms and buttressed trees, supporting epiphytic orchids, ferns and an outstanding diversity of wildlife.

South of the tropics are subtropical and temperate rainforests, and these become less diverse as the latitude increases. Subtropical rainforests are the most wide-spread, and occur in large stands on the northern tablelands, and south to the Illawarra region in New South Wales. The canopy is lower, typically 20-35 m high compared to 30-40 m in tropical rainforests. Ferns and epiphytes are usually more numerous than vines, and just a handful of trees dominate the canopy.

Temperate rainforests are limited to Tasmania and wet montane areas of the south-east, with isolated outliers as far north as the Queensland border. They are damp, quiet and simpler forests with a single canopy layer of smaller leaved trees, giving rise to a denser understorey of filmy ferns, fungi, shrubs and magnificent umbrella-like tree ferns. One or two trees dominate the canopy, including the ancient, beautiful, lichen-draped Antarctic beech, a living link with Australia's Gondwanan ancestry.

Rainforests are, by definition wet, and need at least 1300 mm of rain a year, whether evenly distributed or falling in heavy downpours over a limited wet season. Small patches of monsoon rainforests in Northern Australia survive without rain for half the year, partly by losing leaves during the dry season.

While the majority of species described in the following pages are found only in rainforests, some are seen in wet sclerophyll forests and other moist, sheltered sites.

| FAMILY **ARALIACEAE** | SPECIES *Schefflera actinophylla* | FORM **TREE** | SIZE **TO 16 M** |

UMBRELLA TREE

This small or medium-sized tree has a trunk to 30 cm diameter and is often divided into 2 or more stems at the base. It has a low, compact crown of drooping foliage. **Bark** Greyish-brown with small fissures and horizontal scars.

Leaves Alternate, whorled around the main stems, leathery, paler below. They are divided into 7-16 leaflets, 8-30 cm long and 4-12 cm wide, on reddish stalks 4-8 cm long. These radiate from the end of a thick main stalk, 15-70 cm long. **Flowers** Appear in spring and summer. They are red, cup-shaped, about 4 mm across, with 7-18 petals that fall early to leave a central disc with protruding red stamens. They are clustered on upright spikes to 1 m long. **Fruit** Dark purple, fleshy, globular, ribbed pods, 3-5 mm across, which contain a single seed. Ripe in autumn.
Habitat Clearings and margins of subtropical and tropical rainforests.

| FAMILY **ARAUCARIACEAE** | SPECIES *Araucaria bidwillii* | FORM **TREE** | SIZE **TO 50 M** |

BUNYA PINE

This tall tree has a slightly tapering trunk to 1.5 m diameter, and a symmetrical, dome-shaped crown with leaves clumped at the ends of straight, whorled, horizontal branches. **Bark** Dark brown to black, hard and rough with thin scales. **Leaves** Spirally arranged,

stiff, almost stalkless. They are 10-65 mm long and 5-15 mm wide, and glossy green with a sharp point. **Cones** Male and female cones are borne on the same tree on short branches. Male cones appear in spring and are narrowly cylindrical, with greenish-yellow spikes to 20 cm long. They have many spirally-arranged scales covering the pollen cells. Females appear in summer and are green and ovoid, about 12 mm across, with many sharply-pointed scales. In autumn they ripen into large woody cones, 20-30 cm long, with large scales each bearing a single, flattened, pointed, egg-shaped seed. Seeds are 25-50 mm long with a milky, edible flesh.
Habitat Rich volcanic soils in moist rainforest valleys.

| FAMILY **ARAUCARIACEAE** | SPECIES *Araucaria cunninghamii* | FORM **TREE** | SIZE **TO 60 M** |

HOOP PINE

This tall tree has a straight trunk to 1.9 m diameter and whorled horizontal branches with tufts of leaves clustered at the ends, forming a symmetrical crown. **Bark** Dark greyish-brown, rough, with horizontal cracks forming hoops around the trunk. **Leaves** Scale-like;

3-15 mm long with a sharp point; crowded in spirals around the branchlets. Juvenile leaves are needle-like, flattened, and 1-2 cm long.
Cones Male and female cones are produced on the same tree. Males are light brown, cylindrical, 4-8 cm long and produce wind-borne pollen. Female cones are green, woody and egg-shaped, 7-10 cm long, with long stalks. They occur at the ends of branchlets near the top of the tree. When ripe in summer, they split open on the tree to release numerous flat, wedge-shaped, thinly-winged seeds about 1 cm long. **Habitat** Poor soils in rainforests, rocky gorges and watercourses of the coast and tablelands.

| FAMILY **ARECACEAE** | SPECIES *Archontophoenix cunninghamiana* | FORM **PALM** | SIZE **To 25 M** |

BANGALOW PALM

This tall, single-stemmed palm has a smooth, pale grey trunk to 30 cm diameter, topped by a prominent crown-shaft to 1 m long, and an umbrella-shaped crown of long, feather-leaved fronds. **Leaves** Form fronds 2-4 m long, divided into closely-spaced, opposite, leaflets, which are 60-100 cm long and 3-8 cm wide. The frond bases surround the top of the trunk to form the crownshaft. **Flowers** Produced year-round in large clusters to 1.5 m long, arising from the base of the crownshaft, and initially enclosed in two large, papery bracts. The flowers are pale lilac, stalkless, 3-5 mm across, and spirally arranged in groups of three, with one female between two males. **Fruit** Orange-red berries, 10-15 mm across. These contain a single fibrous seed surrounded by a thin fleshy layer with a smooth, waxy surface. **Habitat** Stream banks, gullies and moist sites in rain-forests and wet sclerophyll forests to 700 m, often forming large colonies.

| FAMILY **ARECACEAE** | SPECIES *Calamus australis* | FORM **PALM** | SIZE **To 20 M** |

LAWYER CANE

A slender, clumping, climbing palm forming impenetrable thickets. The stems and leaves bear sharp spines and the climbing stems have recurved hooks. **Leaves** Up to 2.5 m long, divided into 20-36 unevenly spaced leaflets, 10-30 cm long and 2-3 cm wide with spiny margins. They have flattened stalks 4-5 cm long, sheathing the stem which is covered with reddish spines to 8 cm long. **Flowers** Appear in summer. They are creamy-green, very small, about 2-4 mm long, with 6 lobes. They are borne in long, slender, sparsely-branched clusters arising from the sheaths of the upper leaves. Clusters are 2-3 m long with black-tipped hooks on the stems. **Fruit** Cream to white when ripe, globular with a small point at one end, 8-14 mm across and covered with small overlapping scales. They have a single, ovoid seed, surrounded by a thin, edible, fleshy, outer layer. **Habitat** Grows along the margins and in clearings in lowland and highland rainforests.

| FAMILY **ARECACEAE** | SPECIES *Licuala ramsayi* | FORM **PALM** | SIZE **To 20 M** |

WEDGE LEAFLET FAN PALM

This tall, slender, single-stemmed, fan-leaved palm lacks a crownshaft and has a dense crown of large, shiny green, circular fronds with wedge-shaped segments and long, slen-der, arching stems. **Trunk** Grey to dark brown, to 20 cm diameter, slightly swollen at the base. It is smooth, with small vertical fissures, often with a collar of fibrous leaf bases. **Leaves** The circular leaf blade is 1-2 m across with pleated segments radiating from the end of a slender, arching leaf stalk, 1.25-2.5 m long. The stalks have black spines on the margins of the lower part, and a reddish-brown, fibrous, sheathing base. **Flowers** Cream, very small, in large clusters which are grouped into a much-branched, pendulous inflorescence to 2.1 m long, arising from the leaf bases. **Fruit** Red when ripe, spherical, about 1 cm across, with a single seed sur-rounded by a thin, fleshy layer. **Habitat** Stream banks and swampy sites in low-lying tropical rainforests, often forming extensive colonies.

| FAMILY **ARECACEAE** | SPECIES *Linospadix monostachya* | FORM **PALM** | SIZE **TO 5 M** |

WALKING STICK PALM

This small understorey palm has a slender stem to 3 cm diameter, ringed with brown leaf scars, and a feather-leaved crown of dark green fronds. **Leaves** Up to 1.3 m long with a thin midrib and a smooth, slender, arching stalk to 30 cm long, which partially sheaths the stem. The leaves are divided into broad and narrow, irregularly spaced leaflets, 20-30 cm long. They are sometimes fused at their bases, with toothed tips. The terminal pair form a fish-tail shape. **Flowers** Appear year-round. They are cream, about 8 mm long with three overlapping lobes, and are clustered in a slender, drooping inflorescence to 1.5 m long which arises from the lower leaf bases. Male and female flowers are spirally arranged on the same inflorescence with one female between two males. **Fruit** Bright red, spherical and 10-15 mm across. A thin fleshy layer surrounds a single seed. They form a pendulous spike. **Habitat** Shady stream banks in subtropical and cool-temperate rainforests.

| FAMILY **ARECACEAE** | SPECIES *Livistona australis* | FORM **PALM** | SIZE **TO 30 M** |

CABBAGE (FAN) PALM

This tall, fan-leaved palm has a spherical crown above a skirt of dead leaves. **Trunk** Brownish-grey, to 50 cm diameter, ringed with leaf scars and often retaining the scattered remains of the fibrous leaf bases. **Leaves** Fan-shaped, to 1.8 m across and pleated. They are divided about two-thirds the way down into 30-50 narrow, pointed segments with entire or forked, drooping tips. The stout leaf stalks are up to 3 m long with white scurf below, and partially sheath the trunk. Young palms have sharp spines on the leaf stalks. **Flowers** Cream, 3-5 mm across with three pointed petals, borne singly or in small clusters. The flowers are densely packed along the branchlets of a drooping inflorescence to 1.5 m long, arising from leaf bases within the crown. **Fruit** Dark purple, spherical, 16-20 mm across, with a single seed covered by a thin fleshy layer. **Habitat** Low, moist sites in warm temperate to tropical rainforests and wet eucalypt forests.

| FAMILY **ASPLENIACEAE** | SPECIES *Asplenium australasicum* | FORM **FERN** | SIZE **TO 1.2 M** |

BIRD'S NEST FERN

This large, tufted fern grows on rocks or trees, and has a funnel-shaped rosette of fronds that collects water and organic debris to nourish the plant. **Fronds** Pale to dark green, erect, undivided, usually 60-120 cm long and 3-21 cm wide. They are leathery with wavy margins and a prominent, dark brown midrib, channelled above with a protruding ridge below. Many fine parallel veins run from the central vein to the margins where they are connected to a continuous marginal vein. **Spores** Contained in numerous brown, narrow, linear clusters, 1 mm wide and often 4-6 cm long. These clusters extend along the fine parallel veins from near the midrib to part way across the fertile fronds. **Habitat** Grows in rainforests and protected sites in open forests, on rocks and trees, and sometimes on the ground, preferring filtered sunlight and drier sites.

147

| FAMILY **BIGNONIACEAE** | SPECIES *Pandorea jasminoides* | FORM **SHRUB** | SIZE **TO 30 M** |

BOWER VINE

This vigorous woody shrub produces numerous twining stems 20-30 m long. It climbs strongly into trees and shrubs, sprawls over the ground, or spreads itself over boulders. **Leaves** Opposite, sometimes growing in whorls of 3 around the long stems. They are shiny dark green, 2-7 cm long, and divided into 4-7 leaflets. The leaflets are 45-60 mm long and 15-30 mm wide, the lowest pair being markedly asymmetrical. **Flowers** Appear mainly in spring and summer. They are white to pale pink with a tubular base and a crimson, hairy throat. They are 4-6 cm long and 4-6 cm across, with 5 spreading lobes and 4 stamens. The flowers are grouped in clusters at the ends of the stems. **Fruit** Oblong to ovoid, beaked, woody pods, 4-6 cm long and 1-2 cm across. These contain numerous papery, winged seeds, 10-15 mm across. Ripe in summer and autumn. **Habitat** Wet areas in coastal rainforests.

| FAMILY **COMBRETACEAE** | SPECIES *Terminalia catappa* | FORM **TREE** | SIZE **TO 25 M** |

TROPICAL ALMOND

This medium-sized deciduous tree has a short, cylindrical trunk and a dense, flattened crown with widely-spreading, thick, whorled branches. The buds and shoots are covered with dense brown hairs. **Leaves** Alternate, crowded at the ends of the branchlets, 10-33 cm long and 6-17 cm wide, on stalks 4-22 mm long. Stiff and glossy dark green, they turn bright red when old. They have 8-12 lateral veins and a prominent midrib, dotted with glands below. **Flowers** Appear in spring and summer. They are greenish-white, small and cup-shaped, and have 5 lobes and 10 stamens, grouped in slender clusters 10-25 cm long. Male flowers are about 5 mm across; females 6 mm across; and bisexual flowers 10-13 mm across. **Fruit** Green turning reddish-purple, edible, flattened, leathery spheres, 2-6 cm long and 2-5 cm wide. The small almond-like seed is surrounded by sweet-tasting purple pulp. **Habitat** Along stream banks and beside beaches on the margins of tropical rainforests.

| FAMILY **CUNONIACEAE** | SPECIES *Callicoma serratifolia* | FORM **TREE** | SIZE **TO 20 M** |

BLACK WATTLE

This small to medium-sized tree has a cylindrical trunk to 60 cm diameter, a bushy crown, and slender, willowy branches. The young stems and branchlets are often covered in dense rusty hairs. **Bark** Dark greyish-brown; smooth in young trees, becoming scaly and shedding in longitudinal patches in older trees. **Leaves** Opposite, 4-15 cm long and 2-5 cm wide, with coarsely toothed margins and stalks 1-2 cm long. They are glossy dark green above and covered with dense pale hairs below. **Flowers** Appear in spring and early summer. They are cream and borne in dense, globular, fluffy heads of 1-2 cm diameter, on hairy stalks 1-3 cm long. **Fruit** Small green capsules densely clustered into globular heads, 8-15 mm diameter, each containing 1-2 spindle-shaped seeds. Ripe in autumn. **Habitat** Widespread in damp sites along creeks and rocky gullies in rainforests and their margins, often found in regrowth areas.

| FAMILY **CUNONIACEAE** | SPECIES *Ceratopetalum apetalum* | FORM **TREE** | SIZE **TO 25 M** |

COACHWOOD

This medium-sized tree has a straight, sometimes slightly buttressed trunk, to 90 cm diameter, and a compact crown. **Bark** Light grey, mottled with shades of grey and white lichen; smooth with horizontal raised bands. Older trees have dark, rough and scaly bark on the base of the trunk. **Leaves** Opposite with toothed margins, paler below, 6-15 cm long and 2-5 cm wide. They have a raised midrib and stalks 1-2 cm long. **Flowers** Appear in spring and early summer. They are cream to pink, 6-8 mm across, and have 5 lobes and 8-10 short stamens attached to a flat, yellow, central disc. They are grouped in loose clusters to 12 cm long on hairy stalks. **Fruit** Thin, woody, egg-shaped capsules about 3 mm diameter, surrounded at the base by the enlarged remains of the flower. They contain a single seed. Ripe in summer. **Habitat** Widespread on poorer soils in temperate and subtropical rainforests along the coast and tablelands.

| FAMILY **CUNONIACEAE** | SPECIES *Geissois benthamiana* | FORM **TREE** | SIZE **TO 35 M** |

RED CARABEEN

This impressive tree produces a flush of bright red new growth at the end of summer. It has a cylindrical trunk to 1.4 m diameter, usually buttressed at the base, and a dense crown. **Bark** Grey-brown to dark brown, smooth or with small blisters. **Leaves** Opposite, with stalks 2-5 cm long, divided into 3 ovate to elliptical leathery leaflets radiating from the end of the leaf stalk. The leaflets are each 5-18 cm long and 2-5 cm wide with stalks 5-15 mm long. They are dark green above and paler below, with coarsely-toothed margins. **Flowers** Appear in spring and summer. They are light yellow, open, and about 5 mm across. They have 5-6 tiny sepals and 20-30 stamens 5-6 mm long, borne in dense slender clusters, 7-15 cm long. **Fruit** Light-brown, cylindrical capsules covered with rusty, silky hair. They are 1-2 cm long and 3-5 mm wide, separating into 2 cells with several flat, winged seeds, 5-10 mm long. Ripe in late autumn and winter. **Habitat** Cool sites in subtropical and warm temperate rainforests.

| FAMILY **CYATHEACEAE** | SPECIES *Cyathea australis* | FORM **TREE FERN** | SIZE **TO 20 M** |

ROUGH TREE FERN

This tall, hardy tree fern has a dark brown, fibrous trunk to 40 cm diameter, retaining the old leaf bases towards the top, and thickened at the base with wiry roots. Stiff brown scales, 2-5 cm long, cover the leaf bases and the upper part of the trunk. **Fronds** To 5 m long and 1 m across. The fronds are divided three times into thin, leathery, hairy segments, 4-13 mm long and 2-4 mm wide, with serrated or lobed margins. The main stalk is up to 60 cm long, dark brown and densely covered at the base with coarsely-pointed conical spines. **Spores** Contained in raised, round clusters about 1 mm diameter, on the underside of the fertile leaf segments. There are usually 3-8 pairs per segment, situated at the forks of the lateral veins away from the margins of the leaf segments.
Habitat Moist, shady sites in rainforest gullies and open forests from the coast to 1200 m high.

| FAMILY **DAVIDSONIACEAE** | SPECIES *Davidsonia pruriens* | FORM **TREE** | SIZE **To 12 M** |

DAVIDSON'S PLUM

This small or medium-sized tree has a slender trunk, occasionally with several stems. It has a small crown with few branches and large, drooping leaves. **Bark** Light brown, corky and scaly. **Leaves** Alternate, 30-80 cm long, with stalks 5-20 cm long, divided into 5-19 opposite leaflets. The leaflets are 6-30 cm long and 3-10 cm wide with irregularly-toothed margins, stalkless or with very short stalks. The leaves, branchlets and stalks are often covered with dense, irritating hairs, and the main leaf stalks have irregularly-toothed wings. **Flowers** Appear in spring. They are deep pink, about 6 mm across. They have 4-5 downy lobes and 8-10 yellow stamens, and are borne on the trunk or upper leaf bases in drooping, hairy clusters, 4-10 cm long. **Fruit** Edible, purple to blue-black and plum-like, 3-5 cm long, with a few golden-brown hairs. The tart, crimson flesh surrounds two dark red, flattened seeds about 2 cm long. Ripe in summer. **Habitat** Basalt soils in subtropical rainforests.

| FAMILY **DICKSONIACEAE** | SPECIES *Dicksonia antarctica* | FORM **TREE FERN** | SIZE **To 15 M** |

SOFT TREE FERN

This tall, stout tree fern has a soft, fibrous, dark brown trunk to 50 cm diameter. The top of the trunk bears reddish-brown hairs and the remains of the old leaf bases at the top. The base has masses of fibrous roots. **Fronds** To 4.5 m long, dark green above and paler below. They are stiff, covered with fine hairs when developing, and divided three times into leathery segments, 2-5 mm long with lobed or serrated margins. The main leaf stalk is green to yellowish-brown; to 30 cm long; smooth; and has long, pointed, soft, red-brown hairs, which are 2-4 cm long and cover the base. Up to 40 new fronds unfurl together in spectacular flushes. **Spores** Contained in raised, round clusters about 1 mm across, along the margins of the fertile leaf segments at the ends of their small lateral veins. **Habitat** Prefers deep, shady gullies and creek banks, in cool rainforests and wet forests along the coast and tablelands; often forming large colonies.

| FAMILY **DILLENIACEAE** | SPECIES *Dillenia alata* | FORM **TREE** | SIZE **To 20 M** |

RED BEECH

This small or medium-sized tree has a cylindrical trunk and a dense, bushy crown of large, glossy, dark green foliage. Epyphytic orchids often grow on the trunk and large branches. **Bark** Purplish-red to reddish-brown, loose, papery and flaking. **Leaves** Alternate and whorled around the branchlets. They are thick and slightly rough, 10-25 cm long and 8-12 cm wide, on winged stalks to 55 mm long. **Flowers** Appear mainly in spring and summer. They are bright yellow, 5-8 cm across, have 5 separate spreading petals and numerous red stamens, and are grouped in loose terminal clusters of 2-4 flowers. **Fruit** Edible, bright red, fleshy capsules, opening widely to about 5 cm across. Each capsule has 5-8 cells containing small brown seeds surrounded by a white waxy covering. Ripe in summer and autumn. **Habitat** Stream banks and swampy sites in coastal rainforests and dense monsoon forests.

FAMILY **ELAEOCARPACEAE**   SPECIES *Elaeocarpus reticulatus*   FORM **TREE**   SIZE **TO 22 M**

BLUEBERRY ASH

This small or medium-sized tree has a straight, often slightly flanged trunk to 30 cm diameter, and a dense crown usually bearing a few bright red, old leaves.
Bark Brown, with vertical fissures and irregular blisters.
Leaves Alternate with finely-toothed margins, 5-15 cm long and 1-4 cm wide, on stalks 5-20 mm long. Glossy green above and paler below, they have conspicuous raised net veins on both surfaces.
Flowers Appear mainly in early summer. They are white, occasionally pink; fringed and bell-shaped with a licorice scent; 6-9 mm long. They have 13-20 bristly stamens, and are grouped in simple clusters, 2-10 cm long.
Fruit Shiny, dark blue and globular, 8-13 mm diameter, with a thin, fleshy, outer covering enclosing a single, hard, rough seed. Ripe at any time of year, but mainly in winter. **Habitat** Poorer soils, often in gullies and along watercourses in rainforests and sheltered forests of the coast and tablelands.

FAMILY **EUPHORBIACEAE**   SPECIES *Baloghia inophylla*   FORM **TREE**   SIZE **TO 24 M**

SCRUB BLOODWOOD

This small or medium-sized tree has a cylindrical or slightly fluted trunk to 50 cm diameter, and a spreading crown. Cut stems exude a clear sap that turns bright red. **Bark** Pale brown and grey, smooth with raised dark brown patches and rusty streaks.
Leaves Opposite, thick and stiff with 2 small glands near the base. They are 5-15 cm long and 2-8 cm wide on stalks 4-10 mm long. Glossy green and paler below, they have a prominent midrib. **Flowers** Appear mainly in spring. They are white, cream or pale pink, fragrant, cup-shaped, and about 2 cm across. They have 5 oval petals, and are grouped in loose clusters of either male or female flowers on stalks 6-13 mm long. **Fruit** Hard, globular, 3-celled capsules, brown when ripe, 12-20 mm across. They split at maturity to expose a single oval seed about 8 mm long in each cell. Ripe mainly in winter. **Habitat** Common in coastal rainforests.

FAMILY **EUPHORBIACEAE**   SPECIES *Glochidion ferdinandi*   FORM **TREE**   SIZE **TO 12 M**

CHEESE TREE

This small, ornamental tree has a crooked and often flanged trunk to 40 cm diameter, and a dense, spreading crown. **Bark** Purplish-brown to grey-brown, fissured and falling in patches. **Leaves** Alternate, arranged in two rows to give a divided appearance. They are 3-10 cm long and 15-40 mm wide, on stalks 3-5 mm long. Shiny green above, they are sometimes downy below. **Flowers** Appear mainly in spring. They are small and inconspicuous, greenish-yellow and 2-3 mm long. Male and female flowers are borne separately on the same tree. Males are often clustered in threes, while females are solitary. **Fruit** Red, globular and flattened capsules, 1-2 cm across. They have 5-7 cells with furrows between them giving a pumpkin-like appearance. The cells open to expose a pair of flattened seeds, 4-5 mm diameter, covered by a red skin. Ripe in summer. **Habitat** Sheltered gullies, river banks, and near swamps in coastal rainforests.

| FAMILY **EUPHORBIACEAE** | SPECIES *Macaranga tanarius* | FORM **TREE** | SIZE **TO 7 M** |

BLUSH MACARANGA

This small tree has a short, often crooked trunk to 30 cm diameter, and a bushy, rounded and spreading crown.
Bark Greyish-brown, rough, with pores and pimples forming horizontal bands in older trees. **Leaves** Alternate, 8-23 cm long and 10-20 cm wide, on stalks 8-20 cm long. The stalks are attached towards the centre of the leaf with veins radiating from them. The leaves are greyish-white below, scattered with fine hairs. **Flowers** Appear in spring and summer. Male and female flowers are borne on separate trees in small clusters. They are greenish-yellow, small and cup-shaped. The flowers are enclosed in a broad, fringed, pale green, leaf-like bract, 4-6 mm long in males and 8-12 mm long in females. **Fruit** Greenish-yellow, soft, globular, 3-celled capsules about 9 mm across, with a number of green spikes 3-6 mm long, enclosing a shiny black seed in each cell. Ripe in summer. **Habitat** A pioneer species in cleared sites in subtropical rainforests.

| FAMILY **EUPHORBIACEAE** | SPECIES *Mallotus philippensis* | FORM **TREE** | SIZE **TO 25 M** |

RED KAMALA

This medium-sized tree has a bushy crown and a short trunk to 40 cm diameter, often fluted and flanged at the base in large trees. The ends of the branchlets are often covered with rusty down. **Bark** Grey, smooth or wrinkled with scattered corky blisters. **Leaves** Alternate, 4-13 cm long and 2-7 cm wide, on rusty-brown stalks 2-5 cm long. Glossy green above, they are paler with greyish down below. The midrib is raised below and 2 prominent veins run parallel to the leaf margin for over half its length. **Flowers** Appear in winter and spring. They are yellow-brown, very small and grouped in rusty-hairy clusters, 2-10 cm long, on separate male and female trees. **Fruit** Globular capsules, 6-9 mm across, covered with deep-red granular glands giving it a powdery appearance. The capsules have 3 lobes, each containing a single seed. Ripe in spring and summer. **Habitat** Usually near watercourses in rainforests and forest margins.

| FAMILY **EUPHORBIACEAE** | SPECIES *Omalanthus nutans* | FORM **TREE** | SIZE **TO 6 M** |

BLEEDING HEART

This attractive pioneer tree has a cylindrical trunk to about 13 cm diameter, and a bushy, rounded crown with bright red dying leaves. **Bark** Greyish-brown, smooth and thin, sometimes with numerous pimples. **Leaves** Alternate, broad-ovate or triangular, tapering to a blunt point. They are thin, 3-15 cm long and 3-12 cm across, on stalks 2-12 cm long, with 1 or 2 circular glands at the base of the leaf. Glossy dark green above, they are often greyish below, with a distinct midrib and lateral veins. **Flowers** Appear in spring and early summer. They are yellow-green to red, very small and grouped in slender, terminal clusters, 2-10 cm long. The clusters are comprised of male flowers with a few solitary females at the base. **Fruit** Slightly flattened, ovoid capsules, constricted in the middle, 6-10 mm long, and glaucous-green. Each capsule contains 2 cells each with a single ovoid seed partially enclosed in a fleshy coat. Ripe in summer. **Habitat** Rainforest clearings and wet sclerophyll forests.

| FAMILY **EUPOMATIACEAE** | SPECIES *Eupomatia laurina* | FORM **TREE** | SIZE **TO 15 M** |

BOLWARRA

This shrub or small bushy tree has a crooked trunk to 30 cm diameter, weak branches and a dense crown.
Bark Brown, slightly corky or scaly, with fine vertical fissures. **Leaves** Alternate with a short point at the tip.
They are waxy; glossy green, sometimes coppery, paler below; 5-16 cm long and 2-5 cm wide, with stalks about 3 mm long.
Flowers Appear in spring and summer. They are cream and waxy with a strong fragrance, 20-25 mm across on stalks 5-7 mm long, solitary or in pairs. The petals and sepals form a cap that is shed as the flower opens leaving numerous petal-like stamens, 5-10 mm long. These give the flower a daisy-like appearance. **Fruit** Brown, succulent and edible, the urn-shaped fruits have a flat top, are 15-20 mm across, and contain numerous seeds. Ripe in autumn and winter. **Habitat** Prefers shady streambanks in warmer rainforests and wet sclerophyll forests along the coast and adjacent ranges.

| FAMILY **FABACEAE** | SPECIES *Castanospermum australe* | FORM **TREE** | SIZE **TO 40 M** |

BLACK BEAN

This large tree has a straight trunk to 1.2 m diameter and a dense crown of divided leaves. **Bark** Dark grey to brown with light grey blotches and small vertical fissures. **Leaves** Alternate, 20-60 cm long, divided into 8-17 most-ly alternate leaflets. Each leaflet is 7-12 cm long and 2-6 cm wide, with a blunt tip, distinct veins raised on the undersurface, and stalks 2-6 mm long. The leaves are shiny-green on both surfaces, but paler below. **Flowers** Appear in spring. They are yellowish-red, pea-like, with a broad standard petal 3-5 cm long and 8-10 protruding yellow stamens. Arranged in small clusters 5-15 cm long, they arise from the scars of fallen leaves. **Fruit** Shiny brown pods, 10-25 cm long and 4-6 cm wide. These split open to release 1-5 brown seeds, each 3-5 cm across, separated by spongy partitions. Ripe in summer and autumn. **Habitat** Stream banks in sheltered sites in subtropical and tropical rainforests.

| FAMILY **LAURACEAE** | SPECIES *Cryptocarya laevigata* | FORM **TREE** | SIZE **TO 6 M** |

GLOSSY LAUREL

This large shrub or small tree grows in the rainforest understorey and has a cylindrical trunk with a dense, bushy crown of glossy dark green leaves. New growth has scattered hairs. **Bark** Brownish-black, smooth and finely-fissured, with raised, round blis-ters. **Leaves** Alternate, ovate to elliptical or broad-lanceolate, 5-12 cm long and 1-4 cm wide on stalks 2-5 mm long. They are glossy bright green above and paler below, with 3 prominent main veins.
Flowers Appear in spring. They are cream or greenish, cup-shaped, 2-4 mm across, and have 6 triangular lobes and 9 short stamens. The flowers are grouped in short axillary clusters of 3-7.
Fruit Bright red to orange or yellow, fleshy and globular, 15-20 mm across. They have a single, ribbed, egg-shaped seed. Ripe in autumn.
Habitat Lowland subtropical and tropical rainforests.

| FAMILY **LAURACEAE** | SPECIES *Endiandra pubens* | FORM **TREE** | SIZE **TO 35 M** |

HAIRY WALNUT

Usually seen as a low, bushy tree, the timber of this tree resembles that of the European walnut. It has a slightly flanged trunk to 45 cm diameter and a spreading crown. The branchlets are covered with dense rusty hairs. **Bark** Brown to light grey, smooth, scaly or corky. **Leaves** Alternate and stiff; ovate to elliptic; 6-20 cm long and 2-8 cm wide, on densely-hairy stalks, 5-20 mm long. They are glossy green above and covered with dense, rusty hairs below, with distinct veins. The prominent midrib also has rusty hairs. **Flowers** Appear in autumn and winter. They are white, covered in dense, rusty hairs, bell-shaped, about 3 mm across, and grouped in clusters, 2-5 cm long, on hairy stalks. **Fruit** Pale green turning deep-red and globular, 4-8 cm diameter, with a fleshy exterior. They contain a large, globular seed. Ripe in spring and summer, but only produced every 2-3 years. **Habitat** Cool, moist valleys in subtropical rainforests.

| FAMILY **LILIACEAE** | SPECIES *Crinum pedunculatum* | FORM **HERB** | SIZE **TO 80 CM** |

SWAMP LILY

This erect, bulbous, evergreen, perennial herb aris-es in clumps from a deeply buried bulb. The bulb produces erect, fleshy, flattened stems bearing long, broad leaves. **Leaves** Strap-like, thick and broad, chanelled above, to 80 cm long and mostly 5-7 cm wide. They arise from the base of the stem. **Flowers** Appear in spring and summer. They are white to pale mauve, scented, 4-10 cm long and 4-8 cm across. They have 6 long, narrow, curled and spreading lobes joined at the base to form a tube, and have 6 long, protruding stamens. The flowers are borne in clusters of 10-40 flowers at the end of a stout, fleshy stem. **Fruit** Rounded capsules, 2-5 cm across with a prominent beak, containing numerous small seeds. **Habitat** Wet and swampy sites in rainforests and coastal heaths.

| FAMILY **LILIACEAE** | SPECIES *Tripladenia cunninghamii* | FORM **HERB** | SIZE **TO 40 CM** |

SARSPARILLA LILY

This spreading, perennial herb has many slender, wiry, zig-zag stems, arising from an irregular, knotty, creeping rhizome. The rhizome produces suckers around the base of the plant. The lily is often support-ed by other vegetation and bears one or more widely-opening flowers at the leaf junctions. **Leaves** Stem-clasping, lanceolate to ovate or heart-shaped, 4-9 cm long and 10-45 mm wide. They are shiny mid to dark green above with prominent veins. **Flowers** Appear in spring and summer. They are pink to pale purple, open, 15-25 mm across with 6 oblong lobes. The flowers are solitary or in small clusters on slender stalks 3-6 cm long, growing from the leaf junctions. **Fruit** Ovoid, wrin-kled capsules, 6-8 mm across. The capsules contain numerous, small, yellow or brown seeds. **Habitat** Subtropical and temperate rainforests and wet sclerophyll forests.

FAMILY **LORANTHACEAE**   SPECIES *Amylotheca dictyophleba*   FORM **SHRUB**   SIZE **TO 1 M**

BRUSH MISTLETOE

This is a parasitic, woody shrub that grows attached to the branches of trees by a root-like structure which absorbs nutrient from the host. **Leaves** Mainly opposite on brittle, erect stems. They are thick and leathery with several parallel veins; shiny above and dull below; 6-13 cm long and 2-6 cm wide, with a stalk 2-8 mm long. **Flowers** Appear in summer and autumn. They are orange to red with greenish tips, tubular, and often split on the upper side. They are 3-4 cm long with 4-6 narrow, spreading lobes when opened. They are arranged in axillary clusters of 1-6 three-flowered branches. **Fruit** Red or purple, globular berries, 5-12 mm across, containing a single seed. The seeds are much sought after by mistletoe birds. They are surrounded by a sticky layer that glues the seed to a branch when it is excreted by the bird. **Habitat** Attaches to many host trees in rainforests along the coast and ranges.

FAMILY **MALVACEAE**   SPECIES *Hibiscus tiliaceus*   FORM **TREE**   SIZE **TO 10 M**

COAST HIBISCUS

This medium-sized tree has a cylindrical trunk to 50 cm diameter and a dense, heavily-branched, grey-green crown. **Bark** Grey with black vertical fissures. Small trees are grey and smooth. **Leaves** Alternate, 5-15 cm long and 5-15 cm wide, on stalks to 14 cm long. Bright green above and felty grey below, they have a prominent midrib and net veins below. **Flowers** Appear in spring and summer. They are yellow with a red to purple centre and often turn red before falling. They have a cupped base; 5 overlapping rounded petals, 6-7 cm long; a protruding column of partly fused stamens, and furry stalks 2-4 cm long. The flowers are arranged in a terminal cluster. **Fruit** Yellowish-brown, velvety capsules, oblong to globular, and pointed. They are 15-25 mm long, and split open to reveal 4-5 segments each with several brown, kidney-shaped seeds, 5 mm long. Ripe in winter. **Habitat** Borders brackish swamps and mangroves on alluvial flats in subtropical littoral rainforests.

FAMILY **MELIACEAE**   SPECIES *Melia azedarach*   FORM **TREE**   SIZE **TO 50 M**

WHITE CEDAR

This tall deciduous tree has a cylindrical trunk to 1.6 m diameter and a dense, bushy crown. **Bark** Dark brown with greyish ridges giving a striped effect. **Leaves** Alternate, 12-45 cm long with stalks 5-15 cm long. They are twice-divided into 25-75 opposite, prominently-toothed, lobed or entire leaflets, 2-7 cm long and 1-3 cm wide, on stalks 1-8 mm long. They are glossy green above and paler below. **Flowers** Appear in spring. They are lilac, fragrant, about 18 mm wide, and have 5-6 spreading petals and a purple tube of joined stamens about 8 mm long, fringed at the tip. They are borne in large, loose clusters, 10-20 cm long. **Fruit** Yellowish-brown, ovoid, 1-2 cm long. A fleshy layer encloses a hard, oval, ribbed stone with 5 cells, each containing a single seed. Ripe in autumn and winter when the tree is leafless. **Habitat** Good soils in subtropical and dry rainforests along the coast and adjacent ranges. Naturalised in some inland areas.

| FAMILY **MELIACEAE** | SPECIES *Toona ciliata* | FORM **TREE** | SIZE **TO 55 M** |

RED CEDAR

This medium or tall deciduous tree has a cylindrical, some-times buttressed or flanged trunk to 3 m diameter, and a wide, spreading crown. **Bark** Brown or grey, rough and scaly. It sheds in oblong or irregular patches leaving slight depres-sions. **Leaves** Alternate, 15-45 cm long with stalks 4-15 cm long. They are divided into 5-20 opposite to alternate leaflets, 4-11 cm long and 15-60 mm wide on stalks 3-12 mm long. They are paler below with prominent veins. New growth is reddish. **Flowers** Appear in spring. They are white to pinkish, fragrant, cup-shaped and 5-6 mm long. They have 5 oval petals and 4-6 stamens, and are grouped in large, ter-minal, pyramidal clusters, 20-40 cm long. **Fruit** Dry, light brown, ellip-soid capsules, 1-3 cm long and 6-12 mm broad. These split into 5 valves, each containing 4-5 winged seeds 1-2 cm long. Ripe in late sum-mer and autumn. **Habitat** Scattered in warmer rainforests in moist gullies and along stream banks.

| FAMILY **MIMOSACEAE** | SPECIES *Archidendron grandiflorum* | FORM **TREE** | SIZE **TO 16 M** |

PINK LACE FLOWER

This small tree has a slightly fluted trunk to 20 cm across, and a spreading, bushy crown with purple-green branchelets turning fawn. **Bark** Smooth and usually covered in greyish lichen. It sheds in plates to expose dark brown patches.

Leaves Alternate, divided into 2-4 pairs of opposite leaflets with stalks 2-6 cm long. Each leaf is further divided into 2-4 pairs of leaflets, 3-5 cm long, with purple-black stalks 2-5 mm long.

Flowers Appear in early summer and are strongly perfumed at night. They are crimson with a white base, tubular and stalkless, and 15-26 mm long. They have 4-5 lobes and numerous protruding stamens, 3-5 cm long, and grow in clusters of 4-8 flowers, 5-8 cm across. **Fruit** Flat, woody pods, spirally-twisted, 10-20 cm long and 2-3 cm wide. They curl when opened to reveal glossy black seeds, 6 mm across, embedded in a deep red pith. Ripe in autumn. **Habitat** Occasional trees are scattered throughout rainforests.

| FAMILY **MORACEAE** | SPECIES *Ficus coronata* | FORM **TREE** | SIZE **TO 15 M** |

SANDPAPER FIG

This small tree has a short, crooked trunk to 20 cm diam-eter, long, sprawling, rough and hairy branches, and a bushy crown. **Bark** Dark brown, smooth, but marked with horizontal scars. **Leaves** Alternate, entire or sometimes with small teeth on the margins. They are 5-15 cm long and 2-6 cm wide, on bristly stalks 3-10 cm long. Dark green and sandpapery rough above, they are paler and smoother below with distinct raised veins. **Flowers** Very small and enclosed in a hollow, fleshy receptacle that becomes the fruit. **Fruit** Green-yellow, turning dark purple when ripe; ovoid; densely-hairy and fleshy; 8-20 mm across. They are borne singly or in small clusters on short stalks, 5-12 mm long, which arise from the leaf junctions or from old branches or the trunk. They are edible when ripe in summer and autumn. **Habitat** Stream banks in closed rainforests; sometimes in sheltered, rocky sites and open forests; along the coast, tablelands and inland slopes.

| FAMILY **MORACEAE** | SPECIES *Ficus macrophylla* | FORM **TREE** | SIZE **TO 50 M** |

MORETON BAY FIG

One of the strangler figs, this large tree with a wide, spreading crown, often begins life growing on the trunk of another tree which is eventually enmeshed with aerial roots and killed. It has a flanged and broadly buttressed trunk, sometimes more than 2.5 m across.

Its widely-spreading roots are often visible above the ground. **Bark** Dark greyish-brown and smooth, but marked with numerous blisters, narrow horizontal ridges and small, scattered scales. **Leaves** Alternate, 10-25 cm long and 7-15 cm wide on stalks 3-10 cm long. They are leathery, dark glossy green above and rusty below with conspicuous yellow-green veins. Young buds are enclosed in a brown sheath up to 17 cm long.
Flowers Very small and enclosed in a hollow, fleshy receptacle that becomes the fruit. **Fruit** Brown or purple with white spots, globular and fleshy, 18-25 mm across. They are borne singly on thick axillary stalks 8-25 mm long and ripen throughout the year. **Habitat** Coastal rainforests.

| FAMILY **MYRTACEAE** | SPECIES *Acmena smithii* | FORM **TREE** | SIZE **TO 20 M** |

LILLY PILLY

This small to medium-sized tree has a dense, dark green crown and straight trunk, sometimes slightly buttressed and up to 45 cm diameter. **Bark** Grey-brown, scaly, shed in irregular pieces, cracking longitudinally on older stems. **Leaves** Opposite, 2-11 cm long and 1-5 cm wide, on stalks 2-9 mm long. They are glossy dark green above and paler below with a raised midrib. Lateral veins and oil glands are visible on both surfaces. **Flowers** Appear in late spring and summer. Individual flowers are tiny, cream or greenish with 4-5 rounded petals and numerous protruding stamens 1-3 mm long. They are borne in dense clusters.
Fruit White, pink or lilac globular berries, 8-20 mm across with a circular depression on top. These enclose a single large seed in a succulent, slightly acidic, edible flesh. Ripe in late autumn and winter. **Habitat** Sheltered sites and along waterways, in rainforests and closed forests up to 1200 m on the coast and tablelands.

| FAMILY **MYRTACEAE** | SPECIES *Archirhodomyrtus beckleri* | FORM **TREE** | SIZE **TO 6 M** |

ROSE MYRTLE

This large shrub or small tree has a slender, angular trunk to 25 cm across and a bushy crown. Young branches are red-brown and smooth or sparsely-hairy. **Bark** Light brown and fibrous, with narrow vertical lines dividing it into soft, flaky scales.

Leaves Opposite, 2-8 cm long, thick, glossy above and paler below, on stalks 2-6 mm long. They have a prominent midrib and two longitudinal veins, and are strongly aromatic when crushed. **Flowers** Appear in spring. They are mauve, pink or white; open; and about 1 cm across. They have 5 curled-back petals and numerous protruding stamens, 2-4 mm long. They are solitary or borne in clusters of 2-3 flowers, on a stalk 5-25 mm long.
Fruit Yellow to orange or red globular berries, 5-8 mm diameter, containing 20-40 seeds in 3 cells. Ripe in summer. **Habitat** In or bordering rainforests, particularly regrowth areas; generally on poorer soils.

| FAMILY **MYRTACEAE** | SPECIES *Backhousia myrtifolia* | FORM **TREE** | SIZE **TO 12 M** |

GREY MYRTLE

This tall shrub or small tree has a cylindrical trunk to 30 cm diameter, often slightly flanged or buttressed at the base in large specimens; and a dense, low, spreading crown. Young branchlets have soft hairs towards the tips. **Bark** Brown with vertical fissures and flaking from the trunk. **Leaves** Opposite, 30-75 mm long and 10-35 mm wide, with stalks 2-6 mm long. They are paler below with a raised midrib and conspicuous veins, and are dotted with small oil glands giving them a distinctive smell when crushed. **Flowers** Appear in summer. They are white to pale yellow-green, 15-20 mm across, and have 5 pointed petals and numerous protruding stamens about 6 mm long. The flower tube is clothed with soft white hairs. They are grouped in small leafy clusters on stalks 20-35 mm long. **Fruit** A dry capsule about 1 cm long, enclosed in the persistent hairy floral tube. Ripe in autumn. **Habitat** Along watercourses in rainforests and rainforest margins.

| FAMILY **MYRTACEAE** | SPECIES *Lophostemon confertus* | FORM **TREE** | SIZE **TO 54 M** |

BRUSH BOX

This tall tree has a cylindrical trunk to 3 m diameter, and a dense, rounded crown with tiered clumps of glossy green foliage. **Bark** Light grey to brown, rough and scaly at the base. It sheds higher up to reveal pinkish-brown new bark. **Leaves** Alternate, crowded at the ends of the branchlets, 8-15 cm long and 40-45 mm wide, on stalks 15-25 mm long. Young shoots have silky hairs. **Flowers** Appear in spring and summer. They are 5-10 mm long and about 25 mm across, white, with a short tube, and covered with short fine hairs. They have 5 widely-spreading petals and numerous protruding stamens in 5 feathery bundles, 15-20 mm long. They are grouped in clusters of 3-8 flowers. **Fruit** Bell-shaped, flat-topped woody capsules, 8-13 mm long, with 3 enclosed valves contain narrow, wedge-shaped seeds. Ripe in winter and spring. **Habitat** Rainforests margins, eucalypt forests, and exposed ridges along the coast and tablelands.

| FAMILY **ORCHIDACEAE** | SPECIES *Dendrobium speciosum* | FORM **HERB** | SIZE **TO 1 M** |

KING ORCHID

This robust, perennial herb grows in large, dense clumps on rocks and sometimes on trees. It has thick, succulent brown stems 5-100 cm long and 2-6 cm diameter, which usually taper towards the tip. The stems bear a tuft of 2-5 leaves. **Leaves** Broad oval to oblong, thick and leathery, dark green, 4-25 cm long and 2-8 cm wide. **Flowers** Appear in winter and spring. They are white or yellow, strongly perfumed, to 4 cm across. They have 5 spreading lobes 2-4 cm long, and a purple-striped lip 9-13 mm long and 9-13 mm wide, which embraces the central column of the flower. They are arranged in long, dense, terminal clusters, 20-70 cm long, comprising 20-115 flowers. **Habitat** Usually grows on rocks in moderately exposed sites, and sometimes on rainforest trees of the coast and tablelands.

FAMILY **PITTOSPORACEAE**   SPECIES *Hymenosporum flavum*   FORM **TREE**   SIZE **TO 25 M**

NATIVE FRANGIPANI

This medium-sized tree, sometimes partly deciduous, has a cylindrical trunk to 45 cm diameter, slightly flanged in large trees. Its sparse branches radiate in whorls. **Bark** Grey and slightly rough, with short transverse lines. **Leaves** Alternate; sometimes clustered or whorled at the ends of twiggy branches; pointed; 7-16 cm long and 30-45 mm wide, on stalks 9-18 mm long. Shiny-green above, they are paler and often hairy below. **Flowers** Appear in spring. They are cream turning yellow, fragrant, and have silky hairs on the outside. The tubular flowers are 3-5 cm across, and have a deep-pink throat, with 5 spreading petals 3-4 cm long and 5 protruding stamens. They are grouped in loose terminal clusters, 15-20 cm across, on hairy stalks 3-5 cm long. **Fruit** Brown, hard, compressed, pear-shaped capsules, 2-4 cm long. These split into 2 cells packed with flat, winged seeds, 8-12 mm across. Ripe in summer and autumn. **Habitat** Along stream banks in rainforests and open forests of the coast and adjacent ranges.

FAMILY **PITTOSPORACEAE**   SPECIES *Pittosporum undulatum*   FORM **TREE**   SIZE **TO 30 M**

SWEET PITTOSPORUM

This small to medium-sized tree has a crooked and often flanged trunk to 35 cm diameter, and a dense, rounded crown. **Bark** Dark brownish-grey, rough and scaly in older trees. **Leaves** Alternate and crowded in groups of 3-6 towards the ends of the branchlets. They are glossy green above and paler below with wavy margins, 6-15 cm long and 15-50 mm wide, on stalks 1-2 cm long. **Flowers** Appear in spring. They are white to cream, fragrant, bell-shaped, and about 9 mm long. They have 5 spreading, rounded petals and 5 stamens. The flowers are borne in terminal clusters. **Fruit** Yellow turning orange, fleshy globular capsules, smooth or sparsely-hairy. They are 8-15 mm long and split open in 2 parts to reveal numerous brown or orange angular seeds, 1-3 mm long, with a viscous covering. Ripe in autumn and winter. **Habitat** Gullies and rocky mountainsides in rainforests and open forests along the coast, ranges and inland slopes.

FAMILY **POLYPODIACEAE**   SPECIES *Platycerium superbum*   FORM **FERN**   SIZE **TO 2 M**

STAGHORN FERN

This large, bracketing epiphytic fern has a short-creeping, sparsely-branching rhizome with fine rootlets which are clothed in loose, papery scales and covered by dead fronds. **Fronds** Sterile fronds (nest leaves) are up to 60 cm across and form the domed lower part of the fern, pressed against the host and protecting the root system from drying winds. They fold inwards when mature, catching and holding debris against the root system to create a rich humus that retains water and nourishes the plant. Two fertile, spreading or pendant fronds, 0.75-2 m long, are produced each year. They are forked into 2 narrow segments and often divided into many lobes 15-40 mm wide. **Spores** Produced in large masses to form a brown patch, 10-50 cm diameter, on the underside of the first fork of the fertile fronds. **Habitat** Grows on tree trunks and branches and sometimes on damp rocks, in rainforests along the coast and tablelands.

| FAMILY **PROTEACEAE** | SPECIES *Buckinghamia celsissima* | FORM **TREE** | SIZE **TO 20 M** |

IVORY CURL

This small or medium-sized tree has a cylindrical trunk. In closed sites it has a small, tufted crown, and in open areas a spreading, rounded and bushy crown. Young shoots are covered with grey hair and new growth is pink to red.
Bark Brown, rough and scaly. **Leaves** Alternate, ovate to broad-lanceolate, sometimes with 2-5 deep irregular lobes, 7-20 cm long and 3-79 cm wide, on stalks 1-2 cm long. They are glossy green above and paler below with fine silvery hairs, conspicuous veins and a prominent midrib.
Flowers Appear in summer and autumn. They are creamy-white, fragrant, tubular, and 7-10 mm long. They have 4 curled-back lobes and a protruding, hooked style. They are grouped in pairs on stalks 6-7 mm long, forming dense, cylindrical clusters, 10-27 cm long and 4-5 cm across.
Fruit Dark brown, beaked, woody, ovoid follicles, 15-30 mm long. These split open to release 1-4 flat, winged seeds. Ripe in autumn and winter.
Habitat Subtropical and tropical rainforests.

| FAMILY **PROTEACEAE** | SPECIES *Grevillea robusta* | FORM **TREE** | SIZE **TO 40 M** |

SILKY OAK

This tall tree has a straight trunk to 90 cm diameter, sometimes flanged at the base, and a conical crown of spreading branches. **Bark** Dark grey, furrowed and ridged. **Leaves** Alternate, fern-like, 10-34 cm long and 9-15 cm wide. They are twice-divided into 11-31 segments, each divided into narrow, pointed lobes, 5-80 mm long and 2-10 mm wide. They are smooth above and covered with silky hairs below. **Flowers** Appear in spring. They are orange-yellow, tubular, and 7-10 mm long. They have 4 lobes and a looped style to 2 cm long that straightens when released. They are grouped in dense, one-sided clusters of 60-80 flowers. The clusters are 8-15 cm long, on slender stalks about 13 mm long. **Fruit** Dark brown, woody and boat-shaped, to 2 cm long with a long beak. They contain a flat seed about 12 mm long with a thin wing. Ripe in summer.
Habitat Gullies in subtropical rainforests and wet sclerophyll forests.

| FAMILY **PROTEACEAE** | SPECIES *Hicksbeachia pinnatifolia* | FORM **TREE** | SIZE **TO 12 M** |

RED BOPPEL NUT

This tree usually has multiple stems, each with a high, slender crown. It may have a single, cylindrical trunk to 35 cm diameter, unbranched for most of its length. **Bark** Light-brown, wrinkled and corky. **Leaves** Alternate, stiff, 40-100 cm long, deeply-lobed or divided into 15-25 leaflet-like lobes. Each lobe is lanceolate, 6-25 cm long and 2-6 cm wide, with irregularly-toothed, prickly margins, a sharply-pointed tip, distinct veins and a prominently ribbed and winged primary stalk. **Flowers** Appear in winter. They are fragrant, purplish-brown, slender and tubular. They are silky outside, 10-15 mm long, and have 4 curled-back narrow lobes and a long, protruding, straight style. They are grouped in pendulous, cylindrical clusters, 15-35 cm long, on a stout, reddish, silky stalk arising from leafless stems, the trunk and branches. **Fruit** Red, shiny, fleshy, ovoid, and 2-5 cm long. They have a single edible seed growing directly from the trunk and branches on long, pendulous stems. Ripe in spring and summer. **Habitat** Coastal subtropical rainforests.

| FAMILY **PROTEACEAE** | SPECIES *Stenocarpus sinuatus* | FORM **TREE** | SIZE **TO 45 M** |

FIREWHEEL TREE

This medium-sized to tall tree has a cylindrical, sometimes flanged trunk, to 45 cm diameter, and a compact, domed crown with ascending branches. **Bark** Grey to brown, wrinkled and sometimes corky. **Leaves** Alternate, 15-30 cm long and 2-5 cm wide, with wavy margins, sometimes deeply-lobed. They are leathery, glossy above, dull and paler below with raised veins, on stalks 10-25 mm long. **Flowers** Appear from late summer to early winter. They are bright red or orange, with a globular tip, tubular, and about 25 mm long, on stalks 4-8 cm long. They split open to release a long, slender style. They are grouped like the spokes of a wheel, 5-10 cm diameter, in clusters of 6-20 at the ends of the branches. **Fruit** Grey-brown, boat-shaped follicles, 5-10 cm long. These contain numerous flattened, triangular, overlapping seeds, about 25 mm long, with a membranous wing. Ripe in winter and spring. **Habitat** Subtropical and tropical rainforests.

| FAMILY **RHAMNACEAE** | SPECIES *Alphitonia excelsa* | FORM **TREE** | SIZE **TO 15 M** |

RED ASH

This tree has a straight trunk to 1.25 m diameter and a medium-density crown with layered branches. It is low and spreading in open sites. **Bark** Steel-grey, hard, rough and deeply-fissured in older trees. **Leaves** Alternate, 5-15 cm long and 1-6 cm wide, on leaf stalks 5-20 mm long. It is glossy dark green above and covered with silvery hairs below. New growth is covered with grey or rusty down. **Flowers** Appear in summer and early autumn. They are greenish-cream, open, fragrant, and 2-6 mm across. They have 5 small, hood-shaped petals each enclosing one stamen, and are borne in dense clusters to 10 cm across. **Fruit** Black, flattened, globular, thinly-succulent, and 5-10 mm diameter. They usually contain 2 hard cells, each with a glossy, dark brown, oval seed, covered by a thin, dark orange skin. Ripe in spring and early summer. **Habitat** Rainforests, open forests and woodlands, particularly along watercourses; on the coast, lower tablelands and western slopes.

| FAMILY **RUTACEAE** | SPECIES *Melicope elleryana* | FORM **TREE** | SIZE **TO 25 M** |

PINK EUODIA

Usually seen as a small tree, it flowers prolifically, attracting butterflies and birds. It has a cylindrical trunk to 60 cm diameter and an open, spreading, dark green crown. **Bark** Light grey to light brown, thick, soft and corky. **Leaves** Opposite, 2-11 cm long, divided into 3 ovate to elliptic leaflets radiating from the end of the stalk. The leaflets are 5-22 cm long and 3-8 cm wide on stalks 2-10 mm long with a short point. They are glossy dark-green above and paler below with small oil dots and distinct veins. **Flowers** Appear in summer and autumn. They are pink to mauve, rarely white, cup-shaped, and 5-6 mm long. They have 4 petals and 4 protruding stamens, and are borne in dense clusters to 5 cm long on stalks 3-4 cm long. **Fruit** Dry, 2-4 lobed, grey-brown, ovoid capsules, 7-13 mm long. The capsules split down one side to reveal a single, flattened, shiny, black seed, 4-5 mm long, in each cell. Ripe in spring and summer. **Habitat** Subtropical and tropical rainforests.

| FAMILY **SAPINDACEAE** | SPECIES *Cupaniopsis flagelliformis* | FORM **TREE** | SIZE **TO 12 M** |

RUSTY TUCKEROO

This small tree is common in coastal rainforests and on windswept headlands. It has a short trunk to 30 cm diameter, flanged in older trees, and a spreading crown. Young shoots are bright red with grey, woolly hairs. **Bark** Grey-brown and smooth with pale pustules in vertical lines. **Leaves** Alternate, 20-30 cm long, divided into 8-14 broad-lanceolate to elliptical leaflets. Each leaflet is 4-15 cm long and 2-4 cm wide, on stalks 1-6 mm long, with a pointed tip and sharply-toothed margins. They are shiny-green above and paler below with short hairs and have prominent veins with rusty hairs. **Flowers** Appear in spring and early summer. They are pink to mauve, with rusty hairs outside, cup-shaped, and 5-15 mm across. They have 5 small petals and 8 stamens, and are clustered at the ends of the branches. **Fruit** Dark-red to yellow-brown, globular, stalkless capsules, 12-27 mm across, with 2-3 lobes. Each capsule has a glossy, dark brown, egg-shaped seed, partially covered by an orange skin. Ripe in summer. **Habitat** Subtropical rainforests.

| FAMILY **SAPINDACEAE** | SPECIES *Harpullia pendula* | FORM **TREE** | SIZE **TO 28 M** |

TULIPWOOD

Usually a small tree, older specimens are large and spreading with an irregular, sometimes fluted and buttressed trunk to 60 cm diameter. **Bark** Grey with scales shedding in long flakes, revealing corky blisters. **Leaves** Alternate, 10-30 cm long with stalks 2-5 cm long. They are divided into 3-8 narrowly-elliptic leaflets, each 5-12 cm long and 2-5 cm wide, on stalks 3-5 mm long. They are glossy green above and paler below, with distinct veins and a raised midrib on both surfaces. Young shoots are reddish-brown and downy. **Flowers** Appear in summer. They are white to greenish-yellow, open, with fine hairs, and are 12-16 mm across, on stalks 5-10 mm long. They have 5 oval petals, 5-8 stamens and a spirally-twisted style, and are arranged in clusters in the leaf axils, 10-20 cm long. **Fruit** Bright yellow or orange, 2-lobed capsules, 12-18 mm long and 20-30 mm wide. These split open to reveal 1-2 shiny dark oval seeds about 13 mm long. Ripe in spring. **Habitat** Drier subtropical and tropical rainforests.

| FAMILY **SAPINDACEAE** | SPECIES *Jagera pseudorhus* | FORM **TREE** | SIZE **TO 20 M** |

FOAMBARK

The bark contains a foamy compound used to poison fish. The trunk grows to about 40 cm diameter and is slightly fluted. It has a dense, rounded crown and new growth is clothed in rusty-brown hairs. **Bark** Light to dark grey with raised horizontal ridges. **Leaves** Alternate, 10-50 cm long, with stalks 15-40 mm long. They are clustered towards the ends of the branches, divided into 8-20 toothed, lanceolate leaflets, 2-10 cm long and 6-30 mm wide, on stalks 1-2 mm long. Shiny dark-green above, they are paler below, with rusty hairs and a raised midrib. **Flowers** Appear in late summer and autumn. They are yellowish-brown, downy, 3-6 mm across, with red orbicular petals and ovate sepals about 2 mm long. They have 8-10 stamens and are arranged in much-branched clusters, 5-25 cm long. **Fruit** Yellowish-brown, globular capsules, 15-22 mm across, densely covered in irritating bristles. The capsule's 3 valves each contain a single, dark, egg-shaped seed about 5 mm long. Ripe in autumn and winter. **Habitat** Subtropical rainforests.

FAMILY **STERCULIACEAE** SPECIES *Brachychiton acerifolius* FORM **TREE** SIZE **TO 40 M**

FLAME TREE

This tall deciduous tree has a straight, stout trunk to 1 m diameter, sometimes slightly flanged at the base. Flame-red flowers are massed on the tree when leafless in spring. **Bark** Grey or brown, fissured or wrinkled on older trees. **Leaves** Alternate, entire or shallowly 3-lobed. They are leathery, 8-30 cm long, shiny-green above, paler below with raised veins on stalks 7-20 cm long bearing scattered white hairs. Juvenile leaves often have 5-7 deep lobes. **Flowers** Appear in spring and early summer. They are red, bell-shaped, waxy, 5-lobed, 10-25 mm long and 10-15 mm across. They are grouped in loose clusters, 18-40 cm long, on stalks 7-20 mm long. **Fruit** Boat-shaped, leathery, dark brown follicles, 8-20 cm long, on stalks 6-8 cm long. They open along one side to release bright yellow seeds wrapped in a yellow covering with irritating hairs. Ripe in winter. **Habitat** Prefers sheltered sites on moist soils in lowland subtropical rainforests.

FAMILY **STERCULIACEAE** SPECIES *Brachychiton discolor* FORM **TREE** SIZE **TO 30 M**

LACEBARK TREE

This deciduous tree has a straight, stout trunk to 75 cm diameter, sometimes slightly swollen at the base. Masses of large pink flowers appear when the tree is leafless in spring. **Bark** Grey to brown, mottled with dark red and fawn patches and green fissures. **Leaves** Alternate, 8-20 cm across, with 3, 5 or 7 shallow lobes, on stalks 8-18 cm long. Leaves on young trees have deeper lobes. All leaves are smooth to slightly furry above, and covered with dense, velvety-white down below. **Flowers** Appear in spring and early summer. They are deep pink, bell-shaped with 5 triangular lobes, 4-6 cm long and 3-4 cm across. They are downy and borne in clusters near the ends of the branches. **Fruit** Boat-shaped woody follicles, 7-15 cm long and 3-5 cm wide, covered with stiff brown hairs, with stalks 1-2 cm long. They open on one side to release 10-30 downy seeds. Ripe in winter. **Habitat** Dry rainforests.

FAMILY **URTICACEAE** SPECIES *Dendrocnide excelsa* FORM **TREE** SIZE **TO 40 M**

GIANT STINGING TREE

This large tree has a fluted, buttressed trunk to 2 m diameter, and a spreading crown of large leaves with intensely irritating, stinging hairs. **Bark** Creamy-grey and rough. Large trees have soft, corky markings and scales. **Leaves** Alternate, 10-30 cm long and 7-20 cm wide, with toothed margins and stalks 2-15 cm long. They are thin and covered with downy hairs below. Rigid stinging hairs are scattered on both sides of the leaves and the branchlets. **Flowers** Appear in summer. They are yellowish-green, very small and produced in dense clusters to 12 cm long. Male and female flowers are borne on separate trees. **Fruit** Very small, warty, black, flattened nuts, 1-2 mm across, usually enclosed in a whitish to dull pink, edible flesh. Ripe in autumn. **Habitat** Prefers disturbed sites and clearings in warmer rainforests of the coast and ranges.

| FAMILY **VERBENACEAE** | SPECIES *Clerodendrum tomentosum* | FORM **TREE** | SIZE **TO 15 M** |

HAIRY CLERODENDRUM

This shrub or medium-sized tree has a cylindrical or slightly flanged trunk to 25 cm diameter, and a spreading crown. **Bark** Brown to grey-brown; corky and scaly in old trees. **Leaves** Opposite, 4-14 cm long and 2-5 cm wide, on stalks 1-5 cm long. They are dark green above and paler on the underside, which is covered with dense, soft hairs and has 5-6 raised main veins. Juvenile leaves have coarsely-toothed margins. **Flowers** Appear in spring and summer. They are creamy-white, tubular, 20-25 mm long, and have 5 spreading to curled-back lobes and usually 4 very long, protruding stamens. They are covered with soft down and grouped in loose terminal clusters. **Fruit** Black, shiny, oblong and fleshy, separating into 4 nutlets, 5-10 mm across. These are retained in the enlarged 5-lobed red, fleshy calyx, which is up to 2 cm across. Ripe in summer and autumn. **Habitat** Widespread in rainforests and wet sclerophyll forests. Also found inland on sandhills and rocky outcrops.

| FAMILY **ZAMIACEAE** | SPECIES *Lepidozamia peroffskyana* | FORM **CYCAD** | SIZE **TO 7 M** |

BURRAWANG PALM

This slow-growing, palm-like cycad develops a new, bright green crown every year or two. The fronds are spirally-arranged at the top of a stout trunk to 50 cm diameter. **Trunk** Smooth, woody, patterned with ovate to diamond-shaped leaf scars. **Leaves** Fronds 1.5-3 m long are formed from more than 200 shiny, dark green, stiff and leathery, sickle-shaped leaflets, each 10-32 cm long and 6-15 mm wide. **Cones** Unisexual on separate male and female plants, usually solitary, green turning brown, stalkless, with many tightly-packed, spirally-arranged, scale-like segments. Male cones are cylindrical, usually twisted, 25-60 cm long and 10-40 cm diameter, and open to release pollen. Female cones are conical, 45-80 cm long and 20-30 cm diameter at the base. **Fruit** Orange, fleshy, ovoid, 5-6 cm long and 30-35 mm wide. They contain an ovate seed with a hard woody coat, attached in pairs to the inside of the female cone segments. **Habitat** Rainforest margins, wet sclerophyll forests.

| FAMILY **ZINGIBERACEAE** | SPECIES *Alpinia caerulea* | FORM **HERB** | SIZE **TO 3 M** |

NATIVE GINGER

This perennial herb has a number of thick, erect stems arising from an underground rhizome, which form a dense clump. **Leaves** Alternate, smooth and soft, 12-40 cm long and 2-10 cm wide. They are glossy green above, dull green and paler below, with a prominent, raised midrib. They fold upwards from the midrib and have wavy margins, often purple-edged. The leaf bases wrap around the stem and are often tinged with purple. **Flowers** Appear in spring and summer in a terminal cluster 10-30 cm long. Individual flowers are about 25 mm long, pale yellow with a purplish lip. They have a tubular base 12-14 mm long, 2 petals 5-8 mm long and a circular lower petal about 1 cm across. **Fruit** Globular capsules about 12 mm across, with a brittle blue outer covering. Ripe in summer and autumn. **Habitat** Widespread in rainforests along the coast and lower tablelands.

Forests and Woodlands

Eucalypt trees thrive in Australia's low nutrient soils and dry conditions, and dominate the forests, forming a fairly open canopy above an understorey of shrubs or grasses. In the wet sclerophyll forests of the coast and tablelands they tower over a much denser understorey, reaching heights of 70 m or more. Drier forests with less fertile soils intergrade with woodlands as the rainfall decreases, and are dominated by smaller eucalypts, she-oaks (casuarinas) and wattles (acacias). Many flower profusely and provide copious amounts of nectar to feed brightly coloured parrots, honeyeaters, possums and gliders.

Many Australian plants have to cope with low rainfall and extended periods of drought, and have developed small, linear, thick and drooping leaves to minimise water loss. The soft, greyish-blue colours of the Australian bush come from the oil content and waxy coating of eucalypt leaves. Wax further reduces water loss while the toxic oil deters most herbivores. Evaporating eucalyptus oil creates the blue haze above montane forests and is extremely volatile, leading to frequent bushfires. Most Australian trees outside the rainforests are well adapted to fire, with thick bark, lignotubers and woody seeds or fruits that release their seeds after fire.

Woodlands extend right around Australia and support more than half of Australia's land birds. They are mostly dominated by small to medium-high eucalypts, well-spaced with large round crowns above a grassy understorey, or an understorey of perennial herbs in temperate areas.

Semi-arid and arid woodlands extend to the edges of the dry interior and are scattered patchily through it. They are characterised by low, stunted eucalypts and acacias forming an almost continuous canopy less than 8 m high, with a lower layer of shrubs and some ground cover.

| FAMILY **AGAVACEAE** | SPECIES *Doryanthes excelsa* | FORM **HERB** | SIZE **TO 4 M** |

GIANT LILY

This giant perennial herb produces a very long and straight flowering stem, arising from a basal clump of long leaves. The stem bears spectacular clusters of red flowers. **Leaves** Arise from the root system at the base of the plant. They are fibrous and sword-like, 1-2 m long and 10-15 cm wide with a pointed tip and distinct spines on the margins. **Flowers** Appear in spring. They are pinkish-red or rarely white, tubular, 10-16 cm long with 6 spreading petals and produce large quantities of nectar. They are arranged in a large, globular cluster about 25 cm across with large red bracts at the base. the flowers are produced at the end of a stout solitary flowering stem 2-4 m long. **Fruit** Woody, ovoid, 3-celled capsules, 7-10 cm long, containing many flat, winged seeds, each 15-23 mm long. **Habitat** Forests and woodlands along the coast and adjacent ranges.

| FAMILY **AGAVACEAE** | SPECIES *Doryanthes palmeri* | FORM **HERB** | SIZE **TO 4 M** |

SPEAR LILY

This very tall, perennial herb produces a huge red flowerhead at the end of a long, straight flower stem arising from a cluster of long basal leaves. **Leaves** Fleshy and sword-like, arising from the root system at the base of the plant, 1-2 m long and 5-7 cm or more wide with pointed tips. **Flowers** Appear in late winter and spring. They are red to red-brown, paler or white at the base, tubular to cup-shaped, and about 6-12 cm long. They have 6 fleshy petals and 6 conspicuous stamens. They are arranged in groups of 3 or 4 surrounded by reddish leafy bracts, creating a large conical flowerhead to 1 m long, at the end of a stout solitary flowering stem 2-3 m long. **Fruit** Oval, woody, 3-celled capsules, 7-9 cm long, containing numerous flat, winged seeds, 15-22 mm long. **Habitat** Exposed rocky outcrops, mostly on hillsides in wet sclerophyll forests along the coast and adjacent ranges.

| FAMILY **ARECACEAE** | SPECIES *Livistona humilis* | FORM **PALM** | SIZE **TO 6 M** |

SAND PALM

This small, fan-leaved palm has a sparse, spreading crown of bright green fronds. A skirt of dead fronds usually surrounds the top of the trunk. **Leaves** Up to 1.3 m long including the 40-90 cm long stalk. They are fan-shaped, to 80 cm diameter, pleated at the base and divided one-third the way up into 30-40 narrow segments tapering to long, forked, thread-like tips. The leaf stalks have small, forward-pointing spines on the edges and their fibrous bases sheath the top of the trunk. **Flowers** Appear from September to May in large loose clusters to 2 m long, arising from the bases of the upper fronds. They are yellow, 2-4 mm across, with 3 broad sepals and 3 oblong petals. **Fruit** Purplish-black berries, 10-17 mm across, containing a single seed with a fleshy outer layer. Ripe from January to July. **Habitat** Sandy soils in open forests and woodlands, often forming colonies.

| FAMILY **BLECHNACEAE** | SPECIES *Doodia aspera* | FORM **FERN** | SIZE **TO 45 CM** |

PRICKLY RASP FERN

This small, robust, fern has erect fronds arising from a short-creeping rhizome, which producies long underground suckers to form a spreading, tufted clump. **Fronds** Erect, 10-45 cm long, dissected down to the midrib into numerous linear to triangular segments to 6 cm long. They are coarse with a prominent central vein and prickly toothed margins. The pale green segments are attached by broad bases to a cream-coloured midrib, grooved above and convex below. The lowermost pair are sometimes shortly stalked. New growth is bright pink to reddish. **Spores** Masses of minute spores are grouped in distinct raised round clusters, 1-2 mm across, sometimes joining together with age. They are produced in single or double rows along the whole length of the fertile leaf segments on either side of the main vein. **Habitat** It grows in large colonies in tall open eucalypt forests, rainforest gullies, and among rocks and boulders in woodlands along the coast and tablelands.

| FAMILY **CASUARINACEAE** | SPECIES *Allocasuarina torulosa* | FORM **TREE** | SIZE **TO 30 M** |

FOREST OAK

This medium-sized tree has a straight trunk to 1.3 m diameter and an open crown of spreading branches with pendant foliage clumped at the ends. **Bark** Light brown to black, persistent, furrowed with sharp corky ridges. **Leaves** Minute, 0.3-0.8 mm long with tiny pointed tips, they are grouped in whorls of 4 or 5, at intervals of 3-6 mm along needle-like, pendant branchlets to 14 cm long and about 1 mm diameter. **Flowers** Appear in spring and summer. They are light brown, tiny, on separate male and female trees. Female flowers are globular, hairy, in alternating whorls of 5 along the branchlets. Male flowers form short cylindrical spikes, 1-3 cm long, at the ends of the branchlets. **Fruit** Barrel-shaped, grey to brown, woody, warty cones, 15-33 mm long and 12-25 mm diameter. On slender stalks 1-3 cm long, they open to release brown, winged seeds, 8-12 mm long. **Habitat** Moist open forests on coastal hills and ranges.

| FAMILY **CASUARINACEAE** | SPECIES *Casuarina cunninghamiana* | FORM **TREE** | SIZE **TO 35 M** |

RIVER OAK

This medium-sized to tall tree has a straight trunk to 1.5 m diameter, and a slender, conical crown with fine, pendulous or erect branchlets. **Bark** Dark grey, hard and deeply-furrowed, with conspicuous white, raised blisters on young trees. **Leaves** Minute with tiny pointed tips. They form whorls of 6-10 at intervals of 4-9 mm along the needle-like, dark green, longitudinally grooved branchlets. The branchlets are 10-25 cm long and about 0.6 mm diameter; some are shed after 2-3 seasons. **Flowers** Appear in winter and spring on separate male and female trees. They are small, light brown or red. Female flowers are ovoid, hairy, about 4 mm across, in alternating whorls of 6-7 along the small branches. Male flowers form short, dense, cylindrical spikes, 1-2 cm long, at the ends of the branchlets. **Fruit** Slightly flattened, ovoid, grey to brown woody cones about 1 cm long. On short stalks, they open to release winged brown seeds. **Habitat** Stream banks in open forests.

FAMILY **COCHLOSPERMACEAE** SPECIES *Cochlospermum gillivraei* FORM **TREE** SIZE **TO 12 M**

COTTON TREE

This small deciduous tree has a slender trunk to 40 cm diameter and a small, sparse crown.

Bark Brown to greyish-brown, flaky and fissured with small rectangular scales. **Leaves** Alternate, divided into 5-7 narrow leaflets radiating from the end of the leaf stalks. Each leaf is about 7 cm long and 2 cm wide, dark green and sometimes has slightly toothed margins. **Flowers** Appear in winter and spring when the tree is leafless. They are bright yellow with pink spots and stripes, open, 4-6 cm across, and have 5 notched petals and numerous stamens. They are grouped in short clusters borne at the ends of leafless branches. **Fruit** Brown, globular or oblong capsules, 8-10 cm across. They have 5 valves opening to reveal numerous small, dark seeds embedded in a mass of fine, silky, cotton-like hairs. Ripe in summer and autumn. **Habitat** Rocky sites in tropical woodlands and monsoon forests, in coastal and inland areas.

FAMILY **CYCADACEAE** SPECIES *Cycas media* FORM **CYCAD** SIZE **TO 4 M**

ZAMIA PALM

This stout, palm-like cycad has a crown of dark green leaves emerging from the top of a thick and often fire-blackened trunk, which grows to 35 cm diameter and is packed with triangular leaf scars. **Leaves** Stiff and leathery, to 2 m long and 50 cm across, on a stalk to 35 cm long bearing yellow spines along the margins. They are divided into some 300 closely-spaced, opposite, forward-pointing leaflets with sharply-pointed tips, 10-20 cm long and 7-10 mm wide, becoming smaller towards the base. **Cones** Arise in the centre of the crown on male and female plants. Male cones are yellowish-brown and pineapple-like, 12-25 cm long, with many spirally-arranged segments, opening to release pollen. Female cones are globular, 25 cm across, opening into a rosette of pale brown, leaf-like segments on long scurfy stalks. **Fruit** Orange, globular, 2-4 cm across, borne in clusters of 2-8. They comprise a large seed with a thin fleshy coat. **Habitat** Rocky sites in open forests.

FAMILY **DENNSTAEDTIACEAE** SPECIES *Pteridium esculentum* FORM **FERN** SIZE **TO 3 M**

COMMON BRACKEN

This tall, coarse, fern has a long-creeping, much-branched, woody rhizome giving rise to stout leaf stalks. **Fronds** Stiffly erect, dark green, 0.6-3 m long including the brown stalks. They are twice-divided into numerous coarse and leathery segments with short, fine hairs beneath, deeply lobed at the base of the frond, and often divided again. All segments have a small lobe at the base, and they may have a few reddish hairs near the margins on the upper surface. The leaf stalks are grooved on the upper surface and the midribs may bear a few dark red hairs. **Spores** Contained in continuous linear clusters below the curled-under margins of the fertile leaf segments. **Habitat** It grows in abundance in a wide variety of habitats on well-drained soils in dry open forests; damp, sandy flats; sandstone gullies; at the edge of sand dunes and in pastures.

FAMILY **DICKSONIACEAE**   SPECIES *Calochlaena dubia*   FORM **FERN**   SIZE **TO 1.5 M**

COMMON GROUND FERN

This tall, spreading fern has tough, lacy fronds and a stout, long-creeping, branched rhizome, 8-25 mm diameter, which is clothed with soft, silvery hairs intermixed with golden-yellow hairs. **Fronds** Pale to yellowish-green, broadly triangular in outline, erect with drooping tips, 40-150 cm long, including the yellow-brown stalks which are 30-80 cm long. The fronds are twice-divided into many small, deeply-lobed segments up to 1 cm long with broad bases. The lower ones may be further divided. **Spores** Produced in large masses forming raised, round clusters, 8-15 mm diameter, on the undersides of the fertile leaf segments, close to the margins which are partially folded over them. There are up to 20 clusters per segment, positioned at the ends of the veins. **Habitat** Grows in very large colonies on forested slopes, open gullies and creek flats, usually on poor soils, along the coast and tablelands.

FAMILY **DILLENIACEAE**   SPECIES *Hibbertia dentata*   FORM **SHRUB**   SIZE **TO 2 M**

TWINING GUINEA FLOWER

This is a prostrate or climbing shrub with long, wiry stems. **Leaves** Alternate, 4-7 cm long and 15-30 mm wide with sharply-toothed or lobed margins. The leaves are often purplish, and have stalks 8-12 mm long. **Flowers** Appear in early spring through to early summer. They are yellow and open, 25-50 mm across. They have 5 separate, delicate, spreading petals (sometimes notched at the tip), 5 slightly hairy sepals with pointed tips, and numerous protruding yellow stamens. The flowers grow singly at the ends of the stems. **Fruit** Dry and leathery, opening at the top when mature to release numerous shiny seeds with a reddish-brown, fleshy coat. **Habitat** Tall moist forests and rainforest margins along the coast and lower tablelands.

FAMILY **GOODENIACEAE**   SPECIES *Goodenia ovata*   FORM **SHRUB**   SIZE **TO 2 M**

HOP GOODENIA

This is a weak, erect or scrambling shrub, often with sticky young shoots and leaves. **Leaves** Alternate with finely-toothed margins, thin and minutely hairy. They are very variable in size, ranging from 2-10 cm long and 1-6 cm wide. the leaves are shiny above and slightly paler green beneath, and have stalks 6-15 mm long. **Flowers** Appear mainly in spring and summer. They are bright yellow, tubular, 15-20 mm long and about 2 cm across. They have 5 widely-spreading, rounded lobes, 2 of the lobes arch over the pollen cup. The flowers are arranged in groups of 3-6 in the leaf axils, on stalks to 4 cm long. **Fruit** Narrow cylindrical capsules, 8-15 mm long, containing flat seeds. **Habitat** Widespread, mostly in moist forests and woodlands, also on coastal cliffs and headlands.

| FAMILY **IRIDACEAE** | SPECIES *Patersonia sericea* | FORM **HERB** | SIZE **TO 30 CM** |

BUSH IRIS

This is an erect, perennial, densely-tufted herb growing from a rhizome. Its flowering stem has silky hairs.

Leaves Long, tough and sword-shaped, arising from the base of the stem. They are 15-30 cm long and 2-5 mm wide, with woolly edges at the base when young.

Flowers Appear in succession from late winter to early summer, withering after a few hours to be replaced by others from the cluster. They are purple, 3-4 cm across and 15-30 mm long, with 3 broad, spreading, extremely delicate petals, 3 very small petals and 3 yellow-tipped stamens. They grow in small clusters at the ends of the flowering stems above 2 brown, silky to smooth, sheathing bracts, 2-4 cm long. **Fruit** Cylindrical to ovoid, 3-angled capsules, 15-30 mm long. They contain numerous brown seeds about 3 mm long. **Habitat** Widespread in sandy soils in open forests, woodlands, heaths and the margins of swamps along the coast and ranges.

| FAMILY **LAMIACEAE** | SPECIES *Ajuga australis* | FORM **HERB** | SIZE **TO 60 CM** |

AUSTRALIAN BUGLE

This is an erect or spreading, scented, greyish, downy, perennial herb with toothed leaves that decrease in size towards the top of the stems. **Leaves** Opposite, hairy and soft, forming a rosette around the base of the plant, with a long stalk, bluntly and distinctly toothed. They are 4-12 cm long and 2-4 cm wide, changing gradually into small stalkless upper leaves with entire margins. **Flowers** Appear in spring and summer. They are blue or purple, rarely pinkish; tubular; 7-20 mm long; and have a long, 3-lobed lower lip, and an inconspicuous, 2-lobed upper lip. They are stalkless, with 4 stamens projecting beyond the lower lip, and arranged in false-whorls of 6-20 in the leaf axils, often forming a leafy spike. **Fruit** Wrinkled obovoid nutlets containing a single seed and enclosed in the remains of the flower. **Habitat** Sandy soils and rocky outcrops in open forests and mallee along the coast and inland.

| FAMILY **LAMIACEAE** | SPECIES *Prostanthera nivea* | FORM **SHRUB** | SIZE **TO 4 M** |

SNOWY MINT-BUSH

This is an upright, smooth, sometimes fairly dense, non-aromatic, bright-green shrub belonging to the mint family. **Leaves** Opposite, stalkless, narrow, flat or with the margins turned up. They are 1-5 cm long and 1-3 mm wide, smooth or with dense white hairs.

Flowers Appear mainly in spring and early summer. They are large, white, sometimes mauve-tinged, with orange-yellow spots inside the throat. Hairy and tubular, they are 10-18 mm long with a 3-lobed spreading lower lip and a much larger, erect, 2-lobed upper lip. They are borne solitary in the upper leaf axils forming leafy clusters.

Fruit Comprise 4 small wrinkled nutlets, each containing a single seed.

Habitat Scattered in isolated occurrences, mostly on drier hilly and rocky sites in open forests, woodlands and heaths, on the coast and inland.

FAMILY **LAMIACEAE**   SPECIES *Prostanthera rotundifolia*   FORM **SHRUB**   SIZE **TO 3 M**

ROUND-LEAVED MINT-BUSH

This upright, hairy and bushy shrub is a member of the mint family, and has strongly-scented minty leaves when crushed. **Leaves** Opposite, often appearing clustered, and rather thick. They have obscure veins, are on long stalks, and have entire margins or are cut regularly into rounded teeth. Dull, dark green above and paler below, they are 4-15 mm long and 4-14 mm wide. The branchlets are covered with soft hairs. **Flowers** Appear in spring and early summer. They are purple to blue, sometimes pinkish and rarely white. They are tubular, 10-15 mm long and hooded, with a 3-lobed, spreading, lower lip and an equal-sized, erect, 2-lobed upper lip. They are solitary but crowded into short clusters arising from the leaf axils, or looser clusters at the ends of the branches. **Fruit** Comprise 4 small wrinkled nutlets, each containing a single seed. **Habitat** Widespread in sheltered rocky sites and along streams in open forests and woodlands of the coast and tablelands.

FAMILY **LECYTHIDACEAE**   SPECIES *Planchonia careya*   FORM **TREE**   SIZE **TO 10 M**

COCKY APPLE

This small tree has an open crown and is briefly deciduous in the dry season. **Bark** Grey, rough, fissured and slightly corky. **Leaves** Alternate, 2-14 cm long and 2-7 cm wide on winged stalks 5-30 mm long. They have small, rounded teeth on the margins, are softly-leathery, glossy light green above with distinct veins, and dull below. They turn rusty-orange before falling. **Flowers** Open in the evening and fall by morning. They appear in winter and spring, are large, white with a green tubular base and numerous white and pink, protruding, yellow-tipped stamens to 6 cm long. They have 4 white, fleshy, spreading lobes about 3 cm long, grouped in small clusters arising from the leaf axils. **Fruit** Pale green, fleshy, egg-shaped, edible berries to 10 cm long and 5 cm wide. They have several horseshoe-shaped seeds enclosed in fibrous pulp. Ripe in spring and summer. **Habitat** A common understorey tree in open forests and woodlands.

FAMILY **LILIACEAE**   SPECIES *Dianella revoluta*   FORM **HERB**   SIZE **TO 1.2 M**

BLACK-ANTHER FLAX LILY

This is a tufted or mat-forming perennial herb with rigid stems and long leaves around the base of the plant. **Leaves** The leaves are long and linear and arranged in pairs arising from and sheathing the base of the plant. They are leathery with curled-under margins, 10-85 cm long and 4-15 mm wide. **Flowers** Appear in winter, spring and summer. They are purple to blue, open, 7-12 mm across with 6 rounded lobes and 6 long, thick, yellow-brown anthers. The flowers are borne in a loose, spreading, branched, terminal cluster of 2-9 flowers, 20-90 cm long. **Fruit** Blue to purple berries, 4-10 mm long, with shiny-black seeds. **Habitat** Widespread, especially in wetter sites in sclerophyll forests, woodlands and mallee.

| FAMILY **LORANTHACEAE** | SPECIES *Dendrophthoe vitellina* | FORM **SHRUB** |

LONG-FLOWER MISTLETOE

This parasitic, woody shrub grows attached to the branches of trees by a root-like structure that absorbs nutrient from the host. **Leaves** Mostly alternate and leathery with a prominent midrib. They are 4-16 cm long and 6-30 mm wide. **Flowers** Appear in spring and summer. They are yellow to scarlet, tubular and 25-50 mm long. They have 5 thin, waxy, scarlet, linear, spreading petals, and 5 long, protruding, yellow stamens. They are arranged in dense axillary clusters of 5-20 flowers. **Fruit** Yellow to red ovoid berries, 10-15 mm long, containing a single seed. The seeds are much sought after by mistletoe birds. They are surrounded by a sticky layer that glues the seed to a branch when it is excreted by the bird. **Habitat** Attaches to many host trees in dry sclerophyll forests, especially rough-barked apple, on the coast and ranges.

| FAMILY **MIMOSACEAE** | SPECIES *Acacia longifolia* | FORM **TREE** | SIZE **TO 10 M** |

SYDNEY GOLDEN WATTLE

This wattle varies from a straight, slender tree in shaded bushland to a dense shrub with a low, widely-spreading crown in open sites. The branchlets are angled or flattened. **Bark** Dull grey and finely-fissured. **Leaves** Alternate, stiff and leathery with a small inconspicuous gland on the edge of the leaf near the base. They are 6-20 cm long and 4-35 mm wide, with prominent longitudinal veins and conspicuous lateral veins. **Flowers** Appear in winter and spring. They are packed into golden-yellow fluffy cylindrical spikes, 2-6 cm long, arising from the leaf axils. **Fruit** Rough, leathery beaked pods, green turning pale brown. They are narrow, cylindrical, straight or curved, 5-12 cm long and 3-8 mm wide, and slightly constricted between the seeds. They become curled and twisted when dry, and are ripe in late spring and early summer. **Habitat** Widespread in forests, woodlands and cleared sites, along the coast and tablelands, preferring moist sandy soils.

| FAMILY **MIMOSACEAE** | SPECIES *Acacia stricta* | FORM **SHRUB** | SIZE **TO 4 M** |

HOP WATTLE

This is an erect or spreading shrub with a smooth bark and ascending angular branches. The young branchlets have resinous edges. **Leaves** The leaves are alternate, flat and leathery and rarely have a short point. They are 5-15 cm long and 3-15 mm wide, with a prominent central vein and aromatic oil glands near the base. **Flowers** Appear in winter and spring. Individual flowers are tiny and are packed into pale yellow to white, fluffy, globular flowerheads each comprising 20-30 flowers. The flowerheads are about 8 mm diameter on stalks 2-8 mm long, and are arranged in clusters of 2 or 4 arising from the leaf axils. **Fruit** pale brown, rough, usually flat, thin, narrow pods. They are 3-10 cm long and 2-5 mm wide and are not constricted between the seeds. **Habitat** Often found in moist sites in open forests of the coast and ranges.

FAMILY **MIMOSACEAE** SPECIES *Acacia terminalis* FORM **SHRUB** SIZE **TO 6 M**

SUNSHINE WATTLE

This is usually an erect or spreading shrub, although it rarely grows to a small tree. It has angular branches coloured deep red when young. **Leaves** Alternate, 3-8 cm long, and divided into 1-6 pairs of segments which are 3-5 cm long. These are each further divided into 8-16 pairs of blunt leaflets, paler below, 8-20 mm long and 2-5 mm wide. **Flowers** Appear in late summer, winter or spring. They are packed into pale to golden-yellow or white fluffy, globular flowerheads about 6 mm across, comprising 6-15 flowers. The flowerheads are arranged in loose, terminal clusters. **Fruit** Wrinkled, oblong, slightly curved or straight pods, which are reddish when young. They are flat, 3-11 cm long and 8-17 mm wide with thickened margins, and are not constricted between the seeds. **Habitat** Usually found on rocky hillsides in dry open forests, woodlands and scrubs along the coast and tablelands.

FAMILY **MYRTACEAE** SPECIES *Angophora costata* FORM **TREE** SIZE **TO 30 M**

SMOOTH-BARKED APPLE

This medium-sized tree has a stout trunk to 1.2 m diameter, twisted limbs and an open crown. **Bark** Pink to orange-brown, turning grey before peeling. It is smooth and sheds annually in thin scales leaving a slightly dimpled surface, often stained with exuding red kino. **Leaves** Opposite 7-17 cm long and 15-35 mm wide. Young leaves are bright red becoming mid-green with a prominent yellowish midrib. **Flowers** Appear in spring and summer. They are cream with numerous stamens to 1 cm long spreading from a short, tubular calyx with a hairy, ribbed exterior. They have 5 petals 3-4 mm wide, and are grouped in dense terminal clusters on slightly hairy stalks 7-18 mm long. **Fruit** Grey-brown, soft, woody, cup-shaped capsules. These are 9-15 mm long and 10-15 mm across, with 5 main ribs, a 5-toothed rim and 3-4 enclosed valves with large, flat seeds. **Habitat** Widespread in moist sandstone areas in tall open forests and woodlands.

FAMILY **MYRTACEAE** SPECIES *Corymbia calophylla* FORM **TREE** SIZE **TO 40 M**

MARRI

This medium-sized or tall tree has a thick trunk to 1.5 m diameter and a fairly dense, heavily-branched, spreading crown. **Bark** Grey becoming dark brown, often stained by red gum. It is fibrous, rough and flaky with small square scales. **Leaves** Alternate, 9-18 cm long and 20-45 mm wide, on stalks 15-20 mm long. They are glossy green above and paler below with a prominent midrib and parallel lateral veins. **Flowers** Appear in late summer and autumn. They are pink or white, about 4 cm across, with many stamens spreading from a central disc, grouped in terminal clusters of 3-7 flowers. Buds are ovoid with a short point and a hemispherical, yellowish-green cap, 8-15 mm long and 5-9 mm across. **Fruit** Large, urn-shaped, woody capsules, 3-5 cm long and 3-4 cm across, with 4 deeply-enclosed valves and large black seeds to 2 cm long. **Habitat** Sandy soils in open forests along the coast and nearby ranges.

| FAMILY **MYRTACEAE** | SPECIES *Corymbia ficifolia* | FORM **TREE** | SIZE **TO 15 M** |

RED-FLOWERING GUM

This is usually a small tree with a short, thick trunk, and a heavily branched, broad, leafy crown bearing spectacular red flowers in summer. **Bark** Light grey to dark brown, rough, scaly, short-fibred and persistent. **Leaves** Alternate, 8-15 cm long and 3-5 cm wide on a stout stalk, 1-2 cm long. Glossy dark green above and paler below, the leaves are leathery with a prominent midrib and widely-spreading veins. **Flowers** Appear mainly in summer. They are crimson to scarlet, pink or white, to 4 cm across, comprising many stamens spreading from a central disc. They are grouped in large terminal flowerheads often 25-35 cm across, comprising 3-7 flowered clusters on angular stalks. Buds are cylindrical to conical, 20-25 mm long and about 13 mm across. **Fruit** Urn-shaped woody capsules, 20-35 mm long and 2-3 cm across with 4 deeply-enclosed valves. **Habitat** Sandy soils in open forests near the coast.

| FAMILY **MYRTACEAE** | SPECIES *Corymbia maculata* | FORM **TREE** | SIZE **TO 50 M** |

SPOTTED GUM

This tall tree has a trunk to 1.4 m diameter, and a high, fairly dense, crown. **Bark** Smooth, powdery, and spotted with white, pink, grey and yellow patches. It is often dimpled and sheds in small flakes.
Leaves Alternate with a short stalk, 10-30 cm long and 1-6 cm wide with a prominent midrib and parallel lateral veins. They are dark green above, often paler below. **Flowers** Appear in winter. They are creamy-white, perfumed, about 2 cm across, comprising many stamens spreading from a central disc. They are grouped in terminal clusters of usually 3 flowers on stalks 5-20 mm long. Buds are ovoid with a short point and usually have a reddish-brown cap, 6-11 mm long and 4-7 mm across. **Fruit** Urn-shaped to ovoid woody capsules, 10-18 mm long and 9-12 mm across, with 3-4 enclosed valves. **Habitat** Widespread on sandy soils in taller open forests of the coast and up to 400 km inland.

| FAMILY **MYRTACEAE** | SPECIES *Eucalyptus bicostata* | FORM **TREE** | SIZE **TO 45 M** |

SOUTHERN BLUE GUM

This medium-sized or tall tree has a straight trunk to 1.3 m diameter and a fairly spreading crown. **Bark** White or greyish, smooth and persistent at the base of the trunk. It peels in long strips to leave a smooth surface in pale shades of grey, blue, cream or brown.
Leaves Alternate with fine, regular veins and a prominent midrib. They are 12-35 cm long and 2-4 cm wide, thick, and glossy dark green. **Flowers** Appear in spring and summer. They are cream, comprising many stamens spreading from a central disc. They are solitary or in axillary clusters of 3. Buds are warty, flattened, bluish-green, 14-17 mm long and 11-14 mm across, covered with a whitish bloom. **Fruit** Conical to cup-shaped, ribbed, warty, woody capsules, 8-20 mm long and 10-20 mm across, with 3-4 protruding valves and a broad, usually convex disc. **Habitat** Scattered in moist hilly country in tall open forests in the inland ranges and slopes.

| FAMILY **MYRTACEAE** | SPECIES *Eucalyptus crebra* | FORM **TREE** | SIZE **TO 35 M** |

NARROW-LEAVED IRONBARK

This medium-sized tree has a straight trunk to 1.5 m diameter and a fairly open, straggly crown. **Bark** Light to dark grey or black, hard and deeply furrowed, exuding a reddish gum in places, and persistent to the smaller branches. **Leaves** Alternate with a prominent midrib and thin stalk, 7-16 cm long and 7-17 mm wide, dull green or grey-green. **Flowers** Appear from winter to early summer. They are cream or white, about 12 mm across, comprising many stamens spreading from a central disc. They are grouped in terminal clusters of 4-11 flowers on stalks 4-12 mm long. Buds are diamond-shaped, 3-8 mm long and 2-4 mm across. **Fruit** Ovoid to pear-shaped woody capsules, 3-6 mm across, with 3-4 valves at or below rim level. **Habitat** Widespread in open forests and woodlands on a wide variety of soils, from the coast to the edge of the western plains, on low plateaus and undulating plains.

| FAMILY **MYRTACEAE** | SPECIES *Eucalyptus deanei* | FORM **TREE** | SIZE **TO 75 M** |

MOUNTAIN BLUE GUM

This tall, straight tree is the tallest tree in New South Wales. **Bark** Smooth, grey, usually with a short stocking of rough bark at the base of the trunk. It sheds in plates and ribbons higher up, revealing bluish-grey, fawn or yellowish patches. **Leaves** Alternate, 8-15 cm long and 17-40 mm wide, paler beneath, with faint veins. They often mix with the broad, almost round, juvenile leaves on the tree. **Flowers** Appear in late summer and autumn. They are creamy-white, comprising many stamens spreading from a central disc, grouped in axillary clusters of 7-11 flowers on stalks 10-13 mm long. Buds are acorn-like, often with a short beak. **Fruit** Bell-shaped or urn-shaped woody capsules, 5-6 mm across, on flattened stalks. They have 3-4 broad, triangular valves at rim level or slightly above. **Habitat** Dominant tree in the Blue Mountains Blue Gum forest, growing in deep soils in valleys and sheltered terraces in tall open forests.

| FAMILY **MYRTACEAE** | SPECIES *Eucalyptus grandis* | FORM **TREE** | SIZE **TO 70 M** |

FLOODED GUM

This tall tree has a straight trunk to 3 m diameter, ascending branches and a tufted, fairly sparse crown in forests, dense and conical in open areas. **Bark** White to light grey, often with some rough black bark near the base. It is smooth above, persistent on the lower trunk, shedding higher up in short ribbons or flakes. **Leaves** Alternate, often with wavy margins, 10-20 cm long and 20-35 mm wide, on a stalk about 2 cm long. They are bluish below. **Flowers** Appear in autumn and winter. They are white, about 2 cm across, comprising many stamens spreading from a central disc, and are grouped in axillary clusters of 3-12 on a flattened or angular stalk, 8-18 mm long. Buds are yellowish-green or bluish-green, club-shaped, 5-8 mm long and 3-5 mm across. **Fruit** Pear-shaped, stalkless woody capsules, 5-8 mm long and 4-7 mm wide with 4-5 protruding valves. **Habitat** Moist, well-drained soils in coastal forests and rainforest margins.

| FAMILY **MYRTACEAE** | SPECIES *Eucalyptus marginata* | FORM **TREE** | SIZE **TO 40 M** |

JARRAH

This large tree has a straight trunk to 2 m diameter and a well-developed crown of dark green foliage covering the top half of the tree. On poor sites it may be reduced to a stunted, mallee form. **Bark** Red-brown, weathering to grey, fibrous with longitudinal fissures, rough and persistent to the young branches. **Leaves** Alternate with a fine point; 8-13 cm long and 15-30 mm wide; with channelled stalks 12-16 mm long; glossy dark green above and paler below. **Flowers** Appear in spring and summer. They are creamy-white, to 15 mm across, comprising many stamens spreading from a central disc, and are grouped in axillary clusters of 7-11 flowers on stalks to 2 cm long. Buds are narrow and pointed, 8-17 mm long and 3-5 mm across. **Fruit** Globular woody capsules, 9-16 mm across, with 3 enclosed valves. **Habitat** Common on sandy soils along the coast and adjacent ranges.

| FAMILY **MYRTACEAE** | SPECIES *Eucalyptus miniata* | FORM **TREE** | SIZE **TO 30 M** |

DARWIN WOOLLYBUTT

This small or medium-sized tree has a trunk to 1 m diameter, high branches and a moderately dense, spreading crown. **Bark** Grey or rusty red, spongy, rough and persistent on the lower trunk, shedding in papery flakes higher up to leave a smooth or powdery whitish surface. **Leaves** Alternate, 9-16 cm long and 1-5 cm wide, with a flattened stalk 12-20 mm long. **Flowers** Appear in winter. They are orange or scarlet, to 35 mm across, stalkless or on short stalks, comprising many stamens spreading from a central disc. They are grouped in axillary or terminal clusters of 3-7 on stalks to 35 mm long. Buds are ovate to club-shaped, often strongly ribbed, 11-25 mm long and 7-12 mm across, with a pointed cap. **Fruit** Cylindrical to ovoid, usually ribbed, woody capsules, 3-6 cm long and 17-50 mm across, with 3 deeply enclosed valves. **Habitat** Widespread in low tablelands and undulating sandstone country.

| FAMILY **MYRTACEAE** | SPECIES *Eucalyptus obliqua* | FORM **TREE** | SIZE **TO 70 M** |

MESSMATE

This medium or tall tree has a straight trunk to 3 m diameter and a moderately dense crown. In harsh conditions it is multi-stemmed and mallee-like. **Bark** Persistent to the smaller branches, rough at the base and smooth above. It is thick and grey, fibrous to stringy, and shed in ribbons. **Leaves** Alternate, with an asymmetrical base, prominent midrib and distinct lateral veins. They are glossy dark green, thick, 9-16 cm long and 15-33 mm wide. **Flowers** Appear in summer. They are white or cream, about 15 mm across, comprising many stamens spreading from a central disc, and are grouped in axillary clusters of 7-11 flowers on angular or flattened stalks, 4-15 mm long. Buds are club-shaped, 4-7 mm long and 2-4 mm across. **Fruit** Cup-shaped to urn-shaped woody capsules, 6-11 mm long and 5-9 mm across, with 3 or 4 enclosed valves. **Habitat** Widespread in moist open forests on the foothills and tablelands in cool areas to about 1300 m.

FAMILY **MYRTACEAE**   SPECIES *Eucalyptus oleosa*   FORM **TREE**   SIZE **TO 12 M**

RED MALLEE

This mallee or small spreading tree often has a number of slender stems arising from an underground rootstock, and an open, umbrella-like crown. **Bark** Grey to pale brownish-grey; persistent at the base; rough, fibrous and flaky on lower stems; shedding in ribbons revealing glossy grey to red bark. It is smooth above. **Leaves** Alternate with a prominent midrib, faint veins and many oil glands. They are 5-12 cm long and 8-20 mm wide with stalks 8-18 mm long, shiny dark green or blue-green. **Flowers** Appear mainly in winter and spring. They are creamy-white to pale yellow, about 1 cm across, comprising many stamens spreading from a central disc, and are grouped in clusters of 4-13 flowers on slightly flattened stalks 7-12 mm long. Buds are acorn-like, 5-8 mm long and 3-4 mm across. **Fruit** Conical to pear-shaped woody capsules, 4-7 mm across, usually with 3 fragile, needle-like, protruding valves. **Habitat** Red sandy soils in open woodlands in dry temperate regions.

FAMILY **MYRTACEAE**   SPECIES *Eucalyptus pauciflora*   FORM **TREE**   SIZE **TO 20 M**

SNOW GUM

This medium-sized, often crooked tree has a short trunk to 1 m diameter. It is low-branching with a spreading, open crown. **Bark** Shed in irregular patches in autumn, leaving a smooth white to yellow, olive-green or brown surface, occasionally with scribbly markings from insect larvae. **Leaves** Alternate, variable, with a short stalk, prominent midrib and almost parallel longitudinal veins. They are 6-19 cm long and 12-32 mm wide, thick, leathery and shiny green. **Flowers** Appear in spring and early summer. They are white or cream, about 15 mm across, comprising many stamens spreading from a central disc, and are grouped in axillary clusters of 7-15 flowers on thick stalks 3-16 mm long. Buds are club-shaped, 5-15 mm long and 3-6 mm across. **Fruit** Ovoid to cup-shaped woody capsules, 6-14 mm long and 5-9 mm wide, with 3-4 valves at or below rim level. **Habitat** Open forests and woodlands above 700 m along the coast and tablelands.

FAMILY **MYRTACEAE**   SPECIES *Eucalyptus pilularis*   FORM **TREE**   SIZE **TO 70 M**

BLACKBUTT

This tall tree has a long, straight trunk to 3 m diameter and a fairly open, elongated to spreading crown. **Bark** Greyish-brown, rough and fibrous, persistent on most of the trunk. It sheds in long strips from the upper trunk leaving a smooth, white or yellowish-grey surface, often with scribbly insect markings. **Leaves** Alternate, 9-16 cm long and 15-40 mm wide. They are dark glossy green above and slightly paler below with a prominent midrib. **Flowers** Appear from spring to autumn. They are white, about 15 mm across, comprising many stamens spreading from a central disc, and are grouped in axillary clusters of 7-15 flowers on flattened or angular stalks, 10-17 mm long. Buds are club-shaped, 7-11 mm long and 3-5 mm across, smooth or with 2 ribs. **Fruit** Hemispherical to globular woody capsules, 7-12 mm across with 4 small valves at or below rim level. **Habitat** Tall open forests along the coast and lower slopes to 300 m.

| FAMILY **MYRTACEAE** | SPECIES *Eucalyptus piperita* | FORM **TREE** | SIZE **TO 30 M** |

SYDNEY PEPPERMINT

This small to medium-sized tree is the most common tree in the Blue Mountains, and is named after the peppermint smell of its crushed leaves. It has a short trunk and a low, open and spreading crown. **Bark** Brown to dark grey, fibrous, persistent on the trunk and large branches, falling in ribbons from the upper branches to reveal pale new bark. **Leaves** Alternate, 6-14 cm long and 1-3 cm wide, dull bluish-green, with a prominent midrib and fine marginal veins. **Flowers** Appear in early summer. They are white, comprising many stamens spreading from a central disc, and grouped in axillary clusters of 7-15 flowers on slightly flattened stalks 6-10 mm long. Buds are yellow-green, 4-7 mm long, conical, with a long pointed cap.
Fruit Globular to slightly urn-shaped woody capsules, 6-7 mm long and 6-8 mm wide with 4 enclosed valves. **Habitat** Sandy soils on slopes and ridges in open forests along the coast and ranges.

| FAMILY **MYRTACEAE** | SPECIES *Eucalyptus rossii* | FORM **TREE** | SIZE **TO 25 M** |

INLAND SCRIBBLY GUM

This crooked or gnarled tree has irregular branches on poor sites, and is taller and more shapely on richer soils, with a trunk diameter up to 1 m and a fairly open, spreading crown. **Bark** Smooth, shed in short ribbons, yellow, weathering to grey, often mottled, usually with scribbly insect marking. **Leaves** Alternate with a short stalk and prominent midrib; 7-17 cm long and 6-15 mm wide; dull green, often greyish. **Flowers** Appear in summer. They are creamy-white, about 15 mm across, comprising many stamens spreading from a central disc, and are grouped in axillary clusters of 5-15 flowers on stalks 7-10 mm long. Buds are club-shaped, 3-7 mm long and 2-3 mm across. **Fruit** Ovoid woody capsules, 4-5 mm long and 5-6 mm across, usually with 4 valves at about rim level on a flat or convex disc. **Habitat** Usually on poor soils in open forests and woodlands along the coast and western slopes to 1000 m.

| FAMILY **MYRTACEAE** | SPECIES *Eucalyptus salmonophloia* | FORM **TREE** | SIZE **TO 30 M** |

SALMON GUM

This medium-sized tree has a straight trunk to 60 cm diameter, and a moderately dense, flattish, spreading crown. **Bark** Pale grey, shedding seasonally in large patches to reveal light reddish-brown, smooth new bark, which turns salmon pink and weathers to grey. **Leaves** Alternate, 6-12 cm long and 6-15 mm wide, on narrow stalks 10-15 mm long. They are glossy green with a prominent midrib. **Flowers** Appear in summer and autumn. They are creamy-white, about 12 mm across, comprising many stamens spreading from a central disc, and are grouped in axillary clusters of 7-13 flowers on slender stalks to 1 cm long. Buds are green, ovoid to globular, 3-7 mm long and 3-5 mm wide. **Fruit** Pear-shaped woody capsules, 3-5 mm long and 4-5 mm across, with 3 slender, pointed, protruding valves. **Habitat** Widespread in inland open forests and woodlands.

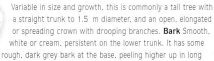

| FAMILY **MYRTACEAE** | SPECIES *Eucalyptus viminalis* | FORM **TREE** | SIZE **TO 50 M** |

RIBBON GUM

Variable in size and growth, this is commonly a tall tree with a straight trunk to 1.5 m diameter, and an open, elongated or spreading crown with drooping branches. **Bark** Smooth, white or cream, persistent on the lower trunk. It has some rough, dark grey bark at the base, peeling higher up in long ribbons during summer. **Leaves** Alternate, 8-20 cm long and 8-25 mm wide, glossy green with a prominent midrib. **Flowers** Appear mainly in summer. They are white, 15-20 mm across, comprising many stamens spreading from a central disc, and are grouped in axillary clusters of 3-7 flowers on flattened stalks 4-8 mm long. Buds are ovoid, stalkless, 5-10 mm long and 3-5 mm across. **Fruit** Spherical woody capsules, 4-9 mm diameter, with 3-4 protruding valves, often grouped in threes with very short stalks. **Habitat** Prefers moist soils near watercourses in open forests and grassy woodlands along the coast and tablelands up to 1400 m.

| FAMILY **MYRTACEAE** | SPECIES *Melaleuca quinquenervia* | FORM **TREE** | SIZE **TO 25 M** |

BROAD-LEAVED PAPERBARK

This small or medium-sized tree has a slender trunk, few branches and compact crown. **Bark** White to light brown, thick, spongy and rough. It peels readily in large, papery sheets. **Leaves** Alternate, 3-15 cm long and 8-30 mm wide, on flat, twisted stalks 4-10 mm long. They are dark green with 5 conspicuous longitudinal veins, mostly hairy. **Flowers** Appear in autumn and winter. They are white to cream or greenish with 5 small petals, 2-4 mm long, and numerous long, protruding stamens fused at their bases into 5 clawed bundles. They are grouped in dense cylindrical clusters, 2-8 cm long and 25-35 mm across, with new shoots often growing from the tip. **Fruit** Woody, cup-shaped, grey-brown, stalkless capsules, 4-5 mm across, which are clustered around the branchlets where they persist for up to a year. **Habitat** Stream banks and swamp margins in low woodlands and heaths, sometimes forming pure stands on moist coastal headlands and hillsides.

| FAMILY **ORCHIDACEAE** | SPECIES *Dipodium punctatum* | FORM **HERB** | SIZE **TO 90 CM** |

HYACINTH ORCHID

This upright, ground-dwelling, perennial saprophytic herb has an extensive system of long, thick tuberous roots and derives its nutrition from decaying organic matter rich in leaf mould. **Leaves** Reduced to small, ovate bracts, 7-30 mm long, sheathing the base of the flowering stem. **Flowers** Appear in summer and autumn. They are waxy, pink to dark mauve or whitish, spotted, 1-3 cm across. They have 5 regular spreading petals, 15-17 mm long, a cylindrical central column and protruding lower petal that offers a good landing place for visiting insects. They are arranged in loose terminal clusters of 6-60 flowers, on long, fleshy, purple-brown or green flowering stems, 30-90 cm long. **Fruit** Dry capsules containing numerous minute seeds and opening along longitudinal slits when ripe. **Habitat** Widespread on various soil types. It has a symbiotic relationship with soil fungi in wet sclerophyll forests and woodlands of the coast, ranges and western slopes.

FAMILY **PAPILIONACEAE**   SPECIES *Erythrina vespertilio*   FORM **TREE**   SIZE **TO 12 M**

BAT'S WING CORAL TREE

This medium-sized, deciduous or partly deciduous tree has a trunk to 80 cm diameter, sometimes flanged. It bears stout conical spikes when young, has a spreading, sometimes sparse crown and spines on the branches. **Bark** Mottled grey-green and yellow, turning brown, corky and fissured. **Leaves** Opposite, divided into 2-3 usually lobed, broad triangular leaflets that resemble bats' wings. They are 2-12 cm long and 4-12 cm wide, on stalks 3-8 mm long, and are often shed before flowering or during the dry season. **Flowers** Appear in spring and early summer. They are orange to scarlet, pea-shaped, 3-5 cm long with an ovate, grooved, standard petal and 10 long, protruding stamens. They are grouped in clusters of about 15 pendant flowers, 10-30 cm long. **Fruit** Brown linear pods, 5-12 cm long and 15-18 mm wide, constricted between the seeds, with 1-8 red or yellow glossy oval seeds, 8-13 mm long. Ripe in winter. **Habitat** Open forests and the margins of dry rainforests.

FAMILY **PAPILIONACEAE**   SPECIES *Gompholobium latifolium*   FORM **SHRUB**   SIZE **TO 3 M**

GIANT WEDGE-PEA

This is an erect, open shrub with several long, slender, ascending branches. **Leaves** Alternate, divided into 3 linear to wedge-shaped leaflets sometimes with curved-back margins. They are dark green above and pale green below, 2-6 cm long and 2-6 mm wide. **Flowers** Appear in winter, spring and early summer. They are deep yellow, pea-shaped, 10-12 mm long and 2-3 cm long, and have a notched orbicular standard petal to 3 cm wide and a densely-fringed keel. They are borne on slender, greenish-black stalks, and are solitary or in clusters of 2-3 in the upper leaf axils. **Fruit** Almost globular, smooth, swollen pods 15-20 mm long and about 1 cm broad. They contain 12 or more small, pale seeds. **Habitat** Widespread on poor sandy soils in sheltered sites, often forming thickets; in dry sclerophyll forests along the coast and ranges.

FAMILY **PAPILIONACEAE**   SPECIES *Oxylobium ilicifolium*   FORM **SHRUB**   SIZE **TO 3 M**

PRICKLY OXYLOBIUM

This is an erect shrub with sharp spines on its holly-like leaves. **Leaves** Variable in shape and mostly opposite, 2-4 cm long and 1-3 cm wide. They are rigid, and usually divided into 3 or more ovate lobes each with a needle-sharp spine at the end. They are shiny dark green above and paler beneath with prominent veins. **Flowers** Appear in spring and early summer. They are bright yellow-orange, usually with a red centre, pea-shaped, 8-12 mm long. They have a broad notched standard petal, 6-8 mm long. The flowers are arranged in short terminal or axillary clusters. **Fruit** Narrow-oblong, swollen, hairy pods, 1-2 cm long and 2-3 mm wide. **Habitat** Widespread in tall, open forests on poor shallow soils along the coast and tablelands.

FAMILY **PAPILIONACEAE** SPECIES *Pultenaea scabra* FORM **SHRUB** SIZE **TO 2 M**

ROUGH BUSH PEA

This is an erect shrub with long, brownish, spreading hairs on the younger stems and undersides of
the leaves. **Leaves** Alternate, variable, 3-15 mm
long and 2-7 mm wide, and narrow to broad
wedge-shaped. They are usually notched at the tip into
two lobes with down-curving pointed tips, turned-down margins and a
depressed midrib. Dark green and roughened with short stiff hairs
above, they are paler green beneath. **Flowers** Appear in spring and
early summer. They are yellow with red centres and slightly silky
bracts, pea-shaped, 4-12 mm long, and have a notched orbicular
standard petal. They are arranged in small terminal or axillary clusters
of 2-5 flowers on very short stalks. **Fruit** Brown ovate, flattened pods,
5-7 mm long, covered with soft hairs. **Habitat** Widespread in open
forests, usually on sandy soils along the coast and ranges.

FAMILY **PITTOSPORACEAE** SPECIES *Billardiera longiflora* FORM **SHRUB** SIZE **TO 6 M**

MOUNTAIN BLUEBERRY

This very attractive twining shrub has wiry, woody
stems and may climb to 6 m over other plants in
damp, shaded forests. **Leaves** Alternate, stiff, dark
green, and ovate to linear. They are 10-75 mm
long and 3-9 mm wide, and stalkless or with very
short stalks. **Flowers** Appear in spring and summer. They are greenish-yellow, sometimes purple-tinted, bell-shaped, and 1-3 cm long.
They have 5 petals spreading only at the top, and 5 slightly protruding stamens. The flowers are terminal and solitary on long, pendulous
stalks. **Fruit** Purple, red or rarely white, spongy ovoid berries. These
are shiny, fleshy and 10-25 mm long, with many seeds. **Habitat**
Widespread in damp, shaded sites in sclerophyll forests and woodlands in the tablelands.

FAMILY **PROTEACEAE** SPECIES *Hakea salicifolia* FORM **TREE** SIZE **TO 8 M**

WILLOW-LEAVED HAKEA

This tall shrub or small tree has an erect, slender, short
trunk, many branches and a dense bushy crown. Young
shoots are often sparsely-hairy. **Bark** Pale greenish-
brown, becoming reddish-brown. **Leaves** Alternate,
5-15 cm long and 5-25 mm wide with a sharply-pointed
tip and a stalk 2-5 mm long. They are reddish with silky hairs when young,
becoming shiny grey-green above and paler below with a prominent midrib.
Flowers Appear in spring. They are white, tubular, 3-5 mm long and have
4 narrow, curved-back lobes and a long, curved, protruding style when
released. They are grouped in short, dense, axillary clusters of 9-20 flowers.
Fruit Grey-brown, globular, warty and woody, 1-3 cm long and 1-2 cm
wide. They have a short, 2-pronged beak, which splits into 2 segments each
with a broad, winged seed. **Habitat** Wet gullies and stream banks in tall
forests, woodlands and rainforest margins along the coast and lower slopes.

| FAMILY **PROTEACEAE** | SPECIES *Lambertia formosa* | FORM **SHRUB** | SIZE **TO 2 M** |

MOUNTAIN DEVIL

This is an erect, bushy shrub with rigid branches.
Leaves Usually arranged in whorls of 3 around the
branches. They are sharply-pointed, tough, glossy green
above and whitish below, with a prominent midrib. They
are 2-8 cm long and 2-5 mm wide with curved-back margins. **Flowers** Appear throughout the year, but mainly in spring and early
summer. They are red, tubular, bearded inside, and 2-5 cm long. The
lobes are rolled back leaving a long, straight, style protruding 10-16 mm
beyond the flower tube. The flowers are stalkless and grouped in clusters
of 7, enclosed in red bracts at the ends of the branchlets. **Fruit** Rough,
hard, woody, and stalkless, they are 15-25 mm long, and contain 2 seeds.
They have a short beak and a long horn on each of the 2-valves, giving
them a devil-like appearance, hence the common name. **Habitat** Sandy
soils in open forests and heaths of the coast and ranges.

| FAMILY **PROTEACEAE** | SPECIES *Persoonia linearis* | FORM **TREE** | SIZE **TO 5 M** |

NARROW-LEAF GEEBUNG

This is a tall shrub or small tree, often with drooping
branches, and reddish branchlets covered with soft
white hairs. **Bark** Reddish or dark brown, loose and
flaking. **Leaves** Alternate, often crowded along the
branchlets. They are almost stalkless, 20-85 mm long
and 1-6 mm wide, and bear minute hairs when young. **Flowers** Appear
in summer. They are yellow, tubular with a bulging base, and covered
with short soft hairs outside. They are about 12 mm long with 4 curled-
back lobes each 11-14 mm long, and 4 curled-back, protruding, brown-
striped stamens. The flowers are solitary or in small clusters arising from
the leaf axils along the terminal branchlets, and grow on a leafy shoot.
Fruit Green, fleshy and globular, often with dark stripes. They are about
1 cm across, containing a single seed. **Habitat** Sandy and rocky sites in
open forests and heaths along the coast and tablelands.

| FAMILY **PROTEACEAE** | SPECIES *Telopea speciosissima* | FORM **SHRUB** | SIZE **TO 4 M** |

WARATAH

This tall, multi-stemmed, stiff and erect shrub bears
large, dense and showy flowerheads. It is the floral
emblem of New South Wales. **Leaves** Alternate,
broad, stiff and leathery, with prominent veins and
unevenly toothed margins. They are 8-16 cm long and
2-4 cm wide, and sometimes divided. **Flowers** Appear in spring and
early summer. They are bright crimson and waxy, tubular with 4
curled-back lobes and a protruding, white-tipped style. They are
arranged in dense, compact, globular, terminal clusters of 90-250
flowers, 8-15 cm in diameter, surrounded by crimson bracts
5-9 cm long. **Fruit** Banana-shaped, woody, 7-15 cm long and
2-3 cm wide. They open down one side while still attached to
the plant to release numerous winged seeds. **Habitat** Sandy soils
on forested ridges, hillsides and valleys along the coast and tablelands.

| FAMILY **PROTEACEAE** | SPECIES *Xylomelum pyriforme* | FORM **TREE** | SIZE **TO 11 M** |

WOODY PEAR

This is a small tree or tall shrub with a slender, cylindrical trunk. **Leaves** Opposite, whorled around the branchlets, 10-20 cm long and 30-45 mm wide on stalks 1-3 cm long. They are leathery, glossy dark green above and paler below with prominent veins and a long pointed tip. Juvenile leaves are soft and rusty-brown, often with prickly, toothed margins.
Flowers Appear in spring. They are yellowish-brown to creamy-white, covered with velvety-brown hairs, tubular, 7-10 mm long, and have 4 curled-back lobes and 4 stamens. They are grouped in dense axillary spikes 4-8 cm long, forming a terminal cluster. **Fruit** Woody, grey-green, ripening to light brown, and pear-shaped. They are covered in small, soft hairs, are 5-9 cm long and 10-18 mm wide, and split open along one side to release 2 seeds, 5-7 cm long and 10-18 mm wide, each with a large brown wing. **Habitat** Sandy soils in open forests along the coast and tablelands.

| FAMILY **RUTACEAE** | SPECIES *Crowea exalata* | FORM **SHRUB** | SIZE **TO 1 M** |

SMALL CROWEA

This is a low shrub bearing minute hairs on its slender, sometimes slightly angular branches. **Leaves** Alternate, flat, thick and smooth, paler below. They are 1-5 cm long and 2-6 mm wide, broadest towards the tip, almost stalkless and are dotted with oil glands emitting an aniseed aroma when crushed. **Flowers** Appear mainly in spring and summer. They are pale to bright pink or mauve, rarely white inside and often greenish outside. They are 10-24 mm across, with a tubular base about 1 cm long and have 5 pointed, spreading, waxy petals and 10 stamens with bearded anther appendages. The flowers are solitary in the upper leaf axils and persist after fertilisation, wrapped around the young fruit. **Fruit** Capsules about 7 mm long, splitting into segments when ripe. **Habitat** Rocky sites or shallow, sandy soils in dry sclerophyll forests of the coast and western slopes.

| FAMILY **RUTACEAE** | SPECIES *Eriostemon australasius* | FORM **SHRUB** | SIZE **TO 1 M** |

PINK WAX FLOWER

This is an erect, open or bushy shrub with minute hairs on the branches. **Leaves** The leaves are alternate, concave, rather thick and leathery, and linear to lanceolate. They are greyish-green to dark green, 15-80 mm long and 2-14 mm wide. The leaves have indistinct oil glands and are hairless when mature.
Flowers Appear in spring. They are pale pink to white or red, waxy and open. The flowers are 2-3 cm across and have 5 separate, spreading petals 10-15 mm long and a prominent central column of 10 protruding stamens. The flowers are solitary in the upper leaf axils.
Fruit Dry capsules, 5-9 mm long, breaking into 5 individual segments when ripe, each containing a single seed. **Habitat** Mainly sandy soils in open coastal forests and heaths.

| FAMILY **RUTACEAE** | SPECIES *Flindersia maculosa* | FORM **TREE** | SIZE **TO 15 M** |

LEOPARD TREE

This small or medium-sized tree has a straight trunk and a spreading crown of graceful, pendulous foliage. Young trees are a tangled mass of spiny branches. **Bark** Grey, scaly and mottled with patches of yellow, brown and orange.

Leaves Opposite, with slightly curved-back margins, occasionally lobed. They are 1-8 cm long and 2-10 mm wide on a stalk 2-15 mm long, glossy dark green above and paler below, and are dotted with oil glands. **Flowers** Appear in spring and early summer. They are creamy-white, open, 6-10 mm across with 5 petals and 5 stamens, grouped in terminal or axillary panicles in showy masses about 75 mm long. **Fruit** Brown, ovoid, woody capsules, 23-40 mm long, covered with small, sharp projections and consisting of 5 valves opening to release flat, winged seeds about 2 cm long. Ripe in autumn. **Habitat** Low rainfall sites in lightly wooded inland areas on sandplains, red soil plains and stony slopes.

| FAMILY **RUTACEAE** | SPECIES *Geijera parviflora* | FORM **TREE** | SIZE **TO 10 M** |

WILGA

This tall inland shrub or small tree has a short, stout trunk and a low, broad, rounded crown of dense, pendulous foliage, often reaching the ground. **Bark** dark grey to brown, rough and fissured. **Leaves** Alternate, 3-20 cm long and 3-10 mm wide, with a raised midrib

below and curled-under margins. They are on flattened stalks 3-12 mm long. The leaves have many oil glands and are aromatic when crushed. **Flowers** Appear in winter and spring. They are small, white to cream, open and 3-5 mm across. They have 5 pointed petals and 5 short stamens, and are grouped in loose terminal clusters, 2-7 cm long. **Fruit** Greenish-brown globular capsules, 4-6 mm across. These split open to reveal a single hard, black, shiny, ovoid seed, about 4 mm across. Ripe in spring and early summer. **Habitat** Mainly on red soils and sandy loams in semi-arid, inland woodlands.

| FAMILY **SOLANACEAE** | SPECIES *Solanum aviculare* | FORM **SHRUB** | SIZE **TO 4 M** |

KANGAROO APPLE

This is an erect, smooth, deep green bushy shrub with purplish-green, angular young stems. **Leaves** Alternate, variable, and deep green. Leaves are lobed or entire. Lobed leaves are obovate to elliptic, 5-30 cm long, with 2-6 narrow lobes 1-10 cm long

and 5-20 mm wide. Entire leaves are lanceolate to narrow-elliptic, 5-25 cm long and 10-35 mm wide. **Flowers** Appear from spring to early summer. They are blue or violet, darker in the centre, broadly cup-shaped, open, and 2-4 cm across. They have 5 papery, pointed lobes and 5 yellow stamens, arranged in loose axillary clusters of up to 11 flowers on stalks to 15 cm long. **Fruit** Smooth, shiny, orange-red to scarlet, egg-shaped, edible berries, with a diameter of 10-25 mm. **Habitat** Often along streams in wet forests, rainforest margins, and disturbed sites.

FAMILY **STERCULIACEAE**   SPECIES *Brachychiton populneus*   FORM **TREE**   SIZE **TO 20 M**

KURRAJONG

This small or medium-sized tree has a tapering trunk to 1 m diameter, and a dense, spreading crown, sometimes semi-deciduous in early summer. **Bark** Grey-brown, hard and granular with shallow vertical fissures. **Leaves** Alternate, narrow to egg-shaped with a sharp point, 5-10 cm long and 2-5 cm wide. They are entire or with 3 or 5 lobes, bright glossy green above and paler below. The leaf stalks are 2-10 cm long. **Flowers** Appear in spring and early summer. They are cream to greenish with dark red spots inside, and bell-shaped. They have 5 petals, which are velvety outside, 1-2 cm long and 13-16 mm across, and are grouped in small clusters in the leaf axils.
Fruit Boat-shaped, beaked, leathery, brown follicles, 2-10 cm long. They have stalks 2-5 cm long, and open on one side to release up to 20 yellow seeds about 7 mm long, held in a mass of irritating, prickly fibres. **Habitat** Stony slopes in open forests, woodlands and dry rainforests below 1000 m.

FAMILY **STYLIDIACEAE**   SPECIES *Stylidium graminifolium*   FORM **HERB**   SIZE **TO 60 CM**

GRASS TRIGGER PLANT

This upright perennial herb has long, leafless, hairy flow-ering stems, and grass-like leaves arising from the base of the plant. **Leaves** Long, stiff and narrow, often with curved-back margins, sometimes finely toothed. They are tufted at the base of the plant, and are 5-30 cm long and 1-5 mm wide. **Flowers** Appear in spring and summer. They are white to pale pink with a white centre, 5-10 mm long and about 2 cm wide. They have a short tube, 4 spreading petals and 2 stamens united into a long bent column held behind the face of the flower. The weight of an insect on the petals causes the column to spring forward, dusting it with pollen. The flowers are grouped in a loose cluster at the top of the flowering stem.
Fruit Ovoid capsules, 5-12 mm long, opening in 2-valves. **Habitat** Often around rocky outcrops in open forests, woodlands and heaths along the coast, tablelands and inland slopes.

FAMILY **VIOLACEAE**   SPECIES *Hybanthus monopetalus*   FORM **HERB**   SIZE **TO 30 CM**

SLENDER VIOLET-BUSH

This is an upright perennial herb with slender, wiry stems. **Leaves** Alternate on the lower part of the stem and opposite higher up, linear with curled mar-gins, 1-4 cm long and about 2 mm wide. **Flowers** Appear in spring and summer. They are blue with a short tube, and 13-20 mm long. They have a spade-shaped, large, spreading lower petal about 12 mm long, pouched at the base; 4 minute upper petals hidden by the calyx; and 5 stamens. The flowers are arranged in small leafless clusters on stalks up to 15 cm long arising from the leaf axils. **Fruit** Smooth globular capsules, 3-6 mm across, surrounded by the persistent remains of the calyx. They open in 3 rigid, boat-shaped valves to release small ovoid seeds. **Habitat** Widespread on sandy soils and rocky outcrops in moist forests and woodlands along the coast, tablelands and western slopes.

Coastal Heaths

Heaths are floristically rich, dense communities of low trees and shrubs, usually less than 2 m tall, interspersed with flowering herbs. Eucalypts, if present at all, are low-branching and rather inconspicuous, while stunted banksias, wattles and tea trees are common and widespread. Heaths develop on sandy, often leached soils of low fertility, mainly near the coast but also in the Grampians in Victoria, the sand-plains of the southwest and the southeastern highlands. Sandy debris and organic matter often impede the drainage, forming permanent peaty swamps where carnivorous sundews and other bog-loving plants thrive.

Heath plants are tough and hardy, with leathery or prickly leaves to minimise water loss and deter herbivores. Theirs is a constant battle for survival against drought, waterlogging, low fertility, and exposure to wind and sun. On windswept coastal headlands the shrubs and trees form a dense, low, carpet-like canopy that hugs the contours of the land. Periodic bushfires contribute to the harsh environment, and many plants have turned this to their advantage, using fire to crack open their tough seed pods allowing them to capitalise on newly-created clearings.

Many of Australia's most distinctive flowering plants grow in heaths, including kangaroo paws, banksias, callistemons and orchids. Many flower prolifically, and in spring and autumn the heaths are alive with brilliant wildflower displays, attracting flocks of birds, particularly honeyeaters, bristlebirds and thornbills.

Included in this section are some of the more conspicuous plants often seen along the shores and watercourses. Among them are the screw palm of the northeast with its huge, pineapple-like fruits and sword-shaped leaves; the dune-colonising pigface; the coconut palm; the giant waterlily, and mangroves that line sheltered bays and estuaries, creating nurseries for vast numbers of marine animals, and important habitats for more than 60 bird species.

FAMILY **AIZOACEAE** SPECIES *Carpobrotus glaucescens* FORM **HERB** SIZE **TO 2 M**

ANGULAR PIGFACE

This perennial herb has long, stout, prostrate stems with roots sprouting from the nodes. **Leaves** Opposite, thick and fleshy but firm. They are triangular in cross-section, blue-green, 3-10 cm long and 9-15 mm wide, with a small pointed tip. **Flowers** Appear most of the year. They are purple with an orange-yellow centre, almost stalkless, and 3-6 cm across. Each flower has 100-150 petals, 16-30 mm long and 1-2 mm wide, arranged in 3-4 rows, with white bases spreading out from a disc. This disc has 300-400 yellow to orange filaments, 3-5 mm long, in 5-6 rows. The flowers are solitary and borne at the ends of the stems. **Fruit** Red to purplish, juicy, edible berries, nearly cylindrical or somewhat elipsoid and slightly flattened with 2 ribs. They are 2-3 cm long and 16-24 mm wide, containing numerous smooth, reddish-brown seeds. **Habitat** Sand dunes and among rocks along the shoreline.

FAMILY **APIACEAE** SPECIES *Actinotus helianthi* FORM **HERB** SIZE **TO 2 M**

FLANNEL FLOWER

This upright annual or short-lived perennial herb has a woody rootstock and is covered with woolly hair. **Leaves** Scattered and variable, to 10 cm long and 7 cm wide, divided into 2-3 linear to oblong segments, 15-30 mm long and about 5 mm wide. The leaves are either entire or divided again into 2-3 lobes. They are grey-green and hairy above, and covered with whitish hairs below. **Flowers** Appear at any time of year. They are very small, white to cream, sometimes tipped with green, and are packed into a globular cluster of many tiny florets surrounded by a ring of 10-18 white, petal-like bracts. The bracts produce an open flower-head, 3-8 cm across, densely covered in soft white hair. **Fruit** Ovate, ribbed, compressed capsules, 3-5 mm long and 2-3 mm wide, covered with silky hairs and containing a single seed. **Habitat** Widespread in heaths and open forests, often on sand dunes along the coast and ranges.

FAMILY **ARECACEAE** SPECIES *Cocos nucifera* FORM **PALM** SIZE **TO 35 M**

COCONUT PALM

This tall, slender, feather-leaved palm has a smooth grey trunk to 30 cm diameter which is ringed with leaf scars. It has a dense crown of arching fronds. **Leaves** Up to 7 m long with a twisted midrib and a long stalk, divided into long, pointed, leathery, drooping leaflets. The leaflets are 1.3 m long and 4-5 cm wide at the base, closely and evenly spaced on either side of the midrib. The leaf stalks have a fibrous base partially sheathing the top of the trunk. **Flowers** Produced year-round in large clusters to 2 m long arising within the crown. They are cream, to 3 cm across, with female flowers at the bases of the branchlets and males at the ends. **Fruit** Green, yellow or brown coconuts, 20-30 cm long. They have a fibrous husk surrounding a woody-shelled seed, lined with a thin, white, oily flesh enclosing a watery fluid. **Habitat** Tropical seashores and sandy plains with underground water.

| FAMILY **CASUARINACEAE** SPECIES *Allocasuarina littoralis* | FORM **TREE** | SIZE **TO 15 M** |

BLACK SHEOAK

This small tree has a slender trunk and a sparse, dark-green, conical crown. **Bark** Brown, hard and closely fissured. **Leaves** Minute, tooth-like, pointed, 0.3-0.9 mm long. They are arranged in whorls of 6-8 at 4-10 mm intervals along needle-like, blackish-green, ribbed, erect, branchlets, up to 35 cm long and 1 mm diameter. **Flowers** Appear in autumn. They are reddish-brown, very small and borne on separate male and female trees. Females form globular hairy spikes to about 7 mm across on the older wood. Males form cylindrical spikes, 1-3 cm long, at the ends of the branchlets. **Fruit** Cylindrical, grey to brown, woody cones, 1-3 cm long and 8-21 mm across, on thick stalks about 2 cm long. They have numerous valves that open to release small, dark, winged seeds, 4-10 mm long. **Habitat** Tall heaths and woodlands along the coast, tablelands and inland slopes.

| FAMILY **DILLENIACEAE** SPECIES *Hibbertia scandens* | FORM **SHRUB** | SIZE **TO 1.5 M** |

CLIMBING GUINEA FLOWER

This shrub is usually vine-like with thick, fleshy stems trailing across the ground or into the understorey. **Leaves** Alternate, soft and fleshy. They are broad and sometimes pointed, taper gradually at the base, and are often slightly stem-clasping. They are 3-9 cm long and 1-3 cm wide, smooth above and covered with silky hairs below. **Flowers** Appear most of the year, although they are short-lived and often peak in summer. They are open and yellow, 2-6 cm across. They have silky-haired sepals; 5 overlapping, delicate, rounded petals; and a central cluster of numerous stamens. They are solitary and arise from the leaf axils on stalks 2-4 mm long. **Fruit** Dry and leathery, opening at the top, containing kidney-shaped seeds with an orange, fleshy coat. **Habitat** Sandy coastal heaths, sand dunes, and heavy soils in forests, along the coast and tablelands.

| FAMILY **DROSERACEAE** SPECIES *Drosera auriculata* | FORM **HERB** | SIZE **TO 50 CM** |

TALL SUNDEW

This erect, slender, perennial herb arises from a globular underground tuber and derives its nourishment from insects trapped in the leaves. **Leaves** Circular to shield-shaped, to 1 cm diameter, with hairs on the upper surface that secrete a sticky liquid, and longer irritable hairs on the edges. Insects are attracted to the dew-like droplets on the hairs, but when the marginal hairs are touched, the leaves curl over and trap the insect, which is dissolved by digestive juices and absorbed by the leaf. The leaves form a rosette around the base of the plant (usually absent when flowering), or are spirally arranged along the stems on long stalks. **Flowers** Appear in spring and summer. They are white or pale-pink, open, and 10-15 mm across. They have 5 rounded and sometimes notched petals, arranged in loose terminal clusters of 2-8 flowers, 3-10 cm long. **Fruit** Small capsules containing numerous black seeds 2-3 mm long. **Habitat** Widespread in moist sites.

FAMILY **EPACRIDACEAE**   SPECIES *Astroloma conostephioides*   FORM **SHRUB**   SIZE **TO 1 M**

FLAME HEATH

This is a small, erect, prickly shrub, compact and rigid. It has soft hairs covering the branchlets. The flowers and succulent fruit are eaten by emus. **Leaves** Stiff and sharply-pointed with the margins more or less turned down, 8-25 mm long and about 2 mm wide. They are hairy or smooth, dark green above, paler and striped below. **Flowers** Appear mainly from winter to mid-summer. They are 18-25 mm long, bright red and tubular, constricted at the top with stamens projecting from the tube. Downy sepals are overlapped at the base by shiny-red bracts. They are solitary and borne on short horizontal or slightly drooping stalks arising from the leaf junctions. **Fruit** Green and berry-like, about 8 mm long, comprising a single seed surrounded by a firm, fleshy layer. **Habitat** Nutrient deficient, rocky or sandy sites in heaths and open forests.

FAMILY **EPACRIDACEAE**   SPECIES *Epacris impressa*   FORM **SHRUB**   SIZE **TO 1.5 M**

COMMON HEATH

This erect, slender, wiry shrub is Victoria's floral emblem. It has small, rigid, prickly leaves and minute soft hairs on the branchlets **Leaves** Rigid, stalkless, and sharply-pointed alternate and crowded around the stem. They are usually smooth, but broader and downy in the Grampians. They are 4-16 mm long and 1-6 mm wide, with a prominent midrib below. **Flowers** Appear most of the year. They are tubular, pink or scarlet, rarely white. They have 5 slightly protruding stamens, 6-20 mm long and 4-8 mm across, with short stalks. The 5 pointed petals are indented at the base of the tube and curl up at the top. The flowers are spreading or drooping and arranged in leafy clusters. **Fruit** Small globular capsules about 5 mm long containing numerous seeds. **Habitat** Widespread on wet soils in heaths and heathy scrubby understoreys in woodlands along the coast and tablelands.

FAMILY **EPACRIDACEAE**   SPECIES *Epacris obtusifolia*   FORM **SHRUB**   SIZE **TO 1.5 M**

BLUNT-LEAF HEATH

This widespread, slender, heath-like shrub is found chiefly in marshy sites, and has an erect stem with hairy branchlets. **Leaves** The leaves are stalkless and held close to the stem at their bases. They are oblong-elliptical to broad-linear with blunt tips, 5-12 mm long and 2-3 mm wide. **Flowers** Appear mainly from June to December. They are creamy-white, honey-scented, stalkless and tubular with 5 curled-back petals, 5-15 mm long and 3-8 mm across, and 5 short stamens fully enclosed in the throat of the tube. Numerous overlapping bracts surround the base of the tube. The flowers emerge from the leaf bases and are arranged among the leaves in long, one-sided clusters along the ends of the branchlets. **Fruit** Dry capsules, 3-4 mm long, opening by valves on the sides to release numerous small seeds. **Habitat** Moist sites in heaths and woodlands of the coast and tablelands to about 1000 m.

| FAMILY **EPACRIDACEAE** | SPECIES *Leucopogon virgatus* | FORM **SHRUB** | SIZE **TO 60 CM** |

COMMON BEARD-HEATH

This is a low, usually erect shrub with weak, wiry, red-brown branches. Flowering branches often zigzag. **Leaves** Alternate, narrow and tapering gradually to very pointed tips. They are concave above, thick, 3-22 mm long and 1-4 mm wide, on very short stalks, often pressed up against the stems. **Flowers** Appear from late winter to early summer. They are small, white to pinkish, tubular at the base, and have 5 spreading petals densely-bearded inside with white hairs, 1-3 mm long and 3-6 mm across. The stamens are enclosed within the flower tube. The flowers are arranged in short, dense clusters of 4-7 flowers, 5-10 mm long. The clusters arise at the ends of the branches or from the leaf axils. **Fruit** Succulent, oblong, 3-5 mm long, containing a single seed surrounded by a fleshy coat. **Habitat** Sandy soils in heaths and open forests of the coast and tablelands.

| FAMILY **EUPHORBIACEAE** | SPECIES *Ricinocarpos pinifolius* | FORM **SHRUB** | SIZE **TO 3 M** |

WEDDING BUSH

This is a lightly-branching, erect to spreading shrub. **Leaves** Mostly opposite or spirally-arranged around the branches. They are long and narrow, 1-4 cm long and 1-3 mm wide, and have curled-under margins. Dull green above, they are paler below. **Flowers** Appear in winter, spring and summer. Separate male and female flowers are borne on the same plant, arranged in terminal clusters of 3-6 male flowers around a single female flower that swells into a globular fruit. They are similar, open, 2-3 cm across, and have 4-6 separate, spreading ivory-coloured petals, 10-15 mm long. The male flowers have a central column of numerous yellow stamens. **Fruit** Globular capsules about 12 mm across, covered with small spines. The capsules open in 3 parts to release fleshy mottled brown seeds 5 mm long. **Habitat** Sandy soils in coastal heaths and open forests.

| FAMILY **GERANIACEAE** | SPECIES *Pelargonium australe* | FORM **HERB** | SIZE **TO 70 CM** |

NATIVE STORKSBILL

This is an erect or semi-prostrate perennial herb arising from a persistent rootstock. It has rather stout stems covered with soft, white spreading, downy hairs. **Leaves** Opposite, 2-9 cm long and 2-8 cm wide. They are entire or deeply dissected into 3-7 toothed lobes, velvety below, on stalks to 15 cm long. **Flowers** Appear in spring and summer. They are pink to white, streaked with dark-purple veins, and about 16 mm across. They have 5 sepals united at the base, one forming a nectary spur 1-3 mm long; and have 5 separate, spreading, unequal petals, 7-10 mm long with 2 broader upper petals. The flowers are arranged in terminal clusters of 4-12, each with 10 stamens united towards the base. **Fruit** Dry capsules which split into 5 hairy, plumed pods, 8-15 mm long, each containing a single smooth seed. **Habitat** Sand dunes, coastal cliffs and rocky inland outcrops.

| FAMILY **GOODENIACEAE** | SPECIES *Dampiera stricta* | FORM **SHRUB** | SIZE **TO 60 CM** |

BLUE DAMPIERA

This is a small, erect or straggly shrub with sharply-angled stems. It is woody near the base, but sometimes soft and herbacious. **Leaves** Vary from elliptical to linear. They are 10-65 mm long and 2-25 mm wide, sometimes with a few coarse teeth on the margins. They are semi-succulent, stalkless and bunched towards the tops of the angular stems. **Flowers** Appear in spring and early summer. They are usually bright blue, although some forms are purple or pink. They are tubular with a pale-yellow throat, 10-15 mm long, and have 5 spreading, unequal, notched petals, clothed with short, flattened rusty hairs outside. They are usually solitary or clustered among the upper leaves. **Fruit** Small ribbed nuts, 4-5 mm long, covered with rusty-hairs. Each nut contains a single seed. **Habitat** Sandy, low-nutrient soils in heaths and open forests along the coast and ranges.

| FAMILY **HAEMODORACEAE** | SPECIES *Anigozanthos manglesii* | FORM **HERB** | SIZE **TO 1 M** |

RED AND GREEN KANGAROO PAW

This perennial herb has a tall, erect, fleshy stem, covered with red hairs, bearing unusual ornamental flowers. It is the floral emblem of Western Australia. **Leaves** Arise from the base of the plant. They are strap-like, grey-green, 10-50 cm long and 5-12 mm wide, with stem-sheathing bases. **Flowers** Appear mainly in winter and spring. They are green with red bases, tubular, and 6-10 cm long. They have 6 curled-back lobes on one side of the flower, long protruding stamens, and are covered in dense green hair, except at the base where it is red. The flowering stem is 30-100 cm tall and covered with red hairs. The flowers emerge from the tip of the stem to form one-sided clusters. **Fruit** Capsules containing 3 cells, with several seeds in each cell. **Habitat** Nutrient deficient sandplains in coastal heaths, low woodlands and open forests.

| FAMILY **LAMIACEAE** | SPECIES *Westringia fruticosa* | FORM **SHRUB** | SIZE **TO 2 M** |

COAST ROSEMARY

This compact, aromatic shrub is a member of the mint family and has whorled leaves and white hairs on the branches. **Leaves** Leathery, crowded in whorls of 4 around the branches, narrow or fairly broad. They are 1-3 cm long and 2-5 mm wide, smooth above and covered with white felted hairs on the lower surface. The leaf margins are curled or rolled under. **Flowers** Appear most of the year. They are white or pale-mauve with orange or purplish spots inside, shortly-tubular, and 10-15 mm long. They have a spreading, 3-lobed lower lip and an erect, flat and broadly 2-lobed upper lip. The flowers are borne solitary in the upper leaf axils. The calyx is covered with short hairs pressed close to the surface. **Fruit** Small, wrinkled nutlets containing a single seed. **Habitat** Heaths and windswept coastal headlands.

PLANTS

FAMILY **LECYTHIDACEAE**   SPECIES *Barringtonia acutangula*   FORM **TREE**   SIZE **TO 8 M**

FRESHWATER MANGROVE

This tall shrub or small tree has a dense, layered and spreading crown, and is sometimes multi-stemmed. In the dry season when it sheds its leaves, Aborigines use the pounded bark and stems to stupefy fish. **Bark** Dark grey, rough and fissured. **Leaves** Alternate, clustered at the ends of the branchlets. They are 4-16 cm long and 2-6 cm wide, on stalks 4-15 mm long; glossy above with prominent veins, paler and sometimes slightly hairy below. The wavy margins are entire or finely-toothed. **Flowers** Bright red, pink or white flowers appear periodically throughout the year. They are about 1 cm across with 4 small lobes and numerous spreading stamens 1-2 cm long. The flowers are grouped in drooping clusters to 30 cm long, with up to 75 flowers. **Fruit** Pale-green fibrous, ribbed capsules, 2-6 cm long, containing a single seed. **Habitat** Freshwater river banks, beside ponds, seasonally flooded lowlands and swampy sites.

FAMILY **LILIACEAE**   SPECIES *Blandfordia grandiflora*   FORM **HERB**   SIZE **TO 80 CM**

LARGE-FLOWERED CHRISTMAS BELL

This is an upright, tufted, perennial herb with fibrous roots and tall, leafless flowering stems which bear large, bell-shaped flowers. **Leaves** Crowded at the base of the flowering stem. They are tough and grass-like with rough margins, cut slightly into rounded teeth. The leaves are up to 80 cm long and 1-5 mm wide. **Flowers** Appear in spring and summer. They are bell-shaped with red lobes tipped with yellow, although the flowers are occasionally all yellow. They have 3 petals and 3 sepals fused into a tube, and the 6 stamens are fused to the inside of the floral tube. The flowers are 35-45 mm long and 25-40 mm diameter. They are grouped in clusters of 3-10 at the end of the flowering stem on slender stalks that bend over so that the flowers droop. **Fruit** Short-stalked capsules with 3 compartments, each containing numerous seeds. **Habitat** Damp sandy or peaty soils along the coast and tablelands.

FAMILY **LILIACEAE**   SPECIES *Sowerbaea juncea*   FORM **HERB**   SIZE **TO 45 CM**

VANILLA LILY

This is a small, grass-like, upright, perennial herb with fibrous roots and a tuft of blue-green leaves. It has a long, leafless flowering stem. **Leaves** Arise from the base of the plant and sheath the flowering stem. They are soft and slender, grass-like, cylindrical, 20-50 cm long and 1-2 mm wide. **Flowers** Appear mainly in late winter and spring. They are pink-lilac to white, papery, with a sweet vanilla perfume. They are 15-20 mm across, and have 6 pointed petals, 8-10 mm long, and protruding yellow stamens. Although the petals are free, they often to form a tube before opening up. The flowers are grouped in dense terminal clusters about 3 cm across, comprising up to about 20 flowers on flowering stems 15-45 cm long. **Fruit** Pale brown, 3-celled capsules, 2-3 mm long. Each capsule contains 3-6 seeds. **Habitat** Widespread in intermittently waterlogged sites in heaths along the coast and tablelands.

FAMILY **LILIACEAE**   SPECIES *Stypandra glauca*   FORM **HERB**   SIZE **TO 1 M**

NODDING BLUE LILY

This is an upright, tufted, perennial herb, with a creeping rootstock and leafy stems. It is woody at the base and often branched. **Leaves** Alternate and linear. The grass-like leaves sheath the stems at their bases. They are bluish-green, 5-20 cm long and 1-15 mm wide. They spread out in one plane along the slender stems. **Flowers** Appear most of the year. They are bright blue, open, and 2-3 cm across. They have 6 pointed lobes and 6 conspicuous yellow, hairy, protruding stamens. They are arranged in loose clusters on slender stalks, 12-20 mm long, that bend down to give the flowers a nodding appearance. **Fruit** Ovoid capsules, 8-12 mm long, with three ridges. The capsules contain numerous black, compressed seeds, 2-5 mm long. **Habitat** Widespread on poorer sandy soils.

FAMILY **LILIACEAE**   SPECIES *Thysanotus tuberosus*   FORM **HERB**   SIZE **TO 60 CM**

COMMON FRINGE-LILY

This is an upright perennial herb with clustered roots expanding into tubers. It has leafless stems and flowers that open for just one day. **Leaves** Arise annually from the base of the plant. They are grass-like, 10-60 cm long, and usually shorter than the flowering stems. **Flowers** Appear in succession from spring to autumn. They are delicate blue or purple, open, and 15-35 mm across. They have 3 broad fringed lobes and 3 narrow pointed lobes, 7-19 mm long, on stalks 6-22 mm long. The flowers are arranged in terminal clusters of 1-8, on flowering stems 20-60 cm long, which branch several times. **Fruit** Cylindrical 3-valved capsules, 3-7 mm across. The capsules split open when ripe to release several black seeds. **Habitat** Widespread in heaths, dry sclerophyll forests and woodlands along the coast and adjacent ranges.

FAMILY **MYRTACEAE**   SPECIES *Baeckea ramosissima*   FORM **SHRUB**   SIZE **TO 60 CM**

ROSY BAECKEA

This heath-like shrub has slender branches and is either upright, spreading and much-branched; or the branches lie close to the ground with their tips ascending. **Leaves** Opposite, narrow, thickish and flat. They are 3-13 mm long and 1-2 mm wide, with scattered, inconspicuous oil dots. **Flowers** Appear in winter, spring and summer and are similar to the flowers of tea-trees. They are red to pale pink or white, open, and 6-10 mm across. They have with 5 separate, orbicular, spreading petals surrounding a central disc with 10 stamens. The flowers are solitary or grouped in small clusters, on short stalks arising from the junctions between the upper leaves and branches. **Fruit** Capsules, opening at the top in 3 valves. Each capsule contains a single, oblong seed. **Habitat** Sandy heaths and open forests.

PLANTS

| FAMILY **MYRTACEAE** | SPECIES *Callistemon citrinus* | FORM **SHRUB** | SIZE **TO 3 M** |

CRIMSON BOTTLEBRUSH

This is a large, erect, rigid shrub with branches that are quite densely entangled. Young branches are covered with soft hairs. **Leaves** Alternate, flat, stiff and sharply-pointed. They are 3-8 cm long and 4-15 mm wide, on very short stalks. Silky when young, they darken with age. **Flowers** Appear in spring, summer and autumn. Individual flowers are small, about 2 cm long, with 5 small petals and numerous long, protruding, crimson stamens. They are grouped in dense, hairy, cylindrical clusters, 5-12 cm long and 4-7 cm across with leafy shoots growing from the tips. **Fruit** Woody, cup-shaped capsules, 4-7 mm across, containing many small seeds. They are stalkless and grouped in cylindrical clusters wrapped around the branches. The capsules persist for many years. **Habitat** Widespread in wet sites, beside creeks and swamps along the coast and ranges.

| FAMILY **MYRTACEAE** | SPECIES *Calytrix tetragona* | FORM **SHRUB** | SIZE **TO 2 M** |

COMMON FRINGE MYRTLE

This is a variable, sprawling or erect, bright green shrub, sometimes with long, drooping branches. **Leaves** Alternate, spirally arranged, often crowded. They are erect on very short stalks, cylindrical or triangular in cross section, 1-12 mm long and about 1 mm wide. Thick and often hairy, they usually have minutely-toothed margins. **Flowers** Appear mainly in spring and summer. They are star-shaped, white to pink, and 7-20 mm across. They have 5 narrow, pointed petals about 6 mm long, and about 20 protruding stamens to 6 mm long. The calyx persists after the flowers have fallen and turns reddish. The flowers are massed in leafy, terminal clusters. **Fruit** A nut containing a single seed. **Habitat** Widespread; often in rocky places on sandy and gravelly soils in heaths, dry sclerophyll forests and woodlands.

| FAMILY **MYRTACEAE** | SPECIES *Chamelaucium uncinatum* | FORM **SHRUB** | SIZE **TO 3 M** |

GERALDTON WAX FLOWER

This is a brittle, spreading shrub bearing a profusion of nectar-filled waxy flowers that attract a wide variety of insects. **Leaves** Opposite, thick and cylindrical in cross-section. They are 1-4 cm long and about 1 mm wide, with a hook at the tip. **Flowers** Appear in spring and summer. They are white, red, purple or pink, and 15-25 mm across. They have a green, funnel-shaped base about 6 mm long, and 5 spreading, rounded, waxy petals surrounding a central tube. This tube is fringed with 10 stamens and has a style protruding from the centre. The flowers are arranged in terminal clusters of 2-4, arising from the ends of the branches or the upper leaf axils. **Fruit** Hard, woody capsules. **Habitat** Common on limestone hills in coastal heaths.

| FAMILY **MYRTACEAE** | SPECIES *Kunzea ambigua* | FORM **SHRUB** | SIZE **TO 3.5 M** |

TICK BUSH

This is an erect shrub with long, arching branches bearing many sprays of flowers crowded on leafy side branches, and hairy lateral young branchlets.
Leaves Crowded, alternate, often tufted on short lateral shoots. They are linear to narrow-lanceolate, concave, 4-12 mm long and 1-2 mm wide, dark-green, and dotted with small oil glands. **Flowers** Appear in spring and summer. They are white, honey-scented, nearly stalkless, and 3-4 mm across. They have 5 small petals hidden beneath a mass of long, white, protruding stamens. They are arranged in dense, globular or cylindrical heads on leafy branchlets, or are solitary, arising from many of the leaf axils on the main stem.
Fruit Globular leathery capsules, 3-4 mm diameter, with spiky valves.
Habitat Widespread in sandy heaths, cleared areas and wet, coastal forests of the coast and tablelands.

| FAMILY **MYRTACEAE** | SPECIES *Leptospermum laevigatum* | FORM **TREE** | SIZE **TO 8 M** |

COAST TEA TREE

This tall shrub or small tree adopts leaning or crooked growth patterns in harsh windswept sites. It has a short, thick and crooked trunk; erect, rigid stems; and a broad, dense crown. The foliage is often slightly drooping. **Bark** Grey or light-brown, fissured and flaking in thin strips from the trunk and branches. **Leaves** Alternate, 1-3 cm long and 5-12 mm wide. They are thick, stiff and dull grey-green.
Flowers Appear in winter and spring. They are white, open and 15-22 mm across. They have 5 separate, spreading petals around a green central disc, which is surrounded by numerous stamens. The flowers are solitary or are grouped in small clusters arising from the leaf axils.
Fruit Flat-topped, cup-shaped capsules, 7-8 mm across, with 6-11 valves.
Habitat Coastal sand dunes, cliffs, heaths, and sometimes dry sclerophyll forests; often in harsh windswept sites.

| FAMILY **MYRTACEAE** | SPECIES *Leptospermum polygalifolium* | FORM **SHRUB** | SIZE **TO 4 M** |

YELLOW TEA TREE

This is usually an erect shrub, but occasionally becomes a small, lightly-foliaged tree with several stems and firm, rough bark. **Leaves** Slightly lemon-scented and fairly thin with conspicuous oil glands. They are alternate, rigid, and usually fairly narrow. The leaves can be flat or have slightly curled-back margins, and are 5-20 mm long and 1-5 mm wide, on very short stalks. **Flowers** Appear in spring and summer. They are white to yellowish, open and 5-16 mm across. They have 5 separate spreading petals around a green central disc, which is surrounded by numerous stamens. The flowers are solitary and arise from the leaf axils or at the ends of short lateral branches. **Fruit** Woody, domed capsules, 5-10 mm diameter. The capsules have 5 valves, opening widely to release very slender seeds. **Habitat** Damp sites in sandy soils in heaths and woodlands of the coast and ranges.

| FAMILY **MYRTACEAE** | SPECIES *Melaleuca squarrosa* | FORM **TREE** | SIZE **TO 10 M** |

SCENTED PAPERBARK

This is a tall shrub or small tree with a spreading crown. **Bark** Pale-grey, corky and peeling in thin, papery strips. **Leaves** Opposite, in pairs at right angles to the stem. They are crowded, pointed, 5-18 mm long and 3-7 mm wide on very short stalks. Stiff and dark green, they have 5-7 indistinct longitudinal veins. **Flowers** Appear in spring and summer. They are cream to yellow, and scented. They have 5 ovate petals to 2 mm long, sometimes tinged with pink; and numerous long, protruding, sparsely-hairy stamens, fused at their bases into 5 bundles of 6-12. The flowers are grouped in dense, terminal, cylindrical clusters, 15-50 mm long and 1-2 cm wide, with new shoots often growing from the tips. **Fruit** Pale-brown, woody, cup-shaped, stalkless capsules; 3-5 mm across and closely clustered around the branchlets. **Habitat** Often forms closed scrubs on peaty sands near swamps and streams in heaths and dry sclerophyll forests along the coast and adjacent ranges.

| FAMILY **NYMPHAEACEAE** | SPECIES *Nymphaea gigantea* | FORM **HERB** | SIZE **TO 50 CM** |

GIANT WATERLILY

This aquatic perennial herb has large floating leaves and upright flowering stems arising from a rhizome buried in the mud. **Leaves** Grow on long stalks that reach the surface of the water. They are pale above and often purplish below, and 10-60 cm across. They have prominent veins and regularly-toothed margins. **Flowers** Appear from spring to late summer, or year-round in the tropics. They are lotus-like, blue, mauve, pink or white, solitary, open, and 6-30 cm across. They have many petals arranged in whorls around numerous yellow stamens. They are borne on long stems standing up to 50 cm above the water. **Fruit** A spongy berry containing many red seeds that turn grey when ripe. The seeds remain dormant in times of drought in the hardened mud. Both seeds and rhizomes are consumed by Aborigines. **Habitat** Still water in permanent rivers and lagoons.

| FAMILY **ORCHIDACEAE** | SPECIES *Cryptostylis subulata* | FORM **HERB** | SIZE **TO 90 CM** |

LARGE TONGUE ORCHID

This is a slender, upright perennial herb arising from a tuberous rootstock, with 2-3 leaves around the base of the plant. **Leaves** Long and narrow, stiff and erect, 4-20 cm long and 1-3 cm wide. They have a prominent midrib and stalks 1-9 cm long. **Flowers** Appear in spring and summer. They are yellow-green with a large red or brown concave lower petal about 25 mm long and 5-10 mm wide. The other petals are long and narrow, 15-30 mm long and about 3 mm wide, spreading out behind the column of stamens and style. The flowers are stalkless and arranged in a tall cluster of 2-14 flowers on a stalk 15-80 cm long. The flowers are pollinated by male ichneumon wasps that back into and try to mate with the flower. **Fruit** A capsule containing numerous small seeds. **Habitat** Sandy soils in moist sites in heaths and swamps of the coast and adjacent ranges.

FAMILY **PANDANACEAE**   SPECIES *Pandanus spiralis*   FORM **PANDAN**   SIZE **TO 12 M**

SCREW PALM

This palm-like tree has a spiral of old leaf bases around the trunk and small prop roots at the base. The trunk grows to 20 cm diameter and is usually forked, with crowns of sword-like leaves. **Leaves** Thick, leathery, M-shaped in cross section, to 2 m long and 8 cm wide. They have long, pointed tips, small spines on the midrib and margins, and broad, fibrous bases partially sheathing the trunk. They are spirally arranged to form a tufted crown with drooping tips. **Flowers** Small, white, sweetly-scented; produced on separate male and female plants. Male flowers form stalkless cylindrical clusters, 3-10 cm long and 30-35 mm diameter, within leafy bracts about 30 cm long. Females arise in the centre of the leafy crowns. **Fruit** Green turning orange, pineapple-like, 15-30 cm across, comprising 8-35 segments. Each segment is 5-10 cm long and 5-9 cm wide, with 5-7 seeds. Fruiting from June to October. **Habitat** Along watercourses, swamps and lagoons.

FAMILY **PAPILIONACEAE**   SPECIES *Dillwynia glaberrima*   FORM **SHRUB**   SIZE **TO 2 M**

SMOOTH PARROT PEA

This is a tough, open, spreading, often wiry shrub, with slender and often arching branches. **Leaves** Alternate, erect or slightly spreading. They are smooth and very narrow to needle-like, cylindrical, 5-20 mm long and 0.5 mm diameter, usually with a small hooked tip. **Flowers** Appear in spring and early summer. They are pea-shaped, 8-10 mm long, yellow, with a large, kidney-shaped standard petal 10-14 mm wide with reddish-brown lines in the centre. They are usually clustered in groups of 2-4 flowers on stalks 3-20 mm long arising from the bases of the upper leaves. **Fruit** Swollen ovoid hairy pods, 4-6 mm long, containing a single seed. **Habitat** Widespread in deep sandy or alluvial soils in heaths and open forests.

FAMILY **PAPILIONACEAE**   SPECIES *Phyllota phylicoides*   FORM **SHRUB**   SIZE **TO 1.5 M**

HEATH PHYLLOTA

This erect, spreading shrub often has reddish stems. **Leaves** Scattered or spirally arranged on the branches. The leaves are linear, almost stalk-less, with curled-under margins. They are rough, yellow-green, 5-20 mm long and 1-2 mm wide. **Flowers** Appear in spring. They are yellow to orange with a red calyx, pea-shaped, and 5-12 mm long. They have a broad folded standard petal, are almost stalkless, and are borne in compact clusters in the upper leaf axils, usually with numerous flowers forming terminal, leafy flowerheads. **Fruit** Small ovate to oblong pods about 5 mm long, containing 2 seeds. **Habitat** Widespread on sandy soils in heaths, scrubs and sclerophyll forests along the coast and ranges, but not in the higher mountains.

FAMILY **PAPILIONACEAE**   SPECIES *Viminaria juncea*   FORM **TREE**   SIZE **TO 5 M**

GOLDEN SPRAY

This small tree or erect shrub has a slender, cylindrical trunk; long, slender, erect or drooping, prickly branchlets; and a sparse crown. **Bark** Greyish-brown, rough and fissured. **Leaves** Alternate, needle-like, 3-25 cm long and about 2 mm wide, bright-green and wiry. Juvenile leaves are divided into 1-3 oblong to linear-lanceolate leaflets, 1-4 cm long. **Flowers** Appear in spring and early summer. They are golden-yellow to orange, pea-shaped, and 7-10 mm long. They have a notched standard petal with red markings near the base. They are grouped in long, slender, terminal, drooping racemes, 20-60 cm long, with stalks about 5 mm long. **Fruit** Soft, stalkless, black, ovate pods, 4-6 mm long, with a short beak. The pod contains a single hard seed, 2-3 mm long. **Habitat** Widespread in moist heaths on sandy soils and swampy sites of the coast and lower mountains.

FAMILY **PROTEACEAE**   SPECIES *Banksia coccinea*   FORM **SHRUB**   SIZE **TO 4 M**

SCARLET BANKSIA

This beautiful banksia is usually a multi-stemmed, erect shrub with furry branches, but occasionaly reaches tree size. **Leaves** Leathery, 5-10 cm long and 4-8 cm wide, with irregular spiny margins. They are stalkless or with very short stalks, and are whorled around the branches. They are dull light green above, white or greyish below, sometimes with a yellow marginal line. **Flowers** Appear in winter, spring and summer. Individual flowers are small and tubular; grey with bright scarlet, wiry, straight, protruding styles, tipped with gold. They are arranged in vertical rows on a terminal, squat, cylindrical flowerhead, 6-12 cm long and 6-15 cm diameter, set in a rosette of leaves. **Fruit** Grey-brown cylindrical cones to about 10 cm long, with numerous small, furry, 2-valved seed capsules. The capsules open to release 2 flat, winged seeds. **Habitat** Gravelly, sandy or marshy sites in coastal heaths.

FAMILY **PROTEACEAE**   SPECIES *Banksia integrifolia*   FORM **TREE**   SIZE **TO 25 M**

COAST BANKSIA

Usually a small tree, gnarled and twisted or straggling along the coast, this banksia is stunted and shrubby in exposed sites, occasionally growing quite tall with a trunk to 50 cm diameter. Young branches are covered in white downy hairs. **Bark** Hard, rough, light grey, sometimes fissured. **Leaves** In whorls of 4-6 with short stalks, becoming alternate when older, 4-20 cm long and 6-35 mm wide. They sometimes have slightly-toothed margins, often curled-under, and are dark-green above, covered with silvery-white hairs below. **Flowers** Appear mainly in summer, autumn and early winter. Individual flowers are pale-yellow, tubular, 22-25 mm long, with long, wiry, straight, protruding styles. They are grouped in cylindrical terminal upright flowerheads, 5-15 cm long and 5-8 cm across. **Fruit** Grey, oblong to cylindrical cones, 7-15 cm long and 7-8 cm diameter, with numerous brown, protruding, 2-valved seed capsules. The capsules are 8-17 mm long and usually contain 2 black, winged, ovate seeds. **Habitat** Poor soils in heaths along the coast and adjacent ranges.

FAMILY **PROTEACEAE**   SPECIES *Banksia prionotes*   FORM **TREE**   SIZE **TO 12 M**

ACORN BANKSIA

This small tree or large shrub has a short trunk, sometimes gnarled and crooked, and spreading branches, giving a fairly open crown. Young branches are covered with dense, woolly, grey hairs. **Bark** Grey-white, becoming darker and marbled in older trees. **Leaves** Alternate and whorled around the branches, 10-35 cm long and 15-25 mm wide. They are glossy green above and greyish-green below, with regular, triangular, toothed, wavy margins and a prominent midrib. **Flowers** Appear in autumn and winter. Individual flowers are orange and woolly-grey, small and tubular with long, wiry, straight, protruding styles when released from the flower tube. They are grouped in dense, acorn-shaped, terminal, upright flowerheads, 10-15 cm long and about 8 cm across. **Fruit** Grey-brown cylindrical cones, 8-12 cm long and 3-5 cm across, with a number of small, furry, deeply-embedded seed capsules. Each capsule has 2 valves opening to release 2 flat, winged seeds. **Habitat** Sandy soils in coastal heaths.

FAMILY **PROTEACEAE**   SPECIES *Banksia serrata*   FORM **TREE**   SIZE **TO 16 M**

OLD MAN BANKSIA

A medium-sized tree or tall shrub, often gnarled and twisted, with a stout, knobbly trunk to about 75 cm diameter, and a sparse canopy. New foliage is soft, hairy and copper-coloured. **Bark** Spongy, dark grey-brown, warty and furrowed on older trees; often blackened by fire with bright orange new bark. **Leaves** Alternate, thick and leathery, 5-20 cm long and 15-40 mm wide. They have regularly-toothed margins, and are entire near the base, often with a flattened tip. **Flowers** Appear mainly in summer and autumn. Individual flowers are silver-grey to cream, tubular, about 4 cm long with long, curved, protruding styles. They are grouped in cylindrical, terminal, upright, silky flowerheads, 7-20 cm long and 5-10 cm diameter. **Fruit** Grey, cylindrical, hairy cones, about 13-15 cm long and 8-10 cm diameter, with 5-30 thick, rounded, protruding, 2-valved seed capsules. The capsules are 25-35 mm wide, and release 2 black, winged seeds after fire. **Habitat** Sandy, often rocky sites in coastal heaths and open forests.

FAMILY **PROTEACEAE**   SPECIES *Dryandra formosa*   FORM **SHRUB**   SIZE **TO 4 M**

SHOWY DRYANDRA

This erect, bushy, dense shrub grows to about 2 m wide and sometimes takes the form of a small tree with many soft, hairy branches. It is the most commonly cultivated dryandra.

Leaves Alternate, soft and narrow, divided almost to the midrib into many curved triangular lobes with curved-back margins. They are soft, paler and slightly hairy below, 5-20 cm long and up to 1 cm wide. **Flowers** Appear in spring. Individual flowers are shiny yellow-orange with 4 long, hairy lobes and a long, protruding style. They are packed into dense, terminal, globular flowerheads, 5-10 cm across, and set in a rosette of floral leaves. **Fruit** Small, nut-like capsules hidden among the spent flowers and surrounding bracts, each containing 1-2 black winged seeds. **Habitat** Stony or peaty soils in heaths along the coast and ranges.

| FAMILY **PROTEACEAE** | SPECIES *Grevillea hookeriana* | FORM **SHRUB** | SIZE **TO 3 M** |

RED TOOTHBRUSH GREVILLEA

This is a widely-spreading shrub with hairy branches, and bears unusual one-sided spidery flowerheads. **Leaves** Divided into 3-9 narrow, wiry segments, 7-20 cm long. They have a pointed tip, curled-under margins and a prominent midrib. **Flowers** Appear most of the year. They are bright-red, curled tubes, and are covered with silky brown hairs outside. They have long, curved, protruding red styles when released from the flower tube. The flowers are crowded into one-sided, spidery-looking clusters to 8 cm long, arising from the base of the leaf stalks. **Fruit** Shell-like, woody follicles about 2 cm long, with 2 valves, opening to release 2 flat seeds. **Habitat** Sandy soils in heaths, often grows among granite rocks.

| FAMILY **PROTEACEAE** | SPECIES *Grevillea lanigera* | FORM **SHRUB** | SIZE **TO 2 M** |

WOOLLY GREVILLEA

This fairly dense, soft and rounded shrub is covered with greyish-green hairs. **Leaves** Crowded around the branches, narrow with rolled-under margins. They are usually fairly soft, 1-3 cm long and 1-5 mm wide, stalkless or with very short stalks, rough and hairy above, and covered with soft hairs below. **Flowers** Appear in winter and spring. They are red or pink and cream curled tubes, bearded inside, about 1 cm long. They have protruding styles covered in silky white hairs, 13-20 mm long when released from the flower tube. The flowers are arranged in small spidery clusters. **Fruit** Hairy, shell-like, thin-walled, woody capsules, 10-12 mm long. The capsules have 2 valves, each opening to release 2 flat seeds. **Habitat** Moist sandy or rocky sites, on stream banks, in heaths and open forests along the coast and ranges as high as the sub-alps.

| FAMILY **PROTEACEAE** | *Hakea sericea* | FORM **SHRUB** | SIZE **TO 3 M** |

NEEDLEBUSH

This is a stiff, erect, slender or bushy shrub with silky hairs on new growth. **Leaves** Alternate, cylindrical in cross-section, stiff, needle-like and prickly. They are 15-80 mm long and 1-2 mm wide, emerging at right angles to the stem. **Flowers** Appear in winter and spring. They are small, scented and delicate, white or pink, tubular, curved-back in the upper part, and 4-5 mm long. They have deeply-cut, rolled-back, hairy petals and long, curved styles when released from the flower tube. They are arranged in clusters of 1-7 flowers arising from the leaf axils. **Fruit** Woody, wrinkled, ovoid and walnut-like with a double-pointed beak, 2-4 cm long and 20-25 mm wide. They have 2 solid valves with flat faces, each containing a single flat, winged seed. The fruits remain on the plant for years. **Habitat** Heaths and open forests of the coast and adjacent ranges.

FAMILY **PROTEACEAE**   SPECIES *Isopogon anemonifolius*   FORM **SHRUB**   SIZE **TO 2 M**

DRUMSTICKS

This is a rigid, erect shrub, usually comprising a dense cluster of straight, sparsely-branched stems arising from the ground. It has drumstick-like fruit and hairy young shoots. **Leaves** Alternate, stiff, flat, 4-11 cm long and 3-5 mm wide. The leaves are on stalks 20-35 mm long, and are divided in the upper half into 3 or more pointed, linear to wedge-shaped, 2 or 3 lobed segments, tipped with red. **Flowers** Appear in spring and early summer. They are yellow, stalkless slender tubes, 10-12 mm long, with 4 small, spreading lobes and a slightly hairy tip. The flowers are arranged in dense, terminal, globular heads, 25-40 mm across with a hard central cone. **Fruit** Hard, spherical cones, 10-16 mm diameter, containing numerous hairy seeds, 2-3 mm long. **Habitat** Sandy soils in heaths and dry forests of the coast and ranges.

FAMILY **RHIZOPHORACEAE**   SPECIES *Bruguiera gymnorrhiza*   FORM **TREE**   SIZE **TO 12 M**

BLACK MANGROVE

This small to medium-sized, spreading tree has a short, slender trunk and many low branches. Its numerous stilt-like roots arch from the lower trunk into the sur-rounding sand or mud, looping out for some distance around the tree. **Bark** Grey and rough. **Leaves** Opposite in pairs at the ends of the branches, thick, leathery and glossy-green, with a prominent raised midrib below. They are 5-20 cm long and 3-9 cm wide, with a reddish stalk 2-4 cm long. **Flowers** Appear in late winter and spring. They are red and cream, tubular and 2-4 cm long. They have 12-13 narrow, pointed and fleshy lobes, are hairy at the base, and are borne singly on stalks 10-25 mm long. **Fruit** Greenish-yellow, cigar-shaped, 20-25 mm long, containing a single seed that usually germinates while still attached to the tree. Seedlings are 30-60 cm long before falling. **Habitat** Saline coastal mudflats and tidal estuaries.

FAMILY **RUTACEAE**   SPECIES *Boronia ledifolia*   FORM **SHRUB**   SIZE **TO 1.5 M**

SHOWY BORONIA

This bushy shrub has hairy young branches and shiny leaves that emit a strong, unpleasant smell when crushed. **Leaves** Opposite, sometimes divid-ed into 3-11 leaflets, with curled-under margins. They are shiny dark green above and densely-covered with a felt of white or grey hairs below, and are 4-40 mm long and 1-7 mm wide. They are dotted with translucent oil glands. **Flowers** Appear in winter and spring. They are pink to red, large and showy, 1-2 cm across, and open. They have 4 waxy, pointed petals, 5-10 mm long, and 8 stamens. They are usually solitary on stalks 6-12 mm long. **Fruit** Dry capsules, breaking into 4 smaller, 2-valved capsules that explode open when ripe to release a single, rough seed. **Habitat** Coastal sandstone heaths and dry sclerophyll forests.

| FAMILY **RUTACEAE** | SPECIES *Correa reflexa* | FORM **SHRUB** | SIZE **TO 1.5 M** |

COMMON CORREA

This shrub may be prostrate or erect and spindly, and has rough branchlets bearing tufts of brownish hairs. **Leaves** Opposite, varying from narrow heart-shaped to elliptic, flat or with slightly curled-under margins. They are 2-5 cm long and 6-30 mm wide, almost stalk-less and stem-clasping. Paler and covered with brownish downy hairs below, they are sometimes slightly rough with tufts of brownish hair above. **Flowers** Appear mainly in winter and spring and are hooded by leafy bracts. They are red with greenish-yellow tips or white, cream or green. They have 4 petals joined into a cylindrical tube for most of their length, 2-4 cm long and downy outside, with 8 protruding stamens. They are solitary or in threes at the ends of short, drooping stalks. **Fruit** Dry capsules, 6-9 mm long. **Habitat** Widespread on various soil types in coastal heaths and dry sclerophyll forests.

| FAMILY **RUTACEAE** | SPECIES *Philotheca myoporoides* | FORM **SHRUB** | SIZE **TO 2 M** |

LONG-LEAF WAX FLOWER

This is a variable tall or rounded erect shrub covered with prominent aromatic glands on the leaves and branches. **Leaves** Alternate, rather leathery, grey-ish-green, stalkless and smooth. They are narrow or broad, 15-110 mm long and 2-60 mm wide, with a prominent midrib and small, prominent glands at the leaf bases. **Flowers** Appear mainly in spring and autumn. They are white and waxy with pink buds, open, and 15-20 mm across. They have 5 separate, spreading, hairy petals and 10 stamens, and are borne singly or in clusters of usually 2-4 flowers on stout stalks about 1 mm thick, arising from the leaf axils. **Fruit** Dry, beaked capsules about 1 cm long, opening in 2 valves, each containing a single seed. **Habitat** Widespread on rocky hillsides in heaths and dry sclerophyll forests.

| FAMILY **XANTHORRHOEACEAE** | SPECIES *Xanthorrhoea australis* | FORM **SHRUB** | SIZE **TO 5 M** |

GRASS TREE

This erect, very slow-growing shrub has an under-ground stem. It develops a tall trunk over many years, sometimes branched, densely packed with the rough leaf bases and usually blackened by fire. The trunk is topped by a tuft of grass-like leaves and a very tall flowering stem. **Leaves** Long, stiff and grass-like, spirally arranged to form a hanging skirt around the top of the trunk. They are triangular in cross section, often more than 1 m long and 1-4 mm wide. **Flowers** Appear in spring, summer and after fire. They are small and cream with 6 lobes and 6 stamens, embedded in smooth brown bracts, and packed in spiral clusters to form a velvety cylindrical flowering spike. This spike with a stout, woody stalk, to 3 m long and 8 cm diameter. **Fruit** Shiny-brown, beaked casules, 14-20 mm long. **Habitat** Sandy soils in heaths and open forests, regenerates quickly after fire.

Dry Country

◊

After Antarctica, Australia is the driest continent on earth, and the interior is an area where rainfall is sparse and sporadic, or absent for years on end. Summer temperatures soar to more than 45 degrees, while winter nights fall below freezing. This is a region of red sand dunes, stony deserts, fiery red gorges, extensive dry claypans and glaring white saltlakes.

The centre is not, however, a barren land, but a place where hummocks of spinifex grasses dot the landscape, mulga woodlands create swathes of green across the tablelands and through the deserts, succulent shrubs take root in saltlakes, while palms and ferns grow around waterholes and river pools. Rain, when it arrives, can occur in massive downpours, inundating thousands of kilometres, turning dry creek beds into raging rivers and filling the vast inland salt lakes. The desert bursts into life, carpets of wildflowers clothe the ground, insects and even fish and frogs appear as if by magic, and huge flocks of birds fly in to feast.

Times of plenty are rare, and the large expanses of low, mulga woodlands belie the fact that the soil is exceptionally low in nutrients. Arid, treeless grasslands cover about 20 percent of the continent. The dominant species grow in spiny humps with bare ground between them where herbs and other grasses spring up after rain. Grasslands support almost 100 species of birds including grass-parrots, grasswrens and finches, a number of rodents, kangaroos, snakes and other reptiles.

Low shrubs with hairy, succulent leaves grow on the red and grey soils and gibber plains of the southern inland. Surprisingly rich in bird and reptile life, they extend as far as the eye can see across the treeless plains. Ephemeral creeks and watercourses lined with river red gums and coolibah trees snake across the landscape. Gorges cut through low mountain ranges and provide shelter for relict species of figs, cycads and palms, remnants of the rainforests that once flourished here.

◊

| FAMILY **AMARANTHACEAE** | SPECIES *Ptilotus exaltatus* | FORM **HERB** | SIZE **TO 1.5 M** |

PINK MULLA MULLA

This is a robust, upright annual or perennial herb with branched or single stems. **Leaves** Alternate along the stems or in a rosette around the base of the plant. They are thick, rigid and fleshy, pointed, to 20 cm long and 7 cm wide at the base of the plant, and to 8 cm long and 45 mm wide on the stems. The leaves are covered with short hairs when young. **Flowers** Appear mainly in winter and spring. Individual flowers are lilac-grey to deep pink, tubular, and to 2 cm long. They have 5 small lobes, long hairs outside and are woolly inside. They are produced in dense, terminal, and conical to cylindrical spikes, 3-20 cm long and 30-45 mm wide, on long stalks. **Fruit** Small and single-seeded with a membranous covering. **Habitat** Widely distributed and locally abundant in limestone and rocky loams, on plains and sand ridges and in mulga woodlands.

| FAMILY **AMARANTHACEAE** | SPECIES *Ptilotus obovatus* | FORM **HERB** | SIZE **TO 1.2 M** |

SILVER MULLA MULLA

This is a compact, stiff, erect, shrubby perennial herb. The stems and foliage are covered in white woolly hair. **Leaves** Alternate broad, sometimes pointed and covered with dense grey hairs. They are 1-6 cm long and 5-20 mm wide, on stalks 1-4 cm long. **Flowers** Appear most of the year. Individual flowers are white and pink to grey, tubular with long white hairs on the back. They have 5 small lobes and are 7-10 mm long. They are produced in dense, terminal, hemispherical to short-cylindrical spikes, usually 1-3 cm long and about 15 mm wide, many on right-angles stems. **Fruit** Small, dry and single-seeded, with a membranous covering. **Habitat** Widely distributed in arid areas on open stony ground, in shrublands and woodlands.

| FAMILY **ARECACEAE** | SPECIES *Livistona mariae* | FORM **PALM** | SIZE **TO 20 M** |

RED CABBAGE PALM

This tall, fan-leaved palm has a spherical crown above a skirt of dead leaves, and belongs to a remnant population that flourished in a wetter climate. **Trunk** Pale to dark grey, to 40 cm diameter, smooth and ringed with horizontal leaf scars. **Leaves** Fan-shaped, to 3 m diameter; pleated and divided more than half way down into, linear, pointed segments with entire or frayed, drooping tips. The stout leaf stalks are up to 2 m long with small spines at the base, and they partially encircle the trunk. Young plants have reddish leaves, hence the common name. **Flowers** Greenish-yellow, about 5 mm across. They are packed along the branchlets of a drooping inflorescence to 1.3 m long, arising from leaf bases within the crown. **Fruit** Glossy black, spherical, 15-20 mm across. They have a single seed covered by a thin fleshy layer. **Habitat** Confined to sheltered gorges and valleys in Finke Gorge National Park, around permanent waterholes.

FAMILY **BIGNONIACEAE**   SPECIES *Pandorea doratoxylon*   FORM **SHRUB**   SIZE **TO 4 M**

SPEARWOOD BUSH

This climbing, multi-stemmed, woody shrub is sometimes regarded as the inland form of *Pandorea pando-
rana*. The long, straight, cane-like stems were used by
Aboriginal people to make spears. **Leaves** Opposite,
divided into 5-11 narrow-lanceolate leaflets, each
15-50 mm long and 2-8 mm wide. **Flowers** Appear in winter and
spring. They are cream with brown-purple markings in the throat, tubular, and densely-hairy inside. They are 14-25 mm long with a 3-lobed
lower lip and 2-lobed upper lip and 4 stamens. The flowers are produced
in short, terminal, leafy clusters. **Fruit** Flat, elliptic, beaked capsules,
6-10 cm long. The capsules open at the top in 2 valves, each containing
more than 30 flat, brown, obovate seeds, 7-10 mm long with wings
5-6 mm long in each of the 2 cells. **Habitat** Sandy and rocky sites in
gorges and sheltered hillsides.

FAMILY **BOMBACACEAE**   SPECIES *Adansonia gregorii*   FORM **TREE**   SIZE **TO 15 M**

BOAB

This small or medium-sized deciduous tree has thick branches and a bottle-shaped trunk to 5 m diameter.
Bark Brown and smooth, turning dull-grey and pock-
marked. **Leaves** Alternate, divided into 5-9 leaflets radiating from the end of the leaf stalk. The leaflets are 5-13 cm
long and 2-4 cm wide, on stalks 1-3 mm long. They are dark green above,
paler with soft whitish hairs and a raised midrib below. **Flowers** Appear mainly in spring when the tree is leafless. They are creamy-white, fragrant, and
broadly tubular, with silky hair. They are 8-12 cm long and about 10 cm wide,
with 5 soft, curled-back petals and numerous white, protruding stamens,
5-6 cm long. The flowers are solitary in the terminal leaf axils. **Fruit** Dark
brown, ovoid, woody pods, 15-25 cm long and 10-20 cm across, covered
with velvety hairs. The pods contain many brown to black, bean-like, edible
seeds about 1 cm across. Ripe in summer and autumn. **Habitat** Rocky outcrops in open woodlands, and along creeks and drainage channels.

FAMILY **BORAGINACEAE**   SPECIES *Trichodesma zeylanicum*   FORM **HERB**   SIZE **TO 1 M**

CATTLE BUSH

This is an erect or spreading, stiff, coarse, woody
annual or perennial herb. It has stiff, long hairs or
short, soft hairs. **Leaves** Alternate towards the
top of the plant, opposite on the lower parts; narrow; 2-12 cm long and 7-25 mm wide.
Flowers Appear most of the year. They are blue, rarely white, cup-
shaped, and spirally-twisted in bud. They are 12-20 mm across, and
deeply divided into 5 lobes, 12-18 mm long, with a protruding column of white stamens. The flowers are borne in one-sided clusters on
hairy stems. **Fruit** Comprise 4, smooth and shiny, one-seeded nutlets.
Habitat Widespread on rocky hills, on deep red sands, sand dunes
and sometimes on heavy clay soils.

FAMILY **CAESALPINIACEAE** SPECIES *Petalostylis labicheoides*	FORM **SHRUB**	SIZE **TO 3 M**

BUTTERFLY BUSH

This is an erect, rounded shrub with downy branches and cassia-like flowers.

Leaves Opposite, divided into 5-21 leaflets, each 1-3 cm long and 3-8 mm wide.

Flowers Appear mainly in winter and spring. They are yellow, often with red markings, open, and 3-4 cm across. They have 5 overlapping, slightly unequal, rounded petals, 15-20 mm long, and a protruding, yellow, petal-like, curved style. The flowers are produced in short clusters of 1-5 flowers. **Fruit** Flat, oblong pods, 2-3 cm long. The pods contain 4-6 flat, obovoid, mottled light and dark brown, shiny seeds about 5 mm long, each with a small cap. **Habitat** Sand plains, dune fields and rocky ridges, in woodlands and spinifex country.

FAMILY **CAESALPINIACEAE** SPECIES *Senna artemisioides*	FORM **SHRUB**	SIZE **TO 3 M**

SILVER CASSIA

This is a very variable, dense, rounded shrub covered with minute white hairs, with many erect, slender branches. There are several subspecies and a number of hybrid forms. **Leaves** Variable in size and divided into 1-8 pairs of needle-like to linear or rarely elliptic leaflets. The leaflets are 7-40 mm long and 2-20 mm wide, with stalks 4-60 mm long, with or without silky or woolly hairs. They are green to grey-green and sometimes have curled-under margins. **Flowers** Appear mainly in winter and spring. They are sweetly-scented, yellow, cup-shaped, about 15 mm across and 7-10 mm long. They have 5 overlapping petals, a cluster of 10 stamens and long, brown anthers. The flowers are produced in short, dense, axillary clusters of 4-12. **Fruit** Flat, shiny brown pods, 4-8 cm long and 6-10 mm wide, mostly straight. **Habitat** Widespread, mostly on rocky rises and hills.

FAMILY **CAMPANULACEAE** SPECIES *Isotoma petraea*	FORM **HERB**	SIZE **TO 40 CM**

ROCK ISOTOME

This is an upright perennial herb, and often forms dense clumps. **Leaves** Alternate, tapering at both ends. They are 15-75 mm long and 5-55 mm wide, and are lobed, or the margins have relatively long, spreading teeth sometimes interspersed with smaller teeth. **Flowers** Appear most of the year. They are delicate, white or pale blue to lilac, with a long slender tube, 15-40 mm long. They are topped by 5 widely-spreading pointed lobes shorter than the tube, sometimes notched on one side, and have 5 yellow stamens. The flowers are produced singly on axillary stalks 8-25 cm long. **Fruit** Ovoid capsules, 10-22 mm long. Each capsule contains numerous tiny seeds. **Habitat** Gorges, canyons, rocky outcrops and hillsides.

| FAMILY **CAPPARACEAE** | SPECIES *Capparis mitchellii* | FORM **TREE** | SIZE **TO 4 M** |

WILD ORANGE

This shrub or small tree has a wide, short trunk and a wide, dense, crown. The branches, leaves and flowers are covered with short, dense, woolly hairs. Juveniles have small, sparse leaves and thorny, vine-like branches. **Bark** Dark brown to black and deeply-fissured. **Leaves** Alternate, dull green, often downy, thick and stiff. They have prominent veins below, and are 20-65 mm long and 1-3 cm wide, on thick stalks 5-15 mm long. **Flowers** Appear in spring and early summer. They open at night and wither before the end of the day. They are white, cream or yellow, open, 5-6 cm across, and have 4 broad petals and numerous very long, protruding, white stamens. They are solitary or in clusters of 2-4 on thick stalks, 2-4 cm long. **Fruit** Edible, rough, globular berries, green to yellowish. The berries are 4-7 cm across, with curved stalks 10-15 cm long, and contain many large, flat seeds embedded in yellow pulp. Ripe in summer. **Habitat** Widespread in arid inland grasslands and woodlands.

| FAMILY **CHENOPODIACEAE** | SPECIES *Enchylaena tomemtosa* | FORM **SHRUB** | SIZE **TO 1 M** |

RUBY SALTBUSH

This is a straggling, often tangled, fleshy, low shrub able to survive in saline soil and tolerate long periods of drought. It has weak slender branches usually covered with short, soft, brown-ish or whitish hairs. **Leaves** Alternate, narrow, almost cylindrical in cross-section, 6-20 mm long. The leaves are fleshy and usually covered with whitish or brownish hairs. **Flowers** Appear most of the year. They are very small and stalkless, yellow or red with 5 whorled lobes and 5 stamens. The flowers are produced singly in the leaf axils and pollinated by the wind. **Fruit** Small and berry-like, red or yellow. They are fleshy, globular, 5-8 mm across, and contain a single seed. **Habitat** Widely distributed in low shrub-lands, particularly on heavy, saline soils around salt lakes.

| FAMILY **COMPOSITAE** | SPECIES *Brachycome iberidifolia* | FORM **HERB** | SIZE **TO 25 CM** |

SWAN RIVER DAISY

This wiry, erect, branching, annual herb is either smooth or covered with soft hairs. **Leaves** Alternate, up to 4 cm long, on stalks 1-8 cm long. They are usually finely divided into 5-13 distant, linear segments, or rarely entire. **Flowers** Appear in winter, spring and summer. Individual flowers are white, blue or violet, narrow and ray-like, and 1-2 cm long. They are arranged in daisy-like flowerheads, 25-50 mm across, with a yellow centre surrounded by 2 rows of bracts, 2-5 mm long. The flowerheads are borne singly on stalks 2-6 cm long at the ends of the flowering branches. **Fruit** Small, dry and narrow with a domed top, 1-2 mm long. They are slightly ribbed and contain a single seed. **Habitat** Sandhills, plains and watercourses.

| FAMILY **COMPOSITAE** | SPECIES *Bracteantha bracteata* | FORM **HERB** | SIZE **TO 80 CM** |

YELLOW PAPER DAISY

Thus is an upright, annual or perennial herb, rough to the touch, or covered with small woolly hairs.

Leaves Alternate, stem-clasping, soft, often bearing a few hairs. They are 2-11 cm long and 5-40 mm wide.

Flowers Appear mainly in spring and summer. Individual flowers are golden-yellow, narrow and ray-like, 8-10 mm long. They are arranged in daisy-like flowerheads 25-50 mm wide and 15-20 mm long, with a yellow centre surrounded by 3 rows of glossy yellow (rarely reddish-brown), smooth, rigid, papery bracts, each 8-10 mm long. They are borne singly or a few together on separate stiff, long or short stalks at the ends of the flowering branches. **Fruit** Small, dry, dark brown and cylindrical. They are about 4 mm long, with a plume of barbed hairs 6-8 mm at one end, and contain a single seed. **Habitat** Widespread, particularly in tall forests and woodlands on sandy soils.

| FAMILY **COMPOSITAE** | SPECIES *Calotis cuneifolia* | FORM **HERB** | SIZE **TO 60 CM** |

BLUE BURR-DAISY

This perennial herb is erect or sometimes prostrate. It has ascending, branching stems bearing stiff hairs.

Leaves Alternate, spatulate to wedge-shaped, toothed or lobed towards the tips. They are 8-50 mm long and 5-20 mm wide, stem-clasping at the base.

Flowers Appear most of the year. Individual flowers are white to bluish or lilac, narrow and ray-like, about 1 cm long. They are arranged in daisy-like flowerheads 6-25 mm wide and 4-5 mm long, with 30-45 rays, and a yellow centre surrounded by 3-4 whorls of hairy bracts, 4-5 mm long. The flowerheads are borne singly in the axils of somewhat reduced leaves on slender stalks. **Fruit** Small, dry, reddish-brown, ovate and flattened, 1-2 mm long. They have 2-4 barbed hairs at one end, and contain a single seed. **Habitat** Widespread in many situations including river floodplains, open forests and grasslands on clay and sand loams.

| FAMILY **COMPOSITAE** | SPECIES *Myriocephalus stuartii* | FORM **HERB** | SIZE **TO 60 CM** |

POACHED-EGG DAISY

This is a rather stout and erect annual herb, covered with soft, cottony or woolly hairs. It is very sticky, and has a single stem or the stem branches at the base.

Leaves Alternate, stalkless, grey-green and woolly. They have a prominent midrib, and are 2-7 cm long and 1-5 mm wide. **Flowers** Appear most of the year, but mainly in spring. The individual flowers are small and yellow with 5 lobes. They are grouped into compound, hemispherical, daisy-like flowerheads, 1-3 cm long and 2-4 cm across. The yellow centres are surrounded by papery, clawed, bracts, 5-7 mm long, with a white tip and green, hairy base. Other, more membranous bracts are scattered throughout the flowerheads. They are borne singly at the ends of the leafy stems. **Fruit** Small, dry and narrow obovoid, 2-3 mm long. They are covered in silky hairs and contain a single seed. **Habitat** Common on sand dunes and sand plains.

| FAMILY **COMPOSITAE** | SPECIES *Podolepis jaceoides* | FORM **HERB** | SIZE **TO 80 CM** |

SHOWY PODOLEPIS

This upright, annual herb has simple or few-branched, woolly stems arising from a perennial rootstock.
Leaves Arranged in a rosette around the base of the plant, and along the stems. Basal leaves are up to 20 cm long and 2 cm wide. The stem leaves are alternate, 1-5 cm wide. **Flowers** Appear at various times in the lowlands; in summer in the highlands. Individual flowers are yellow. Females are ray-like with deeply-cut lobes, 8-15 mm long, and males are shorter and tubular. They are arranged in composite, daisy-like flowerheads, 1-3 cm across, comprising 30-40 flowers, with females around the outside and smooth, pale brown bracts below. They are borne singly or in groups of 2-3 at the ends of long stems. **Fruit** Small, dry and narrow obovoid, about 3 mm long. They have a bristly plume and contain a single seed. **Habitat** Widespread from alpine areas to the western plains in woodlands and grasslands.

| FAMILY **COMPOSITAE** | SPECIES *Senecio gregorii* | FORM **HERB** | SIZE **TO 40 CM** |

FLESHY GROUNDSEL

This is an erect, somewhat fleshy, bluish-green annual herb, branching mainly at the base.
Leaves Alternate, fleshy, broad-linear, 2-9 cm long and 2-5 mm wide. **Flowers** Appear mainly in winter and spring. Individual flowers are brilliant yellow, 1-2 cm long and arranged in composite, daisy-like flower-heads, 2-4 cm across. These flowerheads have 8-12 rays surrounding a central darker yellow disc, with a single whorl of irregularly-fused bracts at the base. The flowerheads are solitary at the ends of the leafy stems. **Fruit** Small, dry, cylindrical, green or fawn, 5-8 mm long, surmounted by a silky-hairy white plume. They each contain a single seed. **Habitat** Widespread and abundant in arid and semi-arid regions.

| FAMILY **COMPOSITAE** | SPECIES *Senecio magnificus* | FORM **HERB** | SIZE **TO 1 M** |

TALL YELLOW-TOP

This is a stout, erect, smooth and woody perennial herb or undershrub. **Leaves** Alternate, crowded, often stem-clasping. They are fleshy blue-green, usually with coarsely-toothed margins, and are 3-9 cm long and 8-30 mm wide. **Flowers** Appear most of the year, but mainly in winter and spring. Individual flowers are yellow, 12-18 mm long and arranged in composite, daisy-like flowerheads. The flowerheads are 3-4 cm across, with 4-8 large rays surrounding a central darker yellow disc, with a single whorl of 12-16 bracts at the base. The flowerheads grow at the ends of long, branching stems, forming clusters of 10-50. **Fruit** Small, dry, cylindrical, hairy, yellow to brown, 5-6 mm long, surmounted by a silky-hairy white plume. They each contain a single seed. **Habitat** Most common in floodways and along roadsides; also on open plains.

| FAMILY **CUPRESSACEAE** | SPECIES *Callitris glaucophylla* | FORM **TREE** | SIZE **TO 18 M** |

WHITE CYPRESS PINE

This small to medium-sized tree has a straight trunk to 45 cm diameter, and a fairly dense, conical or flat-topped crown. **Bark** Dark grey, hard and persistent to the small branches, deeply-furrowed. **Leaves** Green to bluish-grey, reduced to tiny scales, 1-3 mm long and about 0.5 mm wide. They are arranged in alternating whorls of 3, sheathing the needle-like green branchlets. **Flowers** Male and female flowers are produced on the same tree. They are ovoid or cylindrical, 6-10 mm long, whorled and have small pollen- or ovule-containing scales. The flowers are borne at the ends of the branchlets. **Fruit** Spherical, dark brown, wrinkled woody cones, 1-2 cm across. They have 3 large and 3 smaller alternating scales separating to the base, and open widely to release numerous small, light brown, winged seeds. **Habitat** Widespread in woodlands on rolling hills, often on sandy soils, sometimes forming extensive forests; mainly inland, but also along the coast and ranges.

| FAMILY **CUPRESSACEAE** | SPECIES *Callitris preissii* | FORM **TREE** | SIZE **TO 20 M** |

SLENDER CYPRESS PINE

This small to medium sized tree has a slender trunk to 50 cm diameter and a dense, dark green rounded crown. It is sometimes mallee-like with several stems, stunted or irregularly branched. **Bark** Dark grey, fibrous, irregularly-fissured and persistent to the small branches. **Leaves** Dark green, reduced to tiny scales, 2-4 mm long, arranged in alternating whorls of 3, sheathing the needle-like green branchlets. **Flowers** Male and female flowers are produced on the same tree. Males are cylindrical, about 3 mm long and clustered at the ends of the branchlets. Females are globular. **Fruit** Spherical to ovoid, 20-35 mm across, dark brown and woody at maturity. They commonly have scattered warty projections outside, and comprise 3 large and 3 small alternating scales, united at the base on stout stalks. They fruit open to release numerous small, light brown seeds with 2 broad wings. They often persist on the tree for years. **Habitat** Sand dunes and sandy soils in woodlands and low forests.

| FAMILY **GERANIACEAE** | SPECIES *Erodium crinitum* | FORM **HERB** | SIZE **TO 50 CM** |

NATIVE CROWFOOT

This is a low annual herb with scattered long white hairs on stems that often run across the ground before ascending. **Leaves** Arise from the base of the plant on hairy stalks 2-13 cm long. They are deeply dissected into 3 principal ovate, toothed lobes 1-4 cm long and 1-3 cm wide. **Flowers** Appear most of the year. They are blue with white or yellowish veins towards the base, open, and 7-15 mm across. The flowers have 5 separate, spreading petals, and are arranged in terminal clusters of 2-6. **Fruit** Slender, dry, spirally twisted and sharply-pointed. They are 4-7 cm long, and comprise a single seed bearing a long, silky-hairy appendage that becomes straight when moistened. This appendage pushes the seed into the ground. **Habitat** Widespread in sandy soils in open woodlands, saltbush communities and grasslands.

FAMILY **GOODENIACEAE**   SPECIES *Scaevola spinescens*   FORM **SHRUB**   SIZE **TO 2 M**

SPINY FAN FLOWER

This is a rigid, erect, hairy, hard-wooded shrub. It usually has some branches terminating in thorns. **Leaves** Often clustered along the main stem and dwarf branches. A rigid spine usually accompanies each cluster. They are thick and greyish-green,

5-50 mm long and 1-6 mm wide. **Flowers** Appear most of the year. They are fan-like, 9-20 mm long, white to pale yellow. The tubular flowers sometimes have thin purple stripes, and are bearded inside, slit to the base on one side, with 5 lobes spreading to one side of the flower. The flowers are produced singly on slender axillary stalks. **Fruit** Black or purple, ovoid, 5-8 mm across, with a succulent outer layer surrounding a single seed with a hard outer shell. **Habitat** Widespread on hillsides or stony sites, sometimes on deep red sand.

FAMILY **GRAMINACEAE**   SPECIES *Triodia irritans*   FORM **HERB**   SIZE **TO 90 CM**

PORCUPINE GRASS

Often called spinifex, this perennial herb forms dense or sometimes spreading hummocks. Ring-like stands to several metres wide form over a number of years as the centre dies off and the edges regenerate, leading to annual enlargement of the ring.

Leaves Form tussocks at the base of the plant. They are rigid, sharply-pointed, cylindrical and grass-like, 8-20 cm long, sheathing the base of the stem. **Flowers** Appear mainly in winter and spring. They are small, enclosed within yellowish bracts, and arranged in spikelets of 4-12 flowers, 5-20 mm long, on stalks 5-15 mm long. Flowers are produced in a terminal cluster 10-20 cm long, of numerous spikelets, on a flowering stem up to 90 cm high. **Fruit** Dry grain, comprising a single seed closely attached to its outer covering. **Habitat** Common on sandhills and rocky areas, often in mallee.

FAMILY **LAMIACEAE**   SPECIES *Prostanthera striatiflora*   FORM **SHRUB**   SIZE **TO 2 M**

STRIPED MINT BUSH

This upright shrub bears many long, crowded clusters of white flowers. It belongs to the mint family, and its leaves emit a strong aroma when they are crushed. **Leaves** Opposite, mostly with slightly incurved margins, stalkless, 8-30 mm long and

2-10 mm wide, becoming smaller around the flowers. **Flowers** Appear in winter and spring. They are white with purple streaks and yellow spots inside, tubular, hairless or slightly downy outside, and 10-25 mm long. They have a 3-lobed, spreading lower lip and erect, 2-lobed upper lip. The flowers are produced singly in the upper leaf axils forming crowded leafy clusters. **Fruit** Comprise 4 small wrinkled nutlets, each containing a single seed. **Habitat** Widespread in sheltered sites on ridges and rocky outcrops; less common along watercourses in open woodlands.

FAMILY **LILIACEAE**:   SPECIES *Crinum flaccidum*   FORM **HERB**   SIZE **TO 60 CM**

MURRAY LILY

This is an erect, clumping, perennial herb with a large, fleshy and flattened, leafless stem arising from an ovoid, underground bulb, 7-10 mm diameter. **Leaves** Arise from the base of the stem. They are broad and sword-shaped, usually with rough margins, 30-60 cm long and 1-3 cm wide. **Flowers** Appear from summer to early winter. They are white or yellow, heavily scented, tubula and 4-12 cm long. They have 6 pointed, spreading lobes 5-8 cm long and 6 protruding stamens. The flowers are produced in clusters of 4-16 on stalks 2-4 cm long at the end of the stout, fleshy stem. **Fruit** A capsule to 2 cm diameter with 2 or 3 seeds. **Habitat** Moist sites along river banks and floodplains.

FAMILY **LILIACEAE**   SPECIES *Wurmbea dioica*   FORM **HERB**   SIZE **TO 30 CM**

EARLY NANCY

This is a small upright perennial herb with a sweet perfume, arising from a bulbous root-stock. **Leaves** Only 2-3 leaves are produced. They are grass-like, 15-35 cm long and up to 5 mm wide, attached at intervals, and stem-sheathing at the base of the stem. **Flowers** Appear in spring. They are white, pink or greenish-white with faint purple borders, and 10-25 mm across. They have 6 rounded lobes and 6 long, yellow or purple-tipped stamens The flowers are stalkless and produced in a terminal open spike of 1-11 flowers. **Fruit** Brown 3-celled angular capsules, 5-10 mm long. Each cell contains several globular seeds. **Habitat** Widespread on well-drained soils in forests and woodlands, sand dunes and grasslands.

FAMILY **LORANTHACEAE**   SPECIES *Lysiana subfalcata*   FORM **SHRUB**   SIZE **TO 50 CM**

NORTHERN MISTLETOE

This is a parasitic, woody shrub that grows attached to the branches of trees by a root-like structure that absorbs nutrient from the host. **Leaves** Opposite, 2-12 cm long and 4-20 mm wide, broad at the tip and narrow at the base, with distinct veins. **Flowers** Appear most of the year. They are red to yellow with a slender tube, 25-50 mm long, topped by 6 narrow, spreading lobes and 6 long, protruding, red stamens. The flowers are produced in axillary pairs. **Fruit** Pale and somewhat translucent, ellipsoid or pear-shaped and berry-like. They are 8-14 mm long, and contain a single seed. The seeds are much sought after by mistletoe birds. Each seed is surrounded by a sticky layer that glues the seed to a branch when it is excreted by the bird. **Habitat** Attaches to many host trees, including wattles and she-oaks.

| FAMILY **MALVACEAE** | SPECIES *Abutilon halophilum* | FORM **SHRUB** | SIZE **TO 50 CM** |

PLAINS LANTERN BUSH

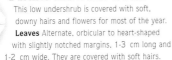

This low undershrub is covered with soft, downy hairs and flowers for most of the year. **Leaves** Alternate, orbicular to heart-shaped with slightly notched margins, 1-3 cm long and 1-2 cm wide. They are covered with soft hairs. **Flowers** Appear in winter, spring and summer. They are yellow, open to cup-shaped, with a calyx about 7 mm long. They are 15-25 mm across with 5 overlapping, rounded petals and a protruding column of fused yellow stamens. The flowers are solitary on long axillary stalks. **Fruits** Papery capsules, 10-15 mm long, depressed and covered with soft hairs. They split open when ripe to reveal about 10 segments, each containing 2 seeds covered with soft hairs. **Habitat** Red gravelly or sandy soils; inland in floodplains and saltbush communities.

| FAMILY **MALVACEAE** | SPECIES *Gossypium sturtianum* | FORM **SHRUB** | SIZE **TO 2 M** |

STURT'S DESERT ROSE

This densely-foliaged shrub is the floral emblem of the Northern Territory, and produces hibiscus-like flowers. It has green stems covered with raised black spots. **Leaves** Alternate, rounded, 25-60 mm long and 1-6 cm wide, dotted with tiny oil glands that emit a pleasing odour when crushed. **Flowers** Appear most of the year, but are most abundant in winter and last only a day or two. They are pink or lilac with a dark red centre, open, and 5-10 cm across. They have 5 overlapping rounded petals and a protruding column of fused stamens, and are solitary, with stalks 5-20 mm long. **Fruit** Black-spotted ovoid capsules, 10-15 mm long and about 1 cm wide. The capsules open in 4-5 valves, each containing a number of whitish, hairy seeds. **Habitat** Widespread in arid, rocky and sandy inland sites along watercourses and drainage lines; often in gorges and gullies.

| FAMILY **MALVACEAE** | SPECIES *Malva australiana* | FORM **HERB** | SIZE **TO 3 M** |

NATIVE HOLLYHOCK

This tall, upright, annual or biennial herb is covered with small hairs and has erect stems that are woody towards the base. **Leaves** Alternate, 2-15 cm across, divided into 5-7 lobes with toothed margins. They are hairy on both surfaces, on hairy stalks 10-15 mm long. **Flowers** Appear mainly in winter, spring and early summer. They are lilac to pink or white, open, about 1 cm long and 3-6 cm across, on stalks 1-4 cm long. They have 5 overlapping, rounded petals 25-30 mm long and a protruding column of fused stamens. The flowers are produced in axillary clusters of 2-5. **Fruit** Dry capsules, 6-7 mm diameter, splitting into 8-16 segments, flat and almost smooth on the back. **Habitat** Prefers sandy soils in sites near watercourses, in areas subject to flooding, and on roadsides.

| FAMILY **MALVACEAE** | SPECIES *Sida petrophila* | FORM **SHRUB** | SIZE **TO 2 M** |

ROCK SIDA

This is an erect, often spindly shrub covered with small hairs. **Leaves** Alternate, 15-60 mm long and 4-30 mm wide with slightly toothed margins. They are covered with dense, greyish, small hairs. **Flowers** Appear most of the year. They are yellow, open, about 2 cm across with 5 overlapping rounded petals 10-12 mm long and a protruding column of yellow stamens. The flowers are borne singly or in axillary or terminal clusters of 2-6, on stalks 7-20 mm long. **Fruit** Dry, hairy and conical capsules, 5-7 mm across with 5-7 segments. **Habitat** Dry, rocky hillsides, often in mulga communities.

| FAMILY **MARSILEACEAE** | SPECIES *Marsilea drummondii* | FORM **FERN** | SIZE **TO 30 CM** |

COMMON NARDOO

This small to medium-sized aquatic or semi-aquatic fern has clover-like leaflets borne in groups on long stalks along a long-creeping, much-branched rhizome, which is covered with orange-brown hairs. **Fronds** Comprise very slender stalks, 2-30 cm long, bearing two pairs of opposite, sterile leaflets at the end. In aquatic sites the sterile leaflets float on the surface of the water. They are silvery-green, broad wedge-shaped to rounded-triangular, and 5-30 mm wide. Hairy when young, the fronds become smooth in aquatic plants and sometimes have slightly indented margins. The veins are fine and numerous, radiating from the base of the leaflets and joined at their ends to form loops. **Spores** Produced in large masses in dry situations and contained in solitary, hard, woody, globular cases (sporocarps). The sporocarps are formed by modified leaves, 4-9 mm long, attached to the rhizome by unbranched stalks 8-90 mm long. **Habitat** Common in depressions and swamps in areas subject to intermittent flooding.

| FAMILY **MIMOSACEAE** | SPECIES *Acacia ligulata* | FORM **SHRUB** | SIZE **TO 5 M** |

DUNE WATTLE

This is a spreading, compact, bushy shrub with smooth, light green, slightly angled or ribbed branchlets. **Leaves** Alternate, thick, linear, 3-10 cm long and 2-10 mm wide. They have 1 vein, are grey-green with yellowish margins, and have a small, inconspicuous gland near the tip and on the upper margin near the base. **Flowers** Appear mainly in winter and spring. They are packed into bright yellow to orange fluffy balls of 15-20 flowers, about 6 mm across. The flowers are solitary or form clusters of 2-5 on short flower stalks arising from the leaf axils. **Fruit** Thick, hard, woody, light brown, straight to curved pods, 3-10 cm long and 5-10 mm wide. The pods are more or less constricted between the seeds, breaking into1-seeded segments. **Habitat** Widespread and scattered, often on sand ridges; inland in mulga and bluebush communities and woodlands.

FAMILY **MYOPORACEAE**   SPECIES *Eremophila bignoniiflora*   FORM **TREE**   SIZE **TO 7 M**

BIGNONIA EMU BUSH

This shrub or small tree has a dense, rounded crown and drooping branches. The fruits are a favourite food of the emu. **Bark** Grey and rough. **Leaves** Alternate, thin, with entire or rarely toothed margins, 3-20 cm long and 3-15 mm wide with a long, pointed tip. They are red-tinged above and pale green below with a prominent midrib. **Flowers** Appear mainly in spring and summer. They are creamy-white with purple spots, fragrant, tubular, 2-3 cm long, and reddish outside. They have 4 stamens and 5 broad, spreading lobes; the upper 2 may appear to be a notched lip and the lowest tongue-like. The flowers are solitary or in small axillary clusters, on sticky stalks 5-24 mm long. **Fruit** Ovoid and fleshy, 10-15 mm long and 10-13 mm across. **Habitat** Floodplains and creek lines on heavy clay soils in open woodlands

FAMILY **MYOPORACEAE**   SPECIES *Eremophila duttonii*   FORM **SHRUB**   SIZE **TO 3 M**

EMU BUSH

This is a compact, rounded shrub with rough branches due to persistent leaf bases. The fruits are a favourite food of the emu. **Leaves** Alternate, crowded, often only at the ends of the branches, 15-50 mm long and 3-5 mm wide. **Flowers** Appear in winter and spring. They are pink or red outside and yellow inside, tubular, and 12-30 mm long. They have a single, narrow, lower lip and a 4-lobed upper lip, with 4 protruding stamens. The flowers are solitary on axillary stalks, 1-2 cm long, curved upwards under the flower. **Fruit** Rather dry, broad, and ovoid, to 11 mm long. **Habitat** Widespread inland on dry red-soils, sandplains and low, rocky hills.

FAMILY **MYOPORACEAE**   SPECIES *Myoporum platycarpum*   FORM **TREE**   SIZE **TO 12 M**

SUGAR TREE

This is a large shrub or a small tree with a cylindrical trunk and a spreading, medium-density crown. It becomes gnarled and crooked with age. **Bark** Dark brown, rough and deeply fissured. It sometimes exudes a sweet resin. **Leaves** Alternate, almost stalkless, with irregular small teeth towards the tip, 25-95 mm long and 3-20 mm wide, on stalks 3-5 mm long. They are thick and fleshy, glossy dark green above and paler below with a prominent midrib. **Flowers** Appear in late winter, spring and early summer. They are white, often with a yellow throat, tubular, 6-8 mm long and 3-10 mm across. They have 5 widely-spreading, rounded lobes, hairy inside, and 4 stamens. The flowers are grouped in axillary clusters of 2-12 on stalks 4-5 mm long. **Fruit** Green dry, flattened and ovoid, 4-6 mm long and 3-4 mm wide, with 2 valves and 2 seeds. **Habitat** Common on sandy soils in woodlands, particularly mallee, casuarina and rosewood communities.

FAMILY **MYRTACEAE**   SPECIES *Corymbia dallachiana*   FORM **TREE**   SIZE **TO 25 M**

GHOST GUM

This small or medium-sized tree has a short, straight trunk to 1 m diameter, dividing early into several large, spreading branches. It produces a fairly tufted crown. **Bark** Light grey to white and smooth, sometimes with persistent scaly bark at the base of the trunk. **Leaves** Alternate, sometimes with wavy margins, 5-20 cm long and 10-45 mm wide, with stalks 10-25 mm long. They are light green or yellow-green. **Flowers** Appear in spring and summer. They are creamy-white to greenish, about 15 mm across, comprising many stamens spreading from a central disc. They are grouped in short axillary clusters of 3-11 flowers on stalks 4-20 mm long. Buds are club-shaped, 5-7 mm long and 3-6 mm across. **Fruit** Conical to urn-shaped woody capsules, 6-11 mm across and 6-9 mm long with 3 enclosed valves. **Habitat** Widespread in undulating open country, hills and plateaus, and along drainage lines; often in open woodlands.

FAMILY **MYRTACEAE**   SPECIES *Eucalyptus camaldulensis*   FORM **TREE**   SIZE **TO 50 M**

RIVER RED GUM

This medium-sized or tall tree to 50 m high has a short, thick trunk, 1-2 m or occasionally 4 m diameter. It has heavy, twisting branches and a large, spreading crown. **Bark** Dull white, usually blotched with creamy-yellow or red, smooth and shed in irregular flakes or short ribbons. **Leaves** Alternate, with a short stalk and a prominent midrib, 8-30 cm long and 7-25 mm wide. They are dull green, often greyish. **Flowers** Appear in spring and summer. They are creamy-white, about 15 mm across, comprising many stamens spreading from a central disc. The flowers are grouped in axillary clusters of 5-11, on slender stalks 2-5 cm long. Buds are globular, contracting to a point, 5-11 mm long and 3-6 mm across. **Fruit** Ovoid woody capsules, 3-7 mm long and 5-10 mm across, with 3-5 (usually 4) strongly projecting valves. **Habitat** Usually along inland watercourses and floodplains.

FAMILY **MYRTACEAE**   SPECIES *Eucalyptus microtheca*   FORM **TREE**   SIZE **TO 20 M**

COOLIBAH

This small or medium-sized tree usually has a short, often slightly crooked trunk to 1 m diameter, and a fairly open crown. **Bark** Grey to black, becoming deeply furrowed at the base; smooth and white or pale grey higher up, sometimes peeling completely leaving a smooth white surface. **Leaves** Alternate, 7-17 cm long and 8-25 mm wide on stalks 8-17 mm long. They are green to greyish-green with a prominent midrib. **Flowers** Appear in summer. They are white to cream, rarely pink, comprising many stamens spreading from a central disc. Flowers are grouped in terminal clusters of 3-7, on a thin stalk 3-10 mm long. Buds are ovoid, 3-5 mm long and 2-3 mm wide. **Fruit** Ovoid to hemispherical woody capsules, 1-5 mm long and 3-7 mm across, with 3-4 broad protruding valves. **Habitat** Near watercourses and seasonally inundated areas in open woodlands; to about 700 m in arid and semi-arid areas.

FAMILY **MYRTACEAE**   SPECIES *Eucalyptus socialis*   FORM **TREE**   SIZE **TO 12 M**

RED MALLEE

This mallee or small tree usually has a number of stems arising from an underground rootstock, and an umbrella-like crown. **Bark** Dark grey, persistent and scaly at the base. It sheds in long strips higher up to reveal white or yellowish new bark. **Leaves** Alternate, 6-14 cm long and 12-20 mm wide, on stalks 1-2 cm long. They have oil glands, a prominent midrib and faint veins, and are dull, greyish-green with reddish new growth. **Flowers** Appear in spring and summer. They are cream to white, about 2 cm across, comprising many stamens spreading from a central disc. The flowers are grouped in axillary clusters of 4-15, on flattened or angular stalks, 8-23 mm long. Buds are somewhat cylindrical with a long, conical cap, 8-14 mm long and 3-5 mm across. **Fruit** Spherical woody capsules, 5-8 mm across, with 3-4 fragile, needle-like, protruding valves. **Habitat** Mallee scrub regions on red sandy soils, usually on the plains.

FAMILY **PAPILIONACEAE**   SPECIES *Crotalaria cunninghamii*   FORM **SHRUB**   SIZE **TO 2 M**

GREEN BIRDFLOWER

This is an erect shrub bearing soft hairs on thick and pithy branches. **Leaves** Alternate, entire or sometimes divided into 3 broad leaflets. They are thick and hairy on both surfaces, 2-9 cm long and 15-60 mm wide, on velvety stalks 10-25 mm long. **Flowers** Appear in winter and spring. They are yellow-green, streaked with fine purple lines, pea-shaped, and 35-60 mm long. they have an ovate, pointed standard petal and a long twisted keel. The flowers are produced in dense terminal clusters to 25 cm long. **Fruit** Hard, swollen, oblong, hairy pods, 3-5 cm long and 10-12 mm wide. **Habitat** Widespread on sandy soils in mulga communities and on sand dunes.

FAMILY **PAPILIONACEAE**   SPECIES *Cullen patens*   FORM **HERB**   SIZE **TO 1 M**

NATIVE VERBINE

This perennial, hairy herb has erect or ascending stems when young, becoming prostrate on maturity. It has several stems clothed in soft, spreading hairs arising from a central rootstock. **Leaves** Alternate, 2-10 cm long. They have stalks 1-4 cm long, and are divided into 3 ovate leaflets with toothed margins, 1-4 cm long and 5-25 mm wide. The leaflets are smooth or with soft greyish hairs above and more densely-hairy below. **Flowers** Appear most of the year, but mainly in winter and spring. They are pink to purple or blue, pea-shaped, and 6-8 mm long. They have a silky-hairy calyx, are on very short stalks, and are arranged in dense or interrupted clusters along a main axis to 14 cm long. **Fruit** Ovoid, hairy, blackish pods, about 3 mm long and 2 mm wide. The pods are more or less enclosed in the calyx. **Habitat** Flood plains and watercourses on sandy soils.

217

FAMILY **PAPILIONACEAE**   SPECIES *Swainsona formosa*   FORM **HERB**   SIZE **TO 30 CM**

STURT'S DESERT PEA

This prostrate, spreading, annual or biennial herb has thick, upright flowering stems and is the floral emblem of South Australia. **Leaves** Are 10-15 cm long and divided into 11-17 narrow to broad leaflets, 1-3 cm long and 5-15 mm wide, grey-green and covered with long, soft hairs below. **Flowers** Appear in winter and spring. They are bright red, white or a combination of these colours, pea-shaped, 7-9 cm long with a pointed ovate standard petal, usually with a large, raised, black, glossy spot at the base, and a long curved keel. They are grouped in dense pendulous axillary clusters of 2-6 flowers. **Fruit** Narrow-elliptic swollen hairy pods, 4-9 cm long, containing many small seeds. **Habitat** Sandy soils in open sites or mulga woodlands, especially on flood plains.

FAMILY **PAPILIONACEAE**   SPECIES *Swainsona phacoides*   FORM **HERB**   SIZE **TO 60 CM**

DWARF SWAINSON PEA

This is a variable prostrate or ascending perennial herb, sometimes no more than 4-5 cm high, with stout, silky-hairy stems, and is poisonous to stock. **Leaves** Are 5-10 cm long, divided into 5-13 narrow to broad elliptic leaflets, 5-30 mm long and 1-5 mm wide, flat or concave with soft hairs on both sides. **Flowers** Appear most of the year, but mainly in winter and spring. They are pale violet to dark reddish purple, rarely white or yellow, pea-shaped, 10-15 mm long with a notched orbicular standard petal, arranged in axillary clusters of 1-10 flowers on hairy stalks. **Fruit** Cylindrical and 10-30 mm long and about 4 mm wide, or ovoid and 10-15 mm long and 7-12 mm wide pods curled longitudinally and covered with short hairs. **Habitat** Arid, sandy sites.

FAMILY **PITTOSPORACEAE**   SPECIES *Pittosporum angustifolium*   FORM **TREE**   SIZE **TO 14 M**

WEEPING PITTOSPORUM

This small tree has a cylindrical, sometimes longitudinally-ridged trunk, long, slender, drooping branches and a fairly open, rounded crown. **Bark** Pale grey and smooth. **Leaves** Alternate, narrow, 4-12 cm long and 3-12 mm wide, with a small, hooked, pointed tip, on stalks about 10 mm long. They are thick with a prominent midrib and aromatic when crushed. **Flowers** Appear in winter and spring. They are pale yellow to cream, tubular, scented, 6-10 mm long with 5 spreading to curled-back petals and 5 stamens. They are solitary or in small terminal or axillary clusters. **Fruit** Compressed ovoid capsules, 8-20 mm long, green turning yellow-orange, thick-walled, somewhat fleshy, splitting open to reveal 6-8 dark orange seeds in a sticky red pulp. Ripe in autumn and winter. **Habitat** A common inland tree in mallee scrub and woodlands in low-lying areas along creek beds and sandy plains.

FAMILY **POLYGONACEAE**   SPECIES *Muehlenbeckia florulenta*   FORM **SHRUB**   SIZE **TO 3 M**

TANGLED LIGNUM

This is an erect, rounded, woody shrub with densely-entangled stiff, grey-green, striated, rigid branches, often ending in a spine. The stems are generally leafless, 2-3 mm thick, with joints at intervals of 4-7 cm. **Leaves** Long and narrow, 15-70 mm long and 2-10 mm wide. They are usually absent from the older branches and do not persist for long on the younger branches. **Flowers** Appear most of the year. They are greenish-white to cream, open, about 5 mm long and 8-10 mm across. They have 5 separate, spreading lobes and 8 stamens, and are produced in interrupted clusters along the stems, 2-12 cm long. **Fruit** Ovoid to conical shiny brown nuts, 3-4 mm long, enclosed in the persistent remains of the flowers. **Habitat** Swampy sites and flood-prone areas in heavy soils.

FAMILY **PORTULACACEAE**   SPECIES *Calandrinia remota*   FORM **HERB**   SIZE **TO 50 CM**

ROUND-LEAVED PARAKEELYA

This is a low, clump-forming, semi-prostrate annual or perennial fleshy herb. It has a tap root and many almost leafless flowering stems. **Leaves** Mainly form a rosette around the base of the plant, with a few leaves on the lower part of flowering stems. They are fleshy, cylindrical, sometimes grooved, stalkless, often red-pink, 15-70 mm long and 1-10 mm wide. **Flowers** Appear from winter to summer. They are mauve-pink to purple, rarely white, with a whitish-yellow centre, open, and about 25 mm across. They have 5 separate, spreading petals, 8-17 mm long, notched at the tips, and have many yellow stamens. The flowers are borne singly or in loose terminal clusters of 2-8 on branching stems 8-50 cm long. **Fruit** Ovate, 3-valved capsules, 5-6 mm long. Each capsule contains numerous tiny red-brown seeds. **Habitat** Red sand soils in arid shrublands.

FAMILY **PROTEACEAE**   SPECIES *Grevillea juncifolia*   FORM **SHRUB**   SIZE **TO 6 M**

HONEYSUCKLE SPIDER FLOWER

This is an erect, straggling shrub with rough, grey bark and long, sparsely-foliaged branches. **Leaves** Linear with curled-under margins, rigid, pointed and covered with soft hair. They are 5-22 cm long and 1-2 mm wide, entire or divided into up to 5 similar segments. **Flowers** Appear year round, especially in winter and spring. They are orange-yellow curled tubes, 7-12 mm long, covered with soft hairs. they have curved, protruding styles, 16-27 mm long when released, and are arranged in terminal, spidery-looking clusters, 7-20 cm long. **Fruit** Flat, ovate, dry and hairy with reddish-brown markings, 20-25 mm long. **Habitat** Sandy soils and sand dunes, often in woodlands.

| FAMILY **SANTALACEAE** | SPECIES *Santalum acuminatum* | FORM **TREE** | SIZE **TO 8 M** |

SWEET QUANDONG

This is a small tree or a tall, erect shrub with a straight trunk, spreading to drooping branches and a fairly sparse crown. It has pale green to olive green foliage. **Bark** Dark grey, rough and furrowed.

Leaves Opposite, thick and leathery, 3-15 cm long and 3-15 mm wide, yellowish-green with a prominent midrib. **Flowers** Appear mainly in spring and summer. They are creamy-white to yellowish-green, small and tubular, and 2-6 mm long. They have 4 slightly spreading lobes and 4 stamens, and are produced in loose terminal clusters on stalks 5-10 mm long. **Fruit** Red and globular, 15-30 mm diameter, with a sweetish, edible, fleshy, outer layer and a light brown pitted stone. They each contain a single, globular seed. Ripe in spring and summer. **Habitat** Widespread on light soils in sandy spinifex areas, often near watercourses, in woodlands and low-open forests.

| FAMILY **SCROPHULARIACEAE** | SPECIES *Mimulus repens* | FORM **HERB** | SIZE **TO 20 CM** |

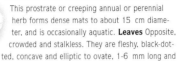

CREEPING MONKEY-FLOWER

This prostrate or creeping annual or perennial herb forms dense mats to about 15 cm diameter, and is occasionally aquatic. **Leaves** Opposite, crowded and stalkless. They are fleshy, black-dotted, concave and elliptic to ovate, 1-6 mm long and 1-7 mm wide. **Flowers** Appear throughout the year. They are blue, violet or pink with yellow and white markings inside, tubular, and 2-5 mm long. They have 5 unequal, spreading lobes and 4 stamens. The flowers are produced singly in the upper leaf axil on stalks 1-10 mm long. **Fruit** Globular capsules enclosed in the remains of the flower, about 5 mm across. Each capsule contains many seeds and opens in 2 valves. **Habitat** Open margins of marshes, lakes, creeks and temporarily inundated areas, sometimes saline.

| FAMILY **SINOPTERIDACEAE** | SPECIES *Cheilanthes sieberi* | FORM **FERN** | SIZE **TO 45 CM** |

MULGA FERN

This is a small, clumping fern with a short to medium, creeping, wiry rhizome, which is clothed with narrow, hair-like scales. **Fronds** Erect, dark green, usually 15-25 cm long (sometimes to 45 cm long) and 2-5 cm wide at the base. They have long, very slender, red-brown to dark brown, shiny stalks. The fronds are twice-divided into many small, lobed segments, some of which may be cut almost to the midrib. The segments are more or less triangular with blunt tips and curled-under margins, 2-8 mm long and 1-3 mm wide. The old, dead fronds may persist for years. **Spores** Produced in large masses forming small, rounded clusters. These clusters are borne on the tips of the tiny lateral veins on the underside of the fertile leaf segments, in short lines beneath the curled margins. **Habitat** Very common in rocky sites, along watercourses, in gorges and as an understorey in shrublands and open forests, both inland and along the coast.

FAMILY **SOLANACEAE**   SPECIES *Duboisia hopwoodii*   FORM **SHRUB**   SIZE **TO 4 M**

PITURI

This compact, erect or straggling shrub grows to 3 m wide. It has many branches and corky bark at the base of the stem. The crushed dried leaves mixed with ashes were traditionally used as a stimulant drug. **Leaves** Alternate with a pointed or hooked tip, thick, 4-12 cm long and 2-13 mm wide. **Flowers** Appear mainly from late winter to summer. They are white with purple stripes inside, funnel or cup-shaped, 7-12 mm long and 4-8 mm across. They have 5 rounded lobes and 4 stamens, and are arranged in terminal, leafy, pyramidal clusters. **Fruit** Purple-black succulent berries, 3-6 mm across. The berries contain brown, kidney-shaped seeds, 2-3 mm long. **Habitat** Widespread in arid regions on red sand soils, in mallee and woodlands.

FAMILY **SOLANACEAE**   SPECIES *Solanum sturtianum*   FORM **SHRUB**   SIZE **TO 3 M**

THARGOMINDAH NIGHTSHADE

This is an erect shrub covered with silvery-green or greyish downy hairs, often with scattered spines on the stems. **Leaves** Alternate, covered in downy hairs. They are silvery below, pale green above, 3-6 cm long and 5-15 mm wide, on stalks 5-15 mm long. **Flowers** Appear mostly in winter and spring. They are purple, broadly cup-shaped, 2-4 cm across with 5 broad and rounded papery lobes and 5 yellow stamens. The flowers are arranged in terminal clusters of 1-12. **Fruit** Dry, yellow to brownish-black berries, 10-15 mm diameter. The berries have brittle skin and break irregularly to release several dark brown to black seeds, 3-5 mm across. **Habitat** Widespread in arid shrublands.

FAMILY **ZYGOPHYLLACEAE**   SPECIES *Zygophyllum apiculatum*   FORM **SHRUB**   SIZE **TO 40 CM**

POINTED TWIN LEAF

This is a low, succulent undershrub with a woody base, fleshy branches and leaves. **Leaves** Opposite, divided into 2 ovate leaflets 15-40 mm long. **Flowers** Appear in winter and spring. They are bright yellow, open, and 15-25 mm across. They have 5 separate, spreading petals, 10-15 mm long, and 10 stamens. The flowers are solitary or in small axillary clusters. **Fruit** Capsules, 5-angled, 7-10 mm long. The capsules have a short blunt appendage at the upper corner of each angle. There is a single seed in each section. **Habitat** Frequent ground cover in mallee scrubs and woodlands.

Glossary

alternate
arranged one by one along a stem, not opposite.

arboreal
living in, or connected with trees.

arthropod
an invertebrate animal with a segmented body, jointed limbs, and an external skeleton.

axil
the upper angle between leaf and stem or branch.

bower
structures created by male bowerbirds, used as display sites to attract females in the breeding season. They usually take the form of avenues of thin sticks, woven upright.

bract
modified leaf, often at the base of a flower or stem.

calyx
outer whorl of the flower, consisting of sepals.

carrion
dead putrefying flesh.

cephalopod
a mollusc with a distinct head and a ring of tentacles round the mouth.

cycad
palm-like plant inhabiting tropical and sub-tropical regions.

dewlap
a loose fold of skin hanging from the throat.

diatoms
microscopic single-celled plants, abundant in plankton.

echinoderm
a group of marine invertebrates, including starfish and sea urchins, many of which have spiny skins and symmetrical bodies. They have a unique system of hydraulic tubes used for locomotion and feeding.

epiphytic
growing on another plant or object, using it for support and not nourishment

gibber
pebbles or boulders, especially wind-polished stones, occurring in arid regions.

herb
a plant without a woody stem.

hermaphrodite
an animal having both male and female sexual organs; a plant having stamens and pistils in the same flower.

inflorescence
the flowering structure of a plant.

keel
the two lower, fused petals of a pea-like flower.

kino
red or black juice or gum.

leaf margins
the edges or a leaf.

leaflet
a secondary part of a compound leaf.

lignotubers
a woody swelling, partly or wholly underground, at the base of the stem.

littoral
on the shore.

lobe
rounded or pointed division of a leaf; the sepal or petal of a flower.

mallee
eucalypts growing with several stunted stems, common in arid and alpine areas.

manna
a sugary substance exuded by sap-sucking insects.

mantle
thin flaps of skin extending from the main body of molluscs and over their upper surface.

marsupial
mammals that produces very small, incompletely-developed young. Some marsupials suckle their young in a pouch.

monotreme
egg-laying mammal.

mulga
scrub vegetation dominated by the acacia species.

nymph
an immature form of some insects.

obovoid
Almost oval, but broader towards the tip.

panicle
a much-branched inflorescence.

polyp
an attached or stationary life stage of marine invertebrates of the phylum Cnidaria, with cup-shaped form and tentacles around the outer rim.

prehensile
adapted for grasping or gripping objects.

prostrate
lying on the ground.

pupate
the process of a larva becoming sedentary, often within a cocoon, and changing into an adult insect.

raceme
an inflorescence with stalked flowers borne along an unbranched axis.

recurved
bent backwards.

rhizome
a stem which is usually underground, producing new shoots and roots.

saprophytic
living on dead or decayed organic matter.

sclerophyll
plants with harsh-textured, tough leaves.

scurf
flakes and scaly matter on a surface.

sepal
a segment of the outer whorl of a flower.

spathulate
shaped like a spatula, tapering from a rounded tip to a narrow base.

spicules
small, often sharp spikes of calcium carbonate or silica, found in sponges, soft corals, sea squirts and sea cucumbers.

spore
a reproductive cell.

stamen
male part of a flower comprising filament and anther.

standard petal
the large, upper petal of a pea-like flower.

tuber
the swollen end of an underground stem containing food reserves.

whorl
a group of three or more structures encircling an axis at the same level.

Index